Whitby looking west from Trafalgar Castle, 1880. This engraving was published in "Picturesque Canada" in 1882.

Chronicles of a County Town

Whitby Past and Present

BRIAN WINTER

"History is the ship carrying living memories to the future."

Stephen Spender,
British Poet

CHRONICLES OF A COUNTY TOWN: WHITBY PAST AND PRESENT

TEXT COPYRIGHT BRIAN WINTER

ISBN 0-9685745-0-5
(BRIAN WINTER, 1947-   )

Contents

Contents

Contents

Contents

Contents

Author's Introduction

For many years, citizens of Whitby have urged me to write a book about the history of the town. After nearly 40 years of research and two years of writing, it is now published, just in time for the Millennium.

Rather than write a formal history of Whitby from its beginning to the present time, I have chosen to publish a collection of stories, many of which are based on columns I have written for local newspapers. Each story is a fragment of Whitby's history. Taken together, I hope they will make interesting reading.

This book would not be possible without the kind help of many hundreds of people, citizens of Whitby past and present and their descendants, who have provided me with information and pictures which are now housed in the Town of Whitby Archives. Indeed, without their help, there would be no archives.

It is impossible to thank every contributor individually, but some deserve special mention. It was Frank Hiusser, my Grade 8 History teacher at Colborne Street Public School who started me on a lifetime search for Whitby's past. At the same time as I was learning about my town in school, my father received a collection of rare documents about the early years of Whitby from the family of John Vandal Ham, the executor of Peter Perry's estate. The combination of these two events determined my life's work.

The Whitby Historical Society deserves particular credit for appointing me as its archivist in 1968 and providing me with space in the newly-opened Whitby Centennial Building. The Town of Whitby

has faithfully supported my work as Town Archivist since I was appointed to that office in 1974, and for the past 10 years it has been a full-time position. The Town of Whitby Archives, the first municipal archives in the Regional Municipality of Durham, marked its 30th anniversary in 1998.

Although the Town of Whitby has supported the concept of this book from the beginning, it is entirely funded from private resources and no taxpayers' money has gone into its production.

I would like to thank my team of special helpers who have provided me with advice and assistance in preparing this book. Without them it would never have been completed. They are: Gerry Emm, Kim Sahadath, Howard Smith, Joe Southwell, and certainly not least, my wife Pat, who suggested the title for the book and was my editor and sounding board throughout the project.

My thanks also go out to Tom Vanderstoop and his staff at David Thomas Printing for their patience and care in typesetting and printing this, the first substantial history of Whitby published since 1907.

"Chronicles of a County Town, Whitby Past and Present", is presented to the people of Whitby as a record of their community's history, in grateful thanks for nearly 40 years of support, encouragement and assistance in my work.

Brian Winter,
Archivist, Town of Whitby,
October, 1999.

Author's Biography

Brian Winter
Archivist, Town of Whitby

Born in Toronto, Brian Winter came with his family to Whitby in 1955 when his father was transferred to the town with the Dunlop Tire and Rubber Company. He attended Whitby schools and graduated in 1970 from a three-year journalism course at Centennial College, Scarborough. He worked as Whitby reporter for the Oshawa Times, community editor of the Whitby Free Press and Secretary-Manager of the Whitby Chamber of Commerce. He has served as full-time Archivist for the Town of Whitby since 1989.

Mr. Winter was introduced to Whitby's history at the age of 13 by his Grade 8 teacher Frank Hiusser at Colborne Street School, and has spent nearly 40 years studying the subject and compiling records of the town. In 1968 he established the Town of Whitby Archives for the Whitby Historical Society and has been Archivist for the Town of Whitby since 1974, with an office in the Centennial Building.

Mr. Winter has written a number of books and pamphlets about Whitby's history, including the Centennial History of the Ontario Ladies' College (now Trafalgar Castle School) in 1974, and tributes to retiring municipal officials. For 30 years he has written historical columns on Whitby in the local newspapers.

Mr. Winter was the youngest recipient of the Peter Perry Award as Whitby's outstanding citizen of 1973 at the age of 26. In 1985 he was presented with the Ontario Volunteer Service award, and in 1998 he received an Achievement Award from the Ontario Heritage Foundation for his 30 years of developing the Town of Whitby Archives.

He is a founding member of the Whitby-Oshawa Branch of the Ontario Genealogical Society, currently serving as secretary; a member of the Ontario Historical Society and has served on the Whitby Local Architectural Conservation Advisory Committee (LACAC) since its founding in 1978. He was a founder of the Whitby Historical Society in 1967.

Mr. Winter has compiled records on nearly 3,000 Whitby families and copied more than 5,000 photographs of the community, dating from the 1860s to the present day.

The First Chronicle

It is no accident that *"Chronicles of a County Town"* was chosen as the title of this book, for the word *"chronicle"* has a special significance for Whitby. The dictionary defines *"chronicle"* as *"a record of historical events arranged in order of time"*. Just such a record was The Whitby Chronicle, a weekly newspaper edited and published by William H. Higgins from 1857 to 1883.

William H. Higgins (1830-1904) was an Irish Roman Catholic, born in Limerick, who came to Canada as a young man in his early 20s. After working as a Parliamentary reporter in Quebec City, then the capital of Canada, he decided to locate in a progressive, growing community where he could publish his own newspaper. In December 1856, he contacted James Wallace (1814-1882), the Mayor of Whitby, and succeeded in borrowing enough money from Wallace to start The Chronicle.

Whitby in 1856 was a new fast-growing town of nearly 3,000 people, with a busy harbour on Lake Ontario and bright prospects for future development. Only four years before, it had been named the County Town of the new county of Ontario, with a court house, jail and land registry office established there in 1853.

Higgins published the first issue of The Chronicle on January 22, 1857, choosing as the paper's motto: *"With calm printed words,*

William H. Higgins

great thoughts and untiring industry, we advocate Peace, Progress, Knowledge, Brotherhood". The Chronicle soon established a reputation as one of the most influential weekly newspapers in the province. Higgins developed a close friendship with many of the political leaders of his time. One of these was the Irish Father of Confederation Thomas D'Arcy McGee, who lived in Montreal. McGee was a frequent visitor in Higgins' home in the years before his death by assassination in April, 1868.

On one occasion, Higgins invited McGee to come to Whitby to deliver a lecture at the Mechanics' Institute, a forerunner of the present public library. McGee chose as his topic, the British writer, Sir Walter Scott. The Mechanics' Institute hall at Byron and Mary Streets where Pearson Lanes is now, was packed to the walls for McGee's lecture, one of the most successful ever held in the Town of Whitby. The attendance was increased by the presence of the members of the Ontario County Council who were in town for their regular meeting that day.

In 1873, Higgins purchased from James R. Armstrong (1787-1873) a large brick home known as *"The Grange"*, at the northeast corner of Mary and Pine Streets. Here he entertained his political friends and raised his family of 10 children. The Grange, home of the Beecroft family after 1918, was demolished in 1976.

In 1862, The Chronicle moved into its own building, north of the Royal Hotel, which was constructed by John Ham Perry (1827-1896) one of Whitby's most prominent commercial men and son of the town's founder Peter Perry. The Chronicle was noted for several special features which were published on a regular basis. Once a year, Higgins listed and described all the new buildings constructed in Whitby, under the heading of *"Town Improvements"*. He was proud of Whitby's development, taking every opportunity to publicize the community. He was also the author of the *"Tim O'Day"* letters which appeared regularly in The Chronicle. Written in an Irish dialect, they were humorous commentaries on life and events in Whitby and the politics of the day. Readers of The Chronicle looked forward to these writings which gained a province-wide following.

William H. Higgins, as well as being Whitby's leading newspaper editor, has the distinction of being the town's first historian. In 1877, he asked, through the columns of The Chronicle, for historical information which he printed in J.H. Beers & Company's Historical Atlas of Ontario County. This atlas, reprinted by three different publishers 100 years later, is the earliest source of history of Whitby and the County of Ontario, which became Durham Region in 1974. In 1887, Higgins republished most of what he had written for the atlas, in *"The Life and Times of Joseph Gould"*, a history of the Gould family and Ontario County.

William H. Higgins (far right) and the staff of The Whitby Chronicle, standing in front of the new Chronicle building, 173 Brock Street North, circa 1863.

Whitby Mayor Jim Gartshore (left) joined Paul Higgins, grandson of the founder of The Whitby Chronicle, on July 30, 1980 in placing a plaque on the old chronicle building.

Joseph Gould (1808-1886), of Uxbridge, was the first Warden of the Provisional County of Ontario, formed from the East Riding of York County in 1852. Without the pioneering research by Higgins more than 120 years ago, much of Whitby's early history would have been lost. Since 1857 he had recorded Whitby's history in the columns of The Chronicle. We of the present generation owe him a great debt of gratitude.

After 26 years of publishing The Chronicle, which he referred to as his *"other self"*, Higgins became discouraged about the future of Whitby. The economic depression of 1857 had halted the town's growth.

Toronto obtained the Government money to build railways to Lake Huron to control the trade routes, and Whitby with its once-active harbour had settled down to be a quiet retired farmers' town. Although he did not specify his reasons for leaving, Higgins published his last Chronicle on March 29, 1883, and left Whitby forever. With his government contacts he obtained a job as a special immigration agent to bring settlers from Ireland to Canada. For a few months after his departure he continued to write his Tim O'Day letters to The Chronicle, describing his *"Forrin Thravels"* in Ireland.

After two years in Ireland, Higgins returned to Toronto where he was appointed inspector of the Division Courts of Ontario, with an office in the Parliament Building at Queen's Park. Here he spent the remainder of his life among his political friends and mentors. He died at his home on Dufferin Street in Toronto on Dec. 5, 1904 at the age of 74. Newspapers hailed him in their obituaries as *"the premier weekly newspaper editor in Ontario"*.

The Chronicle continued publication for 29 years after Higgins sold it to James S. Robertson (1853-1925) and his brother, from Toronto. In 1912 Charles A. Goodfellow (1865-1919) combined it with Higgins' arch-rival, The Whitby Gazette, to become The Gazette and Chronicle. In

January 1942, The Gazette and Chronicle combined with the Oshawa Daily Times to become The Times-Gazette, later The Oshawa Times. The Oshawa Times ceased publication on Nov. 5, 1994, bringing to an end the saga of the Whitby Chronicle and its successors.

Descendants of William H. Higgins continued to occupy prominent positions in Canada, although the family had no further connection with Whitby after 1883. Higgins' eldest daughter, Emma O'Sullivan (1861-1938) was Supervisor of the Andrew Mercer Reformatory for Women in Toronto and publisher of the Catholic Yearbook. Recognized as an authority on penology in Ontario, she represented the province at meetings of the National Prison Association in the Untied States, where she delivered lectures on prison reform and discipline.

Higgins' youngest son, Michael Stafford Higgins (1879-1954) was the founder of Mother Parker's Tea Company. His son, Paul Higgins, president of Mother Parker's, came to Whitby to dedicate a plaque commemorating his grandfather at the old Chronicle building, 173 Brock Street North, on July 30, 1980. Major Jim Gartshore and 14 descendants of William H. Higgins attended the ceremony and ate lunch in the old newspaper office, then a restaurant called Cedrick's Banquet Hall,

operated by the Przybylski family.

Nearly all the issues of The Whitby Chronicle are on microfilm in the Town of Whitby Archives and the public library, but they came close to being destroyed. In the early 1950s, the papers were acquired by Blanche Meeker, a teacher who lived on Gilbert Street East. For many years she typed extracts from The Chronicle, which she provided to the library. The papers were stored on shelves in her basement. On Aug. 28, 1971, four inches of rain fell on Whitby in six hours, flooding many basements including Blanche Meeker's. The sodden papers were retrieved from her basement by the Archives of Ontario and microfilmed in 1974. The Whitby Gazette was not so fortunate. All its files were destroyed in a fire in 1946.

Using Higgins Chronicle newspaper as a major source, this book presents a series of stories from Whitby's past, which are designed to bring to life the people and events that shaped the County Town's destiny over the past 200 years. These new "*Chronicles*" bring Whitby's story up to the end of a century and a millennium in the tradition started by William H. Higgins more than 140 years ago.

THE WHITBY CHRONICLE

IS PUBLISHED EVERY

THURSDAY MORNING,

BY

W. H. HIGGINS,

At his Printing Establishment,

BROCK STREET, WHITBY.

Terms - $1 50, per Annum.

ADVERTISEMENTS. — All Advertisements measured in Nonpariel, and charged at the rate of 8 cents, per line, first insertion, and 2 cents, per line, each subsequent insertion.

Special Reports of Meetings, Financial Statements of Banks, Railway Companies, Insurance Companies, and matters of like description when placed among News Matter ten cents per line.

Special contracts made with advertisers by the year, or otherwise.

*** Orders to discontinue advertisements must be in writing.

This advertisement by W. H. Higgins, for The Whitby Chronicle, appeared in the upper left corner of the front page of every issue. Each advertisement in the paper contained the date of insertion and sometimes appeared for weeks or months. Advertisements were placed at the left side of page 1 and on all of pages 3 and 4. A short story was on the right side of the front page and local, national and international news appeared on page 2.

Whitby, Yorkshire England
Our Ancient Namesake

The Town of Whitby takes its name from the ancient seaport on the north-east coast of England, Whitby, Yorkshire. In the late 18th century, when townships were first set out along the north shore of Lake Ontario, what is now Whitby was first known as Township 8 and then Norwich. When it came time to survey the township between 1792 and 1795, someone from the north of England, it is not known whom, decided to name the townships east of York (Toronto) after towns on the Yorkshire coast. Thus we have, York, Scarborough, Pickering, and Whitby, all in a row on Lake Ontario, just as they are on the north-east coast of England. When Whitby Township received its name, it consisted of all of what is now the Town of Whitby and the City of Oshawa. In 1857, after a bitter debate between the villages of Whitby and Oshawa over which community would become the County Town, the Oshawa faction split the township into two equal halves, Whitby and East Whitby. East Whitby consisted of lots 1 to 17 and Whitby Township was lots 18 to 35. The political headquarters for East Whitby Township was Columbus and Brooklin was the same for Whitby Township. Whitby Town and Township amalgamated as one municipality on Jan. 1, 1968. The present city of Oshawa took over East Whitby when Regional Government

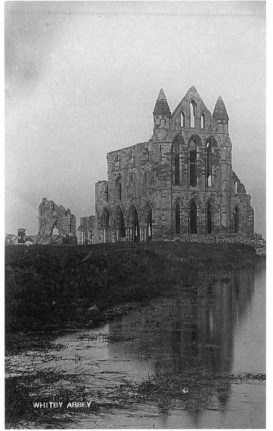
Whitby Abbey and the reflecting pond.

came into effect on Jan. 1, 1974.

The name *"Whitby"* is Danish, dating from a period around 867 A.D. when Denmark invaded parts of what is now England. The name is a contraction of *"Whitteby"*, meaning *"White Village"*. The allusion may be to the white lighthouse on the pier at the harbour. Both Whitby, Yorkshire and Whitby, Ontario have white lighthouses at their harbours.

The Town of Whitby, Yorkshire, has many historical associations. High on the East Cliff overlooking the harbour is the ruin of Whitby Abbey, closed by King Henry VIII when he dissolved the monasteries in 1537. It stands on the site of a much older abbey dating from Celtic times. The Abbess at Whitby was St. Hilda (617-680) who was the spiritual ruler and mother of a large community of people dedicated to religious service. As a land owner, St. Hilda also had in her employ men to care for sheep and cattle, tilling the soil and wood cutting. She was also the Lady of the Village located on the banks of the River Esk, below the monastery, which became the town of Whitby. Kings and nobles came to her for advice. In 664, A.D., the representatives of the Celtic and Roman churches in Britain met at Whitby Abbey to set the date for Easter. The monk Bede, who was one of England's first historians, was a personal friend of St. Hilda, and much of her life story comes down to us through him. Caedmon, *"the father of English sacred music"* was a cowherd for St. Hilda.

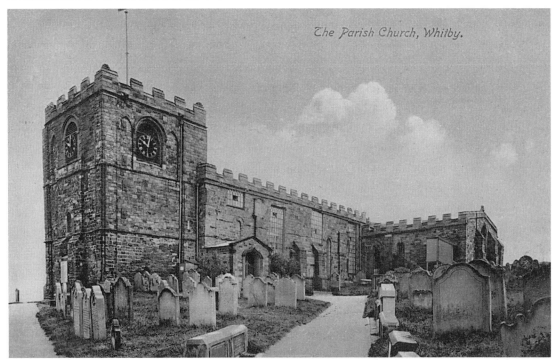

The Parish Church, Whitby.

St. Mary's Church, dating from 1100 A.D.

of Whitby Archives.

Next to the abbey ruin is St. Mary's Church, which dates from about 1100 A.D. With its old box pews it is still in use today, and is reached by 199 steps leading up the cliff from the Town of Whitby. The author of this book has confirmed that there really are 199 steps but he decided to walk down rather than up these steps on a visit to Whitby in 1977!

The most famous resident of Whitby in more recent times was Captain James Cook (1728-1779), who took his apprenticeship as a master mariner at the home of John Walker in Grape Lane. A plaque marks this house for visitors today. It is said that Cook spent winter evenings in the house in Grape Lane, reading by candle-light while other apprentices spent their time in amusement. Cook's ships the *"Endeavour"*, *"Resolution"* and *"Adventure"* in which he explored the south seas were built at Whitby. Today Captain Cook is recognized as one of the greatest surveyors as well as one of the finest sailors and explorers of all time. He was the first navigator to explore Australia and New Zealand. On his memorable third voyage in 1779, he was killed by the natives of Owhyee, one of the Sandwich Islands (now Hawaii). The natives were compelled by his crew to surrender his body and he was buried at sea in Kealakekua Bay. An inter-

Caedmon had a vision in which he was presented with great quantities of remarkable poetry. St. Hilda ordered that these poems be written down. The songs of Caedmon are still being sung in northern England and exercised great influence on later English poets, especially John Milton.

After the Reformation, the Whitby Abbey dating from Norman times was pillaged for building stone. Today it stands as a majestic ruin. It was further damaged in December 1914 when German battleships shelled Whitby from the North Sea. A piece of shrapnel fired by one of these ships was given to Whitby, Ontario's Mayor Harry Jermyn in the 1950s. It is now in the Town

The 199 steps.

A father and son, William Scoresby Sr. (1760-1829) and William Scoresby Jr. (1778-1857) were also navigators from Whitby, Yorkshire. William Sr., a whaler, was the inventor of the crow's nest, from which a lookout man on sailing ships kept an eye open for ice or any other obstructions in the sea. Both father and son were involved in Arctic exploration and invented several nautical instruments. Scoresby Land in east Greenland is named in their honour.

Although perhaps better known as a holiday resort and fishing town in modern times, Whitby has a long history as an industrial port. In the 16th century, alum, mined at nearby Guisborough was shipped from Whitby harbour and coal was imported from Newcastle. By the 18th century, Whitby was the sixth largest port in Britain and the centre of a shipbuilding industry which continued until the early 1900s. The total area of the harbour at the mouth of the River Esk is 80 acres.

Whitby is also well known for a stone used in jewellery, called Whitby Jet. Two theories exist for its origin. One is that it is a form of carbon, like coal or lignite. The other is that the dark black stone was once the sap from prehistoric trees. Geologists say that the jet was exposed when glaciers cut the River Esk Valley through Whitby. Much

esting footnote to the Captain Cook story reveals that John Graves Simcoe (1752-1806), Upper Canada (Ontario's) first Governor, purchased his supplies from the estate of James Cook. The tent he erected as his first habitation at York (Toronto) in 1793, was originally owned by Captain Cook. A bronze statue of the famous navi-gator, on the base of which is carved Captain Cook's coat of arms, was erected on the West Cliff at Whitby in 1912. During the Cook Bicentenary celebrations in 1968/69, commemorative plaques were unveiled by the High Commissioners of Australia and New Zealand to mark Cook's first voyages in the Whitby-built ship

of the jet is found in Bituminous Shale between Robin Hood's Bay and Boulby near Whitby. For centuries, Whitby craftsman have made jewellery from Whitby Jet. Jet beads have been found in prehistoric burial places where bronze age people lived 10,000 years ago. It is thought that the shiny stones were worn to ward off evil spirits. The Romans took a great liking to jet which they made into rings, hair pins and bracelets. In Chaucer's time in the 14th century, jet was a fashionable stone. In the 19th century, Whitby Jet was used in mourning dress. The industry got a significant boost when Queen Victoria (1819-1901) ordered large quantities to wear after the death of her husband Prince Albert in 1861. By 1870, there were 1,500 men, women and children employed in making jewellery of Whitby Jet, which was shipped to all parts of the world. Although mourning gave Whitby Jet its booming trade, it also killed it. It became associated with funerals and gradually fell from favour. A brisk trade in cheaper and inferior jet imported from France and Spain also led to its demise.

Whitby also has a place in literature and entertainment. Bram Stoker created the fictional vampire *"Dracula"* while living in Whitby. Much of the story of Dracula is based on real locations in Whitby. In the book, Mina and Lucy stayed at a home on

G. 7180.   THE QUAY, WHITBY.

Fishing boats at Whitby Harbour.

the West Cliff, as did the lawyer who was hired to import fifty cases of common earth from Transylvania. It was from this cliff that Mina saw the sleepwalking Lucy in the churchyard with *"what looked like something dark bending over her"*. To rescue her, Mina ran up the 199 steps to St. Mary's churchyard. In recent years, a *"Dracula Trail"* was set out in Whitby by the London-based Dracula Society, so visitors could see the sites mentioned in the book.

The area around Whitby is also the setting for the popular television series *"Heartbeat"*, which features a police force in a small Yorkshire village in the 1960s. Some of the scenes are filmed in Whitby.

St. Hilda's School, at Sneaton Castle.

The connection between Whitby, Ontario and Whitby, Yorkshire, is a strong one. In 1939, Whitby's most famous son, Hamar Greenwood (1870-1948) arranged for a stone from Whitby Abbey to be shipped to Canada where it was placed in the wall of All Saints' Anglican Church. During the Second World War, soldiers from Whitby, Ontario visited their namesake town while on leave. In the records of the Town Hall at Whitby, England, are letters from James Wilde (1899-1984) a Whitby, Ontario soldier.

Another wartime link between the two Whitby's is their girls' private schools. In the fall of 1940, when German bombs were raining down on England, eight students from St. Hilda's School in Whitby, Yorkshire, were sent to the Ontario Ladies' College (now Trafalgar Castle School) in Whitby, Ontario. Refugees from the war, these and other St. Hilda's students remained at the Ontario Ladies' College in varying numbers for the next four years. When 25 St. Hilda's students arrived in 1941, the Ladies' College had to find funding to provide for their food. The Whitby War Effort Committee and the Rotary Club came to the rescue along with individual citizens to sponsor the girls' stay in Canada. Ontario Ladies' College provided clothing and travelling expenses, the Brock Theatre offered free admission to movies, and local doctors and dentists provided the English girls with free services. At Christmas the visitors from England were invited to stay at the homes of Whitby residents and received gifts from the community. One of the most emotional moments was the Christmas Festival at the Ontario Ladies' College in 1940 when the English girls, dressed like carol singers from the pages of Charles Dickens' novels, entered the main hall, carrying lanterns and singing an old traditional Christmas song.

Whitby, Yorkshire and Whitby, Ontario were again linked in Whitby, Ontario's Centennial year, 1955, when a mural depicting scenes from both towns was placed in a new British ocean liner, *"Ivernia"*. The two Whitby's were represented in a series of panels of *"City Cousins"* in the smoking room of the new liner. Pictures of Whitby, Yorkshire's harbour and Whitby,

Ontario's Court House (now the Centennial Building) were commissioned by the Cunard Steamship Company Limited, owners of the *"Ivernia"*, from British artist Mrs. D. E. Bates. Whitby, Ontario's Industrial Commissioner and Secretary of the Chamber of Commerce, Charles H. Chaytor (1912-1977) carried on a correspondence with the Cunard Company, the letters of which are in the Town of Whitby Archives. He was particularly pleased that this tribute to the twin towns occurred in Whitby's Centennial year, and sent copies of the town's Centennial booklet to be placed in the *"Ivernia's"* library. The *"Ivernia"* sailed between Britain and Canada until 1963 when it was sold to the Soviet Union. Its whereabouts today are unknown.

A visit by Whitby, England Mayor Ernest Hutchison and Councillor Harry Best to Whitby, Ontario, in March 1977, resulted in an official *"twinning"* of the two Whitbys. Although there are no official visits carried out on an annual basis as with Whitby's twinning partner, Longueuil, Quebec, occasional visitors are always welcomed. In 1997, Whitby, Ontario formally hosted a visit by the 60-voice Dalesmen Singers from Whitby, Yorkshire. Former Mayor Tom Edwards has visited Whitby four times, twice as mayor. In 1992 he was the honoured guest who spoke at the open-

Whitby Harbour and East Cliff with the Abbey ruin.

ing of a 1,000-seat auditorium in the English town.

With a population of a little over 13,000, Whitby, Yorkshire, England, is not only the source of the name of our community, but has developed strong community links with its namesake in Canada. But although our town is named after Whitby, years of research have indicated that not one resi-

dent of Whitby, Yorkshire ever settled in Whitby, Ontario, in pioneer times. The closest one comes to finding a Whitby native in this Canadian town, is Yeoman Gibson (1828-1894) a grocer, who came from the nearby village of Ebberston, Yorkshire.

New Zealand Has A Whitby Too

The bicentennial of the discovery of New Zealand by Captain James Cook gave birth to a new Town of Whitby, the third in the world. Named after Whitby, Yorkshire, where Captain Cook's voyage of discovery originated, Whitby, New Zealand was established in 1969 by Community Developments Consortium, a partnership of The National Mutual Life Association of Australasia and Jubilee Investments Limited. A half-hour's drive from the city of Wellington, Whitby is located on the sea shore near areas known as Paraparaumu and the Gold Coast.

A modern planned community, Whitby, New Zealand is being built in stages. By 1987, 1,700 homes had been built, with potential for another 700 sections by 1996. Whitby is surrounded by a backdrop of green rolling hills and sheltered valleys. The subdivisions as they are built, are contoured into the natural rolling hillsides. Like its counterpart in Ontario, Whitby, New Zealand is experiencing an unprecedented building boom. Each year about 120 new sections are put up for sale as a suburban community to Wellington, the capital city of New Zealand. Whitby won the 1978 environmental award of the New Zealand Institution of Engineers for its town planning and engineering. All its streets are named for associations with Captain Cook and seafaring. Among these streets are Spinnaker Drive, Leeward Terrace, The Anchorage, Capstan Lane and The Quarterdeck.

Like Whitby, Ontario, Whitby, New Zealand possesses a stone from the ancient Whitby Abbey in Yorkshire. The abbey stone came to Whitby in 1980 after several years of negotiations between the Consortium and interested people in Yorkshire. The Hemsworth Rotary Club was responsible for shipping the stone to New Zealand, where it is mounted in a display case in the Consortium office. Another Whitby Abbey stone is located in Tasmania.

Whitby, New Zealand has a population of 7,000, with a final population projected at 10,500. The area of the projected Whitby community is about 3,180 acres.

It is recognized around the world as one of the best model communities ever built.

Community Developments Consortium's

WHITBY

Shows the way

Picturesque Whitby, New Zealand, as shown in an advertising brochure.

The Nine-Mile Woods

The settlement of Whitby Township, which in the 1790s included all of what is now the Town of Whitby and the City of Oshawa, was slow to start. For a number of years, Whitby was known to the early settlers as *"the nine-mile woods on the road to Toronto"*, because of its lack of settlers. The reason for this was an arrangement made between the Government of John Graves Simcoe (1752-1806) and William Willcocks (1736-1813) a citizen of the town of Cork in Ireland. On Dec. 31, 1793, Willcocks was granted 1,000 acres of land in Whitby Township on the condition that he bring settlers from Ireland to his lands. The provision was that the land would be granted free to bona-fide settlers. Willcocks returned to Ireland, where he served as Mayor of Cork in 1794. During his term, he inserted advertisements in most of the newspapers of Britain, offering land to settlers in Whitby Township. He even had them published in Wales in the Welsh language. He advertised free grants if the settlers paid a fee to him, based on the number of acres they wanted. There would also be a small rental fee each year for the land. A ship would be provided for transport to Upper Canada. All passengers were required to provide their own bed and bedding. Tradesmen who could not pay their passage could get special terms.

Willcocks' problems with his immigration

Residence of Charles Lynde in the 4th Concession of Whitby Township in the 1860s. This frame house was replaced by a brick house in 1867.

project began when he could not obtain a ship, even though he said he had 200 families willing to immigrate. A number of these potential settlers decided to back out, because Britain was at war with France and an ocean voyage was particularly hazardous. He had to dispose of his property in Ireland, and finally sailed on an American ship with 33 settlers for Whitby on May 10, 1795. Arriving at New York on July 15, Willcocks and his settlers began to walk to Whitby, but the 500-mile journey was so long that many of the settlers were lured away by better offers of land in the United States. Not one made it to Whitby.

Seeing that it was not possible to entice settlers to come from Ireland, Willcocks began advertising in the United States for settlers to come with him to Whitby. On Aug. 25, 1795, he published the following advertisement in the Mohawk Mercury, at Schenectady, New York:

"Upwards of 30,000 Acres of the most excellent Land on the north side of Lake Ontario, in the Township of Whitby, about 18 miles East of the new Town of York (Toronto), now building for the seat of Government, 20 miles west of the Bay of Canty, and 30 north of Niagara, divided into 200 acre Lots:—Will be disposed of on moderate terms by Wm. Willcocks, Esq'r who will give good Encouragement to the first ten industrious Settlers that close with him before the first day of November next; Apply to him at Niagara or York, or at the printers of the Mohawk Mercury in Schenectady. N.B. This Township is nine miles front on Lake Ontario and twelve miles deep. It has three Good Harbors and several Capital Millseats."

This advertisement and others distributed by Willcocks, incurred the ire of the Government of Upper Canada, for he was offering his land for sale instead of free as per

An early settler's cabin in the 7th Concession of Whitby Township in the 1860s. This was the birthplace of Brooklin's poet, David Burns, August 6, 1850.

the terms of his agreement with the Government. Further problems arose when Willcocks found out that a ship carrying members of his family and some Irish settlers recruited by his son, was captured by the French and all hands were prisoners at Bordeaux. In January 1796, Willcocks was informed by the Government that he was to forfeit all his lands in Whitby Township for contravening the original settlement agreement. On May 25, 1796, Governor Simcoe ordered that Whitby and 11 other townships seized for similar reasons be declared open for settlement by any person who wanted land. Willcocks' agreement was terminated, but a year later, on June 28, 1797, the Government did offer him generous compensation. It was decreed that 1,200 acres in Whitby township would be granted each to Willcocks' wife Phoebe, his daughters, Maria, Phoebe and Eugenia, his son Charles, and his son's wife Ann. The grant amounted to 7,000 acres.

In spite of this offer, Willcocks still felt he deserved *"some token of the Royal favour in this Province"*. He was granted the position of judge of the Court of Common Pleas for the Home District, around Toronto, and was made a commissioner for the purchase of lands from the Mississauga Indians. When other townships were sold to obtain money to build the Danforth Road (Highway 2) Willcocks and members of his family bought five blocks of 3,000 acres each for only 500 pounds ($2,500).

Although it is acknowledged that Benjamin Wilson (1732-1821) was the first settler in Whitby Township, near the present Oshawa Harbour, about 1794, it is not known who was the first settler in what is now the Town of Whitby. Lots were numbered 1 to 35, east to west in Whitby Township and there were nine concessions plus the Broken Front along the lake shore, going south to north. When Whitby Township was split into Whitby and East Whitby Townships in 1857, lots 1 to 17 were in East Whitby (now Oshawa) and lots 18 to 35 were in Whitby Township (now the Town of Whitby). Early records give names of settlers for the entire township, so it is not possible to know who lived in the future Whitby and East Whitby without checking land titles.

The first census of Whitby and Pickering Townships was taken in 1803, showing a total of 130 inhabitants in both townships. In 1804, a census for Whitby alone reveals there were 88 inhabitants. The heads of the households, mostly in the area now occupied by Oshawa, were: George, William and Willard Hall, Benjamin Wilson, Charles Annis, Eleazer Lockwood, Matthew and Claphas Terwilligar, John McGahan, Adam, John and Joseph Stephens, Benjamin and John Smith, Silas Marvin, David Lloyd, Timothy Nightingale, Joseph Wily and Ebenezer Ransom. Later in 1804, Moody Farewell settled in what is now Oshawa, and in 1805, Jabez Lynde settled at Lynde Creek where it crossed the Danforth Road (Highway 2) in Whitby. The Lynde home was located at the *"29-mile tree"*, indicating it was exactly 29 miles east from Yonge Street in York (Toronto).

Before 1830, most of the settlers in Whitby Township were emigrants from the United States. They were not officially classified as United Empire Loyalists, for settlement occurred some years after the Loyalist migration. In 1811 Whitby Township had 279 settlers; by 1820 it had 505 inhabitants. In that year, one of the earliest families from Britain, the Drydens, came to Whitby from Durham County, England. British migration really began about 1830, after a very slow growth in the 35 previous years, most of the settlers coming from Devon, Cornwall and Yorkshire in England, Lanarkshire and Aberdeenshire in Scotland and County Fermangh in Ireland.

Smith's Canadian Gazetteer, in 1846, recorded the following information about Whitby Township, which contained all of what is now Whitby and Oshawa:

"in Whitby, 61,841 acres are taken up, 28,474 of which are under cultivation. This is a well settled township, containing a large portion of excellent land which is mostly rolling. The farms are generally well cleared and cultivated and are in good order. The timber is a mixture of hardwood and pine. There are some excellent mill streams in the township…There are eight grist and twenty-five saw mills in the township. Population in 1842: 5,714 with a mixture of English, Irish, Scotch, Canadians and Americans.'

The War of 1812 – General Brock Visits Jabez Lynde

On June 18, 1812, the United States declared war on Great Britain, and Canada became the battleground. Whitby Township, only sparsely settled, was not the scene of any major battles, but the few settlers there had their own experiences to tell of the war. In 1811, Whitby Township (which included all of what is now Whitby and Oshawa), had a population of 279, mostly emigrants from the United States. The War of 1812 halted all population growth in the township, and it is recorded that there were 289 people in Whitby in 1817, an increase of 10 over 1811.

The Danforth Road (later the Kingston Road, now Highway 2), the only road through the Township, was heavily travelled by soldiers and government officials during the war. The Danforth Road was built some distance back from the shore of Lake Ontario so that it would be out of range of cannon shot from American vessels on the lake. There was a small skirmish at Oshawa's Second Marsh during the war when an American gunboat sailed into the marsh and fired some cannon balls at a house, in an attempt to free prisoners captured by the British. More than 110 years after the war, Tom Henstock (1906-1981) dug a cannon ball out of the beach at the mouth of Lynde Creek, proving that some shots were fired in Whitby Township.

The Jabez Lynde house, circa 1905, Whitby's oldest building.

At the junction of the Danforth Road and Lynde Creek was the home of Jabez Lynde (1773-1856) one of Whitby's earliest settlers. He had settled on this spot in 1804 or 1805 and built himself a log cabin which served as a tavern for refreshing travellers on the Danforth Road. About February, 1811, with rumors of an impending war with the United States circulating freely, Jabez Lynde

received a knock on the door of his log tavern. He was surprised to see two men who identified themselves as General Isaac Brock, Governor of Upper Canada, and his aide-de-camp, Col. Drummond. Dressed in long plaid coats, lined with fur, they asked Jabez Lynde for fresh horses to take them to York (Toronto). *"The King's business required haste,"* they said. Lynde provided his best horses and drove the General and his aide-de-camp to Government House at York, in a record time of three hours and five minutes.

One person who for the rest of her life remembered this historic incident was Jabez's six-year-old daughter Clarissa (1805-1900) who later married William Warren (1800-1887). At the age of 92, in 1897, she recorded her memories of General Brock's visit to the Lynde home, in The Whitby Chronicle.

"The suavity of the commander-in-chief was manifest even in the wayside log inn, and won the heart of the little Canadian girl of the house, who for four score years has not ceased to sorrow for his untimely end."

General Brock was killed a year later on Oct. 13, 1812 at the Battle of Queenston Heights. He became an instant hero, and is commemorated by a monument near the site where he fell.

The other great incident of the war which involved residents of Whitby Township was the capture of York by the Americans on April 27, 1813. The Farewell family at Harmony (now the eastern part of Oshawa) clearly heard the cannon fire from York. The Farewells and other settlers jumped on their horses and rode to the aid of the town, but arrived just in time to be taken prisoners of war. When the Americans left after looting the town, the Farewells were set free.

The capture of York resulted in a panic-stricken exodus of citizens along the Danforth Road east toward Whitby Township. A dispatch rider warned Jabez Lynde of the coming refugees. A short time later, the wounded arrived at Lynde's home accompanied by Doctors Lee and Powell. The doctors asked Lynde if he had any spirits to ease the pain of the wounded men, and when told he had 18 gallons of liquor, they asked him to save it for further wounded that were to follow. Soldiers of the King's 8th Regiment soon arrived and demanded food and provisions at the point of a bayo-

Lynde family reunion, August 14, 1926.

net. Since there were no officers present to control them, the soldiers grabbed all they could from the Lynde home. A number slept on the floor and during the night one of the soldiers snuck into Mrs. Lynde's bedroom and cut a gold necklace from her neck while she slept.

Jabez Lynde submitted a claim for 83 pounds worth of provisions stolen from his house during the flight from York. At that time, all currency was in English money of pounds, shilling and pence. Among the items taken were 18 gallons of rum, a silver watch, eight silver tea spoons, four shirts, a blanket, a set of knives and forks, one pair of pants, a vest, a pair of silver sugar tongs, two handkerchiefs, a coat, a large supply of pork and ham, and Mrs.

Lynde's gold necklace. Lynde had to submit his claim several times, and obtain letters from members of his family and friends to back him up. It was not until 1816 that he was paid 68 pounds for his 83-pound loss.

Under normal circumstances, Jabez Lynde was well paid for his services to the Government during the War of 1812. He kept Government provisions at his home and he and his sons, Hawkins and Sylvester carried despatches for the Government along the Danforth Road. Lynde was paid in gold and at one time had eight pounds of the yellow metal in his strongbox. Soldiers regularly called for lodging and slept on the floor of Lynde's house, sometimes with their wives and children. The despatch carriers, although accompanied by soldiers, were in considerable danger from raiding Americans who crossed Lake Ontario at night to capture messages intended for British Government officials.

With the gold he earned during the War of 1812, Jabez Lynde built a home which was described as the finest house between York and Kingston. Nothing like it existed in Whitby Township at that time. He told his daughter, Clarissa, that his gold would have bought all the land between the Lynde house and Perry's Corners (downtown Whitby), *"a block of land one and a quarter miles square, at least, and probably he meant two and a half miles square."*

It is not known exactly when the Lynde house was built, but it was most likely during the War of 1812. After the death of Jabez Lynde's last child, Elmina (1815-1893), the house was willed to All Saints' Anglican Church. The church sold the Lynde house because it was too far away from the centre of town for it to be of any use. The new owners were Lawrence Heyden (1835-1906) and his sister Barbara (1830-1916), for whom Heydenshore Park was named in 1900. Lawrence Heyden was a Toronto lawyer who rented the house to various farmers. It was purchased in 1920 by William H. Balsdon (1862-1947).

When Balsdon lived in the house, a Lynde family reunion was held at the home on Aug. 14, 1926. Among those attending were George S. Henry, Ontario's Minister of Public Works, W.E.N. Sinclair (1873-1947), leader of the Ontario Liberal Party and Whitby Mayor John W. Bateman (1862-1948). Mayor Bateman dedicated a commemorative stone near the house, on which was inscribed: *"Lot 31, 2nd Con, Whitby Tp. Erected by his descendants in 1926 with the consent of the Minister of Highways to perpetuate the memory of Jabez Lynde who settled on this lot in the year 1800 with crown deed at Lynde Creek."* The inscription is somewhat inaccurate, for Jabez Lynde did not settle there until 1804 or 1805 and he purchased the land in 1811, rather than receiving a Crown Grant.

In 1939, Harry Arnold sold the Lynde farm to Pickering Farms Limited. The clapboard house was covered with stucco at this time, and used as a boarding house for farm laborers. In 1972 it was presented to the Whitby Historical Society for use as a museum, by Loblaws Groceries, which had acquired Pickering Farms. The donation was made with the provision that the house be moved. This was not done because the historical society could not raise the necessary funds to move it. In 1986, Len Cullen, owner of Cullen Gardens, offered to relocate the house to his tourist attraction in order to save it from impending demolition. On Aug. 22, 1986, the Lynde house was moved to Cullen Gardens, and opened as a living museum on June 25, 1988. The house is restored to the time of Jabez Lynde's death in 1856, and is furnished with antique furniture and mannequins of Jabez Lynde and his family.

The Lynde house, recognized as the oldest building in Whitby, was assured a permanent home and saved for future generations to admire. It is Whitby's only tangible link with the War of 1812 that remains to this day.

This Windsor Was Not The Royal Windsor

The first settlement that now makes up part of the Town of Whitby was Windsor, located at what is now Whitby Harbour. In 1802, the land surrounding Big Bay, one of the finest natural harbours on the north shore of Lake Ontario was granted to John Scadding (1754-1824). Born in Devonshire, England, Scadding was property manager for Ontario's first Governor, John Graves Simcoe (1752-1806). Scadding accompanied Simcoe to Upper Canada (Ontario) in 1792 and built a cabin near the mouth of the Don River at York (Toronto) in 1794. This cabin, moved by the York Pioneer and Historical Society to the grounds of the Canadian National Exhibition in 1879, is the oldest building in Toronto.

When Simcoe returned to England in 1796, Scadding went back with him to manage the Simcoe estate in Devonshire. In return for his faithful service, he was granted 1,000 acres of land in Whitby Township, some of which included the harbour known as *"Big Bay."* Scadding returned to Canada in 1818 to manage his land, and about 1819 founded the village of Windsor at Big Bay. He laid out a plan for this village, naming three of the streets after his sons, John, Charles and Henry. Of these three, only Charles Street retains its original name today. John Street's name was changed to Dufferin Street in the 1880s, after Lord

The Goldring Store, south-west corner of Brock and Victoria Streets, demolished in 1967.

Dufferin, the Governor-General of Canada, who opened the Ontario Ladies' College (Trafalgar Castle School) in 1874. Henry Street was changed to Maitland Street after Sir Peregrine Maitland (1777-1854),

Governor of Upper Canada from 1818 to 1828. Part of this street was named Watson Street, east of Dufferin Street, after John Watson (1806-1879), one of the early grain merchants at Port Whitby. In 1955, the

Whitby Harbour Company's grain elevator, 1866-1916, built by Chester Draper.

officially changed in 1847. John Scadding built the first home in Windsor and set out to develop the community. But his time at Windsor was short-lived. On March 1, 1824, at the age of 70, while attempting to chase trespassers off his property at the Don River, Scadding was killed by a falling tree. His sons, John (1807-1845), Charles (1809-1892) and Henry (1813-1901) continued to own the village of Windsor and sold off lots to new settlers over a period of many years. Of all the Scaddings, the most famous was Henry, who served as rector of Holy Trinity Church, built in Toronto in 1847. This church and Henry Scadding's house are located behind the Eaton Centre in downtown Toronto. Henry Scadding's greatest achievement was the writing of Toronto's first history, *"Toronto of Old,"* published in 1873. It is interesting to note that the present Henry Street in Whitby has no relation to Henry Scadding, but was named after Henry Annes (1824-1886).

It was always the intention of John Scadding to provide land for a church in Windsor, but his early death prevented that from happening. In April 1848, John Strachan (1778-1867), the Anglican Bishop of Toronto, officially accepted the gift of land for St. John's Anglican Church from Charles and Henry Scadding. Construction of the church actually began three years pre-

entire street, west to Charles Street was named Watson Street.

John Scadding named his settlement at Big Bay, *"Windsor,"* not after the Royal residence in England, but after a small piece of property he owned in the Parish of Luppitt in Devonshire. Thus Whitby obtained the name it was to bear for 28 years until it was

viously, in 1845.

It is said that Scadding could have called his community *"Scaddington"* or *"Scaddingfield,"* and that name might have existed to this day, but, being a modest man, he did not want his settlement at Big Bay named after him. The name *"Windsor,"* however, soon began to create problems. The post office first opened in Whitby Township in 1824 was called *"Whitby,"* but the harbour was called *"Windsor"* or *"Windsor Bay."* By the 1840s, confusion was occurring in the customs returns and the mails sent to and from Windsor Bay, because of the other town of Windsor, near Detroit. In letter to J.H. Dunn, Receiver General of Canada, William Dow Jr. (1807-1843), Collector of Customs at Windsor Harbour, had to remind his employer that: *"a number of letters sent to me from the Public Offices during the past year have been arrived to Windsor in the Western District. Have the goodness to address to Windsor, Whitby."*

As settlements developed at Hamer's Corners (Dundas and Anderson Streets) and Perry's Corners (Brock and Dundas Streets), the name *"Windsor"* was applied to them as well. Perry's Corners, named after Peter Perry (1792-1851) was also called *"Windsor"* and Hamer's Corners, named after John Hamer (1787-1872) was called *"East Windsor."*

The problem of misdirected mail and produce had become so serious that on July 10, 1847, a public meeting was called at Scripture's Inn, to officially change the name of *"Windsor"* to *"Whitby."* Scripture's Inn at that time was a rough-cast building that stood until 1990 at the corner of Dundas and Euclid Streets where the Canada Trust office is now. Ezra Annes (1796-1857) was elected chairman of the meeting and Alexander McPherson (1803-1861) was Secretary, and the following resolutions were passed:

"Resolved – That the inhabitants of the Village now called Windsor, as also those residing at Windsor Harbour, in the Township of Whitby, having for a long time experienced very great inconvenience on account of there being another Village, Port of Entry and Post Town in the Western District of the same name to which letters and other papers of importance intended for delivery at Whitby Post Office, are frequently sent, thereby occasioning much delay and often serious loss to parties interested, or more immediately connected with the Port of Entry, the meeting therefore deems it proper and expedient to change the name of the Village and Port of Entry of this place, and that henceforth the name of the village be WHITBY instead of Windsor, and the Port of Entry the PORT OF WHITBY, instead of Windsor Harbour.

"Resolved – That it is necessary that the limits of the said Village and Port of Whitby be fixed and determined, and that the same to extend from Lots 22 to 31 inclusive, in the broken front, and to the first Concession, and the South half of the second Concession of the said Township.

"Resolved – That it is expedient to Petition the Governor General and Council, praying that the name of the village now known as Windsor, and the Port of Entry known as Windsor Harbour, be changed, and the limits thereof defined as above mentioned, and that Mr. Perry, Mr. Burnham, Mr. McPherson, Mr. Yarnold, Mr. Laing and Mr. Yule be a Committee to draft the said Petition, procure signatures thereto, and forward the same to His Excellency the Governor-General, and generally to do and perform all such other matters for the promotion of the above object, as to them shall appear necessary.

"Resolved – That copies of the proceedings of this meeting be sent to the Colonist and Globe for publication."

EZRA ANNES, Chairman.
A. McPHERSON, Secretary.

After John Scadding's death, the development of Windsor practically stopped until the beginning of the 1830s when immigra-

St. John's Anglican Church in 1913.

most important function of the port from the 1830s until 1890, when the McKinley Tariff Act put tariffs on Canadian grain shipped to the United States. This political action by the Americans killed Port Whitby as a commercial harbour.

Port Windsor was declared a Port of Entry and a Customs Collector appointed, in 1831. The first Customs Collector was Francis K. Tincombe (1792-1833). He was first buried in a long-gone pioneer cemetery near the Sunnycrest Nursing Home on Highway 2 between Thickson and Kendalwood Roads, and re-interred as the first burial in St. John's Cemetery at Port Whitby, in 1846. William Warren (1800-1887) was the longest serving Customs Collector, for 32 years (1843-1875). He was forced into retirement at 74 because of old age. HIs successor, Dr. George A. Carson (1822-1910) moved the customs office uptown from the harbour. It remained in downtown Whitby, until moving to Oshawa in 1935.

Windsor (Whitby) Harbour reached its peak of commercial activity in 1853, when it was second only to Toronto for the amount of business done by ports on the north shore of Lake Ontario. One of the finest natural harbours on the lake, it was a port of refuge in storms and the arrival point for many settlers coming to Upper

tion from England, Ireland and Scotland to Whitby Township began. Most of the earliest settlers of Windsor Bay were Irish Protestants: James Rowe (1799-1869), John Welsh (1810-1859), John Watson (1806-1879), and William Smith (?-1893). These men and others formed the core of the mercantile and commercial community that grew at Port Windsor. They were involved in shipping grain from the harbour, the

Canada to take up land to the north.

The following is a description of Windsor Harbour, printed in Smith's Canadian Gazetteer in 1846:

"A village and shipping place in the township of Whitby situated on Lake Ontario about 32 miles from Toronto. An excellent harbour has been formed here by constructing a breakwater and building two piers; within the breakwater is enclosed a basin about 120 acres in extent, which when completed will have a depth of ten feet. The width of the channel at its entrance between the piers is 250 feet; and there is a light house on the west pier. Up to July 1st, 1844 £15,355 was expended on this harbour. A plank road is in course of formation from the harbour to Scugog lake. The steamboat "America" (a British boat) calls here daily on her passage to and from Rochester and Toronto. Seven schooners whose collective tonnage amounts to about 400 tons are owned here. Windsor Harbour is a port of entry and has a resident collector of customs. There are two churches in the village; Episcopal (built of stone) and Methodist. Population about 250. Professions and trades — one brewery, three stores, four taverns, one saddler, two blacksmiths, two tailors, one wheelwright, one baker, one ship carpenter."

Exports from the Port of Windsor during the season of 1844

Flour	21,597 barrels	peas	290 bushels
Pork	1,435 barrels	grass seeds	1,175 bushels
Ashes	610 barrels	potatoes	1,240 bushels
Oatmeal	285 barrels	butter	32 firkins
Beer	120 barrels	lard	32 kegs
Wheat	14,563 bushels	hams	14,000 lbs.
Oats	1,682 bushels	lumber	646,000 feet

The Port Whitby Lighthouse, constructed in 1857 and removed from the wharf in 1958. Built by Harbormaster Christopher McDermott (1810-1895), it stood at the end of the west pier for 101 years.

Nothing Remains of Hamer's Corners

The second settlement which makes up the present Town of Whitby is but a very distant memory. Nothing remains today of a thriving business centre which was in existence more than 13 years before downtown Whitby was founded.

The settlement, at the present intersection of Dundas Street with Anderson and Hopkins Streets, was called Hamer's Corners. It was founded as the first settlement in Whitby along the Kingston Road, in the early 1820s, and was joined to Windsor Harbour by a foot path through the woods. The original name of the settlement was Crawford's Corners, named after an early settler, Caleb Crawford, who purchased land at the south-west corner of Dundas and Hopkins Streets in 1807. Nothing is known of this man except his name.

Crawford's Corners first became a settlement of importance when the Government of Upper Canada decided to open the first post office between York (Toronto) and Port Hope, there. John B. Warren (1798-1879) opened a store, likely on the corner where the Hong Kong Bank is now located, about 1823. The post office, known as Whitby Post Office, was opened in his store in March of 1824, with Warren as the first postmaster. The following letter from Postmaster General William Allan, now in the Metro Toronto Public Library, authorized Warren to open the post office:

York, 9th March, 1824.

Mr. John B. Warren:

Sir:

"I herewith enclose you your commission as a Deputy Post Master at Whitby together with a key for the padlock of the post box which you will please acknowledge the receipt of and you will also receive some blank way bills too, in order you may commence after the 5th proximo. You had better put up a notice at Mr. Still's or any other public place that a post office is to be opened at that time. You will upon no occasion detain the courier either going or coming. You must be always ready to receive him, and put up any letters you may have to forward as he happens along.

I am, Sir.
W. Allan

P.S. Any letters on your own business you are entitled to get free of postage or to forward any for yourself from your own office only free also. W.A."

It took a while for the settlers of the area served by the Whitby Post Office to realize that such a facility existed for their use. William Lyon Mackenzie (1795-1861) published the following notice in his newspaper, The Colonial Advocate, on Feb. 28, 1825:

"It seems there is a post office within 28 miles of this place, called Whitby of which Mr. Warren is Postmaster. We give this notice to the public as many may be at this moment ignorant of its existence. It would be well if these alterations were noticed by order of the Postmaster General, in quarterly advertisements, as usual in Britain."

Mr. Still, at whose house a notice was posted, was Deacon John Still (1783-1832), a local Methodist preacher, who has the distinction of having the earliest obituary published for any person living in Whitby. John B. Warren moved the post office after a few years, to a site opposite where the Sunnycrest Nursing Home is now, on Dundas Street between Thickson and Kendalwood Roads. He remained as Whitby's postmaster until about 1836, when he moved to Oshawa and remained there the rest of his life. The second post office in the former Ontario County was opened at Pickering in 1839, and a post office was opened at Oshawa in 1842. The oldest known letter to survive from John B. Warren's post office is one written by Warren himself, on Dec. 15, 1831. It was sent to Montreal, free of postage, as granted by the Postmaster General in his letter quoted above.

In 1835, John Hamer (1787-1872) arrived from Radnorshire, Wales, and opened a general store at Crawford's Corners. Hamer, known to his friends as *"John Bull,"* accumulated a considerable fortune, but lost most of his money by loaning it to other settlers without interest. He built a fine home, called *"Whitehall,"* and the settlement of Crawford's Corners soon became known as Hamer's Corners.

Another early storekeeper at Hamer's Corners was James Wallace (1814-1882) who was the second Mayor of Whitby in 1856. His store was in a brick building called the Emerald House. In 1852, Ross Johnston (1827-1911) took over the Emerald House and found on a shelf in a back room a dog collar with a brass plate on it on which was inscribed: *"I am James Wallace's dog; whose dog are you?"*

A stone blacksmith shop was located on the north-east corner of Dundas and Anderson Streets, the date of which is unknown, but it was likely one of the earliest buildings at Hamer's Corners. It was demolished in 1963. East of this building,

John B. Warren

about where the Harvey's hamburger outlet is now, was a large brick building constructed by Peter M. Nicol (1808-1887) in 1836 as a general store. One of the first brick buildings to be constructed in Whitby, it

housed prisoners after the Rebellion of 1837. In the 1860s it was kept as a hotel called the Victoria House, by John Spurrill (1809-1888), a former sergeant in the British army. The building was demolished in the fall of 1965 when Dundas Street was widened to four lanes of traffic.

On the north-west corner of Dundas and Anderson Streets stood another brick building, the Royal Oak Hotel, which was demolished in 1913. Today, Marigold Lincoln Mercury is on this site. At the back of the Marigold Lincoln Mercury property stood a brick cottage built about 1852 for William Anderson (1786-1862), for whom Anderson Street is named. He retired to this house from a farm north of Rossland Road which he had settled in 1834. There were as many as four hotels at Hamer's Corners, when it was the business centre of Whitby from the 1830s to the 1850s. A school house was also located near the present site of Anderson Collegiate.

On the south side of Dundas Street, opposite East Side Mario's stood the brick house owned by William Till (1810-1867). Till, a cabinet-maker and undertaker, opened his business at Hamer's Corners in 1833 and in the 1850s, moved it to what is now downtown Whitby. The Till house and the Peter M. Nicol house were the oldest brick buildings in Whitby, having been constructed in

Stone blacksmith shop at Hamer's Corners, 1963.

(See the chronicle of James Tweedie's letter of Aug. 21, 1831, for a reference to building this house). The home, in later years known as the Polley house, was moved to Cullen Gardens in the 1980s to be part of Len Cullen's *"Prettiest Little Street in Ontario."* It is the last surviving building from the original settlement of Hamer's Corners.

By the 1840s, Hamer's Corners was known officially as East Windsor or Windsor East, because of its location about a mile and a half east of Windsor (Perry's Corners). The following is the only written description of Windsor East, which was published in Smith's Canadian Gazetteer in 1846:

"Windsor East – A small settlement in the Township of Whitby, about half a mile east from Windsor. It contains one saddler, two tailors, one cabinet maker, one waggon maker, one blacksmith."

In 1850, Perry's Corners began to take over from Hamer's Corners as the commercial centre of Whitby, because it was located at the junction of the Kingston Road and the Centre Road, the main route for taking goods south to Windsor Harbour. By the 1870s, the hotels closed and many of the early buildings of Hamer's Corners were abandoned or converted into dwellings.

the 1830s. The Till house was demolished in 1974.

West of the Till house was a home built of mud bricks and covered with board and batten siding. Dating from the 1830s, it was the only one of its kind in Whitby. It too, was demolished in 1974.

On the south-west corner of Dundas and Hopkins Street stood a brick cottage built in 1854 for William Thorndyke. It was demolished in 1958. South of the Thorndyke cottage was a one-storey frame building, believed to have been constructed in 1831 as the residence of James Tweedie (1803-1857).

Peter M. Nichol's house, Hamer's Corners, 1961.

named, was an uncle of John Hamer Greenwood (1829-1902), one of Whitby's most colourful characters, who served five terms as mayor and was the father of Hamar Greenwood (1870-1948), Whitby's most famous native son.

John Hamer's obituary in the Whitby Chronicle of Feb. 29, 1872 stated: *"The deceased gentleman was born at Cemgrenliug, in Radnor, Wales, on the 7th of December 1787. He was engaged for a number of years as an exciseman and supervisor in the south of England. In 1835 he emigrated to this country, and after knocking about for a short time, settled at 'Hamer's Corners' -- now part of the Corporation of the Town of Whitby -- where he engaged in business as a general storekeeper. He retired from business some nineteen years ago and was reputed to be a man of considerable wealth. This, however, got scattered about, and ran through his hands by loaning it out without interest; and we believe that he died in comparatively narrow circumstances. Mr. Hamer had some peculiarities, but he had many excellent and characteristic traits of the thorough-going Englishman. His remains were accompanied to their last resting place on Tuesday last (Feb. 27) by a large concourse of old friends and neighbours who had known him long."* He died at the home of his nephew, John Hunt (1811-1874) on Feb. 25, 1872.

Today, not a single building from Hamer's Corners remains on its original site. In the 1960s, modern commercial development began to replace the few remaining original buildings of this settlement which was a thriving community 170 years ago. The traveller today would not know that a settlement had ever existed there, for the highway has become a strip of car lots, fast food outlets and other related businesses.

It is of interest to note that John Hamer, for whom this long-gone settlement was

The Almonds Community Was Known For Its Church

At the intersection of Highway 2 and Lakeridge Road, at the western limit of the Town of Whitby, was a small community that is now all but vanished. This community was named *"Almonds"* after James Almond (1809-1894), a native of Lincolnshire, England, who settled there in the 1830s. The story is told that Platt Betts, an American Quaker who owned land at Almonds, was faced with a dilemma because his religion forbade him from taking up arms either for or against the Family Compact during the troubled 1830s. The Reformers, under William Lyon Mackenzie (1795-1861) had been agitating for years against an entrenched government of elite Tories called the Family Compact, which ruled Upper Canada. In December 1837, a rebellion occurred at Toronto and was mercilessly put down by the Family Compact. Not wishing to be drawn into this political conflict, Betts exchanged his land with James Almond and returned to the United States. Almond gave up his land in New York State and settled on Betts' land in Whitby Township. A Justice of the Peace, James Almond was a leading figure in the history of the township for the next 60 years.

The focal point of the Almonds community was its church, which was built about 1837 and demolished in 1977. A frame chapel built by the Wesleyan Methodists, it

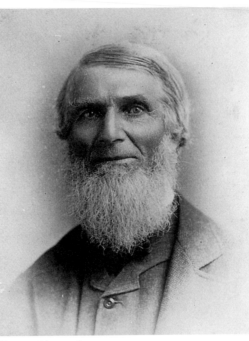

James Almond

stood on the south side of the Kingston Road (Highway 2), west of James Almond's residence. In 1837, Almond and his wife Mary donated the land where the church was built, to the Trustees of the Wesleyan Methodist Church. Previously a congregation had been formed, and worshipped in a local barn. The early history of Almonds Church is not well recorded, but The

Wesleyan, a Methodist newspaper, reported that a chapel was opened in Whitby Township on Aug. 24, 1842. It is believed that this was the Almonds church.

After donating the land, James Almond became one of the leading men in the management of the little church. He served as a lay preacher, class leader, Sunday School superintendent and janitor. Whenever the travelling preacher could not make it to the church on a Sunday, Almond conducted the services himself. In January 1887, when he retired as Sunday School superintendent, Almond was presented with a pair of gold-rimmed spectacles and a printed address of appreciation. Members of the first board of trustees of the church when Almond gave the land in 1837 were: Nathaniel Blow (1810-1881), James Wilson, James Irving, George Clarke, James Storey (1802-1887), Nicholas DeHart (1808-1895) and William Stephenson.

In 1864, Almonds, Whitby, Brooklin, Columbus and Kedron were all served by one minister with Almonds being the senior congregation of the circuit. For many years Almonds was affiliated with the Whitby Methodist Tabernacle (St. Mark's United Church), with one minister serving both churches. It was a struggle for such a small congregation to continue, and the church was nearly closed in 1921, but Almonds

Almonds School, destroyed by fire in 1917. Photo taken in 1907.

Church carried on. In 1948, a 25-foot addition was built at the back of the church to provide a kitchen and Sunday School. In the fall of 1971, the congregation voted to join St. Mark's United Church, and the Almonds Church was closed. It was demolished in 1977.

Today a stone replica of the church, built of materials from the old building, stands on the site, along with a bronze plaque giving its history. The monument was built in 1982 and the plaque dedicated on June 23, 1984. The windows of the model of the church are made from blackboard slate from the old Almonds school.

Almonds Church at the time of its 125th anniversary, 1962.

1917) had a home and blacksmith shop on the south-east corner. The house was demolished in 1969. To the east of the Kempthorne house was a general store which served the community for many years.

After the Second World War, a small subdivision was built south of the Almonds corner by Henry Cresser Gaskins (1881-1959), a civil engineer who had practiced in Montreal and the Eastern United States. He moved to Almonds about 1937. Cresser Avenue in this subdivision is named after him, and Almond Avenue is named after James Almond. While living at Almonds, Gaskins was in the real estate and insurance business.

Little of the old Almonds community has survived to this day. James Almond's brick house, east of the church, is one of the few original buildings still standing.

Considerable changes will come to the Almonds area in the next five years. In 1999, Provincial approval was given to provide an interchange at Highway 401 and Lakeridge Road. There is also a proposal to build a link between Highway 401 and the projected Highway 407 south of Brooklin, which would follow Hall's Road. The Whitby Town Council would like the link to be on Lakeridge Road, but the final location is yet to be decided.

Almonds for many years was a separate and distinct community. A school stood on the north-west corner of Highway 2 and Lakeridge Road. The original brick building burned down in 1917 when a tramp broke into it, and a new school was built. The 1917 school was demolished about 1977. It was known as Union School Number One because it served both Whitby and Pickering Townships. Charles Kempthorne (1846-

The Potash Industry Gave Ashburn Its Name

The village of Ashburn, located at the intersection of the Ashburn and Myrtle Roads, was founded because of the potash industry. As settlers moved into Whitby Township and cleared the land for the establishment of farms, the trees from the dense forest were burned to ashes. In the vicinity of Ashburn, asheries were built for the production of potash from the wood ashes to make soap and candles. As the ashes were burned, thus the name *"Ashburn"* was created for this small community.

The first settler at what is now Ashburn was Richard Butler who built a log house on the south-east corner of the Brock Road and the 9th Concession (Myrtle Road) in 1832. The Brock Road (now Ashburn Road) was built from Whitby Harbour into Reach Township in 1831. The community around Butler's house was originally called *"Butler's Corners"* but became Ashburn about 1850.

By 1847, Noah Bates opened the first store and on Dec. 6, 1852 a post office called *"Ashburn"* was opened, with Edward Olver (1798-1882) as post master. The first church congregation was established at Ashburn in 1849, mainly through the efforts of William Heron (1792-1884). This congregation was Presbyterian, as Ashburn was almost entirely settled by

Ashburn General Store, 1883.

immigrants from Scotland. For many years the only non-Scottish people buried at Ashburn Cemetery were Edward Olver, who was born in Cornwall, England, and the children of Adam Duff (1819-1896) who was born in County Monaghan, Ireland. The Duff children, James and William, were the first to be buried in the cemetery, in 1858. A frame church was built on the site the previous year.

The centre of a rich grain farming community, Ashburn had a population of 200 by 1857, with 11 businesses listed in the Canada Directory for that year.

They were: John Bates, carpenter and painter; Daniel Bowler, wagon maker; John Burchell, shoe maker; William Foley, shoe maker; James Lawrence, saddler; Edward Olver, tailor; Joseph Robinson, hotel keeper; James Ross, general store keeper, George Smith, teacher; Alexander Wilson, hotel keeper and James Lawder, post master.

By 1865, Ashburn had one accountant, a book agent, an architect and builder, two blacksmiths, a bonnet maker, two boot and shoe makers, two second hand brokers, a butcher, a carpenter and builder, a carriage and wagon maker, a druggist, dress maker, two general merchants, a hotel keeper, two justices of the peace, a lime burner, a mason and bricklayer, milliner, paper hanger, ploughmaker, saddle, harness and trunk dealer; sash, door and blind manufacturer, a school teacher, two sewing machine agents, a shingle maker, a stone cutter, two tailors and a post master.

The following description of Ashburn is taken from Mitchell and Company's Gazetteer and Directory of Ontario County, published in 1866:

"*A post village in the Township of Whitby*

The Wilson House Hotel, 1975.

and the South Riding of the County of Ontario. It is situated in the midst of an excellent growing country, 9 miles from Whitby, and was first settled about the year 1832 by Richard Butler, who is still residing in the same log-house. The first post office

was established in 1852, Edward Olver, Postmaster, who was succeeded by Wm. Ross, and finally re-appointed, and is acting at the present time. The village contains one church, viz: Canada Presbyterian, built of frame about seven years ago; there is also one com-

Burns' Presbyterian Church in 1966, a year before the fire.

mon school, numbering about 80 pupils, of whom Benjamin Wood is teacher. The Orange Society, Lodge No. 796 holds its meetings here on the first Tuesday of each month. The business of the village is thriving and consists of two stores, one excellent hotel, kept by George Metcalf; 1 blacksmith; 1 wagon-maker; 1 saddler; 2 tailors; 2 carpenters, etc. Daily mail. Population 250."

One of Ashburn's finest landmarks is the old Wilson House Hotel, built in 1868/69 by Alexander Wilson. It stands on the north-east corner of the Four Corners of Ashburn. Wilson advertised *"wines, liquors and cigars of best brands"* and *"good stabling with attentive ostlers in attendance."* In the early 1900s when Local Option votes did away with serving liquor in Whitby's hotels, the Wilson House became an ice cream bar. Every Saturday, a barber would set up his chair in the hotel and cut hair for 25 cents a head.

Ross Johnston (1827-1911), the travelling salesman for the Whitby Chronicle, spent a night at the Wilson House in 1884 and reported that: *"I cannot in justice to myself or others say that I spent a very comfortable night here, for my room, in addition to being exceedingly cold, was lacking in some of those conveniences that travellers have a right to expect. I have no desire to come down to details."* It is likely that he was referring to the toilet facilities, which at that time would have consisted of a ceramic chamber pot, often called a *"thunder mug."*

"The village of Ashburn is pleasantly situated about a mile and a half west of Myrtle and about 11 miles from Whitby," Johnston continued. *"It is a rather smart little place and somewhat ambitious, as an attempt was made a few years ago to establish a cattle market here. I find that Ashburn has at least one representative in nearly all the departments of business that help make a flourishing village."* Johnston also noted that the Presbyterian Manse, built in 1878, was the only brick building in Ashburn, in addition to the Wilson House hotel.

The Burns' Presbyterian Church, built in 1857, was raised in 1911 and a basement put under it. Tragically, this fine old church burned down on a bitterly cold day, Feb. 12, 1967, and was replaced a year later with the present brick church.

Some of the early Scottish families of Ashburn still remain in the community today – the Herons, Fishers and Gardners, as well as others. The most noted person born in Ashburn was Alice Roger, Mrs. Alexander J. Collins (1878-1955), daughter of the Presbyterian minister, Rev. Walter M. Roger. A concert pianist, she published a number of songs and poems in Canada and England. She was one of Canada's early organizers of the campaign to obtain votes for women and was a member of the Canadian Authors' Association and the Canadian Women's Press Club which was founded by a Whitby man, George H. Ham (1847-1926), in 1904. Mrs. Collins travelled around Ontario with her husband, and retired to Peterborough where she died on Feb. 6, 1955, at the age of 76.

In the 1970s, Ashburn was unofficially twinned with the community of Ashburn in the State of Georgia, U.S.A. Some of the Canadian Ashburn's residents visited their namesake in Georgia, particularly Mr. and Mrs. Edgar Heron. Edgar (Ted) Heron (1908-1992) was a great grandson of William Heron who settled on Dalmore Farm near Ashburn in the 1840s and founded the Burns' Presbyterian Church congregation in 1849. This year the congregation will celebrate its 150th anniversary.

The hub of the community of Ashburn remains the general store, which has stood for nearly 150 years.

A bill from Thomas Allan Fisher, Ashburn General Store, July 15, 1879

Whitby's Settlers Relied On Money From Home To Get Started

Whitby's pioneers 170 years ago found hired help hard to obtain and had to rely on money sent from the old country in order to survive their first years in Canada. Life in the 1830s, when most of Whitby's immigrants began to arrive from England, Ireland and Scotland, is well illustrated by the earliest known letter written by a settler in this community. It was written on Aug. 21, 1831 by James Tweedie (1803-1857), a native of Symington, Lanarkshire, Scotland. At the age of 28, James and his bride Jane Crone (1810-1890) came to Canada on a sailing vessel and looked for a place to settle in Scarborough Township. Not finding this township to his liking, he finally selected some land at the south-west corner of Dundas and Hopkins Streets in Whitby Township. Writing to his brother in Scotland, James Tweedie had the following to say about his new home in the wilderness of Upper Canada:

"We left Scarboro about the 10th of May and came to this township (Whitby). It is about 31 miles from York (Toronto) on the road to Kingston and two miles from Windsor Bay (Whitby Harbour), where all the produce of this part of the country is shipped for Montreal. This part of the country will suit me better than that I sold, for the land is a great deal better here than it is there and our market is as convenient. I have only got 100 acres of land here and the man I bought it of has to build us a farm house 40 feet long and 22 feet wide, a storey and a half high and a cellar 16 by 34, all to be finished off."

This frame house, presumably built in late 1831, is one of the oldest in Whitby. In the 1980s, it was moved to Cullen Gardens to be part of a complex of historic homes called the Prettiest Street In Ontario. This street of boutiques and bed-and-breakfasts has yet to be completed.

James Tweedie continues: *"I bought seven acres of wheat on the ground that is cut and in the barn. It was a very good crop. I have 200 bushels from it. I intend putting it all into wheat this fall. The oats and peas are a very good crop and nearly ripe. There are about 60 or 70 acres*

Jane Tweedie (centre) with seven of her 13 children, shortly before her death in 1890. Back Row: Elizabeth, James Jr., Catherine, Frances. Middle Row: John, Mrs. James Tweedie, Mary. Front Row, Jane, Rebecca.

cleared on this place and the stumps mostly gone, but Mr. Grienchiels can make you understand better than I can by writing to you about it. I have to pay 500 pounds ($2,500) for this farm, the half I have paid down and have taken a bond for a deed and I have to pay the other half in five years in regular installments, six per cent on the money that is to pay. I intend next year to try a small dairy as I think it will pay as well as anything in the country. There is a few things that I should like to get, one is a cheese press and a cheese vat to be a pattern for the coopers around here to hole a cheese of about 18 lbs.

"I should like to get a good ploughman out from our neighbourhood as the land works well with the iron plough and the men here know nothing about ploughing. I have the hired man this summer and it keeps me a little too busy. I bought a pair of very good horses for the plough and have sold all of my oxen. There are two or three men that I have thought would suit me very well. David Brown of Wintermoor had some thought of coming. If he would come to me I would give him $100 a year. That is common wages here and I could get good-like English men for the money but I would rather prefer to have one that I know. So as soon as this comes to hand would you take the trouble to inquire and write me as soon as possible, so that I may not disappoint myself here, for I must have one next summer. You may go about it very quickly and make little sound about it. It is a long way from

The Tweedie home at Broadfield, Cochrane Street and Rossland Road, in the 1880s.

Symington here, but the voyage can be accomplished.

"I intend to get a threshing machine put in next summer as we have millwrights here now. It is a very poor way of threshing out the grain with horses treading on it. Being always impatient about this money coming out, I did not conclude this letter until I came to York to see whether there was any money for me at the bank, but meeting with a disappointment, I was

Broadfield farm house as it appeared in July 1975, 18 years before it was demolished. It was built by George Sonley (1805-1893), a resident of the 4th Concession of Whitby Township.

which he moved, and called the farm *"Broadfield"* after his ancestral home in Scotland. James Tweedie died in 1857 at the early age of 54, but his family continued to farm Broadfield until his son David died in 1912. In 1845, George Sonley built one of the first brick houses in Whitby Township for James Tweedie. The house was demolished in October 1993, to make way for a subdivision. In 1914 the farm's name was changed to Twin Stream Farm, named after the two branches of the Lynde Creek which ran through it. For 66 years it was farmed by the family of James G. Kerr (1866-1949).

James Tweedie had a family of 13 children, the last of which, Rebecca (Mrs. James Campbell) died in Chicago in 1925. A relative of Mrs. Campbell forwarded the 1831 letter to Edwin Storey (1850-1939) who had it published in the Whitby paper, The Gazette and Chronicle, on Oct. 31, 1935. The whereabouts of the original letter today is unknown.

James Tweedie and his family were among the first immigrants from Scotland to arrive in Whitby Township when they settled here in 1831. The last member of the family to live in town was Mrs. James Tweedie Jr. (1854-1945). She had four children, all of whom died under the age of one year. With her death, the Tweedie name died out in Whitby.

rather dissatisfied after mentioning it so often to the whole of you, as James Davidson cannot pay me as much as he had agreed to do, and I am rather at a loss to get along as I expected. In case I do not get a letter written to my brother David, you must try and forward to me all the money you can as quickly as possible for I will want some more building done in the spring."

James Tweedie must have got his money, for he became a prosperous farmer. In 1835 he purchased 200 acres at the north-west corner of Rossland Road and Cochrane Street, to

Glen Dhu School Recalls Home Of One Of Whitby's Earliest Scottish Settlers

Glen Dhu Public School, opened on March 6, 1990, stands near the site of one of Whitby's earliest farms, settled by William Dow in 1833. The name "Glen Dhu" is Gaelic for *"black valley"* or *"Dow's valley"*, in the ancient language of Scotland.

William Dow (1777-1855) was born on Feb. 11, 1777 at Auchinderran, part of Sir Ralph Abercromby's estate in the parish of Marnoch, Banffshire. He was married to Margaret Lumsden (1785-1833), who gave birth to 11 children between 1807 and 1826. The sons became leaders of the community in Whitby and the daughters married into influential families in Whitby and Pickering.

In 1832, Dow, his wife and children and two grandchildren, immigrated to Canada, arriving at Quebec City in August. They spent their first winter in this country in the Eastern Townships of Quebec, and in the spring of 1833, travelled through New York State, via Ogdensburg, to Whitby Township, arriving on March 8. Dow purchased 200 acres of lot 23, third concession, five days later and named his property, between the present Garden and Anderson Streets *"Glen Dhu"*.

William Dow soon established himself as one of the leading farmers of Whitby Township, when settlement was just beginning to occur, with immigrants arriving from England, Ireland and Scotland. He led the way in improving farming methods, and with Francis Leys (?-1853) of Pickering, imported the first bull from the old country to Whitby Township. Dow was a township representative on the Whitby and Pickering Agricultural Societies, and young men who wanted to become farmers would visit Glen Dhu to learn the latest farming methods.

William Dow was one of the founders of the Presbyterian Church in Whitby in the year he arrived, and signed the call to bring Rev. Dr. Robert Thornton (1806-1875) to the township as its first Presbyterian minister. He was also a leading member of the Tory party and took part in a public meeting condemning William Lyon Mackenzie and his radical followers, at Bennett's Tavern, three months before the Rebellion of 1837. The site of Bennett's tavern is now the Canada Trust office at Dundas and Euclid Streets.

When he died on Aug. 2, 1855, at the age of 78, the newspaper The Whitby Commonwealth described Dow in the following terms: *"In his social relations, no man was more beloved. Affability and frankness, combined with a gentlemanly deportment, were his prominent characteristics. His attachment to his Queen and country, based upon an intellect and enlightened understanding of the British constitution, was unflinching and immovable. In all the various relations of life, he commanded respect and esteem, and above all he walked humbly before his God."*

On July 1, 1833, only four months after their arrival in Whitby, Mrs. Dow died from a fever which was common in the summer months in Canada. It was often called *"lake fever"*, for it was prominent in areas around marshes and bodies of water. Since there was no local cemetery in Whitby, her husband had to take her body to York (Toronto) to be buried.

Many members of the Dow family reached prominent positions in the Whitby area. The oldest son, William Dow Jr. (1807-1843) was appointed Collector of Customs at Port Windsor (later Port Whitby) in 1839, but his early death at the age of 35 on Sept. 19, 1843, ended a promising career. The second son, John Dow (1816-1858) took over the management of Glen Dhu on his father's death, but died suddenly and unexpectedly of appendicitis three years later at the age of 42. One of the founders of the Ontario County Agricultural Society in 1853, he was its vice-president when he died, and contributed to making Ontario County (now the Region of Durham) one of the foremost agricultural and stockbreeding districts in the province. His funeral procession to Union Cemetery was one of the largest in the county's history, consisting of more than 100 car-

Glen Dhu as it appeared circa 1925.

riages.

The third son, Thomas Dow (1818-1894) spent his life as a banker, after learning his trade at a store in Oshawa. In 1853, he opened the first bank in Whitby, the Bank of Montreal, in a house where part of the Price Chopper plaza now stands, at Brock and Gilbert Streets. He was subsequently manager of the Whitby branch of the Ontario Bank and the Western Bank of Canada, retiring in 1892.

William Dow's third daughter, Robina (1813-1884) married Dr. Jonathan Foote, one of Whitby Township's pioneer doctors, who lived most of his life in Brooklin. The fourth daughter, Elspeth (1814-1913), married James Wallace, one of the entrepreneurs of Whitby, who was the contractor who built the Court House (now the Whitby Centennial Building). Mrs. Wallace died at Chicago, Illinois, on Dec. 13, 1913, at the age of 99.

Another prominent member of the Dow family was John Ball Dow (1851-1910), second son of John Dow and grandson of William Dow. Born on Glen Dhu farm, he was a lawyer who became Clerk of the County Court and Registrar of the Surrogate Court for Ontario County, in 1907. He was a member of the Whitby Board of Education for many years and was a founder of the Provincial School Trustees' Association of Ontario.

The first house at Glen Dhu was built of stone, with a front addition constructed in 1849. In a letter to a family member, dated Dec. 26, 1849, William Dow stated: *"Our house is all we could wish for after living long in a very humble house, in what I feel well placed. We had at last to build and being most fortunate in our mason and carpenter, our house is allowed to be the best in the township."* Tragedy struck Glen Dhu on Feb. 17, 1868, when the brick portion of the Dow house was gutted by fire. The house was rebuilt, and remained in the Dow family until 1915. In 1984, Glen Dhu was demolished to make way for the Fallingbrook subdivision. However, the naming of the school after Glen Dhu means that this famous name will live on in Whitby's history for many years to come.

Early in 1855, with old age coming on, William Dow purchased a grave stone in Toronto which was erected in Union Cemetery, Oshawa. On the stone was the inscription: "Erected by William Dow who with his wife Margarat Lumsden with ten children and two grandchildren left Auchenderran, parish of Marnoch, County Banff, Scotland, in the year of our Lord 1832 and settled in this Township of Whitby in 1833." At the same time, he had the accompanying portrait of himself painted by a German artist in Toronto.

William Dow, the founder of Glen Dhu.

Whitby's Founder Peter Perry Is Still Honoured Today

Each year, the Whitby Chamber of Commerce presents an award to the outstanding citizen of the town, named after Whitby's founder Peter Perry. Although he died nearly 150 years ago, Peter Perry is still recognized as the man who did more than any other to establish the Town of Whitby as a vibrant and progressive community. If he had lived longer, Whitby could have rivaled Toronto as a commercial centre. Peter Perry was largely forgotten by modern generations until the 100th anniversary of Whitby's incorporation as a town. On a hot June night in 1955, Ontario County Judge John E. Pritchard (1901-1961) told the story of Peter Perry to a packed hall at the old community arena, and asked if there were still any Peter Perrys in Whitby. He answered his own question by stating that there were many people in Whitby of the calibre of Peter Perry. The following year the Chamber of Commerce instituted the Peter Perry Award and Judge Pritchard presented a plaque to record the names of winners.

Peter Perry was the son of United Empire Loyalists Robert Perry (1751-1837) and Jemima Gary Wahsburn (1754-1830). He was born at Ernesttown (now the town of Bath) on the Bay of Quinte, on Nov. 14, 1792, the last of 10 children. Four of his brothers were Methodist ministers. Although he had little formal education, Peter Perry's

Peter Perry and his wife Mary Ham, painted by Toronto artist Nelson Cook in 1836.

will to serve the people was instilled in him by his Loyalist forebearers. He served as a Member of Parliament for the counties of Lennox and Addington from 1824 until 1836, when most of the members of the Reform party, including Peter Perry, lost their seats. Perry was considered the leader of the Reform Party in those days and the

loss of the 1836 election was a bitter blow to him and his supporters.

Three years earlier, on Jan. 5, 1833, Peter Perry had purchased 200 acres of Whitby Township, now the part of the Town of Whitby bounded by Brock, Dundas and Hickory Streets, and Rossland Road. Why he purchased land in Whitby is not known, but it was likely with an idea of future development. In October, 1836, he left Lennox and Addington Counties and began a new life in Whitby. On the site of the Bank of Commerce at Brock and Dundas Streets, Perry built the Red Store, painted red and bearing a sign in white letters which read: *"Peter Perry at Home."* He also built a large frame house behind the present site of the W.C. Town Funeral Chapel, which was demolished in 1982. The house was bricked over in 1900 and changed much in appearance from the original structure.

Soon after his arrival in Whitby, Perry began to develop the harbour at Windsor Bay (Port Whitby) and the road leading to it. His store was strategically located at the intersection of the Kingston Road (Highway 2) the main road through Upper Canada, and the Brock Road which ran from Windsor Bay to a point north of Ashburn. He obtained government grants to build wharves and storehouses at the harbour, and with a number of partners, formed the Windsor Road Company in 1837 to construct a road from Windsor Harbour to Georgian Bay. His ambition was to take the trade from New York and Boston across Lake Ontario to Windsor Harbour and ship it north by road or railway to Georgian Bay. Such a concept would open the farm land north of Whitby to settlement, and eventually the Canadian West.

Peter Perry wrote numerous letters to Robert Baldwin, the leader of the Government of Upper Canada, urging the government to provide money for the road, which he called the Centre Road. This road (now Highway 12) was built as far as Lake Simcoe from Windsor Harbour, and some distance south from Georgian Bay, but the middle portion was not completed in Peter Perry's lifetime. Perry faced the bids of rival road companies in Toronto and Oshawa who were also seeking money to build roads from their harbours to the north. His chief source of concern was the entrepreneurs of Oshawa who wanted to build Simcoe Street as a main road from Sydneham (Oshawa) Harbour to the north. As early as 1848, Peter Perry was urging a railway rather than a road from Windsor Harbour, but the first charter for a railway was granted to Toronto in 1853. Simcoe Street was only partially built, and with the railway, Toronto became the commercial centre of Upper Canada.

In 1853, two years after Perry's death, Whitby harbour was second only to Toronto in the amount of business transacted from harbours on the north shore of Lake Ontario. Had Perry lived, Whitby could have rivaled or surpassed Toronto as a commercial centre if his roads and railway had been completed.

Perry expanded his business interests to include six stores and grain shipping outlets from Whitby to Lindsay. One of these stores was located at a settlement known as Scugog Village, under the management of Chester Draper (1823-1876) who later became owner of Whitby Harbour. After Peter Perry's death, Scugog Village was named Port Perry in his honour.

Through Perry's efforts, the Centre Road was built from Whitby to Lake Simcoe and planked as far as Reach Township. Long thick planks of wood were laid side by side over the mud to make it easier for waggons full of grain to travel to Whitby harbour in the harvest season. The planking was completed by 1848.

When Perry arrived at Whitby, the centres of business were Windsor Harbour and Hamer's Corners (Dundas and Anderson Streets). He managed to draw the trade away from Hamer's Corners to Dundas and Brock Streets which became known as Perry's Corners. In 1846, Perry asked Provincial Land Surveyor John Shier (1808-1882) to draw up a town plan for his land north of Dundas Street, which by that time, extended from Hickory Street to High Street. The land was subdivided into lots and some of the streets named after his family: Perry, Mary (his wife) and John (his younger son). The business centre of Whitby began to

The residence of Peter Perry as it appeared in 1878 when owned by Richard Hatch.

as Colborne Street Senior Public School and was demolished at the end of 1975.

Peter Perry represented Whitby on the Home District Council (covering the area that was later, York, Peel and Ontario Counties) from 1842 to 1845 and again in 1848. He was one of the first people to see the need to separate the eastern townships of Whitby, Pickering, Uxbridge and Reach from the old County of York, because Toronto, the seat of government and the courts, was too far away from the inhabitants of these townships. Along with other leading men of Whitby, he organized public meetings to urge the Government to form these townships into a new county, with Whitby as the County Town, where the court house, jail and land registry office would be located. Although he did not live to see this accomplished, he had done the groundwork for the establishment of the County of Ontario in 1852, a year after his death. Whitby was named the County Town in 1852, due mainly to his influence, and three years later was incorporated as a town. The establishment of Whitby as the County Town initiated a building boom which lasted until the economic depression of 1857 which stopped Whitby's growth. Whitby was to remain a static community until it amalgamated with the Township of Whitby on Jan. 1, 1968. The County of Ontario

grow around the corner of Brock and Dundas Streets, the downtown Whitby of today. Hamer's Corners eventually ceased to be a business centre and the last of its original buildings were demolished in the 1960s.

Peter Perry, along with Ezra Annes (1796-1857) and Samuel Cochrane (1793-1879) was responsible for founding the Whitby Grammar School in 1846. The forerunner of today's high schools, it was located at the corner of King and Colborne Streets. Remodelled several times, it ended its days

became the Region of Durham in 1974.

Peter Perry was responsible for introducing into Parliament the Municipal Act of 1850, which formed township governments and a county system that is still the basis for municipal law today.

From 1849 to 1851, Perry again served as a member of Parliament, this time for the Third Riding of York which included Whitby. Another of his accomplishments was the establishment of a family library in Whitby in 1842.

It is said that Peter Perry eventually died from overwork. On the day he died, he spent five hours writing correspondence. Scores of his letters to the government leader Robert Baldwin can be seen in the Metro Toronto Public Library's Baldwin Room. As his health deteriorated, Perry decided to go to Saratoga Springs, New York, in the hope that the healing waters in this place would restore him. On the way, he stopped in New York City to try to persuade his old friend Marshall Spring Bidwell (1799-1872) to return to Canada. Bidwell, his associate as a Member of Parliament for Lennox and Addington from 1824 to 1836, had been exiled after the Rebellion of 1837. Despite Perry's pleadings, Bidwell refused to return to Canada. Perry himself, took no part in the Rebellion, for he opposed the armed insurrection advocated by William Lyon

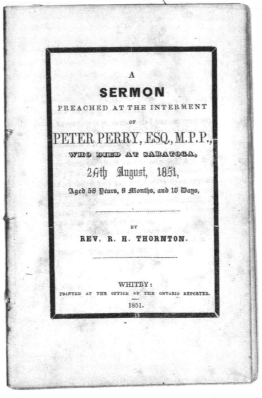

Sermon preached by Rev. Robert H. Thornton at Peter Perry's Funeral, August, 1851.

Mackenzie. On Aug. 24, 1851, Peter Perry died at Saratoga Springs at the age of 58. His body was taken back to Whitby by the steamer Admiral and his funeral to Union Cemetery was the largest ever seen in this community. His death removed one of the most inspired advocates for the development of Whitby. Had he lived, the growth and prosperity experienced by Whitby today, would have occurred 150 years ago instead of in the 1980s and 1990s.

His two sons went on to make names for themselves. Robert Ebenezer Perry (1825-1894) was a businessman in Whitby until 1871 when he moved to Bracebridge and did for that community what his father had done for Whitby. Robert Perry had an outstanding political career, serving as Warden of Victoria County. John Ham Perry (1827-1896) remained in Whitby the rest of his life, serving as Mayor of the Town and Warden of Ontario County. He was Registrar of Deeds from 1853 until his death in 1896.

Peter Perry's philosophy of life may be summed up by the following comments he made at a testimonial dinner in his honour at Scripture's Hotel in Whitby on Jan. 14, 1848:

"May all selfishness, jealousy and sectional feelings beyond legitimate rivalry and competition in trade be forever merged in one common determination to forgive and forget, and may a united effort be made by the men of Whitby for the promotion of the solid and permanent interests of the whole township."

Perry's Corners Became the Business Centre of Whitby

The third settlement which made up the Town of Whitby when it was incorporated in 1855 was Perry's Corners, at the intersection of Brock and Dundas Streets. For more than 160 years this has been the business centre of the town, known as downtown Whitby. It was founded in 1836 by Peter Perry (1792-1851) who came to Whitby from Lennox and Addington Counties, following his defeat in a Provincial election.

A wealthy land owner, Perry had already purchased 200 acres of land from Dundas Street to Rossland Road and from Brock Street to Hickory Street on Jan. 5, 1833. He likely bought it as one of his many investments, but when he lost the election of 1836, and Reformers like himself were being harassed by the ruling government, the Family Compact, he decided to leave his home in Lennox and Addington and start afresh in the wilderness of Whitby Township.

The land Perry had bought in 1833 was strategically located, at the intersection of the Kingston Road (Highway 2) and the Centre Road (Highway 12). The Kingston Road was the main thoroughfare for commercial traffic from Toronto to Kingston, and the Centre Road (or Brock Road as it was sometimes called) had been built in 1831 north from Windsor Harbour. It was to become the main trade route for ship-

Brock Street looking north from Dundas Street, 1863.

ping grain from Georgian Bay and Lake Simcoe to Windsor (Whitby) Harbour. At this crucial intersection, on the site of the present Bank of Commerce, Peter Perry

built the Red Store. Painted red, this frame building had a sign over the door in white letters which read: *"Peter Perry at Home."* The Red Store was demolished in 1866 to build the brick store called the Dominion Warerooms, operated by James B. Powell (1824-1902) and John M. Lowes (1829-1902). This building was replaced by the Canadian Imperial Bank of Commerce building in 1964. Behind his store, in what is now the parking lot for W.C. Town Funeral Chapel, Peter Perry built his home. It was demolished in 1982.

Perry's Corners, or Radical Corners as it was sometimes called because of Perry's radical politics, began to take business away from Hamer's Corners and Windsor Bay. In 1844, Perry hired Provincial Land Surveyor John Shier (1808-1882) to draw up a town plan for his land from Dundas Street to Beech Street and from High Street to Hickory Street. Perry had purchased the 200 acres west of Brock Street to add to his existing property, on May 5, 1842, and the additional 100 acres west of Centre Street on Feb. 8, 1848. It is believed that Centre Street was named because it was the centre of the two half lots of Perry's land north of Dundas Street. Perry's Plan, as the final document was called, was drawn by John Shier in 1844 and registered in 1846.

The 200 acres south of Dundas Street, bounded by Dundas, Hickory, Burns and Henry Streets, had been purchased by Asa Werden on July 2, 1821, many years before Peter Perry came to Whitby. Asa Werden (1799-1866) was born in Connecticut, U.S.A. and settled in Athol Township, Prince Edward County, Upper Canada. He came to Canada with only the clothes on his back and some leather maker's tools, before 1812, but through enterprise and hard work amassed an estate worth $247,000 when he died. Since Crown grants were not available when Werden came to Canada, he had to buy land where he could get it. He owned large tracts of land in Athol Township and in the Picton area, as well as in Whitby and Pickering Townships. As far as is known, he never lived in Whitby or Pickering, but sold off various parcels of his land from 1821 to 1866, making $50,000 on that land before he died.

Asa Werden was a Member of Parliament for Prince Edward County in 1831, at the same time that Peter Perry was a Member for Lennox and Addington. It is interesting to speculate that Werden may have induced Perry to purchase his land in Whitby Township in 1833. Werden was a director of the Prince Edward Agricultural Society, chairman of a temperance society, and owner of a large tannery and several lumber and grist mills in Prince Edward County.

In the 1840s Werden had his 200 acres of Whitby land subdivided into building lots on a plan known as Werden's Plan, although it is believed that he had been selling individual lots before that time. Werden's Plan was registered on Sept. 1, 1854. On Sept. 28, 1865, Werden made his will, giving his 200 acres in Whitby, minus the land which had already been sold, to his sons, John Burns Werden and Sully Paoli Werden. They made a fortune from selling lots in Whitby for the next 10 years. Asa Werden died in Athol Township, Prince Edward County, on May 28, 1866 at the age of 86. Like the Werden sons, Peter Perry's sons Robert E. Perry (1825-1894) and John Ham Perry (1827-1896) made fortunes from selling their late father's land in Whitby after his death in 1851.

There has been much speculation over the years as to why Whitby's streets north and south of Dundas Street do not line up. Various theories have been forth, such as the surveyor being drunk, or the metal chains used in measuring, shrinking in cold weather and expanding in hot weather, but the explanation is likely more simple. Perry's and Werden's Plans were made at different times and for different landowners. Also the size and shape of the lots are different in each plan. Werden's blocks are square, made up of quarter-acre lots. Perry's are of varying sizes, both of blocks and lots. The lots in each plan are so different that it was impossible to line up the streets. Only Byron

Brock Street looking south from Royal Hotel, 1863.

Streets. Kent Street is named after him. All these men had town plans made and sold their lots for building purposes. The Scadding family owned the lots in the town plan for Port Whitby.

Perry's Corners as a settlement grew moderately in the 1840s. The first lawyers to settle in the community were Bernard F. Ball (1819-1856) in 1844, and Zaccheus Burnham (1819-1896) in 1845. Hugh J. Macdonell (1823-1877) opened a law office opposite Peter Perry's residence in 1848. Numerous general merchants began to move into the village in the 1840s, among them being grain dealer Lewis Houck (1817-1887) in 1844 and druggist James H. Gerrie (1821-1872) in 1845.

The following is a description of Perry's Corners, under the name of *"Windsor,"* published in Smith's Canadian Gazetteer in 1846:

"A village in the township of Whitby situated on the eastern road, two miles from Windsor Bay and about thirty-one from Toronto. The plank road from the bay to Lake Scugog passes through the village. There is a Congregational Church in the Village. Population about 500. Post office post every day.

"Professions and Trades – two physicians and surgeons, two lawyers, eight stores, two druggists, one bookseller and stationer, three

Street is perfectly lined up, north and south of Dundas Street.

Land south of Burns Street was owned by John Radenhurst, a Toronto businessman, James Wallace (1814-1882) a Whitby entrepreneur, and Francis Keller (1821-1890), an active man in Whitby in the 1850s who later moved to Uxbridge. Darwin Kent (1822-1884) owned a strip of land north of Dundas Street between Kent and Euclid

taverns, one watchmaker, one ashery, one brewer, three saddlers, two cabinet makers, one chair maker, one fanning mill maker, two wagon makers, one tinsmith, one baker, three blacksmiths, four shoemakers, four tailors.

"About one mile from the village is a small settlement called "Windsor East."

W.H. Smith offered the following description of the village of Whitby, as it was called after July 1847, in this excerpt from *"Canada Past Present and Future,"* published in 1851:

"From Duffin's Creek to Whitby is six miles. This village was formerly called Windsor, and the settlement on the shore of Big Bay was known as Windsor Bay and Windsor Harbour. In consequence of the frequency of mistakes from the name, in order to distinguish it from Windsor in the Western District, an Act of Parliament was obtained, changing the name to Whitby; the village at the bay was included in the limits assigned to it, and it is now known as Port Whitby. Whitby or Windsor, however, has long been known as "Perry's Corners," so called after an old enterprising settler, Mr. Peter Perry; and this name it continues to hold with a large majority of the old settlers in the neighbourhood, and will continue to do so while the present generation lasts, in spite of Acts of Parliament.

*"Whitby is a place of considerable business, notwithstanding it is destitute of what is gen-*erally considered in America a sine qua non in the selection of sites for the erection of towns and villages, namely, a water privilege. The formation some years since of the plank road to Scugog by the Government, as an adjunct to the harbour, has had the effect of considerably increasing the prosperity of the village, by giving the farmer facilities for reaching the market. The exports have rapidly increased, and the revenue arising from both the road and the harbour has been as much as could fairly be expected. The harbour and road cost the Government above thirty-nine thousand pounds, and they were lately sold to a private company for little more than half the original cost.

"A road, called the "Brock Road," runs back from Whitby to the Township of that name, in a N.N. Westerly direction, and the plank road strikes off from the Brock Road a few miles above Whitby, and runs nearly north to Lake Scugog.

"Whitby contains a brewery, tannery, Congregational Church, and a grammar school; and a newspaper, called the "Whitby Reporter," is published here. A small settlement, about half a mile to the east of the village, called East Windsor, is now included in the limits of Whitby. The population, including East Windsor and the Port, is said to be about eleven hundred.

"Between Whitby and the Port, a mile and a half in distance, the land is level, and the soil composed of rich loam. The harbour is capacious, but its borders are bounded by a considerable quantity of marsh, through which a small stream enters the bay. A number of houses have been erected here; but the principal business transacted is in storing and forwarding goods and produce for which there are large warehouses, and others are in course of erection. There is also a brewery, and an Episcopal church built of stone."

Advertisement for store in Perry's Bock, 121 Brock Street North, 1858

Dr. James Hunter, Whitby's Rebel of 1837

Shortly after William Lyon Mackenzie's abortive rebellion at Toronto in December 1837, British soldiers surrounded a house in Whitby to arrest one of his supporters. The home belonged to Dr. James Hunter (1795-1875), who was known to have written criticisms of the government Mackenzie had tried to overthrow. The soldiers burst into the house and found Mrs. Hunter holding the incriminating documents in her hand. They ordered her to turn them over at once or they would shoot her. The soldiers levelled their guns at Mrs. Hunter and waited. Suddenly, she threw the bundle of documents into the fireplace, destroying the evidence against her husband. The soldiers were so surprised that they did not shoot.

The house where these dramatic events occurred, was located on the south side of Dundas Street, east of Kendalwood Road, where Tri-Circle Service was recently located. The frame house was demolished in the early 1960s.

Dr. James Hunter was born in Yorkshire, England, on Sept. 29, 1795. A bright child with a good business ability, he inherited considerable property from his father and was said to be in charge of his own business interests at the age of 12. His guardian, after his father's death, placed him on a ship, intending him to enter the British

Dr. James Hunter in 1856.

Navy, but Hunter had other ideas and ran away.

In 1814, at the age of 19, he married Elizabeth Story (1793-1863) at York Minster Cathedral. In 1822, he sold all his property so that he and his wife and three

children could emigrate to Canada. Dr. Hunter first settled at Niagara-on-the-Lake, where he established a medical practice. He studied medicine at the College of Physicians and surgeons of the Western District of New York, from which he graduated in 1829 and moved to Whitby Township. He was a farmer as well as a doctor.

Dr. Hunter became involved in the politics of Upper Canada in the 1830s when William Lyon Mackenzie's Reformers were opposing the rule of the Family Compact under Governor Sir Francis Bond Head (known as Sir Francis Bone Head to the Reformers).

Hunter was one of 19 persons who signed the Declaration of the Reformers and served as a member of a permanent committee of vigilantes. After his arrest the day his wife threw his political writings into the fire, he was forced to march 30 miles to Toronto where he was jailed with about 600 prominent citizens who had taken part in the rebellion. He was brought before a commission for trial early in 1838, but was acquitted, because the witnesses bribed to testify against him were forced to confess by his lawyer. He testified that he was opposed to armed resistance, and relied on powerful friends to speak on his behalf.

On the same day that Dr. Hunter was

Dr. Hunter's house in the 1920s. Demolished in the early 1960s, it stood at 1913 Dundas Street East.

tried, Samuel Lount and Peter Matthews were hanged for their part in the rebellion. It is said that the judge declared: *"there will be no more hangings,"* and set Dr. Hunter free. One of the witnesses to the hangings was Levi Fairbanks (1829-1907) who later became Whitby's auctioneer.

The Government of Upper Canada, however, was not through with Dr. Hunter. Not long after his acquittal, his house was again surrounded by government troops who tried to smoke him out as he hid in the attic. At night, with the help of Daniel Conant, of Oshawa, he escaped in a boat from Oshawa harbour, ending up in Buffalo, New York. He was hidden under some sacks in a small boat, thus escaping the watchful eyes of the lake patrols.

After living for a while in Hartland, Niagara County, New York, Dr. Hunter returned to Canada, settling at Newmarket. By 1845, he had moved to the village of Winchester (now Brooklin) in Whitby Township, where he carried on an extensive medical practice reaching north to Port Perry and Uxbridge. At Brooklin, his eldest daughter, Sarah Annie (1816-1896) married Rev. Robert Darlington (1807-1881), Brooklin's postmaster and treasurer of Whitby Township. Their daughter, Georgina Hunter Darlington (1845-1923) was the last of the family to live in Brooklin. Robert Darlington's house in recent years was the residence of Dr. John H. McKinney on Cassels Road, east of the brick mill.

Dr. Hunter acquired a considerable amount of land in the Brooklin area in the 1840s and 1850s, but in 1856, he moved to the United States again, never to return to Canada. He settled at Lewiston, New York, became an American citizen, and died at Buffalo on April 20, 1875, at the age of 79.

While living at Brooklin, acting as a magistrate, Dr. Hunter prosecuted a number of members of the Markham Gang, a group of thieves who terrorized settlers between Whitby and Markham, attacking them as they rode through the woods at night. It was said that it was not worth your life to travel on the Kingston Road (Highway 2) through the Rouge Valley at night, because of the Markham Gang and other bandits.

Although it is not known for certain, the Hunters' Lodges, bands of Canadian rebels living in the United States after Mackenzie's rebellion, may have been named after Dr. Hunter. These selfstyled *"patriots"* planned to invade Canada from the United States in 1838 to overthrow the government. One attack occurred at Prescott, where the battle of the windmill was fought. Another attack which did not materialize, was planned for Kingston, the night Nelson Gilbert Reynolds was arrested for treason. Reynolds was appointed sheriff of Ontario County in 1854, and built Trafalgar Castle as his home in Whitby.

Mrs. James Hunter (1793-1863), who threw the papers linking her husband to William Lyon Mackenzie's rebellion into the fireplace.

Whitby Harbour Was The Second Busiest Port On The North Shore of Lake Ontario

Whitby was a prominent community in Upper Canada from the 1830s to the 1890s for two significant reasons. It had one of the finest natural harbours on the north shore of Lake Ontario, and in 1852 it was chosen as the County Town for the new County of Ontario. In 1853, Whitby Harbour was second only to Toronto in the amount of business it conducted as a port.

Whitby Harbour, then known as Windsor Bay, was designated as a port of entry with a customs collector, in 1831, and two years later, John Welsh came from Brockville to build the first grain storehouse and begin shipments of grain to ports in Canada and the United States. In 1833, Welsh (1810-1859) built a tramway across the mud flats at Windsor Bay to a point where his grain could be loaded onto scows. The scows would take the grain to larger boats in the harbour basin. These boats then took the grain to American ports such as Rochester and Oswego and Canadian ports such as Kingston. In the first record ever made of shipments from Windsor Harbour, Welsh stated that in 1833 he shipped 26,000 bushels of wheat, 75 barrels of pork and 387 barrels of potash. By 1835, he was shipping 42,830 bushels of wheat, 170 barrels of pork, 387 barrels of potash, 2,762 barrels of flour and 5,230 bushels of barley. From 1833 to 1840, Welsh was known as one of the largest, if not the largest operator in farming produce west of Montreal. He had such experience in commercial matters that he gained a wide reputation as a successful businessman. In 1836, Welsh became the agent for the *"Commodore Barrie"*, the first passenger steam boat to call regularly at Windsor Harbour. This boat also stopped at Kingston, Bath, Cobourg, Port Hope and Toronto. It likely brought many new settlers to Windsor Harbour on their journey to lands they had purchased in the townships north of Whitby.

An unnamed traveller through Upper Canada recorded the following impressions of Windsor Harbour in his diary:

"Feb. 3, 1837: Went to see Windsor Harbour, an excellent shelter for shipping and a place which in my opinion, will yet come to be one of the most important places on Lake Ontario. What strengthened my opinion is that it is the only outlet for produce of several of the finest townships in Upper Canada. There is a petition brought before the House of Parliament for a grant of £9,000 ($45,000) to improve it, and which has passed the Lower House and there is no doubt it will receive the sanction of the upper one. There is but little done yet in the way of building on it, but there is a great prospect next season. There are five of six schooners lying frozen in there, one of them over 100 tons burden."

Not long after this account was written, Peter Perry (1792-1851) and several other leading men of the township formed the Windsor Road and Harbour Company. John Watson (1806-1879), an Irishman from County Dublin, was hired as Secretary-Treasurer of the company. He had previously worked for John Welsh for two years. In 1841, the Windsor Road and Harbour Company erected a warehouse at the harbour and advertised for a person to take charge of this building. In 1843-44, James Rowe (1799-1869) and James Cotton were given a contract by the Government of Upper Canada to dredge the harbour and build wharves and a lighthouse. This was the first major development at Port Whitby.

After a severe depression in the mercantile trade in 1848, Rowe, Watson and Welsh formed a partnership under the name of James Rowe and Company, and built a large complex of warehouses at the west side of the slip at the end of Brock Street. They dominated the grain trade for 20 years. In 1852, the Government took over control of the road from Whitby Harbour to the north (now Highway 12). The road and harbour were sold to private enterprise in 1863, with Joseph Gould (1808-1886) of Uxbridge taking the road and Chester Draper of Whitby (1823-1876) taking the harbour. In 1866, Draper built a six-storey grain elevator on the east side of the slip and formed what was

The "Nipissing", a dredge at Whitby Harbour, 1901.

Constructing the first concrete docks at Whitby Harbour, 1914.

Sugar Company, which had planned to export sugar from beets out of the harbour. The Keystone Sugar Company failed after a short time, and Whitby Harbour was purchased by the Federal Government in 1910. The Government still owns the main portion of the harbour. The first concrete docks replaced the old wooden cribs in 1914, and the Federal Government did extensive construction of wharves in the 1920s and the 1950s, the last work being completed in 1959 as the St. Lawrence Seaway was opened.

Whitby Harbour thrived as a grain port until the McKinley Tariff Act, passed by the United States Government in 1890, put tariffs on Canadian grain being shipped to the U.S.A. The last shipments of grain were made in 1913 up to the time of the death of John Watson's eldest son, John A. Watson (1841-1913). For a short time in the 1870s, lumber was shipped by rail to Port Whitby from the forests of Victoria County, but by the 1880s, all the timber was gone. Even as late as the 1880s, Whitby Harbour was the place to get a job. Dock hands made two dollars a day, which was good wages, and the best opportunity for employment was during the fall harvest season.

In 1883, the Whitby Chronicle reported regularly on activities at the harbour.

June 29: *"This week has been notable for the*

known as the Whitby Harbour Company. Gould and Draper charged tolls on the road and harbour and came under criticism at times for charging fees that were too high. In 1879, three years after Draper's death, his executors offered the harbour for sale. The Town of Whitby had an opportunity to purchase the harbour, but declined. On April 29, 1879, the harbour was sold to James McClellan (1845-1915) and David Galbraith (1849-1926) of Bowmanville, for $40,100. Galbraith and McClellan moved to Whitby, Galbraith, taking over the home of the late John Watson on Dufferin Street. They operated the harbour until 1905 when it was sold to a short-lived enterprise called the Keystone

A view of Whitby Harbour looking east, from an airplane, 1920. The Watson grain elevators, demolished in 1926, are in the foreground.

large importation by Whitby dealers of that useful mineral, coal, there having been no less than five vessels arrived laden with the 'dusty diamonds'. The dredge is working again and doing good execution after having had some repairs done to the boilers. Lumber shipments have almost ceased, only one cargo having been shipped the past week. The fine weather last week brought out boaters in large numbers to enjoy this beautiful and delightful exercise on the waters of the harbour and lake, but again

the rains have interfered with this pleasurable pastime."

July 13, 1883: "The Harbour Company are taking advantage of the present slack season in the grain shipping business to prepare for the fall trade. The elevator and its appliances are being overhauled, renovated and improved; the engine and boiler house has been torn down and is to be rebuilt on a larger scale to give accommodation to a new boiler which the Company have secured. Mr. Thos. Deverell is

doing the mason work."

August 10, 1883: "*The water level of the lake is now extremely high, having attained the extraordinary height which prevailed several summers ago. Mr. John Watson has moved his office and weigh scales into a more convenient situation facing Brock Street. An inclined driveway and elevated platform to be used for loading railway cars simply by dumping the contents of loaded carts into them, has been erected just west of the turntable and will constitute an expeditious means of handling the mineral. Great quantities of coal have been imported by local dealers, it being the intention to supply by rail the towns and villages to the north, thus materially increasing one branch of commerce through the harbour. The new engine house for the Harbour Co. is completed, but owning to the large quantity of wheat daily coming in by rail it is impossible to put in the new and more powerful boiler which has been secured. The dredging which is nearly completed was interrupted this week by the boilers of the dredge 'Nithsdale' giving out, causing a delay of ten days at least, for repairs. Spearing pike in the bay by jack-light is indulged in nightly by men from the dredge. Fine specimens are caught. The lumber has begun this week to move again; fourteen carloads came down on Wednesday.*"

September 14, 1883: "*The wharves are crowded with lumber as sufficient vessels cannot be got to move the increasing shipments. With commendable enterprise the Harbour Co. have put in a new boiler and have otherwise increased their facilities. Dredging under the Government grant is completed.*"

In the fall, farmers would bring their grain, mostly barley and wheat, by wagon down the Centre Road (Highway 12) to the elevators at Port Whitby for shipment. The bags were unloaded into a hopper and the grain was weighed in a copper pail placed on a scale. One bushel of barley weighed 48 pounds. In one of the elevators there was a team of four horses hooked up with yokes to an apparatus which would carry the grain to the top of the elevator. These horses would walk in a circle, causing the grain to be scooped up to the top where it would wait till the boats came. When the sailing boats were alongside the elevator the grain would slide down a chute into their holds. The engine house referred to in The Chronicle of 1883, contained machinery which replaced the horses as a means of drawing the grain to the top of the six-storey elevator. Behind the grain elevator on the east side of the slip was a turntable in the railway line which could direct cars to the grain elevators, the coal sheds or the main railway line running north to Port Perry and Lindsay.

John Blow (1819-1901) and D. C. Downey owned the coal sheds at the harbour in the 1880s. In the busy season before win-ter, Downey employed as many as 15 men. Coal was weighed in dump carts behind John Watson's office at the end of the slip on Brock Street and placed in railway cars for shipment north to Port Perry and Brooklin. In the 1880s, coal was valued at $4.75 to $5.00 a ton. Today, a 50-pound bag would cost that much. Most of the coal at Whitby Harbour came from Pennsylvania.

Lumber from Victoria County was piled on the east pier after being unloaded off trains from the north. Piles of lath, lumber, shingles and square timer, 12 to 14 feet high, would be piled along the wharf from the Harbour Company elevator to the beach. As many as seven or eight schooners would be in the harbour at one time to pick up the grain or lumber. In the fall season, it was not uncommon to see grain unloaded at mid-night.

At the corner of Brock and Water Streets, opposite Draper's elevator, was the National Hotel, which dated from at least the 1850s. It was the principal hotel for sailors and farmers until it closed in the 1880s. A two-storey frame building, it had a ballroom on the second floor where dances were held. The proprietor, James Pringle (1824-1911) would set up pigeon and snow bird shooting match-es on the lake in winter, and Nathaniel Ray (1817-1891) would organize horse races on the ice. The passenger pigeon, the chief target of hunters, was killed to extinction by 1914. Some of the few stuffed passenger pigeons in existence today were donated to the Royal Ontario Museum at Toronto by Whitby descendants of Charles Fothergill (1792-1840), Ontario's first naturalist, who lived in Pickering Township and Toronto. The pigeons and snow birds were caught by plac-ing feed on the ice and when the birds land-ed, they were scooped up in a net. Later they were released for the hunters.

Besides the large schooners for shipping grain and lumber, there were smaller boats called stonehookers, at Whitby harbour. The stonehookers picked up stones from the bot-tom of the lake with grappling hooks, and their owners sold the stones to builders in Toronto. It is said that the foundation stones for Toronto's old City Hall, built from 1889 to 1899, were supplied by the Goldring brothers of Whitby who operated a fleet of stonehookers at the harbour.

From the early 1900s to the 1960s, Whitby harbour languished as a forgotten remnant of its once busy past. It has enjoyed a new revival after it was designated by the Federal Government as a recreational harbour in 1967. The Waterfront trail in the 1990s has led to the development of parkland around the harbour by the town's Rotary, Lions and Kiwanis Clubs, and a busy yacht club and marina are now located at Whitby Harbour.

The Disunity of Unity Lodge

The Masonic Lodge is known today for its brotherhood and good charitable works, but such was not always the case in Whitby. The community's first Masonic Lodge was founded in 1826 as Unity Lodge, but for a while during its history, there was anything but unity.

The earliest attempt to bring Masonry to Whitby occurred in 1808, when three residents of Whitby Township, Nathan Cummins, David Lloyd and Ebenezer Ransom petitioned the Provincial Grand Lodge of Upper Canada to establish Rising Sun Lodge. No record exists of this lodge being granted a charter, and even if it did come into existence, its work would likely have ended during the War of 1812.

In 1825, Ezra Annes (1796-1857), described as *"the grand old man of Masonry in Whitby,"* petitioned the Provincial Grand Lodge to establish Unity Lodge in the township. Seven residents of Whitby and three of Pickering were charter members of this lodge, which began operation on Jan. 9, 1826. Ezra Annes lived in a white stucco house, built about 1836, at the south-west corner of Dundas and Frances Streets, now the site of the Towne Plaza. His house was moved to 239 Wellington Street in 1960. His brother, Dr. Alvah Annes (1797-1847) lived in one of the earliest brick houses in Whitby, one block east at Dundas and

The old Commercial Hotel (now the Corner Store) at Brock and Colborne Streets, where the split of Unity Lodge occurred in 1842.

Henry Streets. His house burned down in 1902 and the site is today the residence of Mrs. John R. Frost. Both were members of Unity Lodge until a controversial meeting held at the Commercial Hotel on July 21, 1842.

The Commercial Hotel was a frame build-

ing at the corner of Brock and Colborne Streets, which changed its name to the Queen's Hotel in 1875. It was bricked over in 1905 and today is the Corner Store, the oldest building in downtown Whitby. Alvah Annes had been elected Master of Unity Lodge in December 1841, with his term to

Charles Clark (1796-1880), the first Worshipful Master of Composite Lodge in 1852/53, who healed the split of Unity Lodge. A Bible presented to Composite Lodge in 1863 by Clark is still in use in Whitby's Masonic Temple. Charles Clark operated a brewery on Ash Street.

run for a full year. At the July 1842 meeting his election was declared null and void and Ezra Annes was elected Master. When Alvah showed up late for the meeting and was informed of his brother's election, he called it *"irregular"*. He was reported to have used abusive language against the members of the lodge and *"discord reigned supreme"*. When the meeting closed, Alvah, in a great rage, seized the jewels and other official paraphernalia of the lodge and locked them in a strong box. The brethren responsible for Ezra Annes's election had a duplicate key made and removed the jewels from the box, whereupon Alvah seized the constitution and bylaws.

Each brother claimed that the other's election was *"clandestine and irregular"*. As a result, Unity Lodge split in two, half the members going with Ezra Annes and the other half with his brother. For three years the lodge met as two distinct sections, despite Ezra Annes's repeated efforts to make peace with his brother. Unity Lodge was finally reunited in the summer of 1845, with Alvah Annes conspicuous by his absence. He appears to have left Whitby at this time, for his death was recorded at Port Huron, Michigan, on Nov. 14, 1847.

Unity Lodge never really recovered from the split of 1842. It was officially closed in 1851, when 22 of its 35 members were suspended for non payment of dues. Out of the ashes of Unity Lodge grew Composite Lodge No. 30, A.F. and A.M., which was founded in 1852 with 12 charter members. Ezra Annes joined Composite Lodge in 1854 and served as Master in 1855 and 1857. In 1857 he was also Mayor of Whitby, and died on Aug. 25 of that year. He was the only Mayor in Whitby's history to die in office. His was the first Masonic funeral in Whitby, held at St. John's Anglican Church Cemetery. No stone marks his grave today, the original stone having disappeared many years ago.

Composite Lodge is still active in Whitby today, nearly 150 years after its founding and 160 years after the split of Unity Lodge nearly destroyed Masonry in this town.

A Visitor's Impression of Windsor Bay, 1845

The following letter from a visitor to Windsor harbour, dated Sept. 14, 1845, provides a first-hand account of this thriving pioneer community in the days of sailing ships on Lake Ontario. It is written by William T. Jones to his brother Durham Jones, at Maitland, Canada West, near Brockville. The Jones family of Brockville were partners with John Welsh in the grain business at Windsor harbour until the partnership dissolved in 1848. The stone Episcopal Church described by William Jones is St. John's Anglican Church which officially opened for worship on July 5, 1846. Currency was in British pounds until January, 1858.

Whitby, 14th Sept., 1845

Dear Brother:

I promised to write you after being here two or three weeks. Now, as many months have passed, it is time I should say something, even if it is nothing more that I am well. It looks if we were trying each other's patience to see who would write first. Tell Lucia & Dr. Henderson, my two physicians, that I am quite well "From the tip of my nose to the end of my toes."

I am pleased with Whitby, pleased with Windsor Bay, and pleased with being with such an amiable couple as John Welsh & his sister. I have a very comfortable bed in a very comfortable room over the shop and all little comforts attended to down to the blacking of my Boots in the morning.

There are about fifty inhabited houses in this place, one store & that is our own, two or three two-penny concerns besides, one Brewery, three taverns, Two Tailors, Two Shoe Shops, one Bakery and last of all, which I ought to have mentioned first, a stone Episcopal Church is building & will be inclosed this fall. In the mean time the School House is open to all denominations of a Sunday. We have service every second Sunday. The Revd. Mr. Pentland is the name. There will be a splendid harbor here when finished. The pier which is a Government work has already cost £25,000 & will cost £10,000 before completed. There are men at work making a road across the marsh and dredging it. Geo. Munro has a contract for some of it. It is nearly a mile from our store to the end of the Pier where the steamers call and I have very little opportunity of seeing any of my acquaintances who may be passing. The only regular Boats that call here is the America and Admiral & lands passengers at Cobourg in time for the Mail Boats. Since I have been here I have seen a good deal of the country & Whitby well deserves the name of being called a fine Township.

I had a very pleasant ride a short time ago with Mr. Welsh & his sister as far as the Scugog Lake 20 miles from this. The road is planked about 3/4 of the way. We went out to see about some staves he is getting out at the Foot of the lake which is about 30 miles in length. They are brought up in scows to the head of it & conveyed to this place in waggons at 12/ for 100 pieces. Mr. Welsh has not got his store started yet in Pickering, but all things will be ready in the course of Ten days. The goods have been packed this two months. The stock consisted of McGibbons & Co. of Belleville. The store will be a few rods from a Flour Mill in a fine settlement. The gentry of Toronto frequently come down to fish for the little speckled trout that all the little streams abound with here. There is abundance of Wheat. Mr. W. is buying but all open bargains till the next news from England. The mail road is 1 1/4 miles from this. It is a plank road and gives one a very pleasant ride to the Post Office in the morning. It is called Perry's Corners from the founder Peter Perry. I dare say Dr. Henderson recollects him from when he was in the House of Assembly at the same time. Dr. H. will likely know he is a merchant & pretty extensive. There are some half dozen stores besides. You see we are cut off, with opposition to a considerable degree. For some days past Mr. Welsh's has been a little Hospital. The two clerks, Bryan and his little brother & the hired man were all sick with the Fever ague & Lake Fever. I am told this place is always more or less subject to it when the water is low as is the case at present. I have heard of poor Sherwood being at Prescott. I do not know whether you saw him or not. I heard it through Disset. He wrote me wishing to purchase my House. I have had another application from Reid Burnet but none of them will give over £250. I sometimes think I had better take £275 considering the bad state it is in & for a short time the roof will require new shingles. What do you think? I have also heard of that sad affair in Brockville, attempt at suicide. I was in hope at first the reports I heard are not half true, but it proved otherwise. I wonder when poor Alice resides at her home. Now to wind up, as I do know you like writing as well as I do myself. Make Solomon write. If he says why I can't, tell him he should and at the same time you can give him your opinion about my house.

With my love to Amy etc.
Your aff(ectionate)
Brother
W.T. Jones

St. John's Anglican Church, mentioned by William T. Jones in his letter of September 14, 1845.

Myrtle Was An Early Business Centre, But Where Did The Name Come From?

At the intersection of Highway 12 and the Myrtle Road (9th concession of the old Township of Whitby) a settlement known as Myrtle was established in the 1840s. The earliest settlers arrived in the Myrtle area in the 1830s. Three brothers, George, David and William Briggs, arrived from Missisquoi County, Quebec, in 1835. David Briggs (1816-1897) settled east of the corners at Myrtle. His farm remained under the ownership of the Briggs family for 157 years, being sold in 1987. David Briggs' son, Sylvester E. Briggs (1846-1926) along with R.C. Steele of Oshawa, founded the famous Steele-Briggs Seed Company in Toronto in 1873. This company in the early 1900s was known throughout Canada. Another nationally known figure who first settled in Myrtle was Reuben Hurlburt, founder of *"Hurlburt's Shoes for Children."* He started his career as a shoemaker in Myrtle. The Hubbell family came from the United States in the 1830s and established the Hubbell's Cemetery, north-west of Myrtle, one of the oldest pioneer cemeteries in the town. Other early Myrtle settlers were William Blight, Ira Brown, Stephen Hoitt, George Derby and John Carmichael.

About 1836, three Wells brothers, Miles, Jesse and Gardner, settled at Myrtle, having come from the Province of Quebec. The most noted of these was Rev. Gardner Wells (1807-1883), who founded a Methodist Episcopal

Myrtle, looking south along Highway 12, C. 1908. Thomas W. Brookes' general store is at left.

Church at Myrtle and served as pastor from 1846 to 1878. He was responsible for the construction of a frame church built in 1857 where Willy's Car Care Service is now. The church was later moved to Myrtle Station and became Cooke's garage. Gardner Wells is buried in a small cemetery behind Willy's Car Care Centre.

Because of the influence of Gardner Wells,

the little community in the 1840s became known as *"Wells' Corners."* In 1856, the name was changed to *"Lenwood,"* and in 1860 it became *"Myrtle."* The origin of the names *"Lenwood"* and *"Myrtle"* are lost in antiquity, but some people suggest the community was named *"Myrtle"* after the flower called Myrtle which grew in the church yard.

A post office with Selah Orvis as post master,

Myrtle, looking north along Highway 12, C. 1908. The Temperance Hall is at left.

and converted into a community hall. An extension was put on the back in 1931 and a basement and furnace installed. The community centre was moved to the old school house in 1967 and from 1970 to 1972 the Myrtle Community Hall was a museum operated by the Whitby Historical Society. In 1978 it was demolished.

In the 1890's Myrtle was overshadowed by the thriving railway centre at Myrtle Station. The two communities of Myrtle and Myrtle Station became polarized and disputes arose between the two hamlets. One of the most severe was over the relocation of the Church, which is described in another Chronicle in this book.

Another theory for the origin of the name "Myrtle" is that Myrtle was the name of the wife of the community's first post master, Selah Orvis. No record has been found of her name, other than in records of the Canadian Post Office Archives, so it is not certain that this story can be confirmed.

Myrtle is described as follows, in the Province of Ontario Directory for 1869: "A Post Village in the Township of Whitby, County Ontario. It is situated on the gravel road leading to the Town of Whitby, and is distant from there 9 miles. Population 75." This was nine years after the Myrtle Post office was established.

was opened at Myrtle on Nov. 1, 1860. Reuben Hurlburt, of shoe fame, was post master from 1872 to 1874. In the 1860s, Myrtle had a population of 75, but this was reduced to about 50 by the 1870s. In 1871, the Port Whitby and Port Perry Railway was built west of Myrtle and a station established in the community. It was demolished in April of 1937. Myrtle had a school from its earliest days. The last school building was constructed in 1880,

closed in 1966 and was demolished in 1978.

A well-known landmark in Myrtle for many years was the Temperance Hall, later known as the Myrtle Community Centre. It has been said that it was built as early as 1854, but The Ontario Reformer, of Oshawa, records that a temperance hall was opened at Myrtle on June 28, 1872. In 1930, when Highway 12 was widened through Myrtle, it was in danger of demolition, but was moved back from the road

Brooklin – The Village With More Churches Than Taverns

In the 1990s, several large housing developments were constructed around the village of Brooklin, and more are contemplated in the future. This small community is undergoing very rapid change after remaining a quiet village for nearly 160 years.

Brooklin was founded in 1840 as the village of Winchester, named after the community of that name in Hampshire, England. It is not known how that name was chosen or by whom, but the name was short-lived.

In 1846, Smith's Canadian Gazetteer gave the following description of Winchester:

"A village in the township of Whitby situated near the centre of the township, five miles from the village of Windsor. The plank road to Scugog passes through it. It was commenced in 1840 and contains about 300 inhabitants. Professions and trades – one physician and surgeon, one grist mill, one ashery, one tannery, seven stores, three taverns, two waggon makers, three blacksmiths, three coopers, three tailors, three shoemakers, one cabinetmaker."

By 1847, the residents of Winchester decided that they wanted a post office, but they were faced with a problem. There was already a Winchester post office near Ottawa, so the name of the Whitby Township community had to be changed. At a public meeting called on Aug. 11, 1847, the citizens of Winchester voted to change the name of the community to

Mill Street (Cassels Road), looking east from Baldwin Street, 1878.

Brooklin. The post office actually opened a few days earlier on Aug. 6. The following is a report of the meeting, which appeared in the Toronto Globe of Aug. 14, 1847:

"At a meeting of the inhabitants of Winchester in the Township of Whitby,

Canada West, on the 11th inst., the following resolutions were adopted:

"1st. That in consequence of there being two places of the name Winchester in this province, mistakes are daily occurring in the transmission of letters and papers through the post

Methodist Episcopal Church at Church and Albert Streets, 1875.

the creek near Way Street. Two tanneries were located along the creek as well as two or three saw mills.

W.H. Smith provided the following description of Brooklin in his book, *"Canada Past Present and Future,"* published in 1851:

"About five miles and a half before reaching Whitby village, the road passes through a considerable village, formerly called Winchester, but now named Brooklin. It contains a population of about five hundred and fifty, two grist mills with three run of stones each, one of which is built of brick, and another containing two run of stones. There is also a tannery, a woolen factory, foundry, ashery and brewery; two saleratus factories, and a soap and candle factory. The village also contains a circulating library. Lyons's Creek, a small but tolerable mill stream, runs through the village, and after watering the east of the township, enters Lake Ontario about a mile and a half west from Windsor Bay."

The reference to *"Lyons's Creek"* is actually the Lynde Creek, as in the early days, *"Lynde"* was pronounced with a long *"i."* It was not named Bickell's Creek until James B. Bickell arrived in Brooklin in 1859.

An extensive description of Brooklin was provided by Mitchell and Company's Gazetteer and Directory of Ontario County in 1866:

office department and also the forwarding of goods by other public conveyances to the great injury and inconvenience of the business community of this neighbourhood and that in consequence thereof it has become necessary that the name of Winchester should be changed.

"2nd. That the name of this village be henceforth changed to that of Brooklin and that its post office be designated as "the Brooklin Post Office."

The editor of The Globe suggested that the residents of Brooklin should have spelled the name *"Brooklyn"* after Brooklyn, New York. It is not known how the name was chosen. Perhaps it was called after the brook which ran through the village.

Because of the brook, called Bickell's Creek after James B. Bickell (1826-1891), Brooklin was a milling centre. A brick mill was built in 1848 on Mill Street (now Cassels Road East) to replace a frame one that burned down, and Bickell's mill was on

"A post village in the township of Whitby, County of Ontario, situated on Valley Creek, 5-1/2 miles from Whitby, was first laid out in the year 1840 by John Campbell and Daniel S. Way, the eastern portion was afterwards laid out by John McGee, and the northern portion by B.F. Perry; the Post Office was established in the year 1847, Dr. Ware being the first postmaster, and was succeeded by Mr. Robert Darlington, the present postmaster. The village contains three churches, viz: Episcopal Methodist of wood, built in 1846, at a cost of $1,200, and now under the pastoral care of the Rev. O.G. Colomore. The Wesleyan Methodist also frame and rough-cast, built in 1856, at a cost of $1,200, the present pastor being Rev. John Shaw; and the Canada Presbyterian Church, also frame, built in 1862, at a cost of $2,100, the Rev. Mr. LaBelle being the pastor. The Church of England congregation hold occasional services in the town hall. The Town Hall was built in 1849 at a cost of about $1,600. There is one common school under the charge of Mr. John J. Tilly, assisted by Miss Thomas; the schoolhouse is of brick and built about the year 1854. The creek furnishes power for carrying on three good flouring mills and a pump factory. The village also contains two good hotels, the Globe under the excellent management of Mr. A. Alexander, and the Brooklin Hotel by Mr. A. Perrie, two general stores, a large woolen factory carried on by Messrs. Mathewson, Ratcliff & Co., who are also merchants in the village, a fine cabinet factory belonging to Mr. N. Phippen who has lately moved into a new and commodious building, a tin and stove store, several tailoring establishments, two blacksmith and waggon shops, carpenters shops, etc. Daily mail, Population about 600."

On Nov. 27, 1867, the Oshawa Vindicator provided this lively account of the village:

"A description of the village of Brooklin might not be uninteresting to the readers of your paper, not only on account of its proximity to our enterprising and growing town, but also of its own growth and improvement.

"Not the least evidence of real worth is the large number of churches and few taverns which it now maintains.

"There are five religious denominations, viz: The Wesleyan and Episcopal Methodists, the Presbyterian, the English Church and the Millerites. The Methodists are the most important and numerous body, and the new church now being built by the Wesleyans constitutes the chief beauty and improvement of the village. The Episcopals have also an excellent place of worship and a large membership and congregation. The church built by the Presbyterians is large, the interior is very neat and well attended. The English Church members intend building a new edifice in a short time.

"The merchant firms are those of S.M. Thomas and Hayward and Tyler, and their excellent stores are a credit to the village, as are also the factories of Messrs. Phippen and Thomas. The only jeweller's shop is that of W. Hepinstall, Esq. In the manufacture of harness, etc., Messrs. Dale and Maybee do a large and increasing business. The workmen in the blacksmith and carriage shops of Messrs. Hepburn and Roberts, Ketchen and Chamberlain find constant employment and also in the tanneries of Messrs. Cole and Powell. Near the village are the mills of Messrs. Bickell, Campbell and Francis. The apiary of Mr. John Thomas is very large and it is probable that his bees, as regards quality and number are first in the Province if not the Dominion.

"There are two photograph galleries in operation. The artists are Messrs. Campbell, Groat and Brockenshire.

"There are a number of fine private residences, a good Temperance Society has been organized; drunkards are seldom seen, and the youth of the village are, on the whole, industrious and respectable.

"And not the least interesting and noticeable feature is the literary society with its free reading room, connected with which there will be debates, public readings, and free lectures dur-

David W. MacDonald's store and post office, 55 Baldwin Street, C. 1890.

ing the coming winter."

A further outline of Brooklin's churches was provided in a Directory of Ontario County, published in 1876:

"At the present time the village contains several civil and military organizations, among which is one Masonic Lodge, No. 39 named Mount Zion; nights of meeting Tuesday on or before full moon. C.H. Sweetapple W. Bro., Saml. R. Wickett, Secretary. One Lodge of IOGT No. 75.

"The manufactures are represented by three grist mills, one tannery, one planing mill, several stores, telegraph office, etc.

"It also contains one Church of England, which cost about $2,000, is built of wood in the gothic style, and erected in 1870; one Wesleyan Methodist Church, built of brick and erected in 1867 at a cost of $6,000; one Presbyterian Church built of wood in 1862 at a cost of $2,000; one Methodist Episcopal Church built of wood in 1845 at a cost of $1,600, and one drill shed erected in 1867 at a cost of about $600 and is built of wood. Brooklin is connected by the P.W. & P.P. Extension R.R. Population about 700. Postmaster, Robert Darlington."

The four churches described in these accounts were: Church of England (St. Thomas' Anglican), Wesleyan Methodist (now Brooklin United Church); Presbyterian (on site of Mitchell Brothers' store, Church Street, 1862-1926); and Methodist Episcopal (at corner of Church and Albert Streets, 1845-1884). A fifth church, the Bible Christian was built in 1876. It was a Baptist Church from 1884 to 1916 and is now the Brooklin Community Centre. The Bible Christian and Methodist Episcopal Churches amalgamated with the Wesleyan Methodist Church in 1884 and the congregation moved to the present Brooklin United Church. The Presbyterian Church joined the Wesleyan Methodist to become the United Church in 1926 and was demolished. An earlier Wesleyan Methodist Church which was in operation rom 1855 to 1867 on Winchester Road, was moved to Baldwin Street and is now the Brooklin Village Shoppe.

By the 1880s, Brooklin had stopped growing, reaching a population of about 800. There was no significant growth until 1954 when a Toronto developer, George Ferguson announced that he would build 600 homes that became the Meadowcrest subdivision.

Throughout the 1970s efforts were made to extend sewer and water services from Whitby to Brooklin, for the community was served by wells and septic tanks, and no further development was permitted. At the end of the 1980s, the sewer and water services were built, and Brooklin's present-day growth began.

The Brooklin Flour Mill Ground Flour For 130 Years

In the centre of the village of Brooklin stands one of the oldest brick flour mills in Ontario. Built in 1848 by John Campbell and Daniel S. Way, it was been a landmark in the village for more than 150 years. Campbell and Way went to considerable effort and expense to construct this sturdy brick mill after their first mill, a frame building built in 1840, was destroyed by fire in 1847. One of the difficulties they faced, was the fact that the mill site was in the middle of a cedar swamp. Three builders tried and gave up because the foundations kept sinking into the quagmire. Finally, George Sonley (1805-1893), a builder who lived at the north-west corner of Taunton Road and Highway 12, agreed to take on the job. He piled stones into the cedar swamp until they sank 15 feet to bedrock. After this was completed, he was able to start the foundation despite prophecies of his neighbours that the mill would never stand.

They appeared to be right, when a large crack opened in the back wall of the six-storey building, stretching from the foundation to the eaves, but no further structural problems occurred and the mill is as sound today as the year it was built. John Campbell (1794-1876) forbade the serving of liquor on the construction site, thus there were no accidents when the mill was built.

A busy day at the Brooklin Flour Mill, 1953.

The date *"1848"* can be clearly seen in coloured brick under the west eave of the building.

The Brooklin Mill in its earliest days was powered by water that passed through an ingenious mill race built through the village. The mill pond was more than half a mile from the mill, at Vipond's Flats, which are now the site of the Meadowcrest subdivision, built in the 1950s. The mill race ran along Pearl Street after it crossed Highway 12 near Lynde Creek. However, it was soon discovered that the pond did not hold enough water to keep the mill running all day. By noon it would be drained dry when the mill was operating at full capacity. To solve this problem, Campbell built separate bins where local farmers could store tons of grain and come back at a later date when there was enough water to turn it into flour.

In 1887, the Campbell estate sold the mill to John Robson (1859-1902). It was later operated by his brother W.B. Robson and William H. Elviss (1865-1916). The following description of the Brooklin Mill appeared in the Whitby Chronicle in January, 1884:

"The Brooklin Mill stands about a short distance from the Tannery and is a three-storey brick building owned by the Campbell estate, and under the able management of John Robson. The mill has three run of stone and is run by water power. It has had a purifier and smutter lately put in; has also a brush machine, and when in full blast can run off 75 barrels a day. Shipping is done to some extent but business is mainly local; the mill does a large amount of gristing."

Behind the brick mill was one of Brooklin's two tanneries. It was built in 1854 by Moses Bartlett, who later sold it to John and Edward Cole. The tannery was operated by William J. Murray (1849-1932) until it was struck by lightning and burned down in June, 1890. Ross Johnston (1827-1911) the *"Traveller"* for the Whitby Chronicle, gave this description of the W.J. Murray Tannery in 1884:

A bill from the Brooklin Mill, October 19, 1887.

"The premises are extensive and commodious, and present a neat and tidy appearance. No wonder as to that, in view of the vast number of hides and neat stock that receive treatment here. The main building is 102 feet by 56 feet and is fitted up with the most approved machinery and is run by steam power and is heated by steam. Mr. Murray

informs me that from thirteen to fifteen thousand sides of leather are run through during the year. They make a specialty of buff, harness and upper leather, and employ regularly 20 to 25 hands. You will see from this how important an industry this is to the place. A new brick smoke stack was erected last summer, about 70 feet high. The company has been in business here about eight years and everything about the premises gives token of good management and prosperity."

After the tannery fire, which put 25 men out of work, Murray moved to the Maritimes. At the age of 83, Murray died on Sept. 1, 1932, from inhaling calcium cyanide he was using to poison insects in a mushroom barn at Woodville, Ont. A photograph of the tannery appears in the chronicle on the Brooklin flood of 1890.

After the death of William H. Elviss in 1916, a man named Ferguson, and James F. Nelles operated the mill for a short time until on Sept. 17, 1919, it was purchased by Charles M. Wilson (1885-1968) whose family ran it for 59 years. Wilson was born at Maidstone, Kent, England, into a milling family. He worked at his grandfather's mill until it closed in 1908, and came to Canada. For six years he worked at the F.L. Green Mill at Greenwood in Pickering Township, followed by five years at the Maple Leaf Mills in Port Colborne. In 1919

The mill pond in 1912.

brand of flour. By the 1970s, the Brooklin Mill was the only operating flour mill in the Region of Durham, with the exception of the Vanstone Mill in Bowmanville. The Brooklin Mill ended up doing custom flour milling and in later years pastry flour from fall wheat.

In 1978, the last flour was ground by the Wilsons at the Brooklin Mill, 130 years after it was built. In September of that year, they sold the mill to Jim and Jane Hughes who opened a general store on the first floor. A former planner for the Scarborough Board of Education, Hughes wanted to move to a small community and try something different. Alfred Wilson, who with his brothers, sold the mill, started working for his father at the age of 16 in the mill for 50 cents a day in the 1930s.

In 1990, the Brooklin Mill was purchased by Whitby developer Bill Little, who had made the successful Pearson Lanes development in downtown Whitby from a number of old houses. He planned to make the mill into a restaurant and living quarters for his family, but he was hit hard by the recession of 1992 and had to sell the mill. In 1995, Rick and Cathy Ferguson opened a hardware store in the old mill. In September 1998, they hosted a 150th birthday party for the mill, with 50-cent hot dogs and hamburgers and free birthday cake.

he purchased the Brooklin Mill and two years later converted it from gristing to flour exclusively and installed electric motors to replace the old water wheel. Three of his sons, Alfred, Winston and Vernon, carried on the business. During the Second World War the Wilsons converted the electric motors to diesel power and ran the mill 24 hours a day at a capacity of 50 barrels of flour daily. In 1952, they went back to electric power, serving customers from as far away as Kingston to the east and Bobcaygeon to the north. When they started in 1919, the Wilsons had competition from 25 other mills at Greenwood, Whitevale, Hampton, Port Perry and Pickering. They purchased the rights from the Hampton Mill to produce its XXX

Bagotville – A Lost Piece Of Whitby History

As late as the 1920s, the land about half a mile west of Cullen Gardens on Taunton Road (4th Concession of Whitby) was referred to as Baggotsville. By that time there was only a school house to mark the location of the community. Baggotsville was not really the proper name of this place at all. It was named *"Bagotville"* after Sir Charles Bagot (1781-1843), Governor of Upper Canada from 1841 to 1843. A report in the Whitby Gazette and Chronicle in 1917 stated that Bagotville once had a population of 300, but this is unlikely. It is most likely that it was a community of scattered farms surrounding the school house.

The Bagotville school house, a brick building constructed in 1874, was destroyed by fire in 1925 and replaced by another brick school house, now a residence. An interesting story of the Bagotville school was told by the late Keith Lynde (1900-1984). In the 1880s, he said, the school trustees were concerned about

Patly Mills, site of Cottage Country at Cullen Gardens, C. 1870.

someone stealing wood from the school's wood pile. They suspected who was responsible and decided to teach him a lesson. The trustees hollowed out a log, filled it with gunpowder and plugged the ends. The thief took the log home and put it in his stove.

But he had a premonition that something was wrong. He ran out the door, just as his stove exploded.

The 1917 report in the Gazette and Chronicle stated that there were mills at Bagotville. Quinton McGowan had a grist mill about a quarter of a mile south-west of the school, and about half a mile east on Taunton Road, stood the Patly Mills, established by James Mitchell (1811-1853). The mill pond is now site of the lake for Cottage Country at Cullen Gardens. The Mitchell house, built about 1851, still stands south of the Gardens and is owned by Len Cullen. James Mitchell met a tragic death in a ship wreck on Lake Ontario in 1853. His tomb stone in Oshawa Union Cemetery reads: *"In memory of James Mitchell who was lost on the Ocean Wave eight miles from Kingston, April 30th, 1853, aged 41 years. Native of Forfarshire, Scotland."* The *"Ocean Wave,"* was the name of the boat on which he was travelling.

Whitby Becomes A County Town

The second most important factor in Whitby's development, after its fine natural harbour, is its establishment in 1852 as the County Town of the County of Ontario. Even to this day, that designation is still maintained in the names of the *"County Town Singers"* and the *"County Town Carnival"*. The Singers were formed in 1967 by Joe Wainwright (1920-1987) and the carnival by the Whitby Chamber of Commerce in 1966. Ontario County ceased to exist as a municipality on Jan. 1, 1974, when it became the Regional Municipality of Durham, but Whitby still remains the site of the Court House, Jail and Land Registry Office. Due to new Provincial regulations, the Whitby Jail will close within the next year and be replaced with a *"superjail"* in some other municipality. A new Land Registry Office opened on Rossland Road in 1991, and the new Court House was opened on Rossland Road by Ontario Premier John Robarts on Sept. 30, 1964. It remains the meeting place of the Durham Region Council, even though there have been efforts over the past 25 years to move the Court House and Regional Headquarters to Oshawa. A provincial government decision on this is still pending.

The naming of Whitby as County Town for the County of Ontario, initiated a period of rapid growth in the 1850s, but this

The original Ontario County Court House building as it appeared on the Tremaine Map of 1860.

was cut short by an economic depression at the end of 1857. Lawyers, judges and professional men gravitated to Whitby, and many of the town's finest homes were built

by these men. The County Town was selected in March of 1852 and a Provisional County was formed while the Court House, Jail and Registry Office were built. In 1854,

Ontario County was set aside as a separate County. It was called the *"Keystone County"* by Col. John E. Farewell (1840-1923), the County Clerk, because it was long and narrow, shaped like a keystone in an arch. An additional County Building, the House of Refuge (now 300 High Street) was built in Whitby in 1901-1903.

Although the most active movement to create a new county east of Toronto was in the late 1840s and early 1850s, the first meeting to discuss the subject was held at Bennett's Tavern on Dec. 12, 1835. This building stood until 1990 at the corner of Dundas and Euclid Streets where the Canada Trust building is located. Whitby Township at that time was part of the Home District, which included all the townships from Oshawa to Hamilton, with Toronto as the judicial centre where all legal business was conducted. The settlers east and west of Toronto found it a hardship to travel on foot or by horseback to Toronto every time they had to do business with the courts or the Home District Council. Litigants, jurors, witnesses and those wanting to collect debts, all had to travel to Toronto, often on frequent occasions. If trials or council meetings lasted for days, these settlers were away from home for a long time. At the 1835 meeting in Whitby, a resolution was passed to petition the

Legislature of Upper Canada to form a new district east of Toronto. Nothing resulted from this meeting and it was not until about 1848 that Peter Perry (1792-1851) of Whitby became the leader of a group of men from the eastern townships who appealed again to the Legislature for a new district. Perry, James Rowe (1799-1869), Ezra Annes (1796-1857) and Samuel Cochrane (1793-1879) of Whitby organized meetings throughout Whitby, Pickering and the northern townships, to push forward a proposal for a new district. Although Perry, the undoubted leader of these men, died unexpectedly on Aug. 24, 1851, the formation of a new county was assured.

Ontario County as set out in 1852, consisted of the Townships of Pickering and Whitby on the shore of Lake Ontario, and to the north, Uxbridge, Scott, Reach, Brock, Thorah, Mara and Rama. Whitby was split into Whitby and East Whitby Townships in 1857 and Scugog was separated from Reach Township in 1856. The original proposal was to include Georgina Township on Lake Simcoe in the new county, but its inhabitants voted to remain in the old County of York. Rama Township was largely an Indian reservation. When the Region of Durham was formed in 1974, Rama and Mara were transferred to Simcoe County, and Darlington, Clarke and

Cartwright Townships were added to the old County of Ontario. Darlington and Clarke were named Newcastle, but citizens voted a few years ago to change the name to Clarington, a combination of the old names of Clarke and Darlington. East Whitby became the City of Oshawa; Ajax was separated from part of Pickering; Reach, Scugog and Cartwright became Scugog; Uxbridge and Scott combined as Uxbridge Township and Brock and Thorah were amalgamated as the new Township of Brock. Whitby Town and Township amalgamated as the new Town of Whitby in 1968, the only municipalities to do so before Regional Government.

The Provisional Council of the County of Ontario met in two public buildings in Whitby before the Court House was opened in April 1854. The first meetings, in May 1852, were held in a brick school house at 1516 Dufferin Street in Port Whitby, constructed in 1851. This building, although much altered in appearance, still stands. The second place of meeting was a frame building known as the *"Free Church"* which stood on the corner of Brock and Mary Streets. A public building owned by Peter Perry, it was used as a meeting hall and place of worship for the Presbyterian and Methodist congregations of Whitby. By the mid 1850s, with the construction of the

The County Court Room in 1955. Was it really inhabited by a ghost?

architectural designs for the County Buildings. The winning architects were Frederic W. Cumberland (1820-1881) and William G. Storm (1826-1892) of Toronto. Cumberland and Storm were the leading architects of the city. Cumberland and Thomas Ridout had designed St. James' Cathedral in 1850 and the 7th Toronto Post Office (now the Argus Corporation building) and the Normal School in 1851. Cumberland and Storm went on to design University College in 1856 and the centre portion of Osgoode Hall in 1857. They also designed court houses in Lindsay and Cayuga, Ont. The plans by Cumberland and Storm for the Whitby County Buildings are in the Horwood Collection at the Archives of Ontario.

The Ontario County Court House is designed in the Classical Revival style, popular for government buildings in the 1850s. The centre portion is constructed to resemble the Parthenon in Athens, Greece, with its fluted Doric columns, topped by a silver-painted dome. The original building had a one-storey wing to each side, but an addition was made to the north end in 1866 and a second floor added to both wings in 1910.

On Sept. 23, 1852, a small group of officials gathered at the site on Centre Street, selected for the new Court House. In the

Mechanics' Institute Hall and the Methodist and Presbyterian Churches, it became a residence. The old Free Church was demolished in the fall of 1968 and replaced by a Becker's Milk Store.

The Provisional Council argued bitterly over where the County Buildings would be constructed, but finally purchased the block bounded by Centre, Gilbert, King and Ontario Streets, from Asa Werden (1779-1866). A contest with a prize of £25 ($125) was held by the County Council to select

absence of the Provisional County Warden, Joseph Gould (1808-1886) of Uxbridge, James Rowe (1799-1869) of Whitby was asked to turn the first sod. Eli Levens of Pickering Township and Bernard Frey Ball (1819-1856) of Whitby, the first clerk of the peace for Ontario County, also turned a spadeful of dirt.

James Wallace (1814-1882) of Whitby, who had been selected as the contractor to build the Court House and Jail, was a member of the newly-formed Composite Lodge of Ancient Free and Accepted Masons. Along with other Lodge members he arranged for a Masonic corner-stone laying ceremony for the Court House, the first such ceremony ever held in Whitby. Wallace, along with fellow Masons John Welsh (1810-1859), John O. Dornan (1814-1867) and Francis Keller (1821-1890) formed a committee which asked the Provisional Warden of 1853, James Rowe if the Masonic Lodge could take charge of the ceremony. The Masons agreed to pay all the costs involved and solicited funds from the lodge members to cover the expense of erecting a platform for the speakers and stands for the spectators.

June 30, 1853 was a beautiful sunny day as carriages brought Masonic Lodge members and visitors from neighbouring communities to Whitby. The Masons assembled at Scripture's Hotel, now a vacant lot where taxis are parked at Dundas and Byron Streets, where a meeting of the Provincial Grand Lodge was opened. The Worshipful Grand Master of Canada West (now Ontario), Sir Allan McNab, owner of Dundurn Castle in Hamilton, had been invited to lay the corner stone, but was unable to come to Whitby because of illness. The duty, therefore, passed to the Grand Secretary, Very Worshipful Brother Francis Richardson, who along with other members of the Grand Lodge in Toronto, arrived by steamboat at Whitby Harbour.

A procession of Masons, dressed in black suits with white gloves, and wearing their Masonic aprons and other regalia, marched from Scripture's Hotel to the site of the Court House, where a platform and spectator stands had been erected. The procession, led by the Brooklin Brass Band, consisted of sword bearers, the Grand Secretary carrying the constitution book on a cushion, Masters carrying the Doric, Ionic and Corinthian lights and many other colourful symbols of Masonry.

Following an address on the role of the Masons by Brother Richardson, a prayer was offered by Rev. Bro. Vincent P. Mayerhoffer (1784-1859) of Whitby, the Grand Chaplain. Bro. Mayerhoffer, an occasional preacher at St. John's Anglican Church, had once been a Roman Catholic priest. Now he was Grand Chaplain of the Masons and the Orange Order of Upper Canada. The stone, according to Masonic ritual, was laid at the north-east corner of the building. An attempt to find it in 1973 failed to reveal its whereabouts. It was not known until the 1852 architect's drawings were donated to the Archives of Ontario in 1979. They revealed it was below ground level at the north-east corner of the centre portion of the building, and not at the corner of the north wing.

In a cavity beneath the stone, Bro. Richardson deposited the minutes of the County Council; Whitby, Oshawa and Toronto newspapers; Scobie's Almanac; a list of Provincial Government officials; the Canadian Journal; various coins and a letter from Joseph Gould, the first Provisional Warden of Ontario County. A piece of parchment listing the Ontario County Councillors, was placed in a bottle which was embedded in pulverized charcoal inside the cavity.

The Ontario Reporter, published by Bro. John O. Dornan, described the actual laying of the corner stone as follows:

"The mortar being spread, the stone was then slowly lowered to its permanent resting place, amidst the solemn and magnificent strains of the National Anthem by both bands.

The plumb, square and level were each respectively handed by the Chief Architect (William G. Storm) to the Acting Grand Master (Francis Richardson), who, after applying them, pronounced the stone 'well-formed, true and trusty.' Three immense cheers were then given for the Queen and three for the County of Ontario. The silver vessels containing the corn, wine and oil, were then presented to the Grand Warden, and were each successively poured on the stone by the Acting Grand Master. The stone was then struck three times with the mallet, and the ceremony was concluded amidst immense cheering from the vast multitude. The procession then reformed, and proceeded through the principal streets of Whitby, returned to the lodge room at Scripture's and the Masonic Lodge was closed. There was a grand dinner after the ceremony, at which everybody was toasted and everybody's prosperity drunk, as well as the future prosperity of the new county."

The silver trowel used by Very Worshipful Brother Richardson disappeared after the ceremony and was lost for 101 years. It was discovered in an estate in London, Ont., in 1954 and returned to Whitby where it remains at the new Masonic Temple on Cochrane Street in a display case made by Past Master Fred Gale (1883-1972). This historic trowel, presented by Acacia Lodge of London, was used again by Dr. Matthew

Mayor Desmond G. Newman officially opening the Whitby Centennial Building, Feb. 18, 1967.

B. Dymond, MPP (1906-1996), on July 19, 1960, to lay the corner stone for the new municipal building on Dundas Street West (now the Whitby Public LIbrary). Warden J. Sherman Scott of Ontario County and Oshawa Mayor Lyman Gifford employed

the trowel to lay the corner stone of the new Court House on Rossland Road on Nov. 28, 1963. On Dec. 28, 1963, Fred Gale, as the oldest Past Master of Composite Lodge, laid the corner stone for the Masonic Temple with the old silver trowel.

In 1973, Wilfrid Gould, a great-grandson of the first Provisional Warden Joseph Gould, and himself Warden of Ontario County in 1966, wanted to retrieve the contents of the corner stone of the old Court House before the County of Ontario was replaced by the Region of Durham. He was unable to find the stone, as its exact location had not yet been revealed by the plans donated to the Archives of Ontario.

The original County Buildings consisted only of the Court House and Jail. The Land Registry Office was first located on Brock Street, south of the Royal Hotel, in a building owned by the first Registrar, John Ham Perry (1827-1896). A new Registry Office was built beside the Court House in 1873 and additions were made to it in 1929 and 1953/54. It became too small for the growing needs of the Region of Durham, so much so that some business at the end of each month had to be conducted in a tent pitched on the front lawn. In 1987, the Registry Office moved to a plaza in Oshawa, and the new office opened on

Demolishing the Ontario County Jail, February, 1960. The last hanging in Ontario County took place in the room above the door at right, in December, 1946

Rossland Road in 1991.

The old County Jail, built in 1853, was replaced by a new jail on Victoria Street in 1958, and demolished in February, 1960. It was located behind the Court house where the parking lot is now.

In 1964, the County of Ontario moved into the new Court House on Rossland Road. There was some discussion of tearing down the old building on Centre Street and replacing it with apartments, but the old Court House was saved by a citizens' committee which, in the fall of 1964, persuaded the Town Council to convert it into a community centre as Whitby's 1967 project to celebrate Canada's Centennial. The Centennial Building, as it is now called, was officially opened by Mayor Desmond G. Newman, on Feb. 18, 1967. It was so cold that day that the author of this book could not take pictures of the outdoor ceremony as the shutter of his camera had frozen.

The Whitby Centennial Building was saved by an agreement between the Town of Whitby, and the County of Ontario and City of Oshawa, that the building would be leased to the Town of Whitby for 99 years at a cost of one dollar a year. Attempts are now being made to give Whitby ownership of the building so it can be expanded to give new facilities to the town archives and the Whitby Courthouse Theatre, which presents plays in the old court room.

The old Whitby Court House even had its own ghost. As early as 1873, the Whitby Chronicle reported a ghost in the court room, and citizens of the town sat up till midnight, waiting for it to appear. It did not, and the editor, William H. Higgins scoffed at the ghost story. In the 1970s, however, one of the staff of the Whitby Courthouse Theatre saw a figure of a man dressed in a frock coat and top hat, float down from the ladies' balcony at the back of the court room, and walk out through the side wall. In 1988, two psychics were brought in by a local newspaper to try to identify the ghost. They came up with a story that a man, whose son or nephew was on trial for a serious crime (possibly rape), was pacing up and down outside the balcony door, waiting for the verdict. When the judge said *"guilty"*, the distraught man ran onto the balcony, shouted *"you must right the wrong"*, and fell over the edge to his death. The story is interesting, but there is no documented proof that this incident ever happened. It is up to the reader to judge for himself. The psychics reported that they told the ghost that he was dead and he could leave the building in peace.

Whitby's Public Library Is One Of The Oldest In Ontario

No photograph of him is known to exist. His grave in Union Cemetery is unmarked. His name is practically unknown today, but he was one of the chief builders of Whitby's cultural scene. His name was Hugh Fraser, founder of what is now Whitby's Public Library. If it had not been for his foresight and determination, Whitby might never have had a library or been able to sustain one for most of the past 147 years.

Hugh Fraser (1815-1890) was born at Inch, Aberdeenshire, Scotland, on Sept. 17, 1815, and took his apprenticeship as a tailor. When his poor health demanded a change of climate, he sailed for Canada in 1837 at the age of 21, landing at Halifax, where he remained for one year. Travelling to Montreal on foot, he arrived at the time of the Rebellion of 1837, and took up arms on the Government side. After coming to Toronto, a year later, his opinions changed and he became a stalwart member of the Reform (Liberal) party.

Fraser first settled in Whitby in 1840, and after working two years in Brockville, he returned to stay in 1850. With the aid of voluntary subscriptions, he started a circulating library in his tailor shop on Brock Street. In 1852, with Fraser's backing, a Mechanics' Institute was established in Whitby to provide cultural resources for the education of the town's working men. That year a hall and library were constructed for the Mechanics' Institute at the corner of Byron and Mary Streets where Pearson Lanes is now, with Fraser as librarian. This library was open only to members of the Mechanics' Institute, and was not a *"public"* library as we know it today. The Mechanics' Hall provided a reading room and a hall with a stage where lectures and entertainments were presented. Thomas D'Arcy McGee (1825-1868) one of the Fathers of Confederation, and a personal friend of William H. Higgins of The Chronicle, delivered a lecture there.

The Mechanics' Institute flourished in the 1850s and 1860s, but on one occasion, the officers considered that the library was unprofitable and decided to remove the books. When they arrived to do their deed, Fraser barred the door, refusing them entry to the library. He spoke at length on the library's much-needed place in the community and finally forced them to reconsider. The library remained.

On November 27, 1873, after a program which featured the future actresses May and Flo Irwin, the Mechanics' Institute hall burned down, and all the library books were lost. It took several years for Fraser to build up the collection again.

In 1884 a proposal was made to provide a free public library in place of the Mechanics' Institute. New legislation from the Ontario Government was supported by Fraser, but the citizens of Whitby voted down the proposal. He was more successful as a member of the school board for 11 years, convincing the members to amalgamate the public and grammar school boards. The Grammar School, established in 1849, was the equivalent of today's high school.

When Fraser died at the age of 74 on Feb. 1, 1890, his funeral was attended by the directors of the Mechanics' Institute, the Board of Education and the St. Andrew's Society, and all the downtown stores were closed as a tribute to his memory. On Fraser's death, his daughter, Mary Fraser was appointed librarian, serving until her death in 1916. She was succeeded by Fraser's granddaughter, Mary E. Straiton (1868-1947) who was librarian from 1916 to 1938.

It was said of Hugh Fraser when he died that *"His name has been for nearly half a century associated with the cause of education, the cultivation of literary tastes and the intellectual advancement of the people of Whitby"*. For three generations, his family lovingly cared for the town's library, one of the oldest established in a small town in Ontario.

In the early years of the 20th century, the Whitby Library was in rooms above the law

Whitby Public Library in the year it opened, 1914.

office of James Rutledge (1842-1914) in the building south of the Royal Hotel now occupied by the Rainbow Restaurant. In 1911, it was learned that the millionaire American steel magnate Andrew Carnegie was using a portion of his vast wealth to finance the construction of public libraries in Canada and the United States. All he asked was that the town supply a site and form a board to manage the library.

The question of a site was solved by the County of Ontario Old Girls' Association, founded in 1904 at the 50th anniversary of the county as a forerunner of today's service clubs. The Old Girls' Association purchased from Fred L. Green (1864-1945) for $500, a lot at the north-east corner of Dundas and Byron Streets. The town council then formed a library board under chairman Lyman T. Barclay (1855-1925), a local lawyer. The purchase of the library site was approved by a vote of the ratepayers, paving the way for a library grant of $5,750 from Carnegie. However, before the project was completed, he had to provide an additional $4,250.

James Bogue of Peterborough was hired as the contractor to build according to plans by Guelph architect William A. Mahoney. Construction began early in 1913. On June 9, 1913, James Rutledge, Chairman of the Board of Education, and a former mayor,

was called upon to lay the corner stone. On that day, the Toronto Conference of the Methodist Church of Canada was holding its annual meeting in Whitby. The members adjourned to attend the corner stone laying for the library. The silver trowel used for this ceremony was presented to the library board in 1975 by Albert A. Walker (1887-1990), whose father worked in Rutledge's law office. The trowel is displayed in a wooden case made by Walker.

On May 1, 1914, Col. John E. Farewell (1840-1923), Crown Attorney and Ontario County Clerk, officially opened the library. The new building contained separate reading rooms for men, women and children, and eight book stacks containing 5,000 volumes. In order to take out books, a resident had to obtain a library card for five cents, signed by a responsible person who could identify the borrower. The library was open from 2 p.m. to 4 p.m. and 7 p.m. to 9 p.m. on week days. In 1954, a children's library of 2,000 books was opened in the basement under the direction of Mrs. Roy Fowler (1899-1973).

After many years of discussion of the need for a new library, the library moved to the old municipal building on Dundas Street West in 1973. For five years it occupied the basement, moving into the whole building in 1978 after the new municipal building

was constructed on Rossland Road.

The old library served for a number of years as a Canada Employment Centre. It is now the law office of Whitby-Ajax MPP Jim Flaherty, and designated as a historic building under the Ontario Heritage Act. Currently there are plans under way to construct a new library building in the year 2000, to meet again the needs of a growing town.

The deed of land from Frederick L. Green to the Whitby Public Library Boiard, July 26, 1911.

Whitby Incorporated as a Town, January 1, 1855

Two events of major importance occurred within a three-year period (1852-1855) which set Whitby up as an important centre in Upper Canada, or Canada West, as the Province of Ontario was called from 1841 to 1867. In 1857, a third significant event changed Whitby's position and outlook for nearly a century.

On March 11, 1852, a Government proclamation set off the eastern townships of the old County of York as the Provisional County of Ontario, and named Whitby as the County Town. Suddenly this small community of about 1,100 people was to become the political and judicial centre of a new county, the location of a court house, land registry office and jail. The county officials were to have their offices here, and business would boom. And that is exactly what happened. Overnight, land in Whitby increased considerably in value and speculators had a field day selling building lots. Fortunes were made and lost. Whitby's population grew to 1,500 in 1853 and reached a peak of 3,500 by 1857. Long columns of lots for sale were advertised in Toronto newspapers, and businessmen began to open stores in the town. The Centre Road had been completed to Lake Simcoe from Whitby Harbour and planked as far as the middle of Reach (now Scugog) Township by 1848. Trade was pouring down this highway into

James Rowe, Whitby's first mayor.

Whitby. In the fall of 1852, it was recorded that a line of wagons of grain waiting to be unloaded, stretched north from the harbour to Farquharson's (later Rice's) Hill at Brock Street and Rossland Road, and grain was often being unloaded from these wagons

after midnight.

The Ontario Reporter, Whitby's newspaper, had the following to say about the town, on May 15, 1852, two months after the naming of the County Town:

"There is no place perhaps in Canada, the business of which has so steadily and so rapidly increased within the last two years, as that of Whitby. The shipping of our port doubled itself the past year, and from present appearances it will more than double itself on the past during the present year; besides this our mercantile houses have increased their stock nearly fourfold, many of which are in extent equal to some of the largest houses in Toronto, while the great centre road supplies them with a steady and increasing stream of customers from the rich Townships of the north.

"We are led to these remarks more particularly by observing, this early in the season, the incalculable advantages to the rear Townships, of the steamboat on Lake Scugog, built the past season by the enterprise of Messrs. Cotton and Rowe, in affording the people an easy and cheap access to Whitby, and from thence to any part of the province by stage or steamboat. On Monday evening last (May 10) in addition to the two regular daily stages which arrived from the north crammed inside and out with passengers, there were three extras, bringing in all, 65 passengers, down the great centre road to transact business at the front; and every day since

Perry's Block, 121 Brock Street North, destroyed by fire, June 16, 1864.

the growth of our town is correspondingly rapid. Already this spring there are between twenty-five and thirty houses in course of erection and many more are in contemplation, depending only on the choice of the site for the County Buildings. Even while we are writing this, our harbour is filled with craft and our streets lined with wagons. Everything speaks cheerfully of a prosperous future."

With such prosperous times ahead, the citizens of Whitby began planning to have the village incorporated as a town, since it was now officially a *"County Town."* The farmers surrounding the village, all wanted to have their lands included within the town limits, so their property could be divided up and sold for building lots. And so, when an Act of Parliament was passed by the Legislature on Dec. 18, 1854, a town with an area of six square miles was created, of which 3,000 acres were then used exclusively for farming. Whitby, by its act of incorporation, was larger in area than Ottawa and Kingston combined, although the population was much smaller than these well-established towns. Lots were selling for as much as 300 pounds ($1,500). Each farmer thought he was a millionaire, and the whisky flowed freely in the saloons.

The citizens of Whitby Village, in the fall of 1854, petitioned the Government of Canada West to incorporate their communi-

the navigation commenced there had been an undiminished rush of travel to this point. Our town now begins to present a gay and cheerful appearance morning and evening on the arrival and departure of these stages, as they

crack along with their sounding whips and shrill horns among the different hotels, depositing or taking up their passengers, thus giving Whitby the appearance of what she will soon be in reality, a first-class town. In addition to this

ty of 2,300 inhabitants as a town. The Act of Incorporation, dated Dec. 18, 1854, set the southern boundary of the town as Lake Ontario and the northern boundary as the Third Concession (Rossland Road). The eastern boundary was set a short distance east of Anderson Street and the western boundary a short distance west of Jeffrey Street.

For political purposes, the town was divided into three wards: the North Ward consisting of land between Dundas Street and Rossland Road, the Centre Ward between Dundas and Burns Streets, and the South Ward, south of Burns Street to Lake Ontario. The South Ward (Port Whitby) became much of a community on its own, for there was some distance of open space between Port Whitby and the downtown. The South Ward or Port Whitby was often referred to as *"The Bay."*

Sheriff Nelson G. Reynolds (1814-1881) was named as returning officer for the first municipal election which was held on Dec. 21, 1854.

The first Municipal Council of the Town of Whitby was duly elected, with James Rowe (1799-1869) as Mayor, and held its first meeting in the County Court House (now the Centennial Building), on Jan. 1, 1855. The Council proceeded to purchase a block of land from Trent Street to a point south of Burns Street, between Brock and

Byron Streets as a town park and public market. Now Rotary Centennial Park, it is the oldest piece of municipal property in Whitby. The council in 1856, proceeded to build a brick Town Hall at the south-west corner of Brock and Trent Streets. In 1879, the Town Hall was moved to Hopkins' Music Hall at Brock and Colborne Streets, where the fire hall is now, because the old Town Hall was considered too far away from the centre of the community. The old Town Hall finished its days as an apple evaporating works, for making cider and vinegar, and was destroyed by fire in 1900. The strip of land between the existing park and Trent Street was sold by the town in the early 1890s to S.W. Lowell to establish his apple evaporating works. When the town wanted to buy back the land in 1928, the proposal was defeated by a vote of the ratepayers.

In 1856, as Whitby was growing rapidly, plans were made to build a railway from Whitby Harbour to Georgian Bay. Surveys were made and the work was about to begin, when there was a serious economic crash in the fall of 1857. This, although the town did not realize it at the time, was the end of Whitby's growth and prosperity. The population, over the next 30 years decreased from 3,500 to 2,500. The town remained static and did not grow. The railway to Georgian Bay was never built; only a shorter version

was built from Port Whitby to Lindsay in the 1870s. Whitby did not experience another building boom until the 1950s, and again in the 1980s and 1990s. For about 100 years, it remained a quiet little town, surpassed by Oshawa which began to grow after Robert McLaughlin established his carriage factory there in 1877. The carriage factory, the largest in the British Empire, became General Motors of Canada in 1918.

By 1858, the farmers of Whitby who were located within the town limits, found they were paying high taxes, with no hope of developing their land. They petitioned the Legislature to separate from the Town and go back into the Township, but their plea fell on deaf ears. Every time there was a Depression, the farmers again tried to separate from the town. It happened in the 1890s and in the 1930s. In the 1890s, the farmers told the Council they were in the minority in the town and were not being represented fairly. By 1888, the town was in debt by $148,350 for building projects that were of no benefit to the farmers, they said. In 1895, more than 50 farmers petitioned the Ontario Legislature again to be granted the right to separate from the Town, but the Town Council again was able to defeat the proposal. In the disastrous 1930s, the farmers, this time led by a former Town Councillor Charles Broughton (1895-1980) tried again to secede. An agreement which had granted farmers a fixed assessment and some tax exemptions, had expired and the town would not renew it. Sixteen farmers in the east end of town petitioned the Ontario Railway and Municipal Board in 1929 to secede, but an agreement was finally reached. When this agreement ran out in 1935, one of the worst years of the Great Depression, the farmers wanted to secede again. Town Clerk John R. Frost (1901-1983) suggested to Mayor Ed Bowman (1892-1969) that he call the farmers' bluff by telling them that they could secede but they would get no water if they joined another municipality. The farmers finally accepted a nine-mill tax exemption for five years and nothing was heard of the matter again. By 1940, prosperity had returned, with the beginning of the Second World War.

Whitby's population remained static at less than 3,000 people until the First World War. In 1921, the population was 3,597; in 1931, 5,056, and 1941, 5,904. These figures, however, may be misleading, for the 1,500 patients at the Ontario Hospital were often included in the total population figures in order to get higher provincial grants. The actual population may have been about 4,400, as recorded in 1947.

The post-war building boom saw Whitby begin to develop. By 1950, the population

Wolfenden and Lawrie's Monument Works, on Dundas Street East where the dental building is beside the Cenotaph. This building was destroyed in the great fire of October 16, 1877.

was over 7,000 and by 1960 it had reached 12,000, with the construction of many subdivisions in the 1950s. In 1967, a year before amalgamation with the Township of Whitby, the Town of Whitby's population was about 15,000.

During the 1950s, subdivisions were built in the Hillcrest Drive, Nemwan Crescent, Bayview Avenue and Greenwood Crescent areas. Development also occurred in the areas around St. Lawrence Street and Palmerston Avenue. Kathleen Rowe, R. A. Hutchison and Palmerston public schools were built and additions made to King Street (R. A. Sennett) and Dundas Street (Florence M. Heard) Schools.

First Methodist Church Was Built Like A Meeting Hall

Few people who pass the large brick house at the north-west corner of Centre and Mary Streets realize that this substantial two-storey building was once a church. It certainly does not look like a church in the traditional style with high gothic windows and a steeple. Built by the Methodists of Whitby in 1855/56, it was constructed to look like a meeting hall, as was the custom with all early Methodist churches.

Methodism in Whitby dates back to 1826 when the Whitby Circuit was formed from the townships between Hope and Markham, with Whitby as its centre, and visited regularly by circuit riders known popularly as saddleback preachers. Whitby did not get a resident minister until 1854. In 1852, when Whitby was named as the county town of the new County of Ontario, the visiting Methodist preacher, Rev. Peter Kerr, began to raise funds to build a church, for he knew that the new town would grow quickly. He was succeeded in 1854 by the first resident Methodist minister, Rev. David B. Madden, who was in charge of a congregation of about 80 members.

On March 23, 1854, Robert E. Perry (1825-1894) and other members of his family sold two lots at the corner of Centre and Mary Streets to the Trustees of the Methodist Church, William Thorndyke, Jacob Bryan Sr., Robert Morrow, John

Whitby's first Methodist Church as it appeared in 1926.

Welton, George Abbott, James Rice and James Hodgson. Since the trustees did not have a lot of money to spend on the purchase, John Ham Perry (1827-1896), Robert's younger brother, donated half the price of the church site. When the trustees were still unable to raise the necessary funds, Perry donated the balance owing on the lots. Robert and John Ham Perry owned all the

land north of Dundas Street, to Beech Street and from Pine Street to High Street, which they had inherited from their father, Peter Perry (1792-1851), the founder of Whitby. It is interesting to note that John Ham Perry was so generous to the Methodists, for he was an Anglican.

On Oct. 7, 1854, the trustees mortgaged the property to get funds to build the first permanent Methodist Church in Whitby. Up to that time, the Methodists had worshiped in a schoolhouse at Port Whitby, the Free Church at Brock and Mary Streets, now the site of a Becker's store, and in the Mechanics' Institute hall at Byron and Mary Streets, now the site of Pearson Lanes. Construction proceeded throughout 1855 and 1856, at the time that Whitby was incorporated as a town when there was a great building boom in the community. In March, 1856, Rev. Dr. Enoch Wood, President of the Toronto conference of the Methodist Church of Canada, preached the dedication sermon at the Whitby church, assisted by Rev. J. Borland and Rev. Gemley.

When the church was opened in 1856, some members of the congregation thought it was too big and a waste of money, but by 1860 the congregation had reached 490 and was still growing. A Sunday School was built west of the church in the 1870s, and still stands as a private residence at the corner of Mary and Kent Streets.

Nine ministers served in the Whitby Methodist Church between 1856 and 1876, when it was replaced by the Methodist Tabernacle, now St. Mark's United Church. One of these ministers was Rev. John Hunt (1818-1901), whose son, Vincent Perry Hunt (1859-1952) was one of the founders of the Toronto Conservatory of Music and

was music director at Albert College in Belleville and at the University of Alberta. Vincent P. Hunt was born in Whitby while his father was serving as minister. The minister with the most influence who served at the Whitby Methodist Church was Rev. Joseph E. Sanderson (1830-1913) who was in charge from 1871 to 1874. He was the prime mover in the establishment of the Ontario Ladies' College (now Trafalgar Castle School). Sanderson travelled throughout the province to raise funds to acquire Nelson G. Reynolds' Trafalgar Castle, and was appointed governor of the school when it opened in 1874. He returned to the ministry in 1879 and is noted for having written a history of the Methodist Church in Ontario, published in 1910.

By the 1870s, the Whitby Methodists found their church at Mary and Centre Streets to be too small. A building committee under Rev. John S. Clarke (1834-1907) made plans to construct the Methodist Tabernacle, which opened in September, 1876. Rev. Dr. Enoch Wood, who opened the first church in 1856, was called upon again to dedicate the Methodist Tabernacle.

With the old church at Centre and Mary Streets vacated, the congregation was faced with what to do with the building. It was proposed as a music hall or opera house, badly needed at the time, but in 1877,

George Hopkins built a music hall at the corner of Brock and Colborne Streets which became Whitby's town hall. Rev. Clarke, ever resourceful, purchased the old church himself on Feb. 23, 1877 and converted it into a double dwelling house. He added kitchen wings to the west side of the building and bay windows at the front and east side and added a floor to make it a two-storey dwelling. He also converted the Sunday School into a double dwelling and collected rent on these buildings for 30 years, even though he left Whitby after purchasing them. He continued as a preacher until 1895, and died at Niagara-on-the-Lake in 1907. His executors sold the building to James F. Pirie (1860-1940) who divided it into two ownerships when he sold it in 1920.

In 1985 the old Methodist Church was designated as an historic building under the Ontario Heritage Act. Two years later, one of the kitchen wings was demolished because it was structurally unsound, but this did not detract from the appearance of the building. Whitby's first Methodist Church still stands as an example of the boom times of Whitby in the 1850s when many large brick buildings were constructed. The Methodists joined with some Presbyterians and the Congregational Church to become the United Church of Canada in 1925.

The Day The Railway Came To Whitby

When the first railway train arrived in Whitby on Aug. 25, 1856, the whole town turned out for a gala celebration. From 1854 to 1856, the Grand Trunk Railway (now the Canadian National) was constructed from Toronto, east to Oshawa, as part of a line to link Toronto and Montreal. Although Oshawa was the terminus of the line, Whitby played host to the visiting dignitaries because it was the County Town. For many years Whitby took precedence over Oshawa in celebrations of this kind.

A train of 13 carriages set out from Toronto's Don River station at noon on Aug. 25, 1856, to the music of a brass band. Arriving at Oshawa, the invited guests, who were the first passengers on the Grand Trunk, partook of a luncheon in a building adjoining the railway station. After a speech by Oshawa Reeve Silas B. Fairbanks (1820-1871) the train departed for Whitby, where a large crowd jammed the station platform.

Flags and streamers decorated the station, and even the horses and carriages. The Grand Trunk station was located on the north side of the tracks, east of the Victoria Street crossing and west of South Blair Street. In 1903 it was replaced by the station now used by Whitby Arts Incorporated as an art gallery. This station was built at the end of Byron Street, so that it would be closer to the centre of town. The old station was demolished shortly after the 1903 station was built.

After the arrival of the train from Oshawa, Whitby Mayor James Wallace (1814-1882) addressed the directors of the Grand Trunk Railway, expressing praise and appreciation for the way in which the line was built. He was followed by John Ham Perry (1827-1896), president of the Whitby Mechanics' Institute, which housed the town's library.

"The importance to the Province of Canada of this gigantic undertaking is of such magnitude that it is impossible for the human mind to fully comprehend it beneficially and spontaneously," said Perry. He pointed out that the railway had already brought many advantages to Whitby. Since construction began in 1854, the town's population had increased 100 percent and the value of exports had risen to the fifth largest in Canada West (now Ontario). Perry had good reason to be pleased, for he and his brother Robert (1825-1894) owned all the land north of Dundas Street, and were making a fortune in selling building lots as a result of the railroad. In his speech, Perry referred to British capital used to build the Grand Trunk Railway, which would eventually enable a second track to be laid through Whitby. The railway of 1856 was a single track. A second track was not added, however, until 1902.

A representative of the railway replied to Perry, expressing regrets that the president of the Grand Trunk would not be in Whitby because he was on a mission to Europe.

Dinner was served in a large building adorned with evergreens and mottoes, such as *"God Save the Queen"*, *"Grand Trunk Railway – Deeds, Not Words"*, and *"British Capital – Canadian Enterprise"*. Mayor Wallace took the chair, accompanied by Reeve James Rowe (1799-1869) and the Mayor of Toronto, John Beverley Robinson. Wallace opened a series of toasts by proposing the health of Queen Victoria, Prince Albert and the Royal Family, followed by the Army and Navy and the president and directors of the Grand Trunk Railway. J. Beatty of the Grand Trunk responded with an historical sketch of the railway's development.

The chairman next toasted the contractors, Jackson, Peto, Barssey and Betts, followed by a toast to the Town of Whitby by Mr. Tate of the Grand Trunk. Even the press received a toast with all the proper honours. An immense cheer greeted the toast to the prosperity of Canadian agriculture, manufacturing and commerce. The reply from Mr. Bowes, M.P.P. could not be heard amidst the playing of the brass band, the clattering of plates and the popping of champagne corks. The Toronto Leader, which reported the event in great detail, stated it was sufficient to say that he spoke on the future of the rail-

Mayor James Wallace who hosted the reception for the Grand Trunk Railway.

way, communication between Canada and the Motherland and how to defend the railway project against opposition.

The Mayor of Toronto proposed a toast to Mr. Tate, who could not reply because the train whistle was already indicating it was time to leave. After three cheers for the Queen and the mayors of Toronto and Whitby, the guests boarded the train for the return trip to Toronto. Two engines were needed to pull the train, which comprised four passenger cars, a post office car and five platform cars, all of which were crammed with people eager to make the first train ride into Toronto. Passengers were even crammed into the engine and tender.

One passenger on that historic ride was nine-year-old George H. Ham (1847-1926), who in the 1890s, was public relations officer for the Canadian Pacific Railway. In his autobiography, *"Reminiscences of a Raconteur"*, published in 1921, Ham told how he made the trip on the first train from Whitby to Toronto.

"By the fall of 1856, the town schools had a holiday because on that day the first railway passenger train was to arrive at Whitby. The pupils were assembled up-town at the High School, then called the Grammar School. The Public School pupils led the procession, preceded by the town band, and the Grammar School formed the rear of the column, under the command of Mr. William McCabe (1835-1903) who was then the only teacher in the Grammar School.

"Arriving at the station, we were lined up along side the track. About 3 p.m., a train with three passenger cars arrived from Toronto, filled with invited guests. The locomotive was decorated with flags, and on the front and sides was a piece of bunting on which was painted the words 'Fortuna Sequitur'. We were ordered to make note of these words and produce a translation thereof on the following day. We generally agreed that "Let or May Fortune Follow" was about the meaning of these Latin words.

"The train moved on to Oshawa where John Beverley Robinson and

others delivered addresses. On the return of the train from Oshawa, a number of school boys boarded the car during the stoppage at Whitby, and then occurred the first and only time I was ever put off a train. I was bound to Toronto as I had never experienced a ride on a railway train. The conductor put my brother (John V. Ham, 1843-1881), four years my senior, and myself off at the end of the car. We ran to the front end, only to be again ejected. This was a little discouraging, I will candidly admit, but we made another bolt for the front entrance and when the irate conductor threateningly ordered us off, some of the compassionate passengers told him to give the boys a show, which he grudgingly did, and to Toronto we went.

"In the other cars, the invited guests protested against the invasion of the Whitby youths, but they too, notwithstanding the threats and warnings of the conductor, stuck to the train. Neither my brother nor myself had a cent, but that didn't worry us at all, and when we arrived in Toronto it was well after dark.

"No one knew when the train would leave for Whitby, and so we had to sit in that car, hungry as bears, until good old Hugh Fraser of Whitby (1815-1890), loomed up about ten o'clock with some crackers and cheese, after which we didn't take a continental of what old time the train would arrive. Crackers and cheese are very invigorating.

"The other fellows pooled all the money they

George H. Ham and his wife, at Montreal, circa, 1900. He was thrown off the first train from Whitby to Toronto in 1856.

had and Jack Wall who had been attending college in Toronto, rustled some more crackers and cheese, which seemed to be the sole and

only article of food on the menu that night. The clock struck 4 a.m. as we reached home, completely tired out but happy as clams. I was the first boy at school the next morning and was the hero of the day. Rides on trains then were big events of the mightiest importance."

George Ham recalled that the car in which he rode was number 2. Thirty years later he rode on the same car on the Caraquet Railway in New Brunswick, "but as I had a pass, the conductor did not throw me off once — let alone twice."

Although the coming of the Grand Trunk railway was greeted with much rejoicing in 1856, it spelled the end for Whitby harbour as a major shipping centre. In 1853, Whitby's harbour had been second to Toronto in the amount of shipping it handled on the north shore of Lake Ontario. The railway took much of the business from the harbour as trains were faster than sailing ships and did not have to depend on wind to travel. Also, trains could run in the winter when the harbour was blocked with ice.

The Grand Trunk Railway remained a private company until it was taken over by the Federal Government as the Canadian National in 1922. Whitby remained as a stopping point until 1969 when the station at the end of Byron Street was closed. Today the Via trains stop only at the Oshawa station on Thornton Road.

William Laing Provided A Church

The generosity of one man more than 140 years ago provided Whitby with one of its finest churches. The St. Andrew's Presbyterian Church, constructed as a Gothic cathedral at the corner of Byron and St. John Streets is recognized today as one of Whitby's most beautiful buildings. Only a few years ago it was designated as an historic building under the Ontario Heritage Act. It stands today as a Serbian Church, the Presbyterians having moved to a new church on Cochrane Street in 1968.

The man responsible for the construction of the original St. Andrew's Church was William Laing (1819-1891), a native of Morayshire, Scotland, who came to Whitby in 1841. He was one of Whitby's wealthiest grain merchants in the 1850s, with a store at Brock and Dundas Streets where the old Dominion Bank now stands. The store, one of the first in downtown Whitby, was known as *"Old Number 1"* on Laing's Corner. Laing also owned most of the east side of Brock Street South, which he sold as lots for other merchants to build stores.

On June 4, 1857, a number of Presbyterian gentlemen of Whitby met at the residence of the town's postmaster, Alexander McPherson (1803-1861) to discuss the erection of a Church of Scotland. This church was born out of rivalry with other branches of the Presbyterian faith.

St. Andrew's Presbyterian Church in 1914.

The Church of Scotland was founded in Whitby by Rev. James Lambie (1805-1847) in 1841, but was without a pastor after Lambie's sudden death at the age of 42. Those who were still loyal members of the church were concerned that its members

were being signed up by the Free Church at Brock and Mary Streets, and suggested that if they built their own church they could get a minister and their congregation would flourish.

The meeting determined that $3,750 was

available as proceeds from Church land in Scott Township, but this was not enough to build a church. With concern expressed about finances, William Laing decided to come to the rescue. Laing announced that he would purchase a site for the Church of Scotland with his own funds, contribute $1,300 towards the cost of the building, and advance a further loan of $2,500. This was a lot of money in 1857 to come from one person.

It is interesting to note that Laing was not a member of the Church of Scotland, but his wife was. Perhaps she had some influence in his making the offer. Laing at the time, did not know how much money he would actually end up providing for the Church of Scotland. When it was completed in 1859, St. Andrew's Church cost $12,000 half of which was supplied by William Laing.

Two days after making his offer, Laing purchased two lots at the north-west corner of Byron and St. John Streets as a site for the new church. The purchase was made in his name, and he did not sell the land to the church trustees until 1864. The grateful trustees appointed Laing chairman of the building committee and hired Whitby Architect Amos W. Cron (?-1870) to design St. Andrew's Church. Laing advertised for tenders on June 11, 1857. By September the

William Laing

full stone basement was completed. Thomas Deverell (1828-1910) who learned the building trade while constructing St. John's Anglican Church in 1846, had the contract for the stone, brick and plastering work. Others involved in the building were Roderick Ross (1815-1884) and Peter Edgar. Ross's house was built in 1867 on Colborne Street, behind the present public library.

Construction proceeded slowly on St. Andrew's Church throughout 1858 because of the large size of the building and a severe economic depression which began at the end of 1857. Plans were made to place a 150-foot spire on the top of the church tower, but this was never undertaken. On May 6, 1859, tenders were called for the seating, pulpit and stairs of the church and fencing of the grounds. A large carriage shed was built north of the church to accommodate the vehicles of parishioners.

A young lady who visited Whitby in the summer of 1859 described St. Andrew's Presbyterian Church in the following words: *"The Scotch Kirk (Church), a new Gothic edifice, has walls of red brick with splendid and elaborately cut stone entrance. That latter is said to be the purest and most chaste piece of Gothic architecture in America."*

One of the prominent features of the entrance, which can still be seen today, is a bust of John Knox, the founder of Presbyterianism, over the main door.

The Scottish Kirk, as it was commonly called, opened for worship on Nov. 6, 1859, but two weeks after the official opening, services had to be cancelled until a heating system could be installed. On Dec. 12, 1860, Rev. Kenneth Maclennan became the first of a long line of ministers who have served St. Andrew's Presbyterian Church. At the time he came to Whitby there were only 30 families in the congregation, but when he left in 1871 there were more than 60 families.

Over the years, the various branches of Presbyterianism in Whitby joined St. Andrew's Church, the Free Church in 1860 and the Canada Presbyterian Church in 1875. The Canada Presbyterian Church, built in 1869 at Centre and Colborne Streets, became a Baptist Church, and was demolished in 1977. In 1925, when the Methodist, Presbyterian and Congregational Churches of Canada joined to form the United Church of Canada, St. Andrew's congregation split, with the minister, Rev. Edward Turkington, and half the congregation joining the United Church and the remainder deciding to stay as *"continuing Presbyterians"*.

After the new St. Andrew's Church was opened on Cochrane Street in 1968, the old church was used by various small congregations and was vacant for some years before a Serbian Church was founded in the 1990s in the old building.

The fate of William Laing, the man who made St. Andrew's Presbyterian Church possible, is a sad one. His wife died in 1864, giving birth to twin boys, and the following year the grain market collapsed. Laing had to sell his beautiful home, *"Inverlynn"*, built

at Raglan and Giffard Streets in 1860. In the early 1870s, Laing went into partnership with Charles F. Stewart (1845-1913) in a general produce business where Donald Travel is today on Brock Street South.

Another economic depression in 1873 put an end to the partnership and Laing was again without employment. His political friends managed to obtain for him in 1874, the position of Treasurer of Ontario County, in which office he served until 1880 when he moved to Toronto. There he married the mother of his eldest son's wife, Harriet French, and lived the remainder of his life at 79 Seaton Street. It appears that he had little money when he died at the age of 72 on Dec. 4, 1891. He could not afford a tomb stone in Union Cemetery, so one was provided by his sister, Elizabeth (1816-1902), wife of William Smith, M.P. of Columbus.

In his heyday, William Laing was one of Whitby's most influential citizens. He was Whitby's first Reeve when the town was incorporated in 1855 and served as Mayor in 1863-64. A story is told that in 1863, Chester Draper (1823-1876), a rival grain merchant and future owner of Whitby Harbour, wanted to be mayor, and passed a petition around town seeking support. The majority of the citizens who could vote, signed the petition for Draper, but Laing's friends put his name forth on nomination

day and Laing won against the majority.

In the late 1850s and early 1860s, Laing ran for the Provincial Legislature twice against Oliver Mowat (1820-1903) but lost both times. Mowat went on to become Ontario's longest-serving premier and later Lieutenant-Governor of the province.

Laing owed much of his early success to his brother James (1816-1856) who established a store at Oshawa and made William manager of his Whitby branch. When James Laing died suddenly at the age of 40 in 1856, William was well on his way to success in Whitby.

The Town of Whitby, in 1967, was presented with oil paintings of William Laing and his first wife, Louisa Yarnold, by their grandchildren.

William Laing, who was one of the most prosperous merchants in Ontario County, indeed in several counties and according to his obituary in the Whitby Chronicle, was one of the chief builders of Whitby in its early days. His first wife, Louisa Amelia Yarnold (1824-1864), was a daughter of Whitby's first Town Clerk-Treasurer, Benjamin Yarnold (1792-1880) who was dismissed from office for being rude to the ratepayers. She was married to William Laing in 1847 and had a family of seven children.

Rev. Vincent P. Mayerhoffer, The Priest Who Met Napoleon

The little cemetery at St. John's Anglican Church in Port Whitby is the resting place of one of the most remarkable religious figures in Ontario – Rev. Vincent P. Mayerhoffer. When Mayerhoffer died on Jan. 15, 1859, he had been a clergyman for 52 years, and was only 7 days short of his 75th birthday. His life story, published after his death to provide money for his wife and family, reads like something from the novels of Charles Dickens. His funeral was the second held by the Masons of Whitby, with all the pomp and circumstance that could be provided for such a noted figure.

Vincent Philip Mayerhoffer was born in the city of Rabb in Hungary on Jan. 22, 1784. His father, Michael Mayerhoffer, was a Senator (councilman) of that city. The Mayerhoffers were Roman Catholics, and the boy was named Vincent because he was born on the birth date of St. Vincent the Martyr. He was a brilliant scholar, studying the classics at the age of seven. When Mayerhoffer was 11 years old, his father died and his mother put him to work as a grocer's apprentice to help support her family of eight children. He worked for several grocers in various cities and finally ran away from his master after being ill-treated. He sought out an uncle, who sent him to a curate to be trained for the ministry.

Mayerhoffer studied at a seminary for

Rev. Vincent Philip Mayerhoffer

two years and entered the Order of St. Francis at the age of 19. At 21 he took the vows in the Franciscan Order and two years later was ordained as a Roman Catholic Priest. From 1807 to 1811 Mayerhoffer was a curate in several Hungarian parishes. In 1811 he was made a chaplain of an Austrian regiment which was sent to aid Napoleon in his invasion of Russia. Mayerhoffer suffered much during the tragic retreat of Napoleon's army from Moscow in the bitter winter of 1812. After this disaster, his regiment was sent by Austria to fight against Napoleon.

Mayerhoffer was captured as a prisoner of war at Dresden and brought before Napoleon himself to have his fate decided. Napoleon declared he did not want priests for prisoners, and ordered him set free. Despite these orders to release him, he was kept a prisoner until he escaped and was reunited with his regiment who thought he had been killed at Dresden.

Mayerhoffer was present at the capture of Paris and travelled through Italy. At the end of the Napoleonic Wars in 1815, he was given a parish in Bavaria, now part of Germany. In 1819, he decided to emigrate to the United States, where he set himself up as a missionary in Philadelphia, Pennsylvania. He was attached to a Jesuit order but a conflict developed because he would not join the Jesuits, stating that he was a Franciscan. The result of this bitter dispute was that Mayerhoffer gave up his orders in the Roman Catholic Church and opened a drug store in Little York, Pennsylvania. He subsequently married and studied the Bible for two years to decide which church he would join. He chose the German Reformed Brothers of Pennsylvania and went on to take a degree of Master of Arts from Alleghaney College in New York.

After arriving in Buffalo in 1829, Mayerhoffer joined the Church of England and became a missionary in Markham and Vaughan Townships north of York (now Toronto). He preached his services in both English and German. For 20 years he served in Markham, erecting three churches by subscription, two in Markham and one in Vaughan Township. He returned in 1850, moving to Toronto, but in 1851 and 1852 he lived in Whitby, where he became one of the first members of Composite Masonic Lodge, founded in 1852. He was chaplain of the local lodge and Grand Chaplain of the Masons and the Orange Order of Upper Canada. Quite an achievement for a former Roman Catholic priest! On July 12, 1856 (Orangemen's Day) he delivered a sermon to the *"Loyal Orangemen of the County of Ontario at the Town of Whitby"*, which was printed by special request. Under the banner of *"No Surrender to Popery"*, he bitterly attacked the Roman Catholic Church which he had served faithfully for 12 years.

He referred to *"Popery, that dreadfully insatiable and blood-thirsty tiger, (which) overspread since the fifth century, the whole world with superstition, idolatry, and traditions without number – which enslaved our forefathers away from the light of the Gospel revelation, with worse chains than barbarism... Let us follow that example of him whose memory we venerate this day as an instrument in the hand of God for our delivery, the Pious, Glorious and Immortal Memory of King William III, who established our Throne with a truly Protestant Monarch, the gem of all ladies, Queen Victoria, who gave us, and our succeeding generations, the Bible, the Word of God, the privilege to worship God in spirit and in truth. By this we stand or fall, whereby we wish to keep forever the motto – No Surrender to Popery."*

From 1852 to 1854, Mayerhoffer lived at Perrytown, near Port Hope, but returned to spend his last days in Whitby. He was an occasional preacher at St. John's Church and a leading member of the community. One of his daughters, Louisa (1828-1874) married Edmund Humphrey (1825-1904) a millwright and pattern maker at the Brown and Patterson foundry in Whitby. His sons founded the Humphrey Funeral Home in Toronto. In the 1950s, the youngest son Alfred E. Humphrey (1870-1972) restored the Mayerhoffer and Humphrey graves in the cemetery and erected a new stone beside the century-old ones. Above the stones, in the east wall of St. John's Church, is a memorial window to Mayerhoffer, dedicated by the Humphrey family in 1913. One of Mayerhoffer's sons, Julius A. Mayerhoffer (1836-1908) was a partner with William H. Higgins in founding the Whitby Chronicle.

In 1861, likely with the assistance of Higgins, Mayerhoffer's autobiography was published to provide money for his widow and her family. It was entitled: *"Twelve Years a Roman Catholic Priest, or the Autobiography of Rev. V.P. Mayerhoffer, M.A., late Military Chaplain to the Austrian Army, and Grand Chaplain of the Orders of Freemasons and Orangemen in Canada."* A copy of this book is in the Town of Whitby Archives.

Mayerhoffer, with his unconventional religious beliefs, embarrassed Bishop John Strachan (1812-1867), the head of the Anglican Church in Upper Canada.

When Strachan learned that Mayerhoffer had fallen off his horse and ruptured himself, he suggested that the old man be pensioned off. *"He should never had have been received into our Church,"* said Strachan. *"Though a moral and well-meaning man, he is not in manners or qualifications calculated to build up the Church... He is an eye-sore and a great encumbrance."* Henry Scadding (1813-1901), rector of Holy Trinity Anglican Church in Toronto, near the Eaton Centre, described Mayerhoffer as having *"strongly marked and peculiar, perhaps Mongolian"* features, and called him *"a man of energy to the last; ever cheerful in spirit, and abounding in anecdotes, personal and otherwise."* Scadding, whose father John founded Port Whitby as *"Windsor"* in 1819, donated the land for St. John's Anglican Church where Mayerhoffer is buried.

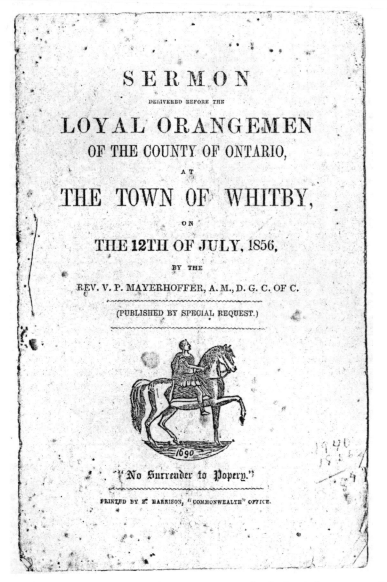

Mayerhoffer's sermon to the Orangemen of Whitby, July 12, 1856

Iron Reynolds
The Man of Trafalgar

Nelson Gilbert Reynolds (1814-1881), who built Trafalgar Castle as his residence 140 years ago, was the kind of man who inspired legends, and many have grown up around his unique personality. The Honourable John Ross, who was responsible for Reynolds' appointment as Sheriff of Ontario County in 1854, referred to him in a letter to a friend as *"large as life and twice as natural"*. A year before his death in 1881, his biography was published in a book entitled: *"The Canadian Biographical Dictionary and Portrait Gallery of Eminent and Self-Made Men"*. His career reads like an account from an adventure novel. In his younger days he earned the nickname *"Iron Reynolds"* because of his great physical endurance. He was married twice and had 12 children by each wife. His last surviving daughter, Annie Caroline Reynolds died in 1959 at the age of 94, exactly 100 years after construction of Trafalgar Castle began.

Reynolds was born at Kingston, Upper Canada, on Jan. 23, 1814, the son of Rev. John Reynolds (1787-1857), a bishop of the Methodist Episcopal Church and a native of County Waterford, Ireland. He was named after Lord Horatio Nelson who had won the Battle of Trafalgar against Napoleon in 1805 – hence the name *"Trafalgar Castle"*.

Young Reynolds was one of the first students to attend Upper Canada College when it opened in Toronto in 1829 and received the remainder of his education at Cazuenrovia Seminary in New York. At 15 years of age he travelled to England where he became an officer in the 11th Lancers, returning to Canada four years later. He remained with his parents in Belleville for a short time, but the spirit of adventure called him again, and he left for service with the Hudson's Bay Company in the Canadian West. He journeyed as far west as Jasper House and the Rocky Mountains through unexplored territory, 50 years before the Canadian Pacific Railway was built.

Returning to Belleville after about a year, he was elected to the

Nelson Gilbert Reynolds

Parliament of Upper Canada for the County of Hastings, but was prevented from taking his seat because he was not 21 years old. His Parliamentary career did not last long, for the House dissolved soon after his 21st birthday. For several years Reynolds was president of the Marmora Foundry and Smelting Company and was involved in banking, mercantile business and railroading. His business ventures flourished until suddenly the country was faced with the upheaval of the Rebellion of 1837.

At the time of William Lyon Mackenzie's march on Toronto in December 1837, Reynolds was a 23 year-old officer in the militia. He raised a company of cavalry to take part in the defence of Upper Canada from the *"Patriots"* who had fled to the United States and were believed to be planning an invasion. Reports of a proposed invasion of Kingston on the night of Feb. 20, 1838 were intercepted, and 1,600 militiamen were ordered to defend the town. Reynolds and his cavalry troop joined the defending forces, but the Government, suspecting his loyalty, sent out its own force to arrest him. When discovered, Reynolds had to fight for his life, receiving three wounds in the resulting skirmish. As he slashed at a charging soldier with his sword, he injured his right wrist on the fixed bayonet of his attacker. A musket ball embedded itself in his right thigh, where it was to remain the rest of his life.

Reynolds escaped and fled to the United States, but three months later, voluntarily surrendered for a trial at Kingston. He was imprisoned in Fort Henry where he received a personal visit from Lord Durham, the new Governor of Upper Canada, who had been sent from England to clear up the political mess left in the wake of the Rebellion. In July 1838, he was tried for treason before Judge Archibald McLean at a special court ordered by Lord Durham. Forty-four witnesses spoke for the prosecution and none for the defence. Reynolds chose to undertake his own defence, explaining that he was loyal to the crown but opposed to the Family Compact which ran the Government. The jury acquitted him without even leaving their seats, and men of all political parties in the joy and excitement, carried Reynolds out of the court house and into the streets where the soldiers saluted him as he passed. Although he protested his innocence, a Kingston newspaper stated very few persons doubted his guilt and he was acquitted only because there was insufficient evidence to convict him. After his acquittal, Reynolds returned to Belleville where he held almost every municipal office in the town and the County of Hastings.

In 1852, Reynolds heard of the formation of the County of Ontario, with Whitby as the County town. With hopes of obtaining an office in the new county government, he approached the Hon. John Ross, Attorney-General of Upper Canada, and was granted the office of Sheriff in January 1854. This came as a surprise to Reynolds, for as he told a friend in a letter, he had been promised *"a much better office"*. The appointment also came as a surprise to the four local politicians who had sought the office, one of whom had been recommended by the provisional council of the new county. The appointment of a stranger from Belleville annoyed some of the county councillors, but within a few months, Sheriff Reynolds was receiving high praise, even from those who formerly opposed him.

Sheriff Reynolds involved himself in many activities in his new home town of Whitby. He was a judge when the Queen's Plate was run at Whitby in 1870, and was Warden of St. John's Anglican Church, where he donated a silver communion set. He was a director of the Port Whitby and Port Perry Railway, and a director of the Ontario Ladies' College, which was established by the Methodist Church in his old home, Trafalgar Castle, in 1874.

A story is told that when the railway was suffering from financial troubles, Sheriff Reynolds was ordered to seize one of its locomotives. He and his deputy set up a barricade of ties on the tracks near the college road, but the company heard of his plan and informed the engineer. When he reached the barricade, the engineer stoked up his engine and smashed through the ties, sending the sheriff and his deputy running for their lives.

In 1835, Reynolds married his first wife, Hannah Mary Eyre. She died in 1850, giving birth to their 12th child. The sheriff chose famous names for his children, naming them after his political and military heroes. One was named John Lambton Baldwin Reynolds, after Robert Baldwin, the Government leader and John Lambton, the Earl of Durham. Another was named Charles Bagot Reynolds after another Upper Canada governor, while another was Arthur Wellesley Reynolds, after the Duke of Wellington, who defeated Napoleon in 1815 at the Battle of Waterloo.

Reynolds' second wife was Frances Eliza Armstrong, daughter of James R. Armstrong (1787-1873), a wealthy Toronto merchant who retired to Whitby and lived at The Grange, a large brick house at the corner of Mary and Pine Streets, demolished in 1976. They were married in 1852 at Toronto and another 12 children were born to the sheriff and his wife. Mrs. Reynolds died at the age of 89 in 1921 at Montreal. The eldest son of the second marriage, George Nelson Armstrong Reynolds (1853-1929) laid the corner stone of Trafalgar Castle at the age of six, and served later as Deputy Sheriff. The stone, inscribed *"N.G.R., 1859"*, is in the wall of the flagstaff tower.

After he left Trafalgar Castle in 1874, Reynolds built a smaller replica of his former home at Byron and Dunlop streets, now the Montessori School. Here he suffered a stroke in 1876 and was bedridden until his death on Jan. 16, 1881 at the age of 66. After such an illustrious life, it is a sad footnote that no stone marks Sheriff Reynolds' grave in St. John's Anglican Cemetery at Port Whitby. Only a tall weathered column marks the grave of his son, John Lambton Baldwin Reynolds (1841-1959) directly behind the church.

Receipt signed by Nelson G. Reynolds, June 20, 1877

Sheriff's certificate signed by Nelson G. Reynolds, January 19, 1871

This Man's Home Really Was His Castle

According to an old legend, jealousy played a part in the construction of Trafalgar Castle, the palatial home of Sheriff Nelson Gilbert Reynolds. Reynolds and John Ham Perry (1827-1896) Registrar of Ontario County, were rivals who constantly tried to outdo each other when opportunity arose. In the summer of 1857 when Reynolds was on a visit to England, Perry built himself a magnificent residence in the Italianate style, which became the talk of the town. It had stained glass windows, silver door hinges and the first gas lights ever seen in Whitby. When Reynolds returned to see Perry's *"castle"* he was said to be so jealous that he set out to build his own castle on an even grander scale.

Reynolds had the dream of building himself a real English castle where he could entertain royalty. He chose as the site for this castle, a hill on the east side of town, and had enough influence with the town council to have them name the roads to it, Gilbert and Reynolds Streets. Gilbert was his mother's maiden name. His trip to England had not been wasted, for there he had studied the ancient baronial castles and made plans for his own Trafalgar Castle.

Reynolds chose Toronto architect Joseph Sheard to design Trafalgar Castle, although much of the structure was designed by

Trafalgar Castle at the time of its completion, C. 1862
Photo from the collection of Laurie Gillespie

Reynolds himself. Sheard was a noted Toronto man who served as mayor of that city in 1871/72. Whitby architect Amos W. Cron (?-1870) was the general contractor, while most of the contractors for masonry, stone work and other fields were from Toronto. William Robinson and William Pirie of Whitby were contractors for the carpentry. As many as 70 men at one time were employed in the building of Trafalgar castle, but no accidents or quarrels were reported because the sheriff had forbidden the use of liquor on the premises. The cost of Trafalgar Castle was an astounding $70,000. By comparison, a bank in the 1850s cost $6,000 to build, and a substantial house, $2,000. Since there were no conflict of interest laws for government officials, the sheriff was able to make a lot of money in land speculation and paid no income taxes.

Trafalgar Castle was built in the Elizabethan style with battlements, turreted towers, and even secret chambers – all the attributes of a real English castle. It is interesting to note that Sir Henry Pellatt, builder of Toronto's better-known Casa Loma, was born in 1859, the year that construction of Trafalgar Castle began.

The castle stands today, much as it was when built, except that the servants' wing to the south was replaced by a larger wing in 1895. Two recumbent cast iron lions flank the front entrance which is crowned with the sheriff's coat of arms cut in stone. Entering the main door, one finds a small vestibule with large bronze lamps in the form of Indians on each side of the doors to the main hall. In the sheriff's time, a fountain was located here, supplied with water from a reservoir in the attic. The oak doors to the main hall are set with hand-painted glass imported from England, in a pattern of yellow roses, and a Canadian beaver over the main door.

The main hall is 105 feet long, leading from the entrance to the grand staircase. To the left of the front door was the sheriff's office and library, now the principal's office for Trafalgar Castle School. The original carved wooden bookcases are still there, along with a white marble fireplace imported from Italy. Across the hall is a reception room, used as a parlour in the sheriff's time. Further down the hall is a massive drawing room, used today as a study hall, with its massive bay window. Here the glittering receptions for noted guests were held, nearly 140 years ago. Magnificent white marble fireplaces carved by Whitby artisan Jonathan Wolfenden can be seen in this room.

Opposite the drawing room are the dining room and breakfast parlour, now known as the Common Room where students at Trafalgar Castle School relax and meet friends. These rooms were once separated by sliding doors. A butler's room and armoury were located at the back of the hall in rooms now used as school offices.

The ceilings of the main hall and adjoining rooms are ornamented with moulded plaster, each room once being lit by a gaslight chandelier. Along the main hall are niches for statuary, most of which now are empty. Only two of the original white marble statues of little girls in Victorian dresses remain in their places. Also in the main hall are four oak chairs and two benches, the last of the original furnishings of Trafalgar Castle. G.P. Walter of Bowmanville made the furniture, with the carving done by a Mr. Maille of Oshawa. On the benches and two of the chairs are carved the sheriff's coat of arms, consisting of a stag and scallop shell. Another piece of original furniture is an octagonal table in the upper hall, believed to have been the sheriff's poker table. It still contains some of his wooden chips.

Carpeting for all the rooms was cut to size in England and transported across the Atlantic Ocean in sailing vessels.

At the end of the main hall is the grand staircase of carved oak. At the head of the staircase is a massive stained glass window which has been an attraction to visitors since the castle was built. Divided into four parts, the great window bears the coats of arms of the Reynolds and Armstrong families, each with a Latin motto. The sheriff's motto is *"Jus Meum Tuebor"* (I will look after my right). Adjacent to the coats of arms are the monograms of the sheriff (N.G.R.) and his wife (F.E.R.). Embossed in the frosted glass at the base of the window are heads representing Queen Elizabeth I and other English monarchs. The monograms O.L.C. (Ontario Ladies' College), were added after

The main hall of Trafalgar Castle, looking toward the entrance, 1913

Trafalgar Castle became a girls' private school in 1874. The cost of the window when it was installed in 1862 was $640.

On the second floor is another grand hall from the staircase to a conservatory looking out through a bay window over the Town of Whitby. At each side of the corridor adjacent to the conservatory were gentlemen's and ladies' sitting rooms. Large oak folding doors were turned back to make these rooms and the hall into a grand ballroom. The remainder of the floor was devoted to bedrooms, some of which opened onto an iron balcony over the bay window of the drawing room below. The third floor was devoted to bedrooms, water reservoirs and a large billiard room at the end of the hall opening onto a balcony over the conservatory. A ladder leads to the

roof, where a fine view of Whitby and surrounding country can be seen. This view from the roof was published in *"Picturesque Canada"* in 1882, the only picture of Whitby in that two-volume book.

In the basement were hot and cold air furnaces and large wine and beer cellars, now all sacrificed to modern renovations. The wing to the south, demolished in 1895 to build Frances Hall, contained a kitchen, laundry, scullery, larder, store room and pantry on the first floor. The second floor contained a nursery, governess' room, gymnasium, servants' rooms, bath rooms and water closets. In the basement was a vegetable cellar.

Trafalgar Castle was lit with gas manufactured on the premises and carried through a half-mile of pipes. Trafalgar Castle was the first building in Whitby to have electric lights, installed in 1890. The castle's 73 rooms were serviced with hot, cold and foul air flues constructed through the towers, and all the main rooms had fireplaces. Thirty-seven bells were installed in the rooms to call servants.

The flagstaff tower where Frances Hall meets the original castle, is the source of many legends. It is said that the sheriff hid from his creditors in a secret chamber between the first and second floors. This padlocked room was discovered by students at the school in the 1920s and sealed up. Legend also has it that a tunnel led from the base of the flagstaff tower to Lake Ontario. Although there is no documented proof of this, some people say it was discovered when Highway 401 was built through Whitby in 1940/41, and a farmer's tractor was swallowed up by a big hole which opened up in a field south of the castle. The base of the flagstaff tower had to be rebuilt in 1959 because it was sinking. When the construction was under way, a large room was found under the tower.

The newspapers of the day described Trafalgar Castle as the largest private detached mansion on the North American continent and filled columns with lavish descriptions of its construction.

Trafalgar Castle was completed in the summer of 1862, when Sheriff Reynolds and his family moved in. Two years earlier when the castle was under construction, Sheriff Reynolds invited the Prince of Wales to visit the site when he paid a visit to Whitby in September 1860, but his itinerary was too tightly planned to allow a visit.

Sheriff Reynolds finally got his wish to entertain British Royalty when Prince Arthur, the third son of Queen Victoria (later the Duke of Connaught and Governor-General of Canada from 1911 to 1916) came to Whitby on Oct. 6, 1869. He was invited to turn the sod for the Port Whitby and Port Perry Railway in front of Trafalgar Castle, before a crowd of 5,000 to 6,000 people. Accompanying the Prince were Canada's Prime Minister, Sir John A. Macdonald; Governor General, Baron Lisgar; Ontario Lieutenant-Governor Sir William P. Howland; Ontario Premier John Sandfield Macdonald and the Mayor of Toronto. The Royal party toured the Town of Whitby in a parade of 100 carriages. After the prince turned the sod in front of Trafalgar Castle with a silver spade, the honoured guests were provided with a luncheon at the castle by Sheriff Reynolds.

In all of Whitby's history, this was the most illustrious gathering of honoured visi-

The Grand Staircase at Trafalgar Castle, 1889.

tors and the crowning achievement for Sheriff Reynolds. Mrs. Reynolds led the Prince into the drawing room, followed by the sheriff, leading Mrs. Young, the Governor-General's wife, Mrs. Howland,

and Miss Macdonald, the Prime Minister's sister. Whitby's Mayor, James H. Gerrie, conducted the introductions.

It was not long, however, before the days of grandeur would come to an end for Trafalgar Castle and Sheriff Reynolds. By 1872, debts haunted the Sheriff's mind and he made plans to sell Trafalgar Castle to whoever would take it. In December, 1872, a delegation of commissioners headed by Ontario's Minister of Agriculture, examined Trafalgar Castle as a possible site for an agricultural college. They took soil samples, lunched at Trafalgar Castle and toured the building, but they chose Guelph as the site for the Ontario Agricultural College.

It was early in 1874 that the Methodist Church of Canada, led by Whitby Methodist minister Rev. Joseph E. Sanderson (1830-1913) selected Trafalgar Castle as the site of the Ontario Ladies' College, which changed its name to Trafalgar Castle School in 1979. The Church paid $35,000 for the castle, only half the cost of its construction, and hired Rev. John James Hare (1847-1922) as the first principal. Ontario Ladies' College was officially opened on Sept. 3, 1874 by Lord Dufferin, the Governor-General of Canada. It remains today as a private girls' school after 125 years.

How John Ham Perry Outwitted the Town Council

One of Whitby's leading citizens was John Ham Perry (1827-1896), the younger son of the town's founder, Peter Perry. He served as Land Registrar for the County of Ontario from 1853 to 1896, and was very active in local politics until a provincial law passed in 1867 forbade registrars from holding political office. Perry was a member of Whitby's first town council in 1855 and served as Mayor in 1858/59. He owned one of the largest mansions in the town, now the site of Kinsmen Park, and was a well respected member of the community. His actions in 1860 when the Prince of Wales visited Whitby, caused considerable comment, however, when he made a little deal with Mayor Hugh J. Macdonell (1823-1877) involving the prince's transportation.

Whitby was fortunate to have the Prince of Wales (later King Edward VII) make a visit to the town. Whitby was not on the Prince's itinerary when it was announced that he would visit Canada in September of 1860. It was planned that he would stop at Cobourg and Port Hope, and make the trip to Toronto by boat. When Whitby's Town Council learned that they would be bypassed, they sent a delegation to the Duke of Newcastle, who was in charge of the arrangements, to ask that the prince make a stop in the County Town. It was therefore agreed that the prince would take

Albert Edward, Prince of Wales

the boat to Toronto from Whitby, instead of Port Hope.

Sept. 7, 1860 was set as the date for Whitby's first royal visit. With a population of nearly 3,500, Whitby expected as many at 10,000 people to attend the welcoming ceremonies. Once the visit was confirmed, a committee was set up by the town to make

the arrangements for a gala reception.

The Town Council's plans called for a procession of carriages to take the prince from the railway station on the Grand Trunk Line at Victoria Street to the steamboat *"Kingston"* at the harbour. Perry, on hearing of this, offered to put his carriage and team of two white horses at the disposal of the committee for the prince's use. Perry's carriage and team were certainly fit for a prince to ride in, but the reception committee was concerned about one citizen having the honour of taking the prince to the harbour, above many other worthy citizens. It would be more fair, the committee stated, if the prince was conveyed to the harbour in another carriage paid for by the people of Whitby. Therefore, no favouritism or jealousy would result.

The committee immediately turned down Perry's offer and made its own arrangements for a carriage. A liveryman in Bowmanville offered the committee his pair of nearly-white horses, while the man who built Perry's carriage had a duplicate nearly finished in his shop. The committee finally agreed to pay Whitby carriage maker David Ford to finish the carriage and pay an additional $60 for its use. The man with the horses was to receive $40.

A rush was made night and day to get the town carriage ready. On the appointed day, it was waiting at the station for the prince. But so was John Ham Perry's carriage. When the official ceremonies were over and bouquets of flowers were thrown to the prince (one hit him on the nose), Mayor Macdonell called for the carriages to come forward. The carriages had been arranged for the procession to the harbour, so that the town carriage for the prince would be last, but the mayor called up Perry's carriage to the head of the line and motioned for the prince to get into it instead.

The program called for enough time for the people to see the prince on the platform for a few minutes while the other carriages were being filled, but at the call of the mayor, the prince was taken away to the harbour immediately in Perry's carriage. Seeing what was going to happen, one of the town committee members rushed up and said to the prince: *"This other carriage is for Your Highness,"* pointing to the town vehicle.

The prince, who was already seated in Perry's carriage beside the Duke of Newcastle, gave a puzzled look. *"It's all right, Your Highness,"* said Sheriff Nelson G. Reynolds, who stood nearby, and the prince kept his seat. Acting on instructions received before the ceremonies began, Perry's coachman set out immediately for the harbour, leaving the committee mem-

John Ham Perry and his family at the time of the Prince's visit. Left to right: Jane Margaret Perry, Peter Perry, Margaret Perry, George D. Perry, John Ham Perry.

bers to scramble into their carriages and get into the procession as best they could.

The Whitby Watchman reporter, who witnessed the episode, commented that Mayor Macdonell *"was successful in carrying out another little private arrangement, concocted it appears from all we learn, between himself and John Ham Perry for the purpose of benefitting the latter individual at the expense of the people and the committee of arrange-*

ments. This conduct caused very general dissat-isfaction among the people of the town, not alone that the prince should have been hurried off by the mayor without regard for the pub-lished program in a carriage with faded trim-mings and seats and sides redolent with cigar smoke, but that their friends from the country should have been cheated out of what they so much desired – a full and satisfactory view of him who is designed under providence to be the future sovereign of the Empire."

Many citizens were not aware of the last-minute switch of carriages. For days after the royal visit, ladies of the town came to Ford's carriage works to sit in the carriage in which the prince had sat. They were natu-rally upset when they found that the prince never did ride in the town carriage, but in John Ham Perry's.

The arrangements committee members were stuck with paying $100 for a carriage and horses which were never used. There is no report on how the Town Council dealt with the mayor who made his private arrangement with Perry at the expense of the town. It is known that he did not serve a second term.

Perry, when he learned that the prince was coming to Whitby, ordered a special set of rosewood furniture from New York City at a cost of $600, hoping to use it to entertain the prince at his palatial home, named

John Ham Perry, as pictured in the Historical Atlas of Ontario County, in 1877

"Dinsbaugh" after one of his ancestors. The furniture, consisting of a settee, two large chairs and two small chairs, sold for only $80 in 1877, when Perry, like Sheriff Nelson G. Reynolds, lost his fortune and had to sell his home and its contents. Until

1920 it remained the property of a store-keeper in Greenwood, Pickering Township. It was then purchased by Frederick L. Green, a Greenwood miller, for $450. In 1974, his estate donated the furniture to the Town of Whitby for a museum. It is often mistakenly reported that the prince sat on one of these chairs while being entertained at Perry's home. At the time of his visit, the program was running late, so the prince had no time to travel through Whitby or make any stops. He was taken directly from the railway station to the Toronto-bound boat at the harbour.

One relic of the visit of the Prince of Wales in 1860 was returned to the Town of Whitby 92 years later. In 1952 at a London auction of royal treasures, Fred W. Browne (1870-1956) of Toronto, a graduate of the old Whitby Collegiate Institute, purchased the original parchment scroll containing the address of the mayor and council to the prince. It is now in the Town of Whitby Archives.

Prince Edward (1841-1910) succeeded his mother Queen Victoria, as the British sover-eign, on her death in January 1901. At that time the Saturday Globe, in Toronto, pub-lished the story of Perry and Macdonell's carriage switch for the first time.

Ashburn Community Centre – A Fine Example of the Stone Mason's Art

Across from Burns' Presbyterian Church in the hamlet of Ashburn, stands a small granite fieldstone building, a monument to the art of stone masonry. It was built about 1861 by William Pearson (1833-1897), a Scottish builder who constructed many fine stone houses in Whitby and Pickering. A community centre since 1967, it served for more than a century as the Ashburn school house.

On January 30, 1861, Abram Madden, an early Ashburn settler, sold a half-acre of land on the north side of the 9th concession (now Myrtle Road) to the trustees of School Section No. 7 of Whitby township. The sale was made *"in trust for the common use of a school in and for School Section No. 7."* The trustees who signed the deed were: P. Montgomery, Timothy Fisher and John Nicol. According to oral tradition, a log school house was built near this site and replaced by the stone school constructed by William Pearson.

Tradition has it that Pearson built the Ashburn School as his *"test piece"* to show off his workmanship so he could get contracts to build other stone structures in the area. Each wall of the school is constructed in a different style. The front is of large square stone blocks, all evenly cut. The sides are of stones cut to various sizes, while the back wall is constructed of rough rubble stone.

As a stonemason, Pearson was often called upon to build foundations for houses and barns, and occasionally a house completely of granite fieldstone. His greatest and one of his last works is the residence of Jeremiah Lick, now the Sunnycrest Retirement Villa. It was built in 1884 of granite fieldstone and was to contain the first indoor plumbing in Whitby Township.

The Ashburn school was a typical one-room schoolhouse of rural Ontario. The farmers' sons and daughters would go to the school in the winter and for the rest of the year, they would work on the farms of the township. Early photographs indicate that some of these children came to school barefoot. In one class picture, the teacher is standing beside her bicycle. All grades, one to eight, were taught by a single teacher. Woman teachers were always single because school trustees would not hire married women. Married women would have children and stay at home to look after them, leaving the trustees without a teacher. One young teacher in Whitby in the 1930s, managed to hide the fact that she was married, for three years before retiring and putting a belated wedding announcement in the newspaper.

The day the photographer came to take the class picture was a very special one. The children would dress up in their finest clothes and one lucky boy or girl got to hold the slate on which the name of the school and the date of the photo was written in chalk. The picture of the Ashburn school accompanying this Chronicle, has a story behind it. The teacher is the young woman in the back row at right. The old lady at left, is *"Granny Tarvis"* who lived in the house west of the school. When she saw the photographer, she ran out of her house and joined the students, so she could be in the picture. This photograph, taken in 1907, was made into a post card.

The Ashburn school was heated in the winter with a wood stove. Old photographs show a pile of wood beside the building. In the early 1900s the interior walls were covered with metal sheeting made by the Pedlar People in Oshawa. It can still be seen today, as well as in St. Thomas' Anglican Church in Brooklin. In the spring and early summer, pots of geraniums were placed on the windowsills of the school.

About 1935, the Ashburn students made a school banner of blue cloth, bearing the words: *"S.S. No. 7, Ashburn, One Flag, One Fleet, One Throne,"* between two Union Jacks. It appears in a number of the class pictures.

After 105 years of use as a school, the old building was closed in 1966, and sold to the Township of Whitby for two dollars. At this

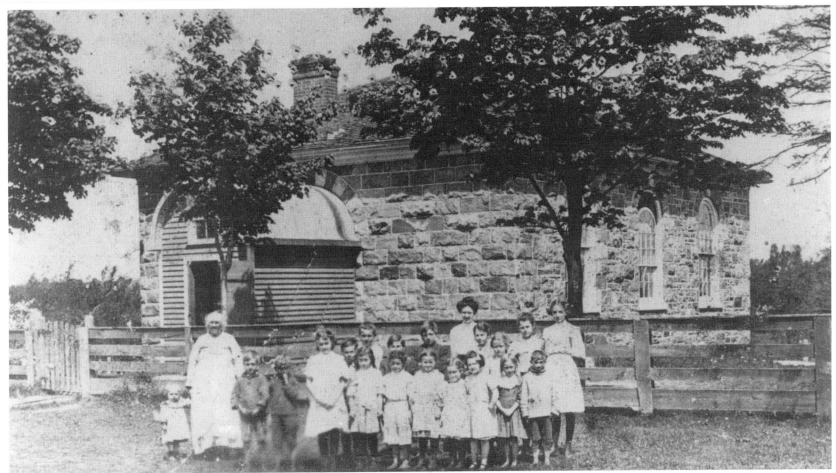

Ashburn Public School, with its 19 pupils and teacher, Mabel White, in 1907. At left is "Granny" Tarvis, who joined the group so she could have her picture taken.

time, most of the rural schools in the old County of Ontario were being closed and the pupils bused to larger schools in Brooklin or the Town of Whitby. In 1967, Canada's Centennial year, the old Ashburn school was made into a community centre, and a kitchen added to the west side.

Now operated by the Town of Whitby Parks and Recreation Department, it was designated under the Ontario Heritage Act as an historic building in 1983.

Whitby's Most Infamous Character – The Notorious Mrs. Glass

It takes many types of people to make a community. Whitby, like any other town had its share of disreputable characters, the worst of which by far was a woman known only as *"Mrs. Glass"*. Mrs. Glass kept what the Victorians delicately called *"a house of ill fame"* in the County Town in 1861 and 1862. Its exact location is unknown. The Whitby Chronicle described it only as *"a neat cottage in a retired part of the town."* There is no record of a Mr. Glass.

Mrs. Glass's bizarre career in *"the world's oldest profession"* was recorded in great detail by William H. Higgins in The Chronicle. The first reference to her activities appeared on April 22, 1861 when she was taken before the Mayor's Court on a charge of keeping a house of ill fame. Alexander Cameron (1804-1881), Whitby's Chief Constable, testified that he saw *"men going to the house at all hours of the night… that he made a descent on the house on Saturday evening, and there were persons there who put out the lights and made their escape."*

Cameron also testified that Mrs. Glass refused him admittance and threatened to shoot him with a loaded pistol. Other witnesses were brought forth at the trial, but The Chronicle considered their evidence was *"unfit for publication"*. The trial concluded with Mrs. Glass being fined five dollars to be paid in three days. She never paid the fine.

On June 18, 1861, Mrs. Glass was again brought to court on a charge of keeping a house of ill fame. She was fined $10 this time and required to pay in two days. It is not recorded whether or not she paid the fine. A man caught in the house was charged with frequenting a house of ill fame and fined $10. He didn't pay his fine either.

These were considered minor incidents in the career of Mrs. Glass, compared with what happened in December 1861 and January 1862. The episode began with a girl aged 13 or 14 who was being sent by train from Toronto to visit her aunt in a town somewhere east of Whitby. Her parents, regrettably, sent her off on the train alone.

The Chronicle, to protect her parents' reputation, did not print any names, but the following account was published about what happened to this young girl:

"While waiting at Toronto to take the train, the silly girl was tempted by the display of knickknacks to spend so much money that she had not enough left for the railway fare to her place of destination. In her distress, the evil tempter, in the shape of a noted woman who goes by the name of Mrs. Glass and keeps a house of ill fame in Whitby, came by. Affecting to take great compassion on her situation, this infamous woman under the guise of a genteel exterior, and well dissembled kindness, suc-ceeded in insinuating herself into the confidence of the innocent, unsuspecting girl. With a promise to provide the girl with sufficient means to get her to her destination, Mrs. Glass took the girl to Whitby and her house of ill fame.

"What followed may be easily guessed," The Chronicle reported. *"The girl's destruction was accomplished. Here she remained up to Thursday last (about a month), leading a life of misery, shame and sin, when she was taken away by her heart-broken father."*

When the girl did not show up at her aunt's home, her father contacted the police. A bulletin containing her description was sent to all towns in the province. Alexander Cameron of Whitby read the bulletin and suspected that Mrs. Glass might be involved in the girl's disappearance. When Cameron went to her house, Mrs. Glass hid the girl, but the constable got enough of a look at her to assure himself that she was the missing girl. He telegraphed her father, but Mrs. Glass also sent the man a telegram under the name of *"Mary Brown"*, claiming that the girl was not his daughter and invited him to come and see for himself. The father arrived in Whitby the same day he received the constable's telegram and the two men proceeded to Mrs. Glass's house.

Mrs. Glass at first denied the girl's presence, but when the father began to threaten her and the constable started searching the house, she gave up the girl.

For fear of adding greater publicity to the whole sordid affair, the father refused to press charges against Mrs. Glass. Editor Higgins of The Chronicle was furious that *"this villainous, wicked woman escapes punishment for one of the most damnable crimes that a debased and depraved wretch could be guilty of committing."* He considered her freedom from prosecution to be almost as great a crime as the one she had committed, and called for the Town Council to do something about the matter.

Mrs. Glass may have got away scott-free that time, but within a week, another of her escapades led her to the county jail. Constable Cameron raided her home a week after the young girl was discovered, and charged Mrs. Glass with selling liquor without a licence. Mrs. Glass received this news by assaulting the constable with an axe. In the Mayor's Court, she was fined $50 levied in distress, for selling the liquor without a licence and committed to the quarter session on the charge of assaulting the constable. No record appears of her trial on the assault charge and the name of Mrs. Glass was no longer seen in The Chronicle after January 1862. What happened to Mrs. Glass and where she went is a mystery. After a year of creating havoc in the Town of Whitby, Mrs. Glass disappeared without a trace.

Constable Alexander Cameron, who tried so hard to bring Mrs. Glass before the law, did not fare very well in later years. He was dismissed by the Town Council for burning down a black man's shanty in 1867, but was rehired for various periods after that. He was so poorly paid by the Council that when he died in 1881, at the age of 76, his family was destitute. On numerous occasions, William Higgins, through The Chronicle, urged the Town Council to provide for this faithful civil servant, but his pleas fell on deaf ears. Constable Cameron is buried in an unmarked grave in Oshawa's Union Cemetery.

No picture accompanies this *"Chronicle"*, for none have been found of Mrs. Glass or Alexander Cameron. And no proof has been found of the location of Mrs. Glass's house of ill fame.

The Whitby Chronicle called Mrs. Glass's escapade a "Great Depravity"

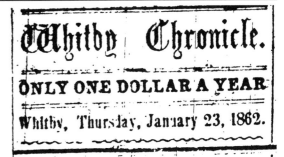

Whitby Chronicle.

ONLY ONE DOLLAR A YEAR

Whitby, Thursday, January 23, 1862.

GREAT DEPRAVITY. A YOUNG GIRL OF FOURTEEN ENTICED TO A HOUSE OF ILL-FAME. HER DISCOVERY AND RESCUE.—The desire to save, as far as possible pain, and public shame to a respectable family, induces the omission of names from the following episode of depravity, which came to light within the last few days, in this very proper and respectable town of Whitby.

About the middle of last month, Eliza ———, aged between 13 and 14, the eldest daughter of respectable parents, residing at ———, left her home to visit an aunt at -———. The aunt's residence being in a town on the Grand Trunk line, of not quite a day's travel from home, the idea of an escort being necessary was not thought of by her friends. The girl herself was very intelligent, very good looking and tall for her age. She had been receiving her education at a boarding school.— While waiting at Toronto to take the train, the silly girl was tempted by the display of nick-nacks to spend so much of the money

Three Generations of Lawlers Have Served the Town of Whitby

For three generations, members of the Lawler family have served Whitby and been an integral part of the town. The first of the family to emigrate to Canada was Thomas Lawler (1828-1895) who made his way to Whitby in 1851 at the age of 23 because of family connections. He was born at Montreath, Queen's County, Ireland, on March 11, 1828, a nephew of Whitby's first Mayor, James Rowe (1799-1869). Rowe operated the largest grain shipping business at Whitby Harbour in the 1850s and was active in politics. Young Lawler began his business career with James Rowe as a clerk and later became a partner in Rowe's grain business. After a few years he began purchasing grain from other Whitby dealers such as William Laing (1819-1891), Yeoman Gibson (1828-1894) and Robert J. Yarnold (1836-1878).

Although the grain business, Whitby's largest commercial enterprise in the 1850s, kept Lawler very busy, he had time to undertake other duties. One of these was to act as a Sheriff's Officer in arresting men accused of serious crimes. On one occasion, the wanted man was an American citizen. Lawler first sighted him as he was crossing the suspension bridge between Niagara Falls in Canada and Niagara Falls, New York. If the man made it across the bridge to his native country, Lawler would be unable to arrest him. Lawler made a dash across the bridge, grabbed the fleeing man by the collar and was dragging him back to Canadian soil when two American police officers rescued the prisoner from the middle of the bridge. Lawler was taken to the police station on a charge of kidnapping a U.S. citizen. He had to do some fast talking to get out of that one. No record remains as to how he did it.

In the 1860s, Lawler decided to go into the grocery business on his own. His first store was located on the corner of Brock and Colborne Streets where Bowman and Gibson's insurance office is now. The shop was a large wooden building painted in white and blue squares, known as the *"Chequered Store"*. For a while, Lawler had a partner, Richard Francis (1837-1925) who later left Whitby for the Canadian West.

By 1865, Lawler was well enough established in business to marry James Rowe's eldest daughter, Mary Charlotte (1844-1911) and have a family of nine children. Some time in the early 1870s, Lawler's prosperity was shattered by a mysterious illness. His health failed suddenly and he was forced to sell his business. No local doctor was able to discover the cause of his illness, so Lawler and his wife went to England in search of professional help. After consulting eminent physicians in London, Lawler was

Thomas Lawler

told he had only a short time to live. He was advised to settle on the island of Jersey in the English Channel and await the end. Such a course did not suit Thomas Lawler at all. He spent only a short time at Jersey before going back to London to seek more advice.

By accident, one day, he met an obscure doctor who was able to cure him in a few weeks and send him back to Canada in good health. He lived for another 20 years. Unfortunately, the family history written by his son James Lawler (1868-1945) does not give any further details on his mysterious illness.

Returning to Whitby, Lawler went back onto the grocery business, purchasing *"Old Number one"*, a store at the corner of Brock and Dundas Streets where the 20/20 Optical store is now. It was not long before tragedy struck again, when a fire began in his store and burned down the entire southeast quadrant of the downtown. The story of the fire is related in another Chronicle in this book. In 1878, Lawler moved into the first store south of the Dominion Bank (20/20 Optical) which is now the dining room for the Golden Gate Restaurant. The store remained in the same location for 50 years, being managed by Lawler's wife and son, Arthur T. Lawler (1866-1928) after his death.

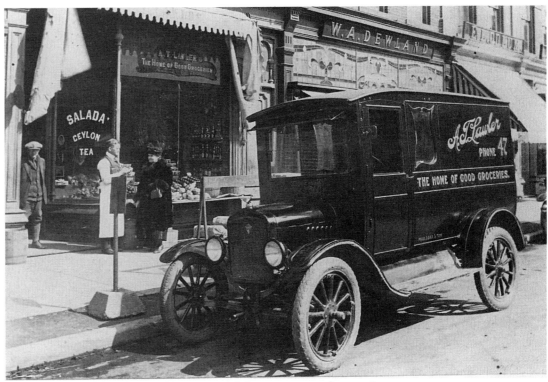

Arthur T. Lawler in front of his store with his grocery truck, 1926.

Thomas Lawler was an active man all his life, with the exception of the year of his strange illness. His love of duck hunting caused him to be often out in boats during stormy weather. He appeared to be quite fearless although he could not swim a stroke. In his youth he played cricket and later enjoyed games of cards. Although he took little interest in politics, Lawler was a man whose influence was considerable. He knew the people of Whitby well and often acted on their behalf. Proof of the high regard in which he was held, is shown in the only time he was elected to the Town

Council. In spite of being confined to a sick bed, he was elected councillor for the Centre Ward in 1894 over two active opponents who were able to get out and run a campaign.

Thomas Lawler died on Jan. 23, 1895 at the age of 66. His funeral was one of the largest in many years, being attended by the members of the Ontario County Council, the Whitby Town Council, the Board of Education and all the male teachers in the town. In those days, it was considered unsuitable for women to attend funerals. The Lawler and Rowe families are buried next to each other in St. John's Anglican Cemetery at Port Whitby.

Arthur T. Lawler, Thomas's eldest son, was actively involved in politics, serving as Mayor in 1906 and for 20 years on the Board of Education. At the time of his death in 1928, a half-holiday was observed by the town schools on the day of his funeral. It was his custom to welcome new pupils and teachers at the opening exercises of the public schools after the summer vacation. He was a leading promoter of the Whitby Horse Show in 1913 and 1914.

Arthur's sister, Elsie M. Lawler (1874-1962) became superintendent of nurses and principal of the nursing school at Johns Hopkins Hospital in Baltimore, Maryland, one of the leading hospitals in the United

Bill Lawler

States. She worked for the noted Canadian physician, Sir William Osler, and trained over 1,700 nurses during her career. On her 25th anniversary as head of the school of nursing in 1935, she was awarded an honorary Master of Arts degree by Johns Hopkins University. She served for many

years as the president of Maryland State Nurses' Association.

James Lawler, who wrote the family history, was on the editorial staff of the Winnipeg Tribune, the Toronto Mail and Empire and the Toronto News. He was secretary of the Canadian Forestry Journal and was editor-in-chief for the Department of the Interior in Ottawa.

Arthur Lawler's son Bill Lawler (1917-1996) served 11 years on the Whitby Hydro Electric Commission from 1985 to 1996 and was deeply involved in the Boy Scouts of Whitby, often attending World Jamborees.

His sister, Betty Weldon (1915-1990) was the winner of the Peter Perry Award as Whitby's outstanding citizen of 1988. Five years earlier, when the Town Council was considering the change of Whitby from a town to a city, she circulated a petition opposing the move. She wanted to see Whitby retain its small town charm, having been born here. In three weeks, she collected more than 3,000 signatures supporting her position and was influential in convincing the council to vote unanimously to keep Whitby as a town. She served for a number of years on the Whitby Local Architectural Conservation Advisory Committee and her sister, Sheila Cormack, was president of the Whitby Historical Society.

John Ham Perry of Whitby Set The Standard For All Ontario

Anyone who travels extensively in Ontario may have noticed that all the 19th century Land Registry Offices in various counties are of the same design. This is the result of the Land Registry Act of 1865, which was drafted by Whitby's registrar John Ham Perry. The Provincial Government of Canada West, as Ontario was then called, asked Perry to prepare a registry act which would set identical standards for all land registry offices in the province.

John Sandfield Macdonald, the premier of Canada West, initiated the project in 1862 by writing to all judges, registrars and lawyers, asking for suggestions on how to establish a uniform Land Registry Act. Perry took a leading role in representing the registrars, and at the request of the Government, attended three sessions of the Legislature in Quebec City from 1863 to 1865 to prepare the new act. He was given *"carte blanche"* as far as his work was concerned and all correspondence on the subject was referred to him by the Solicitor General. When the act was completed, Perry kept a copy of it in his own handwriting as a souvenir.

The Registry Act of 1865 established the principles of registration by duplicate, abstract books of lots, alphabetical records of grantors and grantees, compulsory regis-

The Whitby Land Registry Office, built in 1873, as it appeared in 1929 before the first addition was built.

tration of land titles and fire-proof buildings, all of the same design. Throughout the province the act was considered the basis of the best and simplest system of land registration ever devised. The land registry office in Whitby, located beside the Court House (now the Centennial Building) on Centre Street South, was built in 1873. Additions were made to the building in 1929 and 1954. It ceased to be a land registry office in 1987 when it was too small for the growing Region of

Durham. The new Land Registry Office on Rossland Road opened in 1991.

Until the County of Ontario was set off from York County in 1852, all land registration was done in Toronto. John Ham Perry (1827-1896), the younger son of Whitby's founder, Peter Perry, was appointed Registrar for the new County in 1853 and held the office for 43 years. On Oct. 17, 1853, he entered the first document at the Whitby office. All the documents transferred from Toronto to start the Whitby office, were packed in one large wooden crate. Among those deeds was one granting land in Uxbridge Township in 1819 to Laura Secord, the heroine of the War of 1812 who warned the British of an impending American attack at Beaver Dams.

The first land registry office in Whitby was on Brock Street, south of the Royal Hotel. It was replaced by the building on Centre Street in 1873. John Ham Perry was very active in municipal politics, serving as Mayor of Whitby and Warden of Ontario County, until a new law prohibited registrars from holding political office after 1867. The rules and regulations he drafted were still in use until recent years, when registry offices were computerised.

Senior staff at the Ontario County Land Registry Office in 1922. Left to right, Jack Hay, William Correll (Deputy Registrar), George W. Dryden (Registrar, 1897-1931).

A certificate from the Ontario County Registry Office, signed by Registrar John Ham Perry, February 6, 1860.

Ontario Registry Office, Whitby.

The 6th day of February 1860 at 10 a.m. I hereby certify that since the establishment of this office there has been no Judgments registered against George Anderson.

J Ham Perry
Regr

Lest We Forget Willie Tempest

On Remembrance Day, November 11, we pay tribute to Whitby's servicemen who were killed in action in the First and Second World Wars. Their names are on a plaque on the Cenotaph and they are still remembered as friends and family by the older residents of the town.

One name, however is missing from the list of those to be remembered. He was a young man from Whitby who was killed, defending his country, not in France, Italy or Germany, but here in Canada, more than 130 years ago at the Battle of Ridgeway. His name was Willie Tempest.

The Battle of Ridgeway was an engagement in the Fenian Raids of 1866, when thousands of young Canadians volunteered to repel an invasion of Canada by the Fenian Brotherhood. The Fenians were an Irish organization that tried to gain Ireland's independence from England by invading Canada. Many of them were Americans who had been recruited by Irish insurgents, and were veterans of the American Civil War of 1861-65.

On June 1, 1866, an army of about 1,500 Fenians crossed the Niagara River at Fort Erie, determined to take over Canada. About 1,000 Canadian volunteers and a number of the regular militia were called out to repel the invasion. Among the volunteers were the Whitby Rifles, commanded by Major James Wallace (1814-1882) and the Whitby Infantry, commanded by Captain George H. Dartnell (1834-1899). There were also companies of soldiers from Oshawa, Brooklin and Columbus, who took the long train ride from Toronto to Fort Erie to defend their country.

At 6:15 a.m. on June 2, 1866 the train reached Ridgeway station and the soldiers disembarked there, about five miles from Fort Erie. At 7:30 a.m. they began a march to Fort Erie, which was held by the Fenians. After a mile, they reached a belt of woods. Here they were ambushed by the Fenian army. The Battle of Ridgeway lasted for an hour, until the Canadian volunteers had run out of ammuni-

Members of the Canadian Militia who took part in the Battle of Ridgeway.

tion. Each soldier had been issued with only 40 rounds of ammunition so the Canadians had to retreat when they ran out of bullets. Even though they had superior numbers, the Fenians did not pursue the retreating Canadians. Instead, they retired to Fort Erie. Another battle took place at Fort Erie, forcing the Fenians back into the United States.

Six members of the Queen's Own Rifles were killed in the Battle of Ridgeway and two more died of wounds a few days later. One of those killed was William Fairbanks Tempest, a member of Number 9 Company of the Q.O.R. William Tempest was born in Whitby on Nov. 30, 1845, the son of Dr. William Tempest and Mary H. Fairbanks, and spent his early years in Whitby. His father was a physician in Whitby and Oshawa before moving to Toronto in the early 1860s. His mother's family was very prominent in the Whitby-Oshawa area. One of his uncles was Col. Silas B. Fairbanks (1820-1871), the first commanding officer of the 34th Ontario Regiment which was formed in 1866 after the Battle of Ridgeway and is still Durham Region's local militia unit. Another uncle was Hugh J. Macdonell (1823-1877), clerk of the peace and clerk of the Ontario County Council. A third uncle was Duncan C. Macdonell (1825-1909), division court clerk of Ontario County.

A letter from one of the soldiers at Ridgeway, published in the Whitby Chronicle of June 7, 1866, described how Willie Tempest was killed:

"I saw among others, young Cooper (son of Church of England minister at Etobicoke) who was alongside poor Willie Tempest when he received the fatal shot, which killed him instantly, cutting the jugular vein, and another man of the Queen's Own had a ball enter his shoulder and pass out the back of his neck."

On June 5, 1866, 10,000 people turned out for the public funeral in Toronto for five of the men killed at Ridgeway. Tempest and his comrades were buried in St. James' Anglican Cemetery with full military honours.

In Whitby, the Battle of Ridgeway, and especially the death of Willie Tempest, had a profound effect on the community. On the day of the funeral in Toronto, the Ontario County Council was ready to open its week-long session in the Whitby Court House (now the Centennial Building). County Warden Calvin Campbell (1815-1895) of Brooklin, noted that the county clerk Hugh J. Macdonell was not present because he was attending the funeral of his nephew. John Ham Perry (1827-1896), Whitby's Deputy Reeve, paid a glowing

tribute to Tempest and the others killed at Ridgeway and noted that it was the first time since the War of 1812 that Canadians had died on their own soil defending their country. Reeve Alexander Kennedy of Mara and Rama Townships proposed a motion of condolence to the bereaved families of the volunteers and the council adjourned without doing any further business.

Whitby Mayor Nicholas W. Brown (1821-1889) issued a proclamation closing all the town's businesses from 3 p.m. to 4 p.m. on June 6, in memory of the slain volunteers. The town bells tolled mourning and the Whitby Brass Band marched through the streets for an hour playing the Dead March. All flags on public and private buildings were at half-mast.

Today's historians tend to treat the Fenian Raids of 1866 as something of a joke where more bullets lodged in trees than in men, but they were a matter taken very seriously at the time they occurred. The Fenian Raids resulted in the formation of a national militia by the end of 1866, with the 34th Ontario Regiment being part of this militia, under the command of Willie Tempest's uncle, Col. Silas B. Fairbanks of Oshawa. The Fenian Raids also convinced the political figures of the various provinces to proceed with plans for Confederation in 1867, to make a united country strong enough to repel any further invasions. The Fenians tried again in 1870. Major James Wallace of Whitby was again among those who drove them back.

William Tempest's death notice in the Whitby Chronicle summed up the personal tragedy felt by Whitby citizens over the death of one of their own young men. It reads: *"William Fairbanks Tempest, killed in the Battle of Ridgeway, June 2nd, aged 20 years, 6 months and 2 days."* Accompanying the death notice was the following memorial poem, whose author is unknown:

We shall meet but we shall miss him,
There will be one vacant chair.
We shall linger to caress him,
When we breathe our evening prayer.
When a year ago we gathered,
Joy was in his mild blue eye.
But a golden cord is severed
And our hopes in ruins lie.
At our fireside sad and lonely,
Often will the bosom swell
At remembrance of the story
How our noble Willie fell.
How he strove to bear our banner
Thro' the thickest of the fight
And uphold our country's honor
And the strength of manhood's might.
True, they tell us wreaths of glory
Ever more will deck his brow.

But this soothes the anguish only
Sweeping o'er our heartstrings now.
Sleep today, oh early fallen
In thy green and narrow bed.
Dirges from the pine and cypress
Mingle with the tears we shed.

No photograph of William Fairbanks Tempest has been found, so this chapter is illustrated with a picture of militia volunteers taken at Dunnville, Ontario, near Fort Erie by James Scott, in June of 1866. The man in the front row at far left is Corporal Henry H. Spencer (1831-1894) of the Brooklin Rifle Company.

Willie Tempest's father died in Toronto in 1871 at the age of 52, leaving a widow and at least four children. In 1873, the Federal Government granted a yearly pension of $298 to Mrs. Tempest as compensation for the death of her eldest son at Ridgeway. Mrs. Tempest died at Toronto on July 7, 1902, at the age of 79. Although his death caused much grief in Whitby in 1866, no memorial to Willie Tempest exists in Whitby today, and few, if any, residents of the town have ever heard of him.

There is a memorial in Toronto to the six men who were killed at Ridgeway and the battlefield is recognized as an historic site, visited by tourists who travel to Fort Erie and the Niagara Peninsula.

Five members of the 34th Battalion of Canadian Militia, formed in Ontario County after the Fenian Raids, in the fall of 1866. At upper left is William Warren, and at centre, Henry Warren. Notice the numeral "34" on their caps.

Unmarked Graves Tell a Tale of Tragedy

At the north end of St. John's Anglican Church cemetery are the unmarked graves of five German immigrants who never got the chance to settle in a new land. They were killed in a train wreck at the Whitby station on May 24, 1867. The only record of their names was printed in the Whitby Chronicle at the time of the accident.

In 1867, Whitby's Grand Trunk Railway station was located on what is now the Canadian National Railway, between the Victoria Street overpass and South Blair Street. On the north side of the railway tracks was the station, built in 1856, and on the south side was the Grand Trunk Railway Hotel, which was destroyed by fire in 1896. The station was replaced in 1903 by the building now known as the Whitby Arts Station Gallery, which stood at the end of Byron Street where the Go-Transit station is today.

The fatal accident occurred at 3 a.m. on May 24, 1867, when an unscheduled special freight train smashed into the back of another train stopped in front of the Grand Trunk station. The last three cars of the stationary train were filled with German immigrants, about 40 or 50 in each car. They had come from Hamburg, via Quebec, and were on their way to settlements in Wisconsin.

The special freight train, which no railway official seemed to know about, had stopped

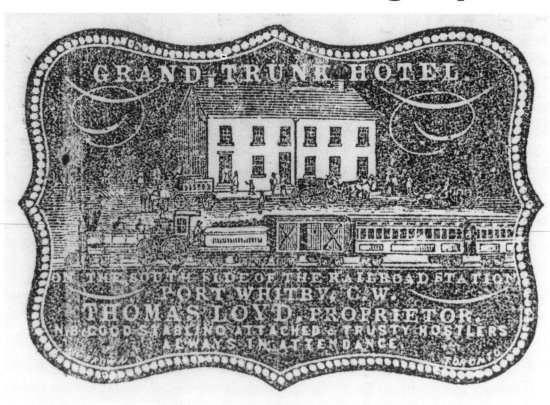

A print from an advertisement in the Whitby Chronicle, of the Grand Trunk Railway Hotel, where the victims of the train wreck of May 24, 1867 were treated.

for water at Bowmanville and was heading toward the Whitby station from the east at about six miles an hour, the speed used when approaching stations.

The semaphore east of the Whitby station showed a green light, indicating the track was clear, but the engineer was horrified to see a red light further ahead at the rear of the immigrant train. He whistled for the brakeman to apply the brakes, but as the track was wet that night, there was not enough time to act. The special freight slammed into the immigrant cars.

Alfred Pentland, the night operator and ticket clerk at the Whitby station, organized a rescue party to take the victims across the tracks to Thomas Totterdale's hotel, and summoned two doctors, Robert J. Gunn (1815-1902), Whitby's Mayor, and William O. Eastwood (1831-1913). At an inquest held the following afternoon, it was established that blame for the disaster lay with Wallace Fraser, the switchman. Fraser, it was discovered, had failed to raise the red light on the semaphore, indicating there was a train stopped at the station. He had been the day switchman at the station for about 10 years, but through a change in staff, he had taken his first night duty the date of the wreck. Instead of raising the red warning light when the first train came in, he had been busy loading wood. No explanation was offered for Fraser's failure to follow the proper procedure, but much sympathy was felt for him since his record had been unblemished up to that time. He was found guilty of manslaughter and sentenced to 12 months of hard labour at the County Jail, the lightest sentence that could be imposed.

Two days after the accident, the five immigrants killed, were buried within sight of the wreck. Mayor Gunn declared a public funer-

St. John's Anglican Church at Port Whitby, from which the funeral of the five German immigrants was held. They are buried in unmarked graves in St. John's Cemetery.

al, which was attended by nearly 2,000 people, almost the entire population of Whitby.

Alfred Pentland, the ticket clerk at the Whitby Station was a son of Rev. John Pentland (1804-1871) who was rector of St. John's Anglican Church, from which the funeral of the five immigrants was held.

Whitby Celebrated Canada's Birthday in Style

Nearly 8,000 people from surrounding townships and villages, crowded into the old County Town on July 1, 1867 to witness Canada's birthday. It was called Confederation Day then, and until recent times it was Dominion Day. Now we celebrate it as Canada Day. The first Canada Day was one to remember for the citizens of Whitby, then a small town of about 3,000 people.

Mayor Robert J. Gunn (1815-1902) proclaimed a public holiday and declared that the Volunteer Militia members of the 34th Battalion (now the Ontario Regiment) were to be the special guests of the town. The 34th Battalion had been formed the previous year to defend against anticipated attacks by the Fenians, Irishmen in the United States who wanted to free Ireland from British rule by capturing Canada.

Special orders were issued that the volunteers were to appear in full uniform, with officers receiving a full day's pay and non-commissioned officers and men 50 cents.

The highlight of the day was a mock battle on the *"commons,"* the fields north of Chestnut Street and south of Rossland Road. Here the 34th Battalion members would fight Major Button's cavalry troop from Markham, dressed in blue uniforms. The 34th Battalion, in red uniforms, had routed the Fenians at the Battle of Ridgeway in June 1866. They were well trained and making their first appearance at the new Battalion headquarters, a drill shed built in what is now Rotary Centennial Park.

Following a luncheon at the Mechanics' Institute Hall, at Byron and Mary Streets, where Pearson Lanes is located today, the 350 soldiers assembled at the Commons and fired a *"feu de joie"* as a salute to the new Dominion of Canada. Mayor Gunn read a proclamation, followed by the mock battle. The soldiers demonstrated the various battle techniques they had learned, but the only casualties this time were a few bloody noses when the mock fighting got too close.

There was some excitement when the Markham cavalry charged

"Dinsbaugh," the residence of John Ham Perry, which was floodlit with gas lights on the first Canada Day, July 1, 1867.

and startled Mrs. Murphy's cow which was grazing on the battlefield. The terrified beast charged into the crowd, ahead of the cavalry, and leaped over a fence to safety.

The 34th Battalion was commanded by Lt. Col. Silas B. Fairbanks (1820-1871) of Oshawa, its first commanding officer. Companies from Whitby, Oshawa, Greenwood, Columbus, Uxbridge and Brooklin, participated in the mock battle.

Between 3 and 4 p.m., dinner was served at the Mechanics' Hall, where speeches were made by several town dignitaries. At 4 p.m. sharp, athletic games, including the three-legged race, sack race, hurdles and the high jump, were held at the fair grounds adjacent to the drill shed. At 8 p.m. a torchlight procession formed in front of the Whitby Chronicle office, north of the Royal Hotel, and marched through the streets of Whitby, headed by the Whitby Brass Band and the 34th Battalion band. The procession was followed by fireworks in a field north of the foundry, on Brock Street North, the present site of Jerry's Drug Warehouse.

The weather for the first Canada Day was excellent, *"Queen's weather,"* according to The Chronicle. The newspaper reported that the celebration of the birth Canada in Whitby was the biggest and best since the visit of the Prince of Wales in 1860. The town cannon, made by Carleton Lynde for the Prince's

visit, was fired off all day, from early dawn until dusk. This cannon stood for many years in front of Trafalgar Castle School, but disappeared some time before the Second World War. Perhaps it was melted down for scrap.

The Whitby Brass Band played in front of the town's various hotels, and John Ham Perry's residence, *"Dinsbaugh,"* which was floodlit with gas lights to celebrate the occasion. Built 10 years before Confederation, Perry's Italianate style mansion was located where the swimming pool used to be in Kinsmen Park. It was demolished during the First World War.

The committee in charge of Whitby's first Canada Day celebrations consisted of Mayor Robert J. Gunn and the Town Council; Major James Wallace, Captain George H. Dartnell and Captain Charles A. Jones of the 34th Battalion; Quartermaster Robert E. Perry, Yeoman Gibson, Samuel H. Cochrane, Hugh J. Macdonell, Hugh Fraser, John V. Ham Jr. and Robert H. Lawder, all leading citizens of the town.

The events of this important day in Canada's history were firmly impressed on all who attended, especially the children. One 10-year-old boy recalled them in 1953 at the age of 95, for the Port Perry Star, providing future generations with the story of Mrs. Murphy's cow on the battlefield.

There was no major celebration of Canada's 50th anniversary in 1917 because of the First World War. Whitby did however, stage a big celebration in 1927 for the 60th anniversary, with a community religious service on the grounds of the Ontario Ladies' College (now Trafalgar Castle School), athletic sports, community singing, a parade, fireworks and dancing.

In 1967, Canada's 100th anniversary was celebrated by converting the old County Court House into a community centre. The town gave certificates to all babies born in Centennial Year, and the Whitby Venturers paddled by canoe to Expo '67. This canoe trip formed the basis for Whitby's twinning with Longueuil, Quebec the following year. Since 1969, there have been annual visits between the citizens of Longueuil and Whitby, representing the longest-lasting twinning exchange in Canada. Last year Whitby celebrated the 30th anniversary of its twinning with Longueuil.

The following Whitby residents recieved Canada Centennial medals in 1967: Edith Bedell, Heber Down, John R. Frost, Dr. John H. McKinney, Omer Edgeley, Thomas W. Sloan and James B. Harder. Twenty-three Whitby residents recieved Canada 125 medals in 1992, when special ceremonies were held in Whitby to mark Canada's 125th anniversary.

The Queen's Plate at Whitby
A Race to Remember

An upset victory by an unknown horse made the Queen's Plate a race to remember when it was run at Whitby on May 24, 1870. On the Victoria Day holiday, 10,000 people converged on the Ontario Turf Club's race track, west of Lynde Creek to witness the 11th running of Canada's most famous horse race. Whitby at that time was a well-known racing centre with a one-mile course built in 1858 north of the Jabez Lynde home (now a museum moved to Cullen Gardens in 1986). In 1870, the house, which stood at the corner of Dundas and D'Hiller Streets, was the oldest home in Whitby, dating from the War of 1812.

Many of Whitby's leading citizens, including Sheriff Nelson G. Reynolds (1814-1881), builder of Trafalgar Castle, were patrons of the Ontario Turf Club. At the Queen's Plate, Reynolds was one of the judges.

For several years before it settled permanently in Toronto in 1883, the Queen's Plate was run in various towns in Ontario that had race courses. When Whitby received the honour in 1870, the Town Council set out to make the race a grand spectacle. Invitations were sent to Prince Arthur, Queen Victoria's third son who was visiting Canada; the Governor-General Baron Lisgar; Sir John A. Macdonald, the prime minister and many other dignitaries.

The Queen's Plate at Whitby as portrayed in "The Canadian Illustrated News" of June 21, 1870.

The only one who actually attended was John Sandfield Macdonald, Premier of Ontario. The Grand Trunk Railway prepared a special train from Toronto to Whitby, furnished with seats and tables made by James Samo, a Whitby cabinet maker.

A grandstand 100 feet long and 12 feet deep was constructed at the track, along with special stands for reporters, pool sellers and distinguished visitors. Six selling booths were auctioned off to the highest bidders, where local merchants sold their wares to racing patrons. The ground in the centre of the course was reserved for parking carriages.

The man responsible for bringing the Queen's Plate to Whitby was Nathaniel

The Robson House hotel, where Major Quimby took the bets on the Queen's Plate.

(Nat) Ray (1817-1891), owner of the town's largest livery stable, and one of Whitby's leading horsemen. His influence convinced the Governor-General to select Whitby as the site for Canada's premier horse race, founded at Toronto in 1860. It is the longest continuously run horse race in the world.

A week before the race, the horses with their owners and trainers began to arrive, using the Robson House hotel as headquarters. An empty lot where taxis park at Byron and Dundas Streets occupies the same site today. Nat Ray's son Charles Ray (1847-1924) purchased the Robson House three years later and named it the British American Hotel. A large two-storey brick building, it was built in 1847 and demol-ished in 1891. Nat Ray's stable at Byron and Mary Streets where Ed Buffett and Associates now have their office, was the site of many spirited poker games during the days before the race.

Trainers exercised their horses by walking them up and down Dundas Street in front of the hotel where the townspeople gathered to admire their favourites. A four-and-a-half year-old boy, William Hewis (1865-1964) recalled the sight to the author of this book 93 years later.

Days before the race, every available household in Whitby was taking in boarders and all the town's hotels were full. There wasn't a bed to be had "*for love or money*", one race patron recalled.

At 8 a.m. on the morning of the race, the pool seller, Major Quimby of Toronto opened the betting in the office of the Robson House. E. King Dodds, a leading track enthusiast, recalled in his book "*Canadian Turf Recollections*", 39 years later that the Robson House was "*packed like a sardine box*". The farmers, always careful with their money, never placed bets over five dollars, but some city dwellers bet much more. Twenty-three horses were signed up for the Queen's Plate, but only 12 lined up at post time for the start. The favourite, Terror, owned by J. White, was such a popular horse that nearly everyone thought he would be the winner.

The Queen's Plate of 1870 was a two-mile dash open to all horses bred, owned and trained in Ontario that had never won public money. The winner received 50 guineas, the gift of Queen Victoria. Rules stated that riders must appear in full jockey costume or pay a five dollar fine for being improperly dressed. Persons entering horses in the Queen's Plate had to pay an entrance fee and a five dollar membership in the Ontario Turf Club.

At 12:15 sharp, the race was under way, after three false starts. Since there was no starting gate in 1870, the horses were lined up beside each other and started with the wave of a flag. Often, a horse would bolt ahead before the flag came down, making another start necessary. Terror, the favourite, led from the start, but with half a mile to go, he fell back to fourth place, much to the dismay of his backers. The winner, a horse named Jack Bell, was a surprise to all, being a relatively unknown horse which received few bets. Even his owner, Charles N. Gates, of Newmarket, advised race patrons not to place a bet on him. One young man, 22-year-old George H. Ham (1847-1926), on being advised not to bet on Jack Bell, was stubborn enough to put all his money on the horse. He was one of the few to win a fortune that day. The Rays of Whitby had two horses in the Queen's Plate, Post Boy, owned by Nat Ray, and Liberty, owned by his son Charles. Liberty placed sixth, Terror placed fifth.

One of the persons associated with the ownership of Jack Bell was Charles Lynde (1827-1912), a grandson of Jabez Lynde whose property was occupied by the race track. Jack Bell's jockey, John Bennett, was especially proud to have been riding the winner, for the race was his first in Canada. Those who had bet on Jack Bell made a great deal of money but the majority of the spectators, who had bet on Terror, lost out. It was considered one of the biggest upsets in the history of the race. It was significant enough to have a picture of the race published in the Canadian Illustrated News in June 1870 and to merit an entire chapter in E. King Dodds' "*Canadian Turf Recollections*", published in 1909.

By the early 1880s, the Ontario Turf Club ceased to exist and Whitby's days as a horse racing centre were over. However, the town continued to make a significant contribution to horse racing in Canada. Nat Ray (1876-1953), a grandson of the Nat Ray who brought the Queen's Plate to Whitby, was a noted jockey in the early 1900s. Born in Whitby, he graduated to steeplechasing and later raced trotters on American tracks. Although he began his racing career in Canada, most of his wins were in the United States. He was considered one of the top jockeys on the North American continent between 1900 and the First World War. Nat Ray was still racing at the age of 76 when he fell during a race in the fall of 1952. He died at Orlando, Florida, on March 3, 1953, and is buried beside his parents in Toronto.

Whitby's racing tradition continued with Sandy Hawley, who won his first of four Queen's Plates on Almoner in 1970. Although born in Oshawa, he grew up in a home on Thickson Road in Whitby and attended Anderson Collegiate. After 30 years of racing, Hawley retired in June 1998, with a record few have ever been able to match. He won 25 per cent of the races he entered, the highest winning percentage among North American jockeys and in 1980 was the youngest jockey to win 4,000 races. He won 6,449 out of 31,455 races, for purses totalling $88.6 million. He was named to the order of Canada in 1976.

In the 1980s, the site of the 1870 Queen's Plate became a subdivision named Queen's Common in honour of that race. Three of the streets are named after horses that ran in the Queen's Plate: Rathowen (misspelled Rothean), New Dominion, and Rapid Roan (Roan Drive).

The Merryweather

The Little Engine That Could

One of Whitby's most prized possessions for 54 years was the Merryweather steam fire engine, a modern marvel of technology in its day, more than 125 years ago. For many years, Whitby had suffered from a lack of adequate fire-fighting equipment. A small hand pumper of 1856 was the only fire engine available to the fire brigade founded six years previously, but it could not do the job at a major fire. When the Royal Hotel on Brock Street burned down on March 6, 1872, the public outcry was so loud that the Town Council under Mayor John Hamer Greenwood began to search for a suitable fire engine.

Later on that year the Council placed an order for a steam pumper from Merryweather and Sons, of London, England, which arrived in Montreal in October. There it was tested against a larger engine from a rival company and surpassed the other engine in its performance. The Whitby Chronicle reported the Montreal test in great detail, so by Nov. 2, 1872, when the Merryweather arrived in Whitby, excitement was running high.

The town councillors were like boys with a

new toy as they set out to see what the Merryweather could do. The steam fire engine, which was pulled by horses, was placed on the front of All Saints' Anglican Church at Dundas and Centre Streets and a

John Sawdon driving the Merryweather at Brock and Dunlop Streets, March, 1934.

line of hose 800 feet long was laid down Dundas Street to a well at the Four Corners. An additional 20 feet of suction hose was put down the well, which was located at the corner of Brock and Dundas Streets where the

Bank of Commerce is now. With ease, the fire-fighters were able to send a stream of water over the roof of the church. Urged on by the excited crowd, they aimed the hose at the steeple and shot a stream of water over its top, a height of 123 feet. Through a shorter hose length of 200 feet, the water was sent over the vane at the top of the steeple, a height of 130 feet. The fire-fighters were so impressed by this accomplishment that they continued pumping until the well ran dry.

The success of the Merryweather at All Saints' Church is all the more remarkable when compared with an incident nearly 100 years later in the summer of 1969. At that time a bolt of lightning struck the steeple, but the fire department's motorized pumper could not shoot the water high enough to reach the resulting fire. It was not until the town acquired its first aerial ladder truck four years later that the feat of the Merryweather fire engine could be equalled.

Elated with their success at the All Saints' Church, the fire-fighters of 1872 took the Merryweather to the harbour to see if it could shoot water over the flagstaff on Chester Draper's grain elevator, a height of 165 feet. Two 40-foot hoses were dropped into the bay. At the sound of two whistles, the fire-fighters succeeded in sending a stream of water at least 25 feet over the flagstaff. The grain elevator was as high as a six-storey building, not counting the flagstaff. The fire-fighters spent all day testing the Merryweather with different lengths of hoses and nozzles. Two representatives of the Merryweather company, Mr. Jakeman and Mr. Gilbert, were in charge of the tests.

Once the Merryweather had proved itself, a lengthy debate ensued at the Town Council on whether the Town of Whitby should purchase it. The cost of the Merryweather was $2,600, a substantial sum in 1872. A man could buy himself a good house for that money. Major Harper (1835-1917), a qualified machinist and member of the Town Council who had a shop on Mary Street East that is now Rousseau Heritage House, reported favourably to the Council on the technical quality of the engine. His testimony convinced the Council to purchase it. Little did the councillors realize that the Merryweather would soon prove its worth by saving downtown Oshawa from destruction.

About 7 p.m. on a Sunday night, Dec. 8, 1872, W.G. Fitzmaurice, a druggist who had fallen on hard times, set a fire in his store to obtain some insurance money. He nearly succeeded in destroying a quarter of downtown Oshawa. More than six stores in the northwest quadrant of the downtown were destroyed. The loss amounted to $60,000, only half of which was covered by insurance. Five fire engines, including one from the Joseph Hall foundry, were called out to fight the fire, but it was Whitby's Merryweather that prevented the fire from spreading to the adjacent residential district.

When it was evident that the entire downtown was threatened, C.W. Smith rushed to Whitby on horseback in the middle of the night to obtain the Merryweather. Smith arranged for a team of fresh horses to meet the fire engine half-way between Whitby and Oshawa to replace the exhausted horses which had left Whitby at a gallop. An hour and 10 minutes after Smith had left Oshawa, the Merryweather was on the scene of the fire, pumping water from a well at King and Simcoe Streets. The Ontario Reformer, one of Oshawa's two weekly newspapers, headlined the story of the fire with the words *"Oshawa Chicagoed"*, a reference to the great Chicago fire of 1871. The Reformer credited Whitby's Merryweather fire engine with saving the stores on the south side of King Street, and called Whitby's fire-fighters *"a noble fire brigade"*.

The Illustrated London News, a popular publication in England, printed a picture of the Merryweather and a story of the Oshawa fire, since the Merryweather was manufactured by an English company. The publicity was of great benefit for future sales.

The druggist, Fitzmaurice, was arrested, convicted of arson, and sentenced to three years in jail. As a result of the fire, the Oshawa Council purchased a fire engine in 1875, but it was not a Merryweather.

With such a successful fire engine in its possession, the Whitby town Council reorganized the fire brigade in February 1873, with John Stanton (1837-1908), the printing foreman at The Chronicle, appointed as chief. He was to serve for 32 years until his retirement in 1905. An engine house was built for the Merryweather on Brock Street, and by 1879 it was housed at the Town Hall at Brock and Colborne Streets. A fire bell was mounted on a tower behind the town hall, which was rung by the caretaker every time an alarm was turned in. Since it was too expensive to keep a team of horses on standby in case of fire, the town relied on local citizens to pull the Merryweather to a fire. When the bell rang, every person within earshot was expected to unhitch his horses from his carriage or waggon and race to the fire hall. The first there would receive five dollars, about three days' wages, and pull the Merryweather to the fire. A supply of wood was kept on hand at the town hall for stoking the fire in the Merryweather's boiler. The engine had the advantage of being frost-proof to meet the needs of Canada's cold climate, but the hoses would freeze on a cold day despite the efforts of fire-fighters to keep them thawed. Frozen hoses prevented the fire brigade from saving Joseph Bandel's Whitby House Hotel on Dundas Street West during a fierce snow storm on Dec. 22, 1879.

By the 1920's, motorized fire trucks were the latest equipment available. They did not require horses and wood, but ran efficiently on gasoline. The Town of Whitby in 1926 purchased a Godfredson pumper and a Chevrolet chemical truck to replace the Merryweather. The new trucks were more cost efficient, but the volunteer fire-fighters had to learn how to use them. It was embarrassing and dangerous when the trucks ran out of gas on the way to a fire and tore the doors off of the fire hall when they were driven out too fast. Ernest Stafford (1907-1989) was hit by a truck on the way to a fire at Almonds in 1928, suffering severe injuries. In 1931, to address these problems,

Harold Boys (1897-1993) was appointed as engineer to maintain and service the new fire trucks. He retired in 1965 after 34 years on the job. The Whitby Fire Department consisted of only volunteers until 1970 when the

Members of the Whitby Fire Brigade in 1885.

first full-time fire-fighters were hired.

After serving Whitby so well for half a century, the old Merryweather met a sad and mysterious end. After it was no longer needed except as an exhibit in parades, in 1930 it was

loaned to the Canadian National Exhibition in Toronto where it was used to cook hot dogs. Four years later, the Town of Whitby donated the Merryweather to the York Pioneer and Historical Society, which put on display at Toronto's old Fort York.

Today, there is no trace of the Merryweather. The York Pioneer and Historical Society no longer has it, and efforts by the Whitby Fire Department to locate it have been in vain. Perhaps it was broken up for scrap metal in the Second World War.

Anyone wishing to see a Merryweather fire engine of the type used by the Town of Whitby, can see one on display at the Chateau de Ramsey in Montreal.

The officers of the fire department at Whitby in 1873, when the Merryweather went into use were: John Stanton, chief engineer; F. Pierson, engineer; H. S. Garrett, fireman; S. Brown, Thomas Harding and George E. Hall, branchmen. Michael O'Donovan was captain; William Epplett, first lieutenant; Edgar B. Clearwater, second lieutenant; Thomas Lawler, treasurer and George H. Ham, secretary.

A Rich Architectural Heritage – The Whitby Buildings of Henry Langley

Whitby is blessed with many fine mid-Victorian buildings designed by the noted Toronto architect Henry Langley (1836-1907). The son of a shoemaker, Langley was educated at the Toronto academy before beginning a seven-year apprenticeship with Scottish architect William Hay. From 1862 to 1869, Langley was a partner with Thomas Gundry, Hay's associate before he returned to Scotland.

In 1865, Gundry and Langley designed All Saints' Anglican Church, the first of 11 known Langley buildings to be constructed in Whitby. A quaint and picturesque example of Victorian village life is depicted in the architect's print of All Saints' Church, showing sheep grazing on the front lawn amongst the parishioners on their way to church. A number of these 70-year-old prints were found in the church in the 1930s by the rector, Rev. E. Ralph Adye (1897-1982), who sold them to raise much-needed money during the Great Depression.

Langley became well known as a church architect, specializing in the Gothic style. He designed more than 70 churches across Ontario, and at least one as far east as St. John, New Brunswick. He was responsible for designing the spires and belfries of two of Toronto's most famous cathedrals: St. Michael's and St. James's. He also designed

Residence of George H. Dartnell: 320 St. John Street West, 1881.

Ryerson Hall, Trafalgar Castle School, 401 Reynolds Street, 1877 (at left of photo)

the original Metropolitan United Church in 1870 which was rebuilt after a fire in 1928.

In Whitby, Langley, designed the first St. John the Evangelist Roman Catholic Church at the corner of John and Palace Streets. Built in 1867/68, it burned down on Dec. 9, 1901. The present building on the site (now a bed and breakfast) was built in 1902 according to Langley's original plans, and continued as a church until the present St. John's Church was built on Giffard Street in 1958. From 1959 to 1975 it was a hall known as the Amber Room.

In Brooklin, Langley designed St. Thomas' Anglican Church, built in 1869. A quaint frame church, it has been the subject of many artist's sketches over the years. A large memorial hall was added to this church in 1987. The original plans for St. John's and St. Thomas' Churches are at the Archives of Ontario in Toronto.

After Gundry's death in 1869, Langley formed a partnership with his brother Edward and nephew Edmund Burke, as Langley, Langley and Burke. This firm was responsible for many commercial buildings in Toronto, as well as Whitby's Royal Hotel and the Watson and Allin Blocks on Brock Street South.

Henry Langley was a founder of the Ontario Society of Artists in 1873 and the Royal Canadian Academy of Arts in 1880. Proud of his profession, he helped to create an architects' association in Toronto in 1876 and the Ontario Association of Architects in 1889. He was also responsible for the endowment of a chair in architecture for the School of Practical Science at the University of Toronto. His high standards inspired his students to take an active interest in their chosen profession.

Many examples of Langley's work still stand in the small towns of Ontario as a testimonial to his skill in design.

All Saints' Anglican Church: 300 Dundas Street West, 1865/66. Spire added 1870.

All Saints' Parish Hall: Centre Street North, 1870. Demolished, 1980.

St. Thomas' Anglican Church, Brooklin: 101 Winchester Road East, 1869.

Watson's Blocks: 107 Brock Street South, 1878.

Royal Hotel: 171 Brock Street North, 1872/73.

Hopkins' Music Hall: 201 Brock Street South, 1877. Demolished, 1961/62.

Whitby High School: 315 Colborne Street West, 1872/73. Demolished, 1975/76.

St. John's Roman Catholic Church: 508 John Street West, 1867/68. Destroyed by fire in 1901. (Ontario Archives photo)

Mansard roof on residence of John V. Ham Jr.: 408 Byron Street South, added c. 1875 to an 1853 Regency cottage.

How Whitby Saw Itself In The 1870s

Whitby was experiencing a building boom in the 1870s. Many of the town's finest residences and business blocks in the downtown were constructed between 1870 and 1880. William H. Higgins, editor of The Whitby Chronicle, never missed an opportunity to outline the advantages of Whitby for his readers. On Feb. 27, 1873, he wrote the following summary of Whitby in a special edition of his newspaper and had extra copies printed for distribution throughout Ontario:

WHITBY AND SURROUNDINGS

"Whitby, the County Town of the County of Ontario, is situated on the margin of the beautiful lake of that name and possesses one of the safest harbours on the north shore of Lake Ontario. Population, three thousand. It is distant thirty miles from Toronto, the capital of the Province of Ontario, and 303 miles west of Montreal. There is a large mercantile business done in the town. It is well known as a first-class market for all kinds of produce, especially grain. Its harbour is open nearly throughout the year, making it a cheap and convenient shipping point. The harbour is well protected and has accommodation for a large fleet of vessels. There is also splendid wharfage and warehousing room. Vessels load beside the warehouses of Messrs.

Michael O'Donovan's Carriage Works, now the site of the Price Chopper Plaza on Brock Street South.

Jas. Rowe & Co. and of Mr. Chester Draper. The grain elevator is owned by the latter gentleman and is a remarkably imposing structure; it is worked by steam and is admitted to be one of the best of the kind in the Province. Whitby is an important Port of

Entry – the sixteenth in the Province as to Exports – the value of which, according to the last Government returns, amounted to $396,498; the value of Imports $87,219; and the duties collected $15,058.48.

"There is a station of the Grand Trunk

131

iron and machine shop, two large planing mills, and door and sash factories, large carriage factory, wagon and blacksmith's shops, extensive marble works, large tannery, a clock factory – recently established – the only establishment of its kind in the Dominion, complete in every respect and capable of turning out four thousand clocks per month; a sewing machine factory; two extensive furniture factories, harness shops and other industries which will be found more particularly described in advertising columns. There are numerous stores and places of business built in good style, some very extensive and elegant and well supplied and having a much superior stock to those found in most country towns, the principal of which will be found advertised in this paper.

"As the County Town, Whitby contains the usual public buildings and county offices – court house, county gaol, etc. Also a commodious Town Hall, Mechanics' Institute and Library, High and Public Schools (both free) under a Head Master and a staff of capable teachers and several public and private buildings remarkable for their architectural beauty. Amongst the latter, "Trafalgar Castle," the splendid residence of Mr. Reynolds, Sheriff of the county – noted as the largest detached private dwelling in the Province. The churches are amongst the most conspicuous public buildings. They embrace

Gerrie's Block, built in 1873, now Van Belle's flower shop.

Railway at Whitby and it is also the terminus of the Whitby and Port Perry Railway. The manufacturing interests of the town are represented by a large foundry and agricultural implement manufactory at which are turned out the celebrated mowers and reapers of the Brown & Patterson manufacture. Also Clayton's agricultural implement factory, an

two Episcopal (All Saints' and St. John's); a Roman Catholic: St. Andrew's (established Church of Scotland); Canada Presbyterian, Wesleyan Methodist and Congregational. All Saints' with its magnificent spire 150 feet high and built after the old Gothic style, is a model of architectural style and beauty. St. Andrew's is also a fine Gothic edifice, and when surmounted with a tower and spire, is well calculated to present a commanding appearance.

"Within the corporation are situated extensive agricultural buildings and show grounds where the exhibitions of the County Agricultural Society are held. These exhibitions are usually open for competition to the Province and the large number of entries and amount of prizes partake more of a Provincial than local character. Whitby has two Volunteer Companies, a Fire Brigade – possessing a "Merryweather" steam fire engine (the first imported into Canada) and Hook and Ladder Company. Also Masonic, Foresters and Odd Fellows' lodges; National and Temperance Societies, chess club and various other local organizations including a Brass Band. It has also two Telegraph offices, branches of the Ontario and Dominion Banks, Express office, etc., and this paper is a specimen of what it can turn out in the Newspaper and printing line. There are daily mails from all points – not less than 23 mails

Brown and Patterson's Agricultural Implement Foundry, now the site of Coffee Time Donuts on Brock Street North.

are made up and distributed during the day, and the Toronto daily papers are delivered in town at as early an hour as they are distributed in the city. The Hotel accommodation is ample and of the best character. Omnibuses run to and from the railway stations. Convenient and well supplied livery stables. Whitby is very healthy and delightfully situated and well laid out with every regard to sanitary considerations. It would prove an admirable point for the establishment of additional manufactures which would also be liberally aided by municipal and local assistance. The town is divided into three wards – North, South and Centre – the Corporation consisting of a Mayor, Reeve,

Hatch and Brother's Hardware Store, built in 1874, first building north of the Bank of Commerce on Brock Street North.

Deputy Reeve and nine Councillors – three from each ward."

When another newspaper reported that Whitby was dull, Higgins printed the fol-lowing reply on July 9, 1874:

"Within fifteen years most of the substantial brick stores on the principal business streets of the town have been built. The fine building of the Dominion Warehouse has replaced the old "Red Store", most of the brick buildings, including Allin's stationery, Campbell's Glasgow Warehouse, down to Richardson's handsome brick block, in which are Goldsmith's hall and Saunders' boot and shoe store, on the east side of Brock Street, have been built within that time. On the west side there is a large double store and three storey brick block of Mr. Gross. Further on, at the corner, there is the fine Gerrie Block, the substantial three-storey building erected for the Express and Montreal Telegraph Company by Mr. Yule; the brick store occupied by Messrs. Gibson & Sparvel, erected by Mr. Richardson, on Dundas Street, and we believe also the adjoining store occupied by Mr. Jameson, were all put up within the time spoken of. There is the Ontario Block of two storey buildings, put up by Col. Wallace, the handsome Ontario Bank block, and passing over to the east side of Brock Street again, McMillan's block in which are the offices of the Dominion Bank and the stores of Messrs. Hickie and Pringle. There are brick buildings put up by the late Mr. Cochrane, now Mr. Farewell's law office and Mrs. Knowling's store, and various other places of business on the principal streets which we cannot stop to enumerate. There are also O'Donovan's Carriage factory, Cormack's planing factory and large lumber premises, the new organ factory of Mudge & Yarwood, the foundry rebuilt and enlarged, the splendid elevator (one of the best if not the very best on the north shore) erected at the bay by Mr. Draper, and various improvements carried out at the harbour. We have the Whitby and Port Perry Railway, its stations, workshops and surroundings, a large number of handsome residences which meet the eye at every turn, and in fact the signs of substantial, if not immoderate progress on every hand. Three churches – the splendid edifice of All Saints', and the Catholic and U.P. edifices have been erected within a few years past, and also the very creditable High School building. We have now in course of erection the splendid Odd Fellows' Hall building, the large brick building, nearly completed, for Messrs. Hatch as a hardware store, and the new building of the Dominion Bank. And artisans can be seen engaged in putting up many fine residences and buildings all over town. There is not a house in town to rent; not a man out of employment; in two years, property within the corporation has risen twenty per cent in value."

A Student's Letter From College, 1875

Life for a student at the Ontario Ladies' College (now Trafalgar Castle School) was organized and strict in the 1870s when the school opened. Students were usually in their '20s or '30s in those days, for the College was more like a university than a secondary school. Fees for the Collegiate department were $6.00 per term, plus room and board $2.75 per week, and fuel, light and laundry 50 cents per week. The College offered two certificates: Mistress of Liberal Arts (M.L.A.) and Mistress of English Literature (M.E.L.). Students came from all parts of Canada and some from the United States, to receive a higher education. Only daughters of well-to-do families could afford

Students at the Ontario Ladies' College in the 1880s.

such a luxury in the 1870s. Although Sheriff Reynolds had to give up Trafalgar Castle to the school because of financial restraints, he was still able to send at least one of his daughters there. His granddaughter, Cort Reynolds, was May Queen at the school in 1921.

A fascinating insight into student life at Ontario Ladies' College is provided in the following letter from M.E. Bowman, to her sister, Mrs. A. Arnot, Londesboro, Ontario, dated April 18, 1875, seven months after the school opened.

Dear Sister:

I have no doubt you will be surprised to hear that on the 8th I started to College. I am in the Collegiate apartment (which is the highest to be obtained). There are three apartments, Primary, Preparatory & Collegiate. I have to study very hard for we have long lessons & a very great many of them. But I have received a card of high value and only have been here 10 days which is considered to be a great honour to any pupil. But you will ask if it is very expensive; it costs about $50 a quarter, i.e. (ten weeks). I like it well so far. We board and sleep in the College & never leave the playground without one of the teachers with us. It is lonely sometimes for I have not seen any person that I was acquainted with since I have been here. No Gentlemen are allowed to converse with any of the ladies without a note from the Parents & if they suspect any correspondence with Gentlemen they will not send the letters or allow them to be sent to the P.O. I do not expect that I will be here more than 12 wks. (that is a term & ¼). On the 30th of June there will be a concert. I suppose there will be a great number of Ladies and Gentlemen attend at which the pupils all dress in white. (I am taking up English Branches with Music). But you are tired of this now. I will conclude by stating that we have six teachers, 3 Ladies and 3 Gentlemen, one of which is M.A., another B.A. another a music teacher from Toronto. The Ladies all have First Class Certificates. It is the Sheriff's house converted into a College. Dear sister, I was very much pleased to hear from you that you are well & permanently settled, that Sarah Jane is getting big and making such rapid progress. Give my best respects to Albert, kiss Sarah for me. I would like to see you all very much but you will surely make us a visit before long. So good bye this time, for the girls are come from church and you know where there is so much talk, there is no writing. Write soon & tell me all the news, everything you can talk of. I still remain your true & affectionate sister.

M.E. Bowman

(Please excuse this scribble, for it is lamplight and I am in a hurry for I wish to be in bed by ½ past 9 o'clock).

Downtown Whitby's Finest Building

Many of the early buildings of downtown Whitby, dating from the 1850s to the 1880s, are still standing as a testament to the craftsmanship to our forefathers. Among these buildings, some stand out particularly as fine examples of Victorian architecture. One of these buildings, which is recognized as significant by Heritage Canada, is the Bigelow Block at 106 Dundas Street West. Now occupied by the Lafontaine Trading Post, it is the finest example of mid-Victorian commercial architecture in Whitby.

The main feature of the Bigelow Block is the stone work around the windows and along the cornice of the building. The ornamental Corinthian pillars on the ground floor are still intact, as are the stone quoins at the corners of the brickwork on the facade. Although it stood empty for nearly 20 years, the Bigelow Block now enjoys a new lease on life with tenants on the second and third floors as well as the ground floor.

The man who built this fine building was Joel Bigelow (1828-1896), twin brother of Joseph Bigelow (1828-1917), one of the founders of Port Perry. He was married in 1856 to Mary Ann Dryden (1830-1912), a sister of Ontario's Minister of Agriculture, John Dryden. Bigelow rose to a prominent position in the community, being secretary-treasurer of the Port Whitby, Lake Scugog, Simcoe and Huron Road Company in 1857. This company owned what is now Highway 12 from Whitby to Lake Huron, and charged tolls to farmers who used the road to convey their produce to Whitby Harbour. In 1859, Bigelow served one term on the Whitby Town Council, representing the North Ward, which included the built-up part of the town between Dundas Street and Rossland Road. For a number of years, he kept a store on Brock Street North before purchasing the site of his new building on Dundas Street in November 1859.

In 1860 he opened in his new building as a dry goods shop called *"The People's Cheap Cash Store"*. A rubber stamp on a school exercise

Bigelow's Block as pictured on the Tremaine Map of Ontario County, 1860.

book sold by Bigelow to a student at the Whitby Grammar School in the 1850s reads: *"Joel Bigelow, dealer in dry goods, groceries, boots and shoes, ready-made clothing, china, glass and earthenware, school books, Brock Street, Town of Whitby, C. W.".* The initials *"C. W."* stood for Canada West, the old name for Ontario before Confederation in 1867.

The status of Bigelow in Whitby's business community was such that his new store was pictured on the Tremaine Map of Ontario County, produced in 1860. A copy of this map hangs in the

Joel Bigelow.

entrance of the Whitby Public Library and another is located in the ante-room to the Durham Region Council Chambers. Bigelow was a wealthy and prosperous businessman in Whitby until a financial slump in the grain market in 1864, in which he lost much of his fortune. At this time he decided to leave Whitby and seek better opportunities in the United States. For two years he lived in Milwaukee, Wisconsin, moving to Chicago in 1866, where he remained for the rest of his life. Bigelow took an active part in business affairs in Chicago and amassed a considerable fortune in real estate. He died at Chicago on Feb. 11, 1896.

After Bigelow left Whitby, his building was occupied by a succession of businessmen. In the 1870s it was a grocery store called *"the Italian Warehouse"*, operated by Robert H. Jameson (1844-1929), who listed himself as an *"importer and dealer in family groceries, wines, liquors, etc."*. In 1876, Jameson was the first merchant in Whitby to have his store lighted by gas. Previously the stores of Whitby were lit by coal oil lamps. The Whitby Chronicle reported that the light given by gas, was equal to that of four coal oil lamps. The gas, called *"Canadian Air Gas"*, was supplied to the burners through pipes leading from a gas-making machine and air pump. The entire system was installed in four days by a Toronto firm and was said to be 50 per cent cheaper than city gas. Jameson was active in community affairs, being president of the St. Andrew's Society and the Whitby Curling Club. He was a member of the Town Council in 1879 and later served on the Board of Education.

In 1880, when Jameson moved his store to Brock Street South, the Bigelow Block was taken over by John Ferguson, a tailor. In 1908, the store was purchased by Richard N. Bassett (1880-1940) who, over a period of nearly 40 years, ended up owning most of downtown Whitby. He served as Mayor of Whitby in 1923-24. From 1908 to 1915 he operated a jewellery store in the Bigelow Block. In 1915, the store was sold to Samuel F. Murdoch (1879-1961) who operated a bakery and confectionery shop. He was succeeded by bakers Charles and Albert Sturgess. In the 1930s and 1940s, the Bigelow Block was a Diana Sweet's Restaurant, and in the 1950s Top's Grill. In 1963 the popular restaurant, Le Chalet, was opened in the building, and in the 1970s it was expanded into the two neighbouring buildings to the west. The Whitby Chamber of Commerce and other organizations held luncheon meetings at Le Chalet. The restaurant moved to Brock Street North, about 1980.

On the upper floors, a number of professional men had offices. In 1861, a Mr. Summers opened a photography studio in the Bigelow Block, and in 1872, dentist Dr. Wellington Adams (1848-1918) opened an office on the second floor. He was succeeded in 1914 by Dr. Blake Beaton (1891-1982).

McMillan's Block Housed Three Banks And A Post Office

One of the oldest and most attractive business blocks in downtown Whitby is the McMillan Block on the east side of Brock Street North, opposite Elm Street. For more than 80 years its brick front had been painted, but in the mid-1970s it was sandblasted to reveal a front of light yellow brick and sides of red brick.

The McMillan Block is the second business building on the site, the first being Perry's Block which was destroyed by fire on June 10, 1864. It was constructed in 1858 by John Ham Perry (1827-1896), son of Whitby's founder Peter Perry, who owned most of the land on Brock Street North, east of the Four Corners. It was divided into two stores, the north shop being occupied by Thomas H. McMillan (1839-1917) and the south store by Robert Campbell (?-1915). Both these men were dry goods and grocery merchants.

About 4 o'clock in the morning of June 16, 1864, McMillan, who was sleeping in an apartment above his shop, smelled smoke and found his store to be on fire. Since Whitby did not have an adequate fire engine, a runner was sent to bring one from Oshawa. By the time the Oshawa fire engine arrived, the building was a total loss. The visiting firefighters, however, were treated to a breakfast after the fire, courtesy of John Agnew (1800-1872),

Perry's insurance agent.

On Aug. 16 of the same year, exactly two months after the fire, John Ham Perry sold the site of the burned building to Thomas H. McMillan, who immediately began construction of a three-storey brick building to replace it. McMillan's new block was divided into three stores on the ground floor and apartments on the second floor. The third floor was never finished inside and was not divided into offices until the 1970s. Above the windows on the third floor was placed a date stone which reads: *"T.H. McMillan, 1864"*.

Thomas H. McMillan was born in Pickering Township in August 1839, and started in the dry goods and grocery business in Whitby about 1860. He left Whitby during the recession of 1873, and settled in Oshawa, where he did much to revive the sagging economy of that industrial town. Along with Thomas N. Gibbs (1821-1883) and W.F. Cowan (1830-1918), he founded the Ontario Loan and Savings Company in Oshawa and was its first and only manager. In 1882, he became the founding general manager of the Western Bank of Canada, with its head office in Oshawa. The Western Bank amalgamated with the Standard Bank of Canada in 1909, and it joined the Canadian bank of Commerce 20 years

later. Thomas H. McMillan died at Oshawa on May 6, 1917 at the age of 77.

The McMillan Block in Whitby was for many years associated with banking. In 1866 the centre store became the home of the Royal Canadian Bank, with Arthur Richardson as manager. The bank's vault can still be seen at the back of the Go Natural health food store, which now occupies the building. After the Royal Canadian Bank failed, the first branch of the Dominion Bank outside of the head office in Toronto, opened in the McMillan Block in February 1871. Whitby got the first branch of this national institution because of the influence of James Holden (1828-1881) of Whitby, who was one of the directors. In 1874, the Dominion Bank constructed the brick building at the south-east corner of Brock and Dundas Streets, which is now the home of 20/20 Optical. The bank remained in this building until 1970. When he founded the Western Bank of Canada in 1882, McMillan opened the Whitby branch in the south store of his building. Here too, can be seen the old bank vault at the back of the store. The bank remained there until 1914, when as the Standard Bank, it moved to the corner of Brock and Dundas Streets now occupied by the Canadian Imperial Bank of Commerce.

McMillan's Block, 121 Brock Street North, in the 1920s.

building to two brothers, William Hewis (1865-1964) and George Hewis (1877-1945), who established a butcher shop in the north store. To many residents of Whitby the building was known as the Hewis Block, for the family owned it for 61 years. William Hewis in his later years was known as Whitby's *"grand old man"* who lived to be 98 years old. In 1958, William Hewis sold the building to his son Harry Hewis (1894-1968). Harry Hewis's executors sold the building to Bruno Harilaid in 1973.

In 1913, a large advertising sign for Coca-Cola was painted on the north wall of the McMillan Block. It appears in the photograph accompanying this Chronicle. In the earlier years, the price of *"five cents"* was included on the sign.

An interesting story lies behind the photograph of McMillan's Block which accompanies this Chronicle. In the 1920s, travelling photographers went from town to town, photographing store fronts and selling the pictures to the merchants as post cards. About 15 of these post card photos of Whitby stores are in the Town of Whitby Archives.

From 1880 to 1910, the north store of the McMillan Block was the home of Whitby's post office. John D. Howden (1841-1927) was postmaster most of that time. In September 1910, the post office moved to the corner of Brock and Dundas Streets where until recently the Bank of Montreal had a branch. When the third floor of the McMillan Block was renovated in the 1970s, a number of wickets and boxes from the old post office were found in the empty rooms. There were also screens from the windows of the old Western Bank, with signs painted on them, advertising mortgage rates.

In 1912, Thomas H. McMillan sold his

Two Royal Hotels Have Served Whitby For 137 Years

One of the most familiar landmarks in Whitby is the Royal Hotel on the east side of Brock Street North. For almost a century it was the leading hotel in the town. Although its function has changed in the last 30 years, it remains as the finest example of 19th century hotel architecture left in Whitby.

It is not generally known that the present Royal Hotel is the second building of that name to stand on the site. The first Royal Hotel, one of the earliest brick buildings in downtown Whitby, was built in 1862 at a cost of $3,000 by Jacob Bryan (1823-1887) who had been in the hotel business in Whitby for 12 years. The Whitby Chronicle, which occupied part of the new building, reported that the Royal Hotel had 26 apartments, including the basement. As one entered through the front door, the bar was on the right and a large sitting room 22 feet square was on the left. The dining room was in the south wing. The rooms were all panelled with oak and the ceilings were 12 feet high. On ascending the main staircase, one found a ladies' sitting room and private parlor at the top of the stairs and a number of large bedrooms. On the third floor, along with more bedrooms, was a billiard room, 23 by 50 feet, well lighted and well ventilated. Behind the hotel were two wells and stabling for 50 horses.

The Royal Hotel was designed primarily for farmers coming south to Whitby from the northern townships to sell their grain during the fall harvest season. An advertisement in the Chronicle when the hotel opened in September 1862, stated that the farmers would be able to meet wheat buyers in their rooms at the Royal. The ad concluded with the words: *"It is particularly requested that any lack of attention will be made known at the bar."*

In 1868, Darwin Kent (1822-1884) and Thomas Walker, a son-in-law of Jacob Bryan, purchased the Royal Hotel and completely renovated and refitted it throughout. In 1870, the Royal was taken over by James Pringle (1824-1911) who stated in his advertise-

The first Royal Hotel, 1862-1872.

ments that the hotel provided spacious, well-fitted sample rooms for commercial travellers, and a horse-drawn bus travelled between the Royal and the railway station on the Grand Trunk line, near St. John's Anglican Church. When Jacob Bryan retired from the

The second Royal Hotel, opened on April 23, 1873.

All the Oshawa Fire Department could do was to prevent the spread of flames to adjoining buildings, which, fortunately were built of brick. The north wall of the Royal Hotel collapsed against the south wall of the Whitby Chronicle Building (now Liberty Mutual), causing considerable damage. The Chronicle did not miss its regular publication date, but had to print the story of the fire from its rival, The Gazette, because much of its type had been destroyed.

The damage to the first Royal Hotel and its contents amounted to $10,000, about three-quarters of which was covered by insurance. Mayor J. Hamer Greenwood (1829-1902), Deputy Reeve Thomas H. McMillan (1839-1917) and Deputy Reeve Michael O'Donovan (1834-1918) directed the fire fighting operations, and Major Harper (1835-1917), another member of the Town Council, was seriously injured when he fell from the roof of the nearby Hatch building while trying to save it from destruction.

The fire had scarcely ceased burning when James Pringle announced that he would build a new Royal Hotel. Cleaning up of the debris began immediately. One of the immediate results of the fire was the plan of the Town Council to purchase a new fire engine as soon as possible. The

hotel business, he served from 1873 until his death in 1887 as Whitby's Chief Constable.

The first Royal Hotel met an unfortunate end on May 6, 1872, when it was completely destroyed by fire. A great uproar was heard in the town because there was not a sufficient fire engine which could have saved the hotel. With no fire engine, the Whitby Town Council had to telegraph to Oshawa to obtain one, which arrived about an hour after the fire alarm was turned in.

Merryweather steam fire engine, ordered from England, arrived in Whitby in November, 1872 and in less than a month proved its worth by saving downtown Oshawa from destruction.

James Pringle selected noted Toronto architect Henry Langley (1836-1907) to build his new hotel. Local contractors were Thomas Deverell (1828-1910) for the brick and plaster work, Stephen Grose (1807-1889) for the carpenter work and Alexander C. Wilson (1826-1908) for the painting. Furniture was supplied by James H. Samo of Whitby. Samo also supplied 40 mattresses, spring beds and toilet sets to match. The cost of the new Royal Hotel, built in 1872-73 was $13,000. It was described by The Chronicle as *"one of the most commodious and best fitted up buildings of the kind between Toronto and Kingston."*

Patrons entered through a spacious hall on the ground floor, to the left of which was a dining room which could seat 180 people. To the right was a room for commercial travellers, a reading room and a sitting room. At the rear of the building was a bar and a 20 by 30-foot billiard room. A staircase eight feet wide led to the second floor where there were two front sitting rooms and 13 bedrooms. On the third floor were 15 bedrooms for guests. All the ceilings were 12 feet high and the rooms were elegantly furnished.

The grand opening of the new Royal Hotel, on St. George's Day, April 23, 1873, took the form of a banquet for 150 invited guests, with Mayor Greenwood acting as chairman and John Ham Perry (1827-1896) and Michael O'Donovan acting as vice-chairmen. John Ham Perry, the son of Whitby's founder Peter Perry, was Registrar of Deeds for Ontario County. Michael O'Donovan was a carriage maker and Reeve of the Town.

Such festive dinners of the 19th century were freely punctuated with toasts, with the chairman paying tribute to Her Majesty the Queen, the Prince and Princess of Wales, the Royal Family, the Army and Navy, the Volunteer Militia, the Governor-General of Canada and the Lieutenant-Governor of Ontario. The new hotel and its proprietor James Pringle, were also toasted, along with St. George, the patron saint of England. At appropriate times the Whitby Brass Band played the National Anthem and other musical tributes. After the toast was drunk to St. George's Day, the band played *"The Homes of Merry England,"* and the vice-chairmen proceeded to toast the municipal institutions of the Town of Whitby, the industries of Canada, education, Canadian railways, and anything that came to mind as the banquet lasted far into the night.

The opening of the Royal Hotel was a grand occasion in a grand age. One of the highlights of the banquet was the presentation of a set of silver-plated dish covers to the proprietor, by the Hatch brothers, Richard and Samuel, local hardware merchants.

The Royal Hotel in its early days had its share of distinguished visitors. On May 2, 1877, Canada's first Prime Minister, then leader of the opposition, Sir John A. Macdonald, paid a visit to make a speech in favour of the local Federal Member of Parliament, Thomas N. Gibbs (1821-1883) of Oshawa.

About 1914, the plate glass windows on the front of the first floor were replaced by a brick wall with smaller windows, which remains to this day. Above the first floor was an ornamental wrought iron balcony which was removed in the 1970s. In 1914, the hotel was operated by Thomas Cussion, a groom for Sir Henry Pellatt (1859-1939), the builder of Toronto's Casa Loma, who kept a farm and horse stable in Pickering Township. From 1927 to 1969, the Royal Hotel was owned by the Rousseau family, who advertised *"excellent dining room service, home cooking and rooms with bath or running water."* In recent years, the Royal Hotel has offered a bar and live entertainment.

The Ontario Bank Was Built In The Year of Canada's Confederation

In 1989, Charles and Ron Schaaf restored one of downtown Whitby's finest architectural landmarks, the old Ontario Bank, at the corner of Brock and Elm Streets. One can easily tell by looking at the three-storey brick building, that it was designed to be a bank. Construction began in the fall of 1867, the year of Canada's Confederation, and the bank opened in March of 1868.

The Ontario Bank had its head office in Bowmanville and several branches throughout what is now the Region of Durham. Chester Draper (1823-1876) a wealthy entrepreneur who owned Whitby Harbour in the 1860s and 1870s, paid for the construction of the Whitby branch of the Ontario Bank, which cost $6,000 to build. The architect was George Cormack (1830-1894), a Whitby lumber dealer and carpenter who obtained his architectural training while building Balmoral Castle for Queen Victoria in the early 1850s. Cormack also had the contract for all the carpentry work in the building, and William Dunkley (1831-1904) and William Weeks were the contractors for the masonry.

One of the features of the Ontario Bank was a wrought iron balcony over the main entrance at the corner of Brock and Elm Streets. The Schaaf brothers had a replica of the original balcony built during the renovations. When the bank was built, a brick vault was constructed on a mound of earth in the back part of the building. The rest of the building was constructed around this vault. During the 1989 renovations, the vault was removed because it took up too much valuable retail space. When the bank was built, the manager, K.F.

The Ontario Bank building, 122 Brock Street North, when it was Edmund Stephenson's telegraph office, Circa 1907.

Lockhart, lived in an apartment on the third floor, which was reached by a staircase at an entrance on the north wall.

The following is a description of the interior of the main floor, published in The Whitby Chronicle on March 12, 1868:

"Substantial oaken counters extend the entire length of the counting room, about 26 feet, the counters surmounted by a stained glass screen. At the farther end, a wide convenient desk is provided for the general public, a great desideratum to all who like to do whatever writing they want to do at a bank, without having people look over their shoulders at the general counter before the teller. Passing along the teller's compartment, a convenient place is provided midway for communicating with the accountant, handing in cheques to be certified, etc. Two doors communicate with the manager's room, a snug, cosy, nicely carpented sanctum — one from the outside and the other from behind the counter. The ample vault has been heretofore mentioned. It is built solid on a mound left in the excavation for the purpose, flagged, cemented, ironed and with — we forgot the thickness of the brick all round — and thoroughly fire-proof. On the very entrance to the building, one involuntarily pauses at the vestibule, before opening an inner door which is lined with red baize, to

The old Ontario Bank Building in July, 1975

look upon the air of warmth and comfort all around. All the offices are airy, well lighted and well ventilated, with lofty ceilings, and while they are superior to most, will compare favourably with any other banking offices in the Province."

The stone used for the quoins and over the windows, was quarried in Ohio and

Georgetown, Ontario. The original windows on the ground floor were glazed with the best English sheet glass, and over them were shutters which were raised and lowered with a crank. These windows had to be replaced during the reconstruction because the old wooden frames had rotted in some places.

About 1890, the Ontario Bank closed its doors, and the building became a ticket and telegraph office operated by Edmund Stephenson (1848-1920). Stephenson, an early version of a travel agent, was also agent for the Great Northwestern Telegraph Company and ticket agent for the Grand Trunk Railway. He was the local agent for the Canadian Express Company until 1914. Because of a childhood injury, he was lame, but this disability did not interfere with his work. After being in business for more than 50 years, Stephenson died on Nov. 22, 1920.

After Stephenson's death, the Ontario Bank building was divided into apartments and remained as such for 70 years. The north wall was somewhat disfigured when small windows were cut into it for washrooms.

In 1936, the Eastern Star Lodge of the Independent Order of Oddfellows moved into the upper floors of the building where they established their lodge rooms.

At Whitby's Greatest Fire, They Pumped Till The Wells Ran Dry

Whitby fire fighters pumped water until the wells ran dry, in an effort to save the downtown from destruction on Oct. 16, 1877. The fire, which destroyed almost all the buildings on the east side of Brock Street between Dundas and Colborne Streets, was the worst in Whitby's history. Whitby was no stranger to fires in the 19th century. A serious blaze in 1857 destroyed all the wooden buildings at the north-west corner of Brock and Dundas Streets, now the site of Van Belle Flowers. Individual buildings had succumbed to the flames also, such as the Perry Block on Brock Street North in 1864, the Gerrie Block at Brock and Dundas Streets in 1873 and the first Whitby House Hotel on Dundas Street West in 1879. But nothing could compare to the great fire of 1877, which resulted in damage exceeding $150,000 and left a quarter of downtown Whitby in ashes.

Shortly before 6 p.m. on Tuesday, Oct. 16, 1877, a delivery man was carrying a tray of lighted coal oil lamps to the back door of Thomas Lawler's grocery store on Dundas Street East, where the Best Little Tirehouse is now. The man tripped and dropped the tray of lamps just as he entered the frame store. The broken lamps burst into flame, and soon Lawler's store was engulfed. It took 12 minutes for the Merryweather fire engine to reach the scene, although some spectators

The brick Hamilton and Company building that stopped the fire but was gutted by the flames on October 16, 1877.

thought it took much longer. There was no hope of saving Lawler's store, so the fire fighters with their new engine concentrated on trying to save the Dominion Bank at the corner of Brock and Dundas Streets.

Although the roof of the Dominion Bank caught fire several times, the fire fighters succeeded in saving the building because it was

The block of stores built south of the Dominion Bank after the great fire, as it appeared in 1906.

made of brick. It was the only building on the east side of Brock Street to survive the fire. Occupants on the upper floors above the bank, including Mayor George Y. Smith (1833-1920), a lawyer, began carrying furniture, files and other contents out of the building as the flames roared up behind it. It appeared for a while that the fire could be stopped at the Dominion Bank, but a light wind caused it to spread to a nest of wooden shacks and piles of lumber south of the bank.

The lumber was being used by John Watson (1806-1879) to build a block of stores on Brock Street which were only partially completed at the time of the fire. If there had not been so many loose construc-tion materials lying around the building site, the fire might not have spread to Brock Street. It was not long before the fire began to proceed south along Brock Street consuming the frame stores one after another.

As the progress of the fire became evident, there was a general rush by spectators and storekeepers to save the contents of the stores on Brock Street. As cinders rained down upon them, the citizens used axes, hooks and chains in an effort to pull down some of the wooden buildings before the fire got to them. The one hope of stopping the fire was the brick Hamilton and Company building situated in the middle of the block. If the work of the fire fighters at the Dominion Bank could be duplicated there, the fire might be halted.

There were cheers when the Oshawa Fire Brigade arrived with its engine as the flames reached the Hamilton Block. Both Whitby and Oshawa's steam pumpers were soon shooting streams of water over the roof. Then a calamity occurred. The wells being used by the two pumpers ran dry. In the 1870s there was no modern waterworks system in the town. The fire engines worked by dipping hoses into wells which had only a limited water capacity. When they ran dry, it would take hours for them to refill. Much valuable time was lost as the fire engines and hoses were moved to other wells in the downtown, farther away from the fire.

By the time the fire engines were hooked up at the other wells, the flames burst out again, this time inside the Hamilton Block. In a few minutes the fine brick building which had been constructed in 1858, was gutted. However, the brick walls prevented the flames from progressing any further south.

Although the great fire did not actually reach Colborne Street, all the buildings south of the Hamilton Block were damaged either by cinders or by the townspeople attempting to tear them down to stop the fire. The Chequred Store at Brock and Colborne Streets, one of the oldest landmarks in the downtown, was badly damaged by wrecking crews even though it was never reached by the flames. In all, the entire block of stores with the exception of the Dominion Bank, built in 1874, had to be replaced.

The day following the fire, the merchants who had been burned out moved into other premises. Two set up shop in the new Hopkins Music Hall (later the Whitby Town Hall) at Brock and Colborne Streets where the fire hall now stands. At least 16 merchants had sustained losses, less than half of which were covered by insurance.

About 50 years after the fire, James Lawler (1868-1945), Thomas Lawler's second son, wrote his memoirs of the fateful night of Oct. 16, 1877.

"That year, mother, Arthur and I were visiting Aunt Sarah at Aspdin, Muskoka, when a telegram came to say that Old No. 1 (the Lawler store) had been burned down," he said. *"It put us all in a panic. It appeared that the delivery man at dusk had dropped a tray of lighted coal oil lamps and the fire was on. In addition to Old No. 1, the whole of the new Watson Block which was nearly completed but in which no stores were rented, had burned down also. Father, who was to occupy the store next to the bank on the corner as soon as the new building was ready, had been laid up with sciatica a short time after we left for Muskoka, was unable to get a chance to see the fire except from a back window. It was a great shock to him but he rented the store in the corner of the present town hall (Hopkins Music Hall) and remained there until the second Watson Block was finished when he moved into the store next to the bank."*

Another person who never forgot the great fire of 1877 was Frances Wilson, later Mrs. William Bobier. An immigrant from Ireland, related to Albert W. Jackson (1870-1939) a future mayor of the town, she arrived in Whitby on the night of the fire and witnessed all the excitement. When she died in St. Thomas, Ontario in 1929 the fact that she had arrived on the night of the great fire was mentioned in her obituary.

Wolfendien's new Marble Factory, built in 1878, after the fire.

Between 1878 and 1883, all the existing stores on Brock Street south of the old Dominion Bank were constructed to replace those lost in the great fire. Wolfenden's Marble Works, on Dundas Street east of Lawler's Store was also destroyed in the fire. In 1878 a new brick building replaced the old tombstone factory. It stood until 1970 when it was demolished and replaced by the dental building beside the Cenotaph.

These Stores Once Served As A Hotel

The stores on the west side of Brock Street South, from Donald Travel to the Loonie Bin, are among the finest examples of mid-Victorian architecture in downtown Whitby. Although stripped of much of their ornamental woodwork, they still attract the eye as one passes down the street.

These five stores, built in 1878, were known a Deverell's Block, named after their owner and builder Thomas Deverell (1828-1910). Deverell, born in Ireland, came to Whitby in the 1840s. He learned the trade of masonry during the construction of St. John's Anglican Church in 1845/46 and is believed to have been the first person married in that church, on Nov. 11, 1850. For the next 50 years, he was one of the leading builders in Whitby. In the 1890s, he owned most of the land on the south side of Dundas Street from Byron to Brock Street and half the block south on Brock Street toward Colborne Street. In 1891 he bought the old Ray's Hotel at Byron and Dundas Streets where the taxis now park, and built a new frame hotel. Two days before it was due to open, in January 1892, a worker dropped a lighted cigarette into a pile of wood shavings, and the building burned to the ground.

For 17 years the Deverell Block was used as a hotel. In 1900, Van Buren Woodruff (1860-1935) converted the Deverell Block into the New Armstrong Hotel. The name was later changed to the Windsor Hotel, after Whitby's original name, and operated until it closed in 1917 and its contents sold by public auction. After the hotel closed, the building was converted back into stores.

The first store, Donald Travel today, was originally occupied by the dry goods firm of Laing and Stewart. When William Laing (1818-1891) moved to Toronto in 1881, his partner, Charles F. Stewart (1845-1913) carried on the store into the 1890s. Stewart advertised *"staple and fancy goods, millinery, gents' furnishings and clothing made to order"*. In 1911, Jacob McIntyre (1855-1927) moved his hardware store to this location in the Deverell Block where he sold hardware, stoves, paints, oils, glass and furnaces, and specialized in plumbing and tinsmithing. After his son, Francis McIntyre (1891-1958) took over the business, he moved it in 1929 to the second store of Deverell's Block. From 1930 to 1935, the first store was the Royal Bank, which closed after five years, a victim of the Great Depression. In 1954 the Bank of Montreal opened in this store, after an absence of nearly 100 years. It moved into the new Brock Building in 1960 and was replaced by Donald Travel.

From 1878 to 1886, the second store, now the Money Mart, was occupied by James S. Robertson (1853-1925) and his brother as a publishing, stationery and book store. The Robertsons had moved from Toronto to Whitby in 1874, and published The Whitby Chronicle from 1883 to 1886, along with two other weekly papers, The Whitby Saturday Night and Our Own Fireside. After the Robertsons returned to Toronto in 1886, another bookselling firm of Stafford and Cormack took over. Richard S. Cormack (1837-1912) operated the business until the hotel moved in.

The third store, now called Cash or Deals, was the office of the Canadian Bank of Commerce from 1919 to 1929 and was later ladies' clothing stores operated by Hilda B. Sleeman and Agnes Disney.

The fourth store, now Vera's Cafe, was in the 1880s and 1890s, Matthew B. Collins' (1828-1898) shoe store. From 1932 to 1969 it was a barber shop operated by Hilliard Millard (1891-1970).

The south store, now the Loonie Bin, was occupied from 1878 to 1900 by Edward J. Johnston (1845-1902), a cabinet-maker, upholsterer and undertaker. In those days, before the modern funeral homes, the local cabinet-maker doubled as an undertaker because he had the ability to

J. S. Robertson and Brother's stationery store, 106 Brock Street South, in 1880.

make coffins. When Whitby was a small town there was not enough business to keep an undertaker busy on a full-time basis. Johnston, who moved to Toronto in 1900, advertised himself as a chair and cabinet maker, *"with painted window blinds a specialty,"* and *"undertaking in all its departments"*. For many years after 1917, the store was a bakery operated by Maitland Martin (1885-1958) and Guido De Agnese (1911-1991). In July 1997 the store was severely damaged in a fire, but was repaired within a few months. In 1965 the stores of Deverell's Block were painted white, but the brickwork was cleaned and restored in 1978.

A bill from J.S. Robertson and Brother, March 20, 1882.

Windsor Hotel logo, 1914.

The Bandels Operated The Whitby House Hotel For 68 Years

On Dundas Street West, across from the new Medical Centre stands the old Whitby House hotel. In recent years it has been a bar under the names Cokee Joe's, The Late Night Cafe and Rolling Rock. Built in 1880 by Joseph Bandel (1826-1896) it was one of the last of downtown Whitby's many hotels.

Joseph Bandel was born in Wurtemburg, Germany on Jan. 27, 1826 and came to Canada in 1852, landing at Toronto. In the fall of 1858, he moved to Whitby and for about 10 years was in the boot and shoe business. About 1870, he gave up shoemaking and went into the hotel business, which proved to be a very lucrative career. In 1875 he replaced his first hotel, the Western House, with a new building on Dundas Street West, which he called the Whitby House, designed by Oshawa architect Hiram R. Barber (1843-1914).

Tragedy struck on Dec. 22, 1879, when a fire which originated in a stable near the hotel spread to the Whitby House and burned it to the ground. The hotel might have been saved, said the Whitby chronicle, if spectators had leant a hand to the fire department. The fire was well under way, when the *"Merryweather"* fire engine arrived. It took 20 minutes to drag it through deep snow from the fire hall at Brock and Colborne Streets, only two and a half blocks away from the hotel. The fire fighters were

The Whitby House Hotel, 207 Dundas Street West, in the 1920s.

also severely hampered when their hoses froze during the fire.

After the fire, Bandel hired architect Barber to build him a new hotel in 1880, which stands to this day. Joseph Bandel continued to operate the Whitby House until his death on June 5, 1896 at the age of 70.

The Whitby House was very popular with the members of the Ontario County Council who travelled as much as 100 miles to attend council meetings at the Court House (now the Centennial Building), in January and June. Many of the council members stayed at Bandel's hotel when the

Joseph and Mary Bandel and family in the year the Whitby House was built, 1880. Back Row: Emeline, George, Joseph Jr. and Mary. Centre Row: Annie, Victoria and Ottilia. Front Row: Anthony, Joseph and Mary Sr. and Louis.

council was in session.

When Joseph Bandel died, his family discovered that they did not have a suitable portrait of him. The only picture in which he appeared was a family group photo taken about 1880. The family took the group photo to Whitby photographer William E.

O'Brien (1858-1925) who made an enlargement of Joseph Bandel alone. Copies of both photos are in the Town of Whitby Archives.

Joseph Bandel's wife Mary (1834-1914) continued to run the hotel until her death at the age of 81 on Aug. 18, 1914. Her son Anthony (1866-1946) took over after her

death and in 1921 he sold it to his brother Louis S. Bandel (1868-1932). Louis' son Joseph P. Bandel (?-1933) inherited the hotel from his father but died within a year. It was then taken over by Louis S. Bandel's wife Mabel (?-1943). The last Bandels to operate the Whitby House were her son and daughter Louis and Mary. In January 1948, they sold the Whitby House to the Alliance Hotel Company. One of the reasons for selling was the difficulty in getting staff to run the hotel.

In the 1940s, a porch was built over the sidewalk in front of the Whitby House. It was removed in the early 1960s, when the hotel was an entertainment spot known as Jim's Stage Door. Inside was a coffee shop called the Melody Grill. The Whitby House has changed much in appearance, having been painted in the 1940s and covered with stucco in the 1960s. A major renovation took place in the mid-1990s when the old building was gutted and completely rebuilt inside for the Late Night Cafe.

The Whitby House was the first meeting place of the Whitby Rotary Club, which was founded in 1933. The first executive of the club was photographed at the front of the hotel at that time.

Members of the Bandel family still live in Whitby, although the family ownership of the old Whitby House ended 51 years ago.

Canada's Greatest Political Cartoonist Got His Start In Whitby

Canadians today usually recognize our first Prime Minister, Sir John A. Macdonald through the drawings of a brilliant cartoonist named John W. Bengough. Bengough (1851-1923), pronounced *"Ben-goff"*, published a magazine of political satire called *"Grip"* from 1873 to 1892, which was illustrated with his cartoons of the great political figures of 19th century Canada. Many of his cartoons are reproduced in modern history books, but little is known by today's generation of the man who drew these cartoons.

In the early 1850s, the Bengough family, recently arrived from St. Andrew's, Fifeshire, Scotland, came to Whitby where they were to make their home for about 30 years. John W. Bengough's grandfather, John Bengough Sr. (1792-1867) was a ship's carpenter who likely found his first employment at a shipyard at Port Whitby operated by James Rowe, the first mayor of the town. Bengough's father, John Bengough Jr. (1819-1899) was a carpenter who built houses in Whitby and was streets foreman for the town in the 1850s. He was one of the tradesmen who helped build Trafalgar Castle for Sheriff Nelson G. Reynolds. His specialty was building stairs and cabinets. Some members of the Bengough family married into the Sleep family of Port Whitby. The stairs in the home of Emanuel

John W. Bengough

Sleep on Victoria Street, east of the C.N.R. crossing, were constructed by John Bengough Jr. and Sleep's second wife, Christina Bengough, was his sister.

Young John W. Bengough attended the old Henry Street Public School, which stood on the site of the present R.A. Sennett School. His schoolmaster, George Y.

Smith (1833-1920) was the subject of some of Bengough's earliest attempts at cartooning. Smith was so impressed with his pupil's work that he gave him a box of paints as a Christmas present. While at the Whitby Grammar School, Bengough was an average student, but his artistic talent was recognized. Thomas Kirkland (1835-1898), the headmaster, awarded him a general proficiency prize, a book entitled *"Boyhood of Great Artists"*. After Kirkland's death many years later, Bengough published a poem in tribute to his former teacher in the Toronto Globe.

Bengough's younger brother Thomas (1853-1945) recalled that John's first real cartoon was of his older brother George (1846-1900). Young Bengough was laid up with a fever, and counted on George to bring him the Toronto daily papers. One day, when George forgot the papers, John drew a cartoon of George walking nonchalantly down the street, while he had left his head on the mantlepiece.

As a youngster, Bengough had access to the American magazine Harper's Weekly, which featured the political cartoons of Thomas Nast. He studied Nast's cartoons and decided that he wanted to be a cartoonist himself. He took every opportunity to sketch people he saw in Whitby, including Matthew Crooks Cameron, a Queen's

Counsel who appeared regularly at the Ontario County Court House to conduct the Assize Court. The court house is now the Whitby Centennial Building. Bengough continued drawing Cameron in *"Grip"* when the lawyer became leader of the Liberal opposition in the Ontario Legislature.

Bengough figured the best way to become a cartoonist was to enter the newspaper business, so he applied to George Ham (1847-1926), editor of the Whitby Gazette, for a job. In the late 1860s, a small-town local newspaper did not have the resources to print cartoons, so Ham decided to hire Bengough as a type-setter in the composing room. Bengough got his opportunity to get into the editorial side of the Whitby Gazette in 1870 when the Franco-Prussian War broke out in Europe. Ham decided to publish a daily edition of The Gazette, a weekly paper, featuring the latest war news, but found that the dispatches from Europe did not supply enough copy to fill his four-page paper.

Young Bengough came to his rescue by offering to write a serial story to fill the empty space. Entitled *"The Murder's Scalp or the Shrieking Ghost of the Bloody Den"*, the story was supposed to keep the reader guessing as to what it was all about. There was much comment in Whitby about

Bengough's story, which never did end, for the war was a short one and Ham went back to publishing a weekly paper. Unfortunately, all the Gazette files were destroyed in a fire at the newspaper office in 1946, so we have no copies of Bengough's never-ending story.

By 1871, when Bengough reached his 20th birthday, he realized that The Whitby Gazette was too small for his ambitions, so he went to Toronto and got a job as a reporter for The Globe, the leading Liberal newspaper in Canada (now the Globe and Mail). The Globe was published and edited by a Father of Confederation, George Brown.

After two years as a Globe reporter, Bengough published his first issue of *"Grip"*, on May 24, 1873. He named the magazine after the raven in Charles Dickens' novel, *"Barnaby Rudge"*. *"Grip"* was not an instant success, but soon fortune, in the form of the Pacific Scandal, made John W. Bengough a national figure. Prime Minister, Sir John A. Macdonald was accused of taking money for political purposes from the men he was hiring to build the Canadian Pacific Railway. Bengough's cartoons, ridiculing Macdonald, became an overnight success and established Bengough as one of Canada's leading journalists. For 19 years, Bengough continued to publish *"Grip"*,

mainly because of his caricatures of Macdonald. When Sir John died in 1891, Bengough was without his favourite subject, and a year later, *"Grip"* ceased publication.

Bengough met his favourite subject only once, when he was introduced to Macdonald by another Member of Parliament in a side room at the House of Commons in Ottawa. *"I was indeed much affected by the air of humility and even bashfulness which our great leader displayed, though he assured me that they all enjoyed the hits I made at them,"* Bengough recalled years later.

After 1892, Bengough became a cartoonist for the Montreal Star, and later the Toronto Globe. In addition to his newspaper work, Bengough made a name for himself on the lecture circuit for his *"Chalk Talks"*. His favourite ploy at a chalk talk was to ask a member of the audience to draw a line on a sheet of paper on a large easel on the stage. From that line, Bengough would construct a caricature of the man who drew it. Bengough was always a popular crowd-pleaser when he returned to Whitby on several occasions to give his chalk talks at the old town hall at Brock and Colborne Streets.

In addition to his illustrated lectures, Bengough published a number of books of cartoons and political commentary. Among

WHITHER ARE WE DRIFTING?

"Whither Are We Drifting", Bengough's famous cartoon of Sir John A. Macdonald during the Pacific Scandal, published in "Grip", August 16, 1873.

the titles were: *"Motley: Verse Grave and Gay"*, *"The Up-to-Date Primer: A First Book of Lessons for Little Political Economists"*, and *"A Caricature History of Canadian Politics"*.

As an artist, Bengough was a charter member of the Royal Canadian Academy in 1880. As a teacher, he was a professor of elocution (public speaking) at Wycliffe College in Toronto. As a politician, he was a member of the Toronto City Council in 1907 and was president of the Single Tax Association and of People's Reform. He was also a director of the Canadian National Exhibition. Described as *"one of the ablest cartoonists in the world,"* he toured Australia and New Zealand, giving his Chalk Talks. The Toronto Methodist newspaper, The Christian Guardian, called him *"a genial companion, a brilliant conversationalist, a peerless cartoonist and as an author his works lie close to the purest and simplest passions of the human heart."*

John W. Bengough died at his Toronto home at the age of 72 on October 2, 1923. His brother William (1867-1932) was a prominent artist in New York City and another brother, Thomas, was an official reporter for the Senate of Canada for 23 years and organized the first convention of shorthand writers in Canada.

Colonel John E. Farewell – A Community Leader

On November 17, 1983, Ontario's Minister of Education Bette Stephenson officially opened the Col. J.E. Farewell Public School in the Otter Creek subdivision. This school is named after one of the most influential personalities in the history of Whitby, who contributed to the development of this town in many fields.

The story of Col. Farewell's life begins with the fact that he was not a Farewell by birth. At an early age, probably five, he was adopted by Abraham Farewell (1812-1888), an influential resident of Whitby Township who lived at Harmony, now part of Oshawa at the intersection of Highway 2 and Harmony Road. Abraham Farewell represented Ontario South riding in the Provincial Legislature from 1871 to 1875 as a Liberal. He first ran for election in 1854, but lost to John M. Lumsden. The same year he was elected as the first Deputy Reeve of Whitby Township. He contested another provincial election in 1865, but was defeated by Thomas N. Gibbs (1821-1883) of Oshawa. The Farewell family settled in Whitby Township, now part of Oshawa, in 1804 and remained active in the local area for more than a century.

It is believed that Col. John Edwin Farewell was a son of Franklin A. Kellogg (1808-1878) and Mary E. Galloway (1813-1845). When Mrs. Kellogg died on Nov. 14, 1845, her husband was left with six children and no way to care for them all. John Edwin, the first son, was adopted by Abraham Farewell and took the name of Farewell for the rest of his life. He was born in Whitby Township on Feb. 18, 1840. His biological father, Franklin A. Kellogg, married a second time and moved to the United States where he died in 1878 at New Oregon (now Cresco), Iowa.

Educated at Whitby and Barrie High Schools, Col. Farewell graduated in law from the University of Toronto in 1864. He practised law in Bowmanville, Oshawa and Whitby before being appointed Ontario County Crown Attorney on the death of Samuel H. Cochrane in 1872. In 1877 he was appointed Clerk of the Peace, and

Colonel John Edwin Farewell

in 1882, County Clerk and Solicitor. In 1916, he was elected president of the Ontario Bar Association. As Crown Attorney, he was prominent in prosecuting political bribery cases. Under his direction, Ontario County had more convictions for this crime than any other county in the province.

Col. Farewell had a prominent military career which began in the University of Toronto Rifles in 1862. He served in the militia which repulsed the Fenian Raids at Fort Erie in 1866 and later served as president of the Toronto Veterans' Association. He was commanding officer of the 34th (now Ontario) Regiment from 1898 to 1902 and retired with the rank of Lieutenant-Colonel. He was instrumental in obtaining medals and recognition from the Federal Government for Canada's Fenian Raid veterans.

A member of Eastern Star Lodge of the Independent Order of Oddfellows, in Whitby, Col. Farewell was elected Grand Master for Ontario in 1899. A member of the Whitby Board of Education for more than 30 years, from the 1870s to the 1900s, he was chairman of the board on a number of occasions. He was the founder of the Ontario Provincial Association of Public and High School Trustees in 1887, was the first president of the association and was later president of the Provincial Educational Association. Col. Farewell began his life's

work as a teacher at the old Henry Street Public School, on the site of the present R.A. Sennett School, in the 1850s when he was still in his teens.

Col. Farewell was a great promoter of Whitby and Ontario County. In the early 1900s he named Ontario *"the Keystone County of the Province of Ontario"*. This resulted in a new Whitby newspaper founded in 1903 by Charles A. Goodfellow (1865-1919) being named *"The Whitby Keystone"*. It is believed that Col. Farewell had a hand in designing Ontario County's Coat of Arms in 1895 and selecting the county motto: *"Peace, Plenty, Progress"*. He is best known today for the writing of a history of Ontario County, published in 1907, which is one of the few reference books available on the county's history and development.

Col. Farewell died at the age of 83, on Dec. 29, 1923, as a result of injuries received in one of Ontario County's first automobile accidents. His dog was later buried with him at Union Cemetery in Oshawa.

The influence of Col. Farewell extended beyond his death. In 1925, a memorial plaque honouring the men of Ontario County who were killed in the First World War, was dedicated at the Court House, with money supplied from his will. This plaque was moved to the new Court House on Rossland Road in 1964. Col. Farewell also

left a sum of $3,000 to build a general hospital in Whitby. Since 1921 the town had been struggling to raise funds to provide the community with a hospital. Since the will gave a time limit of three years for the hospital to be started, or the money would be diverted to other causes, a special sod-turning was held for the hospital in 1926 at a site in Kinsmen Park. However, no hospital was built, so the Farewell legacy was dispersed to other charities. The total value of Col. Farewell's estate was $65,000, a considerable sum in 1923. He was married twice, but had no children.

Col. Farewell purchased in 1877 the home of former County Clerk Hugh J. Macdonell (1823-1877) at the north-west corner of Byron and Ontario Streets. This house was completely remodelled in the 1970s and covered with white stucco. The yard extended back to Centre Street. For a number of years, Col. Farewell's neighbour Judge Robert Ruddy (1861-1940) urged the county to purchase the lot for a park or to relieve overcrowding at the Court House, but this was never done. In 1968-69, senior citizens' apartments were constructed on this lot.

Col. Farewell's biography was published in a number of books during his lifetime. In Henry James Morgan's *"Canadian Men and Women of the Time"*, published in 1912, he is described as *"A man of active temperament with many admirable qualities."*

Whitby And The *"National Dream"*

Whitby might have played an important part in the *"National Dream"* of the Canadian Pacific Railway, had it not been for the untimely death of one of the town's leading citizens, James Holden. On Oct. 24, 1881, James Holden (1828-1881), Managing Director of the Whitby, Port Perry and Lindsay Railway, died of pneumonia at the age of 53 in the far-off community of Dominion City, Manitoba. Holden was on a business trip to the Canadian West to secure financial support for a transcontinental railway from Whitby when he died. Four years earlier, he had obtained a railway charter that would allow him to build anywhere in Canada.

Railways were very important to the commercial development of Canada in the 19th century. As early as 1848, Peter Perry (1792-1851) had proposed the construction of a railway from Port Whitby north to Lake Simcoe and Georgian Bay on Lake Huron. In 1853 a charter was obtained to build this railway but before construction could begin, the plan was killed by a severe economic depression at the end of 1857. Whitby's growth stopped, and Perry's dream of bringing trade from New York and Boston to Georgian Bay through Whitby harbour died.

It was 10 years before another proposal was made to construct a railway north from Whitby. In 1867, interested men from

James Holden

Whitby and Port Perry met to build a smaller version of the railway planned in the 1850s. They hoped to open up the grain trade of northern Ontario County by shipping it to market through Whitby Harbour. James Holden was not involved in the initial meetings, but was brought into the project when it was in financial trouble in 1873.

The railway had been completed from Port Whitby to Port Perry in 1871, but was not paying for itself. It was officially called the Port Whitby and Port Perry Railway, but the local citizens called it the *"Nip-and-Tuck"* because it was nip-and-tuck whether the trains got to their destination and nip-and-tuck whether the line could pay its way.

Holden as Managing Director of the *"Nip-and-Tuck"* succeeded in clearing the debts, and in 1877 extended the railway from Port Perry to Lindsay, to open up the lumber trade of Victoria County. Squared timber from Victoria County was shipped to Whitby Harbour where it was then taken on sailing vessels to England to be made into ships' masts. For 10 years in the 1880s, the *"Nip-and-Tuck"* did a good business, but by 1890, all the lumber was gone and the McKinley Tariff Act in the United States stopped grain shipments from the harbour to the States. The *"Nip-and-Tuck"* ended its days taking rural children to High School in Whitby.

After Holden's death in 1881, the Whitby, Port Perry and Lindsay Railway was taken over by the Midland Railway of Canada, and in 1893 by the Grand Trunk Railway system. In 1922 it became part of the Canadian National Railway.

Although its promoters took great pride in the railway, it was something of a joke to the

A railway pass signed by James Holden, 1876

baggage car and helped themselves to cartons of bacon and eggs which they fried on the wood stove in the caboose.

The steep grade was a problem for trains going up-hill from Whitby to Brooklin and points north. The school trains would move so slowly up the grade that the students would jump off the front of the train to pick raspberries and climb back on as the last car passed them.

The major directors of the Port Whitby, Port Perry and Lindsay Railway were James Holden, James Dryden (1806-1881) of Brooklin and Joseph Bigelow (1828-1917) of Port Perry. Construction of the railway was financed by bonuses granted by the councils of Whitby and Port Perry. When the money subscribed was not enough to complete the railway extension to Lindsay, Joseph Bigelow resigned as president of the railway to lend an additional $40,000 of his own money. Another director was James Austin of Toronto, the first president of the Dominion Bank (now the Toronto-Dominion Bank). Three American locomotives purchased by the company were named the *"James Austin"*, *"James Dryden"* and *"James Holden"*. The *"James Dryden"* was destroyed in an engine house fire in Whitby in October 1875. Another official for the railway was its solicitor, William Mulock (1844-1944) of Toronto who had an office upstairs in the Whitby station which stood where Hickory Street runs south of Dundas Street. As Sir William Mulock, he served as Chief Justice of Ontario, was Postmaster General in Sir Wilfrid Laurier's Cabinet, and was responsible for starting future Prime Minister William Lyon Mackenzie King on his political career. Sir William celebrated his 100th birthday in January, 1944.

When the charter for the extension of the railway to anywhere in Canada was granted, James Holden travelled to St. Paul, Minnesota to meet with American railway magnate James J. Hill to plan a transcontinental railway from Whitby. From St. Paul he went to Winnipeg, where he contracted pneumonia and died before he

local population. It was not uncommon for a train to lose its brakes on the steep grade from Port Perry to Whitby. On one occasion, a train loaded with ships' masts lost its brakes near Brooklin and roared down the line, out of control. It nearly pitched off the end of the dock into Lake Ontario at Whitby Harbour, but was stopped just in time.

On another occasion, when an engineer was ill, James Holden Jr. (1861-1946), son of the Managing Director, was called upon to drive the train from Port Perry on a school run to Whitby. When he reached Manchester, Holden tried to push the train through a heavy snow drift and got stuck. His young students had to spend the night in the snow drift, but they did not go hungry. They broke into the

could return home. He was opposed to Government subsidizing the Canadian Pacific Railway and wanted to see a transcontinental line built with private funding.

James Holden was a man of many parts, of which railway building was only one. He was born at Markham on Feb. 29, 1828 and moved to Prince Albert (now part of Port Perry) in 1857 where he published a newspaper called the North Ontario Observer. In 1864 he moved to Whitby to become official assignee for Ontario County. His house was on Dundas Street East, opposite Florence M. Heard School. It was demolished in 1980 to be replaced by apartments.

A Liberal in politics, a Methodist in religion, Holden was a personal friend of George Brown (1818-1880), the owner of the newspaper, *"The Globe"* (now the Globe and Mail) in Toronto. Other close friends included Alexander Mackenzie, the second Prime Minister of Canada; Dr. John Potts, a leader of Canadian Methodism, and Sir William Mulock. In 1873, Holden ran as a Liberal in the federal election in the riding of South Ontario, but was defeated by his Conservative opponent Thomas N. Gibbs (1821-1883) of Oshawa. The Liberals won the election throughout most of Canada, following the disgrace of Sir John A. Macdonald's Conservatives in the Pacific

Scandal. In municipal politics, Holden was Deputy Reeve of Whitby in 1868 and Mayor in 1878.

James Holden was also one of the founders of the Dominion Bank in 1871. In the late 1860s, he enlisted the support of prominent financiers in Toronto and Ontario County to establish the new bank. The head office opened in Toronto in April, 1871, and Whitby obtained the first branch office of the bank, because Holden was the first person to raise the required amount of money to open a branch. The Whitby branch of the Dominion Bank opened in the T. H. McMillan Block at 121 Brock Street North in 1871. In 1874, a new building was constructed for the bank at Brock and Dundas Streets, with the name *"Dominion Bank, 1874"* over the third storey. It is now an optical shop.

Holden was also a founder of the Ontario Ladies' College (now Trafalgar Castle School). Working with Whitby and Toronto Methodist leaders, he helped to acquire Sheriff Nelson Gilbert Reynolds' Trafalgar Castle for the school in 1874. From its founding in 1874 until his death in 1881, Holden was president of the College's Board of Directors. With five girls in his family, he took a keen interest in the higher education of young ladies.

A member of the building committee of

the Whitby Methodist Tabernacle (now St. Mark's United Church), Holden was called upon to lay the corner stone of the church on Aug. 12, 1875. Among the special guests on this occasion was Rev. Dr. Egerton Ryerson (1803-1882) the founder of Ontario's education system. Ryerson laid the corner stone for an addition to the Ontario Ladies' College named *"Ryerson Hall"*, in 1877, and was married to a sister of the second wife of Sheriff Reynolds.

After 1890, James Holden's railway declined in use until in the 1930s, several efforts were made by the Federal Government to close it. Those who did use the *"Nip-and-Tuck"* managed to stall the closure until 1941 when it was officially shut down. The last train ran on July 3, 1941. An honoured guest who took that ride was 84-year-old John Jeffrey of Prince Albert, who was a passenger on the first train in 1871. The rails from the *"Nip-and-Tuck"* were removed north of the C.P.R. tracks in Whitby and melted down as scrap metal for the Second World War. A spur line remained between the C.P.R. and C.N.R. tracks in Whitby until this line was removed in 1978. The Whitby station was demolished at the end of 1969. Nothing remains of James Holden's part of the *"National Dream"* except some early freight bills in the Town of Whitby Archives.

Residence of James Holden 601 Dundas Street East, with Trafalgar Castle in the background, 1877

His name is generally unknown in Whitby today, but James Holden deserves to be remembered as one of the "might-have-beens" of Whitby's history. Had he lived longer, Whitby might have become the terminus of a transcontinental railway, and a large commercial centre. James Holden belongs in the same category as Peter Perry as one of the chief builders of Whitby until called by an early death.

Brooklin Has Had Four Schools In More Than 150 Years

Meadowcrest Public School in Brooklin is at least the fourth school to have served the village in more than 150 years. As far as is known, Brooklin's first school was built about 1855, a one-storey frame building which stood near the eastern portion of what is now the Community Park on the south side of Winchester Road. In the early 1870s this building was replaced by a brick school house on the north side of Winchester Road, nearly opposite the Luther Vipond Memorial Arena. The site is now a vacant lot. In 1886, the old school was purchased by William J. Murray (1849-1932) who converted it into a dwelling house.

The new school consisted of two classrooms, the downstairs room for the beginners and pupils up to the Senior Reader class and the upstairs room was for Third and Fourth Form pupils. These rooms were heated with two stoves to each room – a large coal stove at the back and a box stove for wood at the front of the classroom. During the day, the teachers and the older pupils were responsible for keeping the fires going. On the coldest winter days the pupils moved their benches up to the stoves, for the rooms would not be fully heated until about 10 or 10:30 a.m.

Old records indicate that there were 163 pupils on the roll in 1877, with an average

The second Public School, C. 1872-1923.

attendance of 93 per day. Many farmers' sons would be absent from school because chores had to be done at home. The first teachers in the new school were Mr. Dobbin, at a salary of $525 per year and

Mr. Edwards at $350. Salaries were paid to teachers quarterly.

Two new classrooms were added to the brick school in 1880. The contracts were let by the Whitby Township School Board to William Pearson (1833-1897) of Ashburn, for $1,070 for the brick work, Maxwell Hamilton for $1,327 for the carpenter work and glazing as well as painting and McPherson and Campbell for tinsmithing.

By 1886 the staff had increased to three teachers, the principal receiving $575 a year and the junior teachers, $187.50. The principal in the 1880s was John Spence (1857-1918) who moved to Toronto about 1890, where he was principal of several city schools.

The brick school had a tall, rather heavy tower which was struck by lightning in 1896 and was replaced with a smaller dainty tower, where the school bell was hung. As the building aged, it eventually became unsafe for use as a school. In February 1923 the trustees discovered that the ceiling had dropped four inches and the roof was sagging. The building was abandoned immediately and pupils took their classes in the Masonic Hall across from the Methodist (now United) Church and the Township Hall (now the Brooklin Community Centre). The pupils who studied in the Masonic Hall had their group pictures taken in 1923 on the front steps of the United Church. The students who studied in the Township Hall had to miss some school time until a furnace could be installed in that building.

A building committee of Dr. John Moore (1862-1937), John Vipond (1849-1926) and Job White (1855-1936) was appointed to act with the township school board consisting of Ernest Patterson (1879-1935), William Ormiston (1882-1943) and William Croxall (1875-1950) to build a new school immediately. Several sites were visited in other communities to try to find the most modern and economical design for the new building. Mr. Hornsby of Lindsay was selected as the architect and T. G. Morrow who had built a school on the same plan at Woodville, was selected as the contractor. The school board purchased three

The Public and Continuation School, 1923-1982.

acres of land from Luther Stainton (1880-1963) at the south-east corner of Highway 12 and Winchester Road where construction began. The cost of the new building, which was a public and Continuation school for some High School grades, was $35,000. Equipment for the new school cost $3,700. Pupils moved into the

Public and Continuation School in December 1923. It was officially opened on Jan. 20, 1924 by George McMillan, Reeve of Reach Township, Warden of Ontario County for 1924. By this time, the old brick school had been demolished.

The first teacher at the Continuation School was Miss C. B. Ross, who was principal until 1929. Mr. Burton was principal of the public school section, with Elsie West and Miss Stillman as assistants. One of the first teachers was Stan Ireland (1908-1996) who later taught at Henry Street High School.

A unique feature of the old Public and Continuation School was a long metal pipe leading from the second floor to the ground at the back of the school which served as a fire escape. The Brooklin Public and Continuation School closed in 1970 and was demolished in 1982.

By the 1970s, public school students were attending the Meadowcrest Public School, opened by the Hon. Matthew B. Dymond, M.P.P. (1906-1996), on Nov.28, 1958. High School students were sent by bus to Henry Street High School and Anderson Collegiate.

Room 3, Brooklin Continuation School, October 26, 1926.
Back Row: *Edith Holliday, Margaret Akey, Jean Weller, Mary Luke, Doris Moore, Hazel Nesbitt, Fenimore Cooper, Gordon Hunter, Ken Fraser (teacher), Charlie Brignall, Everett Tink, Ken Holliday.*
Centre Row: *Elsie Dyer, Mildred Webber, Stella Watson, Margaret White.*
Front Row: *Mary Harris, Mary Hunter, Ethel Brooking, Bernice Eddy*

This Building Served Two Church Congregations and a Municipality

Brooklin's Community Centre, built in 1876, has seen many uses. Located at the corner of Church Street and Cassels Road, it was originally constructed as a Bible Christian Church. Church Street is aptly named, for there were once three churches on that street. The first was the Methodist Episcopal Church, a large frame building known as the "*white Church.*" It was built in 1847 at the corner of Church and Albert Streets. After it was closed in 1884, the building was moved to the corner of Baldwin and Roebuck Streets where it was used as a store and a bank until demolished in 1929 and replaced by the building now housing the Brooklin Antiquarian.

The second church was a Presbyterian edifice, built of wood, with a large steeple, located on the east side of Church Street where Mitchell Brothers Building Supplies is now. It was demolished in 1926 after the Presbyterians joined the Wesleyan Methodists to become Brooklin United Church.

The Bible Christians were a sect of the Methodist Church which chose their preachers more for their eloquence than learning, according to a local historian. It was said that many Bible Christian ministers were unable to read or write, but what they lacked in education, they made up in speaking ability. Since the 1850s there had

been a small society of Bible Christians meeting in Campbell's school house, two miles west of Brooklin, where the Spencer Community Centre is now.

By 1875, it was felt that efforts should be made to establish a larger congregation, so on July 11 of that year the Bible Christians rented the old Masonic Hall in Brooklin, a frame building replaced by the present Masonic Hall in 1951. The Masonic Hall, which could seat 300 to 400 people, was a frame structure built in 1871. Rev. E. Roberts of Lindsay preached the first sermon, to a crowd of about 400 Brooklin residents. The following day, James B. Bickell (1826-1891), one of the leading citizens of Brooklin, chaired a public meeting, at which he congratulated the Bible Christians on coming into the village. He said he had a special interest in this denomination, for his mother was a member and his brother, a preacher for the church. Bickell led the hymn singing and invited Rev. Roberts to give an account of his recent trip to England.

By December 1875, the Brooklin Bible Christians had established a society of 24 members and a congregation of about 100. An organ was purchased from Oshawa, and when a Mrs. Kenner of that town, preached in Masonic Hall on Dec. 12, nearly 500 people attended. The crowd was so large

that not everyone could get into the hall, so the doors were left open so those standing on the sidewalk could hear Mrs. Kenner's sermon.

Tea meetings were popular with the Bible Christians, with the ladies of the church supplying food free of charge. Tickets of admission at 25 cents each were sold to obtain money for a building fund. Construction of a permanent church building began in December, 1875, with the mason work done by Messrs Gale and Dinnes of Oshawa and the woodwork and painting by Messrs Stephenson and Kirby, also of Oshawa. The building was 35 by 50 feet, with basement, according to plans prepared by J.P. Rice of Bowmanville. The "*Observer,*" the Bible Christian newspaper published in Bowmanville, printed the following description of the Brooklin Church at the time of its dedication on December 17 and 18, 1876:

"The building is a handsome brick structure 50 x 35 with a full stone basement and a classroom partitioned off one end. The audience room is neatly furnished, the walls being blocked and the ceiling having four ornamental centrepieces. In the front gable there is a neat inscription stone, containing the name and the date of the erection of the church. In the rear of the church the friends have erected a shed 80 feet long, and the whole is enclosed

Brooklin Community Centre, as it appeared in 1909 when it was a Baptist Church.

with a neat picket fence."

The dedication days were bitterly cold, but the church was crowded, so much that one member of the congregation preached an overflow service at the same time as the dedication service, in the Methodist Episcopal Church, only a block away.

A highlight of the dedication was the presentation of a Bible and hymn book by 85-year-old Harriet Cook of East Whitby Township. In presenting the hymn book, she commented that *"when you are singing*

Brooklin Community Centre, 1975.

Christians in Eldad and Hampton in Darlington Township, the centre of the Bible Christian movement in this part of Ontario. The Bible Christian faith began at Shebbear, Devonshire, England in 1815 and started in Ontario in 1833 at Cobourg.

In 1884, the Bible Christians joined with the Methodist Episcopal Church and the Wesleyan Methodists. All three congregations then used only the Wesleyan Methodist Church (now Brooklin United Church). The Bible Christian Church was immediately taken over by the Baptists, who moved from a small church on the 7th concession (Columbus Road) east of Thickson Road, where the Dryden Baptist Cemetery is located. In 1888, the Baptists removed the old wood stoves from the church, replacing them with a furnace. In 1916, the Baptist congregation disbanded, and did not reorganize until the 1960s when the Meadowcrest Baptist Church was founded.

After four years of neglect, the old church was taken over in 1920 by the Township of Whitby for use as a Township Hall. The Township Council moved from the old Balfour building, north of the present Legion Hall. In 1932, the Township spent $700 to place a concrete floor in the basement and construct a porch around the front entrance, with assistance from the Brooklin Women's Institute. The Women's Institute and the township library were provided with quarters in the new hall.

After 46 years of use as a Township Hall, the old building was replaced by a modern township hall, directly behind it on Church Street in 1966. The following year, the old Bible Christian Church was converted into a community centre. Operated by the Town of Whitby, the Brooklin Community Centre has seen many improvements in recent years, the latest being the installation of an elevator, with the assistance of the Brooklin and District Lions Club, in 1996.

the praises of God on earth, I hope to be singing the praises of God in Heaven."

Although there was a heavy snow storm on the second day of the dedication, a large crowd turned out to a public meeting at which the financial statements for the construction of the church were read and an appeal made to pay off the debt. The total cost of the church, including lot, shed, fence and furnishings, was $2,907.42. By the time the day was over, money to cover the debt was fully subscribed, with a surplus of $10.99. The church received substantial contributions not only from Brooklin residents, but from Bible

Honest John Dryden – The Farmer's Friend

The first Ontario Cabinet Minister to live in Whitby was John Dryden (1840-1909) who served as the province's Minister of Agriculture from 1890 to 1905. Much of Ontario's agricultural legislation in the late 19th century was prepared by him. He was so well regarded that he was known as *"Honest John Dryden, the Farmer's Friend."* When he died at the age of 69, the 1909, his funeral at the Baptist cemetery near Brooklin was attended by Ontario Premier Sir James Whitney, former Premier George W. Ross, Attorney-General J.J. Foy and G.C. Creeland, president of the Ontario Agricultural College at Guelph. In 1995, a new public school in Whitby was named in his memory as the John Dryden Public School.

The entire Dryden family made significant contributions to Whitby and Ontario for four generations. John Dryden's son, William A. Dryden, founded the Royal Agricultural Winter Fair in Toronto, and three generations of Drydens were Reeves of Whitby Township prior to amalgamation with the Town of Whitby in 1968.

The Drydens of Whitby began with James Dryden (1806-1881) who was born at Sunderland, Durham County, England, on Feb. 22, 1806. An only child, his father's name is not known and his mother's name was Elizabeth Liddle. When James was an infant, his parents moved to Wolsingham, in Durham County, where his father was killed in September 1806 when thrown from a horse. James and his mother emigrated to Canada in 1820 and settled in Whitby Township. Mrs. Dryden subsequently married William Paxton (1791-1877) and had a family of six children.

About 1827, when he had reached the age of 21, James Dryden settled on 40 acres on Rossland Road, west of Highway 12. He was married in 1830 to Abiel Groat, who died giving birth to a daughter, Mary Ann, a year later. Mary Ann Dryden married Whitby merchant Joel Bigelow who moved to Chicago where he made a fortune in real estate. In 1832, James Dryden moved to the north-east corner of Thickson and Columbus Roads where he established *"Maple Shade Farm"* which remained in the Dryden family for 133 years. He had to walk from Whitby to Kingston to make the first payment on this farm.

James Dryden was an early Justice of the Peace and Magistrate in Whitby Township, and eventually held nearly all the municipal offices in the township. He was Deputy Reeve in 1852 when the Provisional County of Ontario was formed, councillor in 1854 and Reeve in 1856-58 with a seat on the Ontario County Council. He was a director of the Ontario Bank, which had its head office in Bowmanville, and also a director of the Port Whitby, Lake Scugog and Huron Road Company in the early 1850s. He was president of the Port Whitby and Port Perry Railway in 1870-71 and had one of its locomotives named after him. The *"James Dryden"* was destroyed by a fire in the engine house in 1875.

A busy man, Dryden was constantly attending meetings of the organizations to which he belonged. In his diary of Jan. 7, 1861, he recorded: *"To Brooklin Town Meeting. Made a perfect ass of myself by being too excited."*

In 1835, James Dryden married Elizabeth Marsh, daughter of Rev. Israel Marsh, a pioneer Baptist minister in Whitby Township and granddaughter of Rev. William Marsh. Rev. William Marsh established a Baptist Church and cemetery on the south side of Columbus Road near Maple Shade Farm in the 1840s. Four generations of Drydens were trustees for this cemetery, and many of the family are buried there. It is said that the brick house at Maple Shade Farm was constructed as a wedding present from James Dryden to his new wife, who provided James with five children. Elizabeth Dryden died in 1852, and James married for a third time to Mary Stephenson.

James Dryden died at Maple Shade Farm on July 31, 1881 at the age of 75. Many

Four Generations of Drydens

James Dryden
(1806-1881)

John Dryden
(1840-1909)

William Arthur Dryden
(1881-1949)

John Dryden
(Born 1913)

County officials and Members of Parliament attended his funeral to the Baptist Cemetery.

John Dryden, James's eldest son, was born at Maple Shade Farm on June 5, 1840. He left school at the age of 19 to work for shares on his father's farm. At the age of 21 he was renting Maple Shade Farm and over the years increased its size to 400 acres by purchasing neighbouring farms. Maple Shade Farm under John Dryden developed a national and international reputation when he was Minister of Agriculture. Among the many visitors to Maple Shade Farm was the Premier of Manitoba.

John Dryden entered politics at the age of 24 in 1864 when he served as a Whitby Township Councillor. He subsequently served as Deputy Reeve and Reeve, with a seat on the County Council, as his father had before him. He also served as a trustee for the Dryden Public School, located west of the farm.

In 1879, John Dryden was elected as the Liberal Member of the Ontario Legislature for South Ontario Riding, with a majority of more than 400 votes over his Conservative opponent. He served as local MPP for 26 years, until he was defeated by his neighbour, Charles Calder (1852-1920), a Conservative, in 1905.

Besides being a Member of the Legislature, John Dryden was president of a loan and savings company, a director and shareholder in the Port Whitby and Port Perry Railway and a prominent figure in the

Baptist Church. Since his mother and grandfather were Baptists, John became deeply involved in church work. A Bible Class teacher in the Brooklin Baptist Church for 40 years, he re-established the Whitby Baptist congregation in 1876, and arranged for the purchase of a former Presbyterian Church building at Colborne and Centre Streets. This baptist congregation moved to Gilbert Street East in 1967 and is still active today. John Dryden was president of the Baptist Union of Canada, a director of the Home Missionary Society of Ontario and one of the original members of the Board of Governors of McMaster University in Hamilton.

John Dryden gained fame as one of the most outstanding agriculturalists in Canada. He was a member for many years of the South Ontario Agricultural Society which held a fall fair at Whitby. He was president of the Dominion Shorthorn Breeders Association, director of the American Clydesdale Association, and director of the American Shropshire Sheep Association. He later became president of the International Shropshire Sheep Association of the United States and Canada, the largest stock association in the world.

Maple Shade Farm gained an international reputation as one of the cleanest and best kept farms in Canada. John Dryden was recognized as a world-class breeder and importer of Shorthorn cattle, Clydesdale horses and Shropshire sheep. He travelled extensively in Canada, the United States and Britain, addressing meetings of farmers wherever he went. He possessed one of the finest herds of Cruickshank Shorthorn cattle in North America, importing many cattle from the internationally known breeder Amos Cruickshank of Aberdeen, Scotland. One of his Cruickshank bulls won 17 prizes and was never beaten in the show ring in Canada. In 1892, the Dryden herd numbered 70 head of Shorthorns. In 1908, a special train brought 500 stock breeders from Canada and the United States to a Shorthorn sale at Maple Shade Farm. Three hundred and fifty people sat around a show ring in a massive tent set up beside John Dryden's home. Twenty-one animals were purchased by Americans, and the sale raised nearly $10,000.

It was as Ontario's Minister of Agriculture from 1890 to 1905 that John Dryden gained lasting fame. He was the second person to hold that office in the Provincial Government, succeeding Charles Drury who was appointed in 1888. John Dryden organized Farmers' Clubs before the Farmers' institutes were established, and assisted in the founding of the Women's Institute, the first having been founded at Stoney Creek by Adelaide Hunter Hoodless. In 1896, John Dryden established an experimental farm in Northern Ontario. The town of Dryden, associated with that farm, was named after him. He enlarged the Ontario Agricultural College, established in 1874, and opened dairy schools at Guelph, Strathroy and Kingston. He also established 12 experimental fruit farming stations throughout the province.

In 1896, John Dryden was appointed to a commission to revise the Ontario Statutes, and was selected by the British Government to serve on a Royal Commission to investigate agricultural conditions in Ireland. He was the first colonial to serve on such a commission.

John Dryden moved from Maple Shade Farm to Toronto in 1903 because of the pressure of his legislative duties, but was out of office two years later. He remained in Toronto, where he died on July 29, 1909 at the age of 69. He had eight children, three of his daughters being married to Baptist ministers, one to a noted Toronto doctor and one to a professor at the Ontario Agricultural College. Two of his sons died as infants, as a result of catching cold while being bathed in front of a draft of air from the fireplace at Maple Shade Farm. After these tragic deaths, John Dryden bricked up the fireplace. It was not opened again until the house was remodelled for his only surviving son, William A. Dryden, in 1926.

William Arthur Dryden (1881-1949) was John Dryden's youngest son, born at Maple Shade Farm on May 29, 1881. He attended Woodstock Baptist College and the Ontario Agricultural College, taking over Maple Shade farm in 1903 when his father moved to Toronto. Considered to be one of the leading Shorthorn cattle breeders in Canada, he wrote a number of articles on these animals for agricultural publications. In 1924, he purchased 400 acres of land in Cartwright Township for a sheep ranch, and also bred silver foxes for the fur trade.

William A. Dryden was named a member of the Ontario Advisory Committee on Industrial Research in 1929 and in 1943 was appointed as livestock representative to the Ontario Agricultural Commission of Enquiry. As chairman of the livestock committee he helped plan future government policy. He judged sheep and cattle at shows in Canada and the United States and was a senior director of the Canadian National Exhibition in Toronto. He also was chairman of the Canadian National Livestock Records, President of the Dominion Shorthorn Breeders Association and president of the Dominion Sheep Breeders Association.

His most outstanding achievement, how-

Maple Shade Farm, circa 1900.

ever, was the founding of the Royal Agricultural Winter Fair, in 1922. The idea for what is now the world's largest indoor fair, originated with William A. Dryden in 1919. He served as the fair's first president from 1919 to 1923 and was a director for the rest of his life. In 1936, he was the unanimous choice of the directors for the position of General Manager. He served in this position until ill health forced him into retirement in 1949. On the local level, he was president of the Brooklin Spring Fair in

1921-22.

William A. Dryden died at Maple Shade Farm, on Nov. 18, 1949, at the age of 68.

John Dryden, a son of William A. Dryden, who still lives in Whitby, was the fourth generation of this illustrious family to serve his community. In 1925, at the age of 11, he won a gold medal as champion public speaker in Ontario County. At the age of 15, in 1929, he won third place in Ontario for public speaking. His subject was *"Canada Among the Nations."*

In 1937, John Dryden took over his father's farm after graduating from the Ontario Agricultural College. One of the founders of the Brooklin Junior Farmers, he was president for 20 years. He continued the family tradition of raising Shorthorn cattle until he changed to general cattle and poultry in 1948. He had 5,000 hens laying eggs for a Port Perry egg distributor. Like his father, John Dryden was a president of the Brooklin Spring Fair, and was a director of the Oshawa Fair.

He also carried on the family tradition of politics, serving as a member of the Whitby District High School Board from its founding in 1949, until 1960, and was a member of the building committee for Meadowcrest School in Brooklin. John Dryden also served on the Whitby Township Council as Deputy Reeve and Reeve and was involved in the township's negotiations for amalgamation with the Town of Whitby in 1968. After amalgamation he served on the Whitby Planning Board. He retired from farming and sold Maple Shade Farm in 1965. John Dryden was awarded the Ontario Bicentennial Medal in 1984, and Dryden Boulevard was named after him in 1987.

Another noted member of the Dryden family was George Dryden (1844-1931), a younger brother of the Minister of Agriculture, who served as Ontario County Registrar of Deeds from 1897 until his death at the age of 87 on April 9, 1931.

Few families in Whitby can claim to have been as active in community service as the Drydens, or have been members of the Whitby community for nearly 180 years. The farm house at Maple Shade Farm, to which a second floor was added in 1926, was designated as a historic building under the Ontario Heritage Act in 1997.

The Drydens are among the first settlers to come to Whitby Township directly from Britain, in 1820. Prior to that time, almost all the settlers in the township were from the United States. It was not, however until about 1830 that the mass British migration into Whitby began. In continued until the end of the 1860s.

Maple Shade Farm in winter, after the second storey was added to the brick farm house in 1926.

James B. Bickell Was "The Old War Horse" Of Whitby Politics

One of Whitby Township's most colourful politicians was James B. Bickell (1826-1881), known throughout the township as *"The Old War Horse."* He served as Reeve of Whitby Township for a record 14 years in the 1860s and 1870s and operated a flour mill on Way Street. His influence in Brooklin was considerable, as was his support of the Conservative party and Sir John A. Macdonald.

James B. Bickell was born at Stowford, Devonshire, England, on Dec. 7, 1826, and came to Canada in 1843 at the age of 17. His family settled in the vicinity of Peterborough and farmed in Mariposa Township. After a few years, Bickell moved to Bowmanville where he entered the milling business. When Queen Victoria's husband, Prince Albert, inaugurated the Great Exhibition in London, England in 1851, Bickell sent a sample of his flour to the exhibition and won first prize over exhibits from several other nations.

In 1859 he moved to Brooklin and built the Whitby Mills on the stream which ran through the village near Way Street. This waterway became known as Bickell's Creek. A four storey frame building, Bickell's mill had the words *"Whitby Mills, J.B. Bickell, Cash for Wheat,"* painted on the north wall.

As well as business, politics took up much of Bickell's time. He served as a Whitby

James B. Bickell

Township Councillor in 1862, 1865-66 and was Reeve of the township in 1863-64, 1867-68 and 1872-1881. A member of the Ontario County Council, the forerunner of Durham Region Council, he was chosen by his fellow councillors as warden (chairman) of Ontario County in 1868.

A Mason, Bickell was Master of Mount Zion Lodge in Brooklin in 1867-68. He was also an officer of the Grand Lodge of Canada, a member of the Sons of England, and of several other societies.

But like so many other 19th century entrepreneurs in Whitby, his success was not to last. On March 18, 1881, the Bickell mill was destroyed by fire, the cause being determined as an overheated shaft. Nearly 1,000 bushels of wheat and a large quantity of flour were destroyed. The loss of the building and machinery was estimated at $12,000. Bickell was on a business trip to Delaware at the time of the fire, so there was little he could do about this catastrophe. It was said that the flames could be seen as far away as downtown Whitby. With his business ruined, Bickell decided to leave Brooklin and move to Toronto. By coincidence, another leading Brooklin merchant, Samuel R. Wickett (1844-1932) had lost his business, a tannery, in the spring of 1881, so the two men decided to open a tannery in Toronto under the name of Bickell and Wickett. There were rumors at the time that an arsonist was on the loose in Brooklin, for several other fires occurred in the village, but nothing was proven. The result was that Brooklin lost two of its leading industries. On his removal to Toronto in 1882, Bickell was given a testimonial

James B. Bickell's mill, as pictured in the Ontario County Atlas of 1877.

Way Street and his portrait is among those of the past Wardens of Ontario County in the Durham Region Court House.

By coincidence there was another miller near Brooklin of almost the same name. He was Henry Bickle (1829-1913) who spelled his name slightly differently. Another Devonshire man, he was born at Milton Abbot, and kept the Centre Mills about two miles east of Brooklin on Winchester Road. The Centre Mills were also a victim of fire, in 1886.

Advertisement for James Bickell's rival, W. B. Robson of the brick mill, Brooklin, 1881, the year Bickell's mill burned down.

dinner by the citizens of Brooklin.

James B. Bickell was married twice. His first wife, Mary Jane Davey of Cobourg died in 1863, and a year later he married her sister, Johanna Davey. From his first marriage, Bickell had twins who died at birth. His second family consisted of four sons and four daughters. His youngest daughter, Muriel Bickell (1881-1945) was a graduate of the first occupational therapy class at the University of Toronto and was secretary for 20 years of the Canadian Women's Club. Another daughter, Mrs. John Turnbull (1878-1957) was superintendent of a military hospital in France during the First World War. She received several military medals and a life membership in the Canadian Red Cross for her overseas service.

James B. Bickell's house still stands on

Legion Saved Fine Brooklin Landmark

One of Brooklin's most significant landmarks, the old Brooklin House Hotel, was saved for posterity by Brooklin Branch 152 of the Royal Canadian Legion. Built in 1882/83, it served as a hotel for more than 80 years, and was purchased for use as a Legion Hall on May 15, 1967.

In August of 1882, the site of the hotel was purchased by Benjamin McQuay (?-1928), a member of an old Pickering Township family, who hired Whitby builder William Westlake (1847-1916) to construct for him a brick building two stories high, with a belvedere on the roof. The hotel was completed in June of 1883, but not without problems for both McQuay and Westlake. The land title reveals that Westlake issued a mechanic's lien against McQuay when he was not paid for his work. The issue ended up going to court, with Westlake receiving a cash settlement from McQuay. The amount of payment is not recorded. Once the court case was settled, McQuay leased his new hotel to George H. Henderson.

An advertisement in The Brooklin Times for the new hotel read: *"The McQuay House, Baldwin Street, Brooklin, G.H. Henderson Proprietor. The house has been built by the proprietor with a view to supplying the best accommodations for the travelling public. Every attention will be paid to ensure the comfort of guests. A well stocked larder, best wines, liquors and*

The McQuay House hotel, Brooklin, as it looked in 1892.

cigars. Good stables, large yard room and an attentive hostler." The hostler was the man who took care of guests' horses at the hotel.

In August 1884, the McQuay House was taken over by Thomas Chinn (1836-1887) whose Globe Hotel, where Grass Park is today, was the oldest hotel in the village. On

Feb. 11, 1885, the Globe Hotel burned down, ending a colourful era in Brooklin's history.

When Thomas Chinn died, his son, George Washington Chinn (1860-1892) took over the hotel. He was succeeded by Oliver Sebert (1855-1931) who operated it until 1910. One of Oliver Sebert's sons was Louis Joseph Sebert (1886-1942) who was a track star at the Whitby Collegiate Institute and represented Canada at the 1908 Summer Olympics at London, England.

Sebert sold the Brooklin hotel when the residents of Whitby Township voted under Local Option to prohibit the sale of liquor in hotels. His successor, Norman W. Colwill (1876-1963) renamed it the *"Temperance House"*. Several structural changes were made to the hotel over the years. Some time before 1907 the belvedere or observatory on the roof was removed. In 1915 a long verandah was placed along the front of the hotel, remaining until the 1960s. In 1925 the Temperance House was sold to John W. Graham (?-1948) who formerly kept a hotel at Markham. An expert horse judge at fairs, Graham was a director of the Oshawa Fair for many years and was later an honorary director. When he retired in 1946 he sold the hotel to William J. Goodwin (1901-1964), the last proprietor. Goodwin, a former police officer from Belfast, Northern Ireland, made the Brooklin House famous for its chicken dinners. He met a tragic death in a car accident at Rossland and Thickson Roads on Oct. 7, 1964, before there were any traffic lights at that intersection. Goodwin's son John Goodwin was a member of the Whitby Town Council for many years and served as Reeve of both Whitby Town and Township.

The old hotel as a Royal Canadian Legion Hall, 1970.

With the hotel empty after Goodwin's death, the new Brooklin Legion Branch No. 152 under Fred Phillips a Brooklin barber, purchased the building for a legion hall in 1967. Using volunteer labour, work began in 1968 to convert the hotel into a Legion Hall, starting with the first floor. On June 6, 1970, the 26th anniversary of D-Day, Donald Wilson, Dominion Legion First Vice-President, cut a ribbon to officially open the new hall. When General Motors workers went on strike in the fall of 1970, those who were members of the Legion set to work to renovate the second floor of the old hotel. About the same time the mortgage on the hall was burned, setting a record for the youngest Legion branch in Canada to discharge its mortgage in the short span of three years.

Brooklin Legion Branch 152 was not really as young as it appeared, having been organized in 1966. It actually dates back to 1929. But that is another *"Chronicle"*.

Myrtle Station Was Created By A Railway

The community of Myrtle Station, on Highway 12 at the northern limits of Whitby, owes its existence to the Ontario and Quebec Railway, which was built through Whitby Township in 1883/84. The tracks crossed Highway 12 about a half-mile north of the old village of Myrtle, so a new community was formed around the railway station and freight yards. The two communities became known as North Myrtle and South Myrtle, or Myrtle Station and Myrtle. Myrtle Station originally consisted of a hotel, general store, grain elevator and several residences, as well as a railway station. A post office was opened on March 1, 1896, with store keeper William G. Armour as post master. It closed on March 31, 1970.

In the early months of 1884, Italian railway workers started preparing the grade for the Ontario and Quebec Railway tracks, which were to run from Toronto to Montreal. These tracks formed a junction with the Whitby, Port Perry and Lindsay Railway, a short distance west of Highway 12. While the work was being carried out, the railway men boarded in local farm houses. One traveller commented that he could not find a place to stay for the night in Myrtle because the homes were all full of railway men. This traveller was Ross Johnston (1827-1911), salesman for the

Myrtle Station, looking east from Highway 12, 1906.

Whitby Chronicle. In The Chronicle of Feb. 29, 1884, Johnston wrote:

"Well, here I am at the road-bed on the site of the new station. The building material is mainly on the ground, lying about in piles here and there, as is also the material for the immense tank, the water for which is being brought in underground pipes from Mud Lake, a half mile or more north. I am told the water has a fall of 66 feet in that distance. Malcolm McTaggart, Esq. has the contract for cutting the water way and laying the pipes and a big job it is. It was nearly completed by the time of my visit.

The Myrtle Station grain elevator, destroyed by fire in 1968.

"Leaving the site of the station, I proceeded westward along the road-bed, the cutting of which commences just about the intersection of the road-bed with the gravel road (Highway 12) a little west of the station. Unless due precautions are taken, this point will be one of great danger to passing teams. The natural outlook of a coming train is so limited and difficulty of getting out of the way so great that without safeguards of a very reliable kind, accidents will be almost inevitable.

"Going westward, the cut increases in depth until the intersection with the Midland Railway (Whitby, Port Perry and Lindsay) is reached at which point the depth is said to be 26 feet. Beyond the intersection the depth rapidly lessens and as you go westward, the cutting seems turned upside down and becomes an embankment running through a deep and long ravine.

"The work seems immense when closely examined. The tough blue clay looks almost as difficult to manage with a pick and shovel as if it were so much gutta-percha (rubber). A huge pile of this material immediately below the rails of the Midland was still awaiting removal at the time of my visit but a sufficient space on each side was cut through to allow of building the bridge, the foundation of which was in course of erection and is composed of immense blocks of blue stone brought out on the Midland from Bobcaygeon.

"Quite a number of Italians were engaged on the works, and seemed to be doing their part very efficiently, notwithstanding the severity of the weather and the unpleasant nature of the work. The large blocks of stone were being raised to the proper height by the aid of a derrick worked by a rat-tailed scraggy-looking old rack of bones of a horse that

Myrtle Station looking west from the grain elevator, Circa 1887.

might have been taken for the ghost of Rosinante, the famous steed of Don Quixote, on the back of which he made the noted attack on the windmills."

The first storekeeper at Myrtle Station was William Ledingham (1834-1901), who built a grain storehouse on the north side of the tracks opposite the station, in addition to his store. Both buildings were constructed in 1887 to take advantage of the lucrative grain market in Ontario County. Ledingham was killed by a train at Myrtle

Station in 1901, and was not the last resident of this community to meet that fate. Frank C. Harrison (1898-1947) was also killed by a train, while trying to clear ice from the tracks.

At this time, Myrtle Station was becoming an important trading centre as a cattle and grain market. In 1887, efforts were made to bring telephone service to the community. Cattle pens were built on the north side of the track and a livery stable was built on the south side.

In 1887, McKay brothers of Toronto built a tall grain elevator beside Ledingham's storehouse, and a home for Mr. Mosier, the manager of the elevator. This grain elevator was purchased in 1890 by Cephas Goode, whose family operated it until it was destroyed by fire on Jan. 25, 1968.

Fire was a frequent occurrence at Myrtle Station. The first store burned down and James E. Beacock's (1861-1943) store burned down twice, in 1909 and 1933. Beacock was postmaster at Myrtle Station from 1906 until forced into retirement by the Federal Government in 1936 at the age of 65. His wife was a sister of Sir Sam Hughes, Canada's Minister of Militia in the First World War. Fire also destroyed the Myrtle Station hotel, on Mar. 29, 1919.

A noted resident of Myrtle Station was John Bright (1865-1917) who served as Dominion Livestock Commissioner at Ottawa from 1912 to 1917. He lived in the brick house behind the store called The Whistle Stop. Bright was Reeve of Whitby Township from 1902 to 1907 and Warden of Ontario County in 1907. The County Warden was similar to today's Regional Chairman.

Myrtle Station was at its peak in the 1890s, when as many as 26 trains, passenger and freight, passed through in 24 hours. The Ontario and Quebec Railway had been taken over by the Canadian Pacific. When the C.P.R. opened its southern line through the Town of Whitby, in 1914, the stage coach service between Whitby and Myrtle Station was withdrawn and the number of trains decreased by half. The coming of the automobile and truck in the 1920s further reduced the railway activity at Myrtle Station. During the Great Depression of the 1930s, the station agent and telegraph operator were removed from Myrtle Station, but in 1946, an agent was reinstated because of an increase in business. The last agent was taken from Myrtle Station in 1968, when the old railway centre was designated as a flag stop. In 1927, the livery stable was demolished and the wood used to build hen houses. The site of the cattle sheds and pens was made into a playground in 1948. The station, empty for seven years, was demolished about 1975.

In the 1970s and 1980s, Myrtle Station again received a new lease on life, with the establishment of a commuter train from Havelock to Toronto, used by about 200 travellers. Myrtle Station was one of its stops. The Federal Liberal Government cancelled the commuter train in 1981, but it was reinstated in 1985. By the time of the 1991 recession, the train was again discontinued and Myrtle Station ceased to be a Toronto commuter stop.

The railway crossing at Myrtle Station had a reputation for having one of the worst bumps on Highway 12. It was featured in an article in the Toronto Globe and Mail in 1957 and was the scene of a number of accidents. It was common for speeding gravel trucks to go off the road at the crossing. On one occasion a farmer's truck loaded with pigs, hit the bump at the tracks and sent pigs flying in all directions. The ladies of Myrtle Station were called into service to round them up. On another occasion, the ladies of Myrtle Station were called out in the middle of the night in their night clothes to extinguish a fire on the tracks, started by a spark from one of the coal-burning locomotives.

How About This For Family Connections?

Writing and journalism are in the family of James Cuttell (1833-1908) who published a newspaper called the Brooklin Times from 1880 to 1889. James Cuttell was born in Leeds, Yorkshire, England, and came to Canada at the age of 14. His mother, Charlotte Lockwood, had a sister Maryia, who married Rev. John Kipling in England. Their grandson was the famous British writer Rudyard Kipling. In 1865, James Cuttell was a grocer in Orono, where his brother John published a newspaper. About 1867, James moved to Brooklin and went into the printing trade. According to the numbers on surviving copies of the Brooklin Times, he published his first edition of that paper on Dec. 14, 1880, and the last edition on May 14, 1889, before moving to Toronto. One of the reasons for leaving Brooklin was a severe fire on Dec. 16, 1888 which destroyed his office on Baldwin Street where the Bank of Commerce now stands. He tried to continue publishing his paper for a few months, but the financial loss was too great. Only five copies of the Brooklin Times have survived to this day; the others were undoubtedly destroyed in the fire.

Another newspaperman, Philip Thompson, married Louise Cuttell, a granddaughter of James. His sister was

The family of James Cuttell, publisher of the Brooklin Times, Circa 1900. Back Row: Thomas James Cuttell, William Lockwood Cuttell, Samuel James Cuttell. Front Row: James Cuttell, Jessie Esther Cuttell, Mrs. James Cuttell.

Laura Beatrice Berton, mother of Canada's most famous popular historian, Pierre Berton. But the journalistic connection with famous names does not stop there. A great-great-grandchild of James Cuttell is Kathie Lee Gifford, the noted American talk show host. Her mother, Joan Epstein, visited Whitby and Brooklin a few years ago to look into the family history.

James Cuttell lived in Toronto from 1889 until his death on Jan. 26, 1908. He is buried in Mount Pleasant Cemetery in that city. Accompanying this Chronicle is a portrait of James Cuttell and his family, taken about 1900. Few Whitby families are likely able to claim connections to so many famous literary personalities from the mid 19th century to the present day.

Kathie Lee Gifford, photo taken by her mother Joan Epstein.

THE BROOKLIN TIMES
IS PUBLISHED EVERY
TUESDAY MORNING,
—— BY ——
JAMES CUTTELL,
At his Printing Establishment,
BALDWIN STREET, BROOKLIN,
TERMS 25 CTS. PER ANNUM.
Special contracts made with Advertisers by the year or otherwise.

The Brooklin Times.

TUESDAY, MAY 10th, 1881.

James Cuttell's advertisement for The Brooklin Times, May 10, 1881.

Telephones Have Served Whitby For 120 Years

On March 9, 1938, Whitby's Mayor Fred Rowe (1873-1959) made an historic telephone call to Reeve Albert W. Jackson (1870-1939). Seated at a desk in the new telephone exchange building on Brock Street South (now the Tap and Tankard pub), the mayor placed the first dial phone call in Whitby. The two officials discussed the history of the telephone in Whitby and congratulated each other on bringing this new advancement in technology to the town.

In 1938, Whitby had 600 telephones. Up to that time, all phone calls had to be made through the operator at the central switchboard. Dial calling meant that there was no delay in getting through to the person on the other end of the line.

When the first dial phone call was made, Whitby had been served by telephones for 59 years. The first six telephones in Whitby were installed by the Dominion Telegraph Company in October, 1879, a year before Bell Canada was established and three years after Alexander Graham Bell patented the invention. The six party line subscribers were: Farewell and Rutledge (law office), G.Y. Smith (law office), Judge George H. Dartnell (residence), Lyman T. Barclay (residence and office in the Court House) and Edmund Stephenson (local agent for the Dominion Telegraph Company).

By 1880, both the Dominion and Montreal Telegraph Companies were installing telephones in Whitby. The following year, Whitby's first telephone exchange was opened in the rear of Thomas. G. Whitfield's (1854-1928) drug store, at 109 Brock Street South. By that time, the Bell Telephone Company had acquired the rights to all telephones in Whitby and Whitfield was the first Bell Telephone agent.

In 1882, George E. Gibbard (1850-1923) purchased the Whitfield drug store and became Whitby's second Bell agent.

Whitby's first telephone directory, in the form of a small pamphlet, was published in November 1883. It listed 18 telephone subscribers and stated that the telephone central operator was on duty

Mayor Fred Rowe making the first dial telephone call in Whitby, March 9, 1938.

from 8 a.m. to 8 p.m. on weekdays and 2 p.m. to 4 p.m. on Sundays. The first commercial telephones had a range of about 20 miles. In August, 1884, the Bell Telephone Company extended phone lines from Whitby to Brooklin, Manchester, Port Perry and Uxbridge. In 1889, the Bell exchange went through another change of ownership when the drug store was purchased by James E. Willis (1863-1938). Fanny A. Willis (1866-1956), the proprietor's sister, was operator for 40 years, retiring in 1933. When she started in 1893 there were only 35 telephones in Whitby, serving a population of 2,800. When she retired, there were more than 500 phones, serving a population of 5,000.

In 1905, the Home Telephone Company, an independent business, sought permission from the Town Council to operate in Whitby. The Council refused the request and Bell was given an exclusive franchise for five years. At the end of the five years, in 1910, Bell tried to renew its franchise but was met with opposition. The Ontario Reformer, one of Oshawa's two weekly newspapers, stated: *"There is much objection to this, as the company offers practically nothing in return, and Independent Telephone Co., if allowed to come in, would bring new business from the surrounding townships where they have upwards of a thousand subscribers."* After some deliberation, the Council granted a franchise to both telephone companies in 1911. The Markham and Pickering Telephone Company, as the independent firm was now called, was given a five-year franchise in exchange for paying the town $60 a year for the first three years and giving the municipality free use of six telephones

for the remaining two years.

This agreement did not find favour in the business community, for the local merchants had to pay for two phones in their stores, one for each company, in order to do business with all subscribers. They were particularly annoyed that a connection could not be made between the lines of the two companies. To meet the challenge of the independent company, Bell extended its long distance lines from Whitby and inaugurated 24-hour phone service in 1905. The unnatural competition between the two phone companies did not last long. The independent company withdrew from Whitby before the agreement terminated.

Whitby's 200th telephone was installed in 1911. The increasing importance of the town as a telephone centre prompted the Bell company to change its office from a commission status and began to pay James E. Willis as a salaried manager. He was succeeded as manager by his sister Fanny in 1914. Telephone service grew rapidly with the 300th phone being installed in 1915 and the 400th in 1920. A reorganization of the Bell system in 1923 brought Whitby under the control of H.M. Black, the manager at Oshawa, while Fanny Willis remained as Whitby representative.

From time to time, telephone operators are called upon to perform heroic deeds in

time of emergency. In 1937, the two Whitby operators, Connie Rainnie (1913-1985) and Jean Heard (1909-1979) received a special commendation from the Town Council for staying at their posts during a downtown fire. On Feb. 8, 1937, a fire broke out above a store at 129 Brock Street South, one door south of the Bell Telephone exchange. Three stores were gutted by the fire which caused $40,000 damage. As smoke and water poured from the upper floors of the adjacent building, during the fire, the two operators carried on business as usual, protected by a tarpaulin provided by the Oshawa Fire Department. For five hours, these two brave women continued to relay phone calls as firefighters battled the blaze next door. Jean Heard became Whitby's local representative of Bell Canada in 1938, the year the dial phones came into existence. She moved to the Oshawa exchange in 1957, when the Whitby exchange was automated, and retired in 1967, after 40 years of service with the company.

Another Whitby telephone operator, Viola MacKenzie, later Mrs. Harold Parrott (1899-1986) had the duty of telling the Town of Whitby about the beginning and end of the First World War. Hired as an operator at the age of 14 in 1914, she received a call after her lunch break on Aug. 4, from Edmund Stephenson, the telegraph operator in Whitby. *"I have to ask you to spread some terrible news,"* he told Miss MacKenzie. *"Britain has declared war on Germany, so that means we are all in the war."* Stephenson asked her to call the local newspaper, the Gazette and Chronicle, and all the Bell subscribers, to inform them about the war. Miss MacKenzie realized that many of the women of Whitby would be deeply affected by the news she was passing on, because their husbands and boyfriends would have to leave home to fight in the war, and many would not come back. Indeed, she lost four cousins during the war.

Four years later, on Nov. 11, 1918, 17-year-old Viola MacKenzie received another call from telegraph operator Stephenson to inform her that the war had ended. *"I have good news for you,"* he said. *"The Armistice has been signed. Thank God!"* "Thank God", said Miss MacKenzie, and she proceeded to call all her subscribers to give them the good news. But there was more work ahead for her. In the fall of 1918, Whitby, like the rest of the world, was being ravaged by the Spanish Influenza. With all the other operators sick with the 'flu, Viola MacKenzie handled the switchboard for 36 straight hours before she fainted and had to be taken home unconscious in a taxi. She caught the 'flu a few weeks later and was confined to her bed for four months. She suffered a heart attack

during this time, which ended her telephone career, but she lived to the age of 86, dying on Feb. 9, 1986 at Lindsay. She had been hired by Fanny Willis in 1914 because she had long arms which could easily reach the terminals on the telephone switchboard.

Whitby telephone numbers adopted the Mohawk exchange about 1955 and this became 668 in the early 1960s. A new automated telephone switching centre was constructed beside the 1938 building on Brock Street South, in 1974.

Although Bell Canada has served Whitby since 1881, in the early days of telephones, not everyone wanted to be a Bell subscriber. One hold-out who decided to *"go it alone"* was Dr. Wellington Adams (1848-1918), who constructed his own private phone line between his home and office, based on plans printed in the magazine Scientific American. Adams, a dentist, had an office above the store now occupied by Lafontaine Trading Post on Dundas Street West, while his home was in The Terrace on Byron Street North. Since he was not serviced by Bell, he had to purchase and install his own telephone line and poles. For two years he could not obtain a bell for his phone, so when the town bell at the municipal building rang at regular hours or for a fire, Adams and his wife would rush to their respective phones to make a call. He finally got some phone bells

from New York and no longer had to rely on the sound of the town bell. Dr. Adams' private phone was a source of wonder and fear to the residents of Whitby and a source of amusement to telephone mechanics who saw it. A plug was attached to the phone to be used as a ground for the current during thunderstorms. Telephone subscribers in the earliest days were warned not to use the telephone during a thunderstorm for fear of being electrocuted.

Patients from the rural areas who came to Dr. Adams' office to see his phone marvelled that the wire wasn't heavier and hollow like a pipe. After the doctor's death in 1918, the Bell Telephone Company asked for the phone so it could be placed in their archives, but it had already been destroyed by his family when they cleaned out the house.

Dr. Adams came to Whitby from Port Hope in 1872 and married Ellen I. Huston (1855-1917), daughter of Whitby's Town Clerk-Treasurer Thomas Huston (1825-1896). They had two children, Allan H. Adams (1878-1928) who was a well-known Toronto physician, and Clara E. Adams (1882-1978) who married a student minister at St. John's Anglican Church and lived to the age of 96. Dr. Adams retired in 1918 and moved to Toronto to live with his son.

Unique Stone House Is Now Part of a Nursing Home

On the south side of Dundas Street between Thickson and Kendalwood Roads stands a unique stone farm house, the centrepiece of the Sunnycrest Nursing Home and Retirement Villa. Built by William Pearson (1833-1897) of Ashburn, in 1884, it is the last of many granite fieldstone houses built in Whitby and Pickering. The fieldstone farm house was popular in the 1850s and 1860s, but the Sunnycrest Nursing Home is a late example of the stone mason's art. Known as *"The Stone Lodge"*, this fine house was built for Jeremiah *"Jerry"* Lick, a wealthy Whitby Township farmer.

Jeremiah Lick (1830-1906) was born at Richmond Hill on July 28, 1830 and at the age of three, moved with his parents, William and Zephia Lick to Darlington Township. When he reached the age of 26 in 1856 he started farming on his own in the sixth concession of East Whitby Township, now part of Oshawa, south-east of Columbus. There, he and his wife Martha McNeal (1840-1902) raised a family of one son and six daughters. While living in East Whitby, Lick sat on the Township Council for 10 to 15 years, and was Reeve of the Township in 1877.

In 1880, Lick purchased a new farm in Whitby Township and had his fine stone residence constructed there four years later.

The Stone Lodge as it appeared, Circa 1900.

Each stone was cut or *"dressed"* into a block and laid in the walls like bricks. One can hardly imagine the time required to cut these stone blocks from solid granite and transport them from the rocky areas north of Whitby to the building site. The Stone Lodge was a modern marvel for its day. It was said to be the first farm house in

The Lick family's 1903 Ford, one of the first automobiles in Whitby.

the enterprising farmer travelled to Holland at his own expense and hired a Dutch interpreter so he could learn all he could about the pioneer Dutch dairy farms. At the time, Holland was the leading dairy farming country in the world. The Lick farm was also the site of one of the largest apple orchards in Ontario, being one of the first from which apples were shipped to England in the 19th century. Always at the forefront of the latest technology, the Lick family owned one of the first automobiles in Whitby, a 1903 Ford. The family was so well known that the site of the Stone Lodge was called *"Lick's Hill"*.

Jeremiah Lick died at the age of 76 on Aug. 4, 1906 and is buried in Oshawa Union Cemetery. His only son, Elmer Lick (1861-1926) was a pioneer of the Farmers' Co-operative movement in Ontario and a prominent figure in the United Farmers of Ontario (U.F.O.) who governed the province in the early 1920s. A founder of the United Farmers' Co-operative, he was one of the organizers of the first local co-operative association for fruit growers in Oshawa. For more than 30 years he was active in the Ontario Fruit Growers' Association. Elmer Lick built a concrete block house, one of the first in Ontario County, beside his father's home in 1904. It was demolished in 1979 after vandals set

Whitby Township in which *"modern conveniences"* (indoor plumbing and toilets) were installed. The house acquired a provincial reputation along with its owner, who was described as one of the most progressive farmers in south Ontario County.

When dairy farming started in Canada at the time Jeremiah Lick's house was built,

fires in it.

Elmer Lick's sister, Adelina (1874-1944) married John Arthur Jeffrey and continued to live in the Stone Lodge after her father's death. One of the few highly educated women of her time, she was a teacher at the Ontario Ladies' College (now Trafalgar Castle School) at Whitby and Alma College in St. Thomas, specializing in mathematics and physics. She was a noted authority on fine art and an accomplished wood carver. After her husband's death at the age of 44 in 1922, she opened the Stone Lodge as a tourist home.

Roy F. Lick (1895-1960), Elmer Lick's second son, was Reeve of Whitby Township in 1936 and served for 18 years as a director of the Dairy Farmers' Association of Canada. He was also a member of special agriculture committees appointed by the Ontario Government. In 1948, he was a member of a delegation which went to Britain to inquire into milk marketing methods.

By the early 1950s, the Lick family had sold the Stone Lodge, and attempts were made unsuccessfully to run it as a restaurant. It became the Arden Nursing Home in the 1950s and later changed to Sunnybrae Nursing Home. In 1967 the nursing home was purchased by the Leroy family, and the name changed to Sunnycrest. Additions were made to the back of the house in 1971 and 1982, making it one of the largest private nursing homes and retirement villas in the Whitby area. The original Stone Lodge is still well preserved, facing Dundas Street, displaying its beautiful workmanship to anyone who stops long enough to look.

The Stone Lodge on Lick's Hill is associated with several other features of the landscape which predate it by many years. In the 1830s, the Whitby post office stood near the site of the home, and also nearby was one of the earliest cemeteries in Whitby. More than 70 years ago the stones were removed from what was latterly known as *"Lick's Cemetery"* and no trace of it remains today. We know it dates back to at least 1833, for the body of Francis K. Tincombe, Port Whitby's first collector of customs, was laid to rest there in 1833 and moved to St. John's Anglican Cemetery at the harbour in 1846. East of the Stone Lodge is Lick Pond, a popular place for skating since pioneer times. Identified as a marl bed in the Historical Atlas of Ontario County in 1877, it was a marshy area which provided rich soil for fertilizer on Whitby's pioneer farms. In past years, Lick's Hill was much bigger than it is now. In the 1920s, the Ontario Government scraped down the tops of several of the hills between Whitby and Oshawa to provide a more level roadbed for Highway 2.

Jeremiah Lick as he appeared in 1892, from a photo taken for Composite Lodge No. 30, AF and AM, Whitby, by William E. O'Brien, the town photographer. The site of his home on the Kingston Road between Whitby and Oshawa was known for many years as "Lick's Hill."

Whitby Collegiate Institute Was Second Best In Ontario

In 1884, the Whitby Collegiate Institute was considered one of the best in Ontario — second best according to the school's record in Departmental Examinations.

"The year just closed has been one of the most successful in the history of the Institute," the Whitby Board of Education reported at the end of 1884. *"At the Toronto University Matriculation Examinations of this year, the Institute carried off 10 first class and 11 second class honours, taking the rank at the head of all the Collegiate Institutes and High Schools in the province, with but one exception; 26 honours in all and a General Proficiency Scholarship were carried off by the pupils of the Institute during the year. Twenty-eight pupils also successfully passed the Departmental Examinations. The school has been maintained with an efficient staff of five masters, four of them being honour graduates and all being specialists in their several departments. Owing to the large attendance of pupils, and especially in the upper forms, it was found necessary to engage the services of an additional assistant master."*

The Whitby Collegiate Institute, under principal Luther E. Embree (1844-1929), enjoyed its highest standing throughout the 1880s. In 1881, it had been elevated from a high school to a Collegiate Institute because it had more than 60 Latin scholars. It did not revert back to high school status until

Major James McBrien with Whitby Collegiate Institute's callisthenics class of 1888. Photo from Scugog Shores Historical Museum.

1911. In 1885, the Provincial Inspector reported that the Whitby Collegiate Institute *"continues to maintain its high standing as regards both success at Departmental and University Examinations and general tone. The staff is efficient all round, the commercial department being a good deal above the average."*

The Whitby Collegiate Institute began as a Grammar School, established it is believed, in 1846, although other sources indicate it did not open until 1849. A two-storey brick building was constructed for the Grammar School on the south side of

Whitby High School in 1916 after major renovations were completed.

Colborne Street between King and Centre Streets, where the Windsor Place senior citizens' apartments are now. The first Head Master was James Hodgson (1812-1890) who later was a school inspector for York County. Peter Perry (1792-1851), Samuel Cochrane (1793-1879) and Ezra Annes (1796-1857) were the founders of the Grammar School. Among the noted principals of this institution were William McCabe (1835-1903) who was later general manager of North American Life Assurance Company, and Thomas Kirkland (1835-1898) who became principal of the Toronto Normal School, the leading teacher's college in the province. Kirkland married a daughter of Whitby's first Presbyterian minister, Rev. Dr. Robert H. Thornton (1806-1875) and wrote a number of school text books in the 1870s and 1880s.

In 1872/73 a new building, designed by Henry Langley (1836-1907) of Toronto was added to the front of the Grammar School. It was considerably remodelled in 1915. After Henry Street High School opened in September 1954, the old building became the Colborne Street Senior Public School. It was demolished at the end of 1975. Thousands of Whitby children received their education at this site. All that remains of the old school is its bell, placed on a concrete pedestal behind the seniors' apartments.

The classics were very important to the Victorians in the last half of the 19th century. One could not enter university to study law unless one was fluent in both Latin and Greek. The Whitby Collegiate Institute had its own motto: *"Per Aspera Ad Alta"*, which was Latin for *"Through Difficulties to the Heights"*. Adopted as early as 1882, the motto, in Latin, Greek, French and English, was printed on a banner in the assembly hall.

The Whitby Collegiate staff were proud that two of their students matriculated into university in 1881. This may seem a small number by today's standards, when the school had an enrolment of 211, but in the 1880s, few students could afford to attend university. One student from Whitby was awarded the highest standing at the Ontario Agricultural College in Guelph in 1881.

Commercial education received more attention in 1881 than in past years. There were also drawing and music classes. In 1882, the Board of Education imposed fees for students attending the Collegiate Institute because irregularity in attendance jeopardized the county and provincial grants received by the school. These fees amounted to 75 cents a month for Ontario County pupils and one dollar per month for non-residents of Ontario County. In 1883, the Board of Education reported: *"During the last year, $111 in fees have been received from the pupils engaged in the study of classics and as anticipated, the attendance at the Collegiate Institute has been much more regular since fees were imposed."* The board also reported: *"The low salaries paid in the lower divisions of the Institute render it difficult to retain efficient teachers for any great length of time. The Board regrets that from this cause a most efficient teacher has declined to continue in the service of the board."*

Despite the low pay for teachers, the Board of Education was able to purchase additional land for the Collegiate Institute in 1883, extending its property east to Centre Street. To maintain the school's status as a Collegiate Institute, the Board of Education erected a gymnasium on the new land in 1889. The land purchased in 1883 cost the Board $250, and it was expected that increased county and provincial grants would pay for the construction of the frame gymnasium. James McBrien (1832-1909), an officer in the 34th (now Ontario) Regiment, and County Public School Inspector, was hired to teach gymnastics, which in the 1880s were called callisthenics. It was the custom at that time for military men to teach such subjects and they appeared at the school dressed in their uniforms. The girls went through various drills with brooms and Indian clubs, under the watchful eye of Major McBrien. He was succeeded by another military officer, Anson G. Henderson (1852-1928).

In 1890, William W. Tamblyn (1844-1912), the principal, received a salary of $1,000, while the other teachers received $800 to $900 a year. Tamblyn left a sum of $200 in his will as prize money for a public

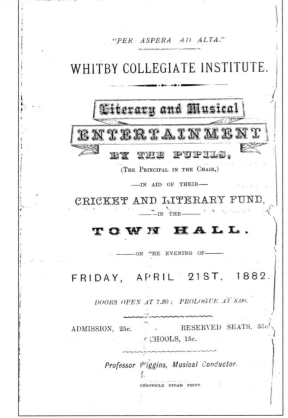

"PER ASPERA AD ALTA."

WHITBY COLLEGIATE INSTITUTE.

Literary and Musical ENTERTAINMENT BY THE PUPILS,

(THE PRINCIPAL IN THE CHAIR,)

—IN AID OF THEIR—

CRICKET AND LITERARY FUND,

—IN THE—

TOWN HALL.

—ON THE EVENING OF—

FRIDAY, APRIL 21ST, 1882.

DOORS OPEN AT 7.30; PROLOGUE AT 8.00.

ADMISSION, 25c.   RESERVED SEATS, 35c.

SCHOOLS, 15c.

Professor Wiggins, Musical Conductor.

CHRONICLE STEAM PRINT.

Literary and Musical Entertainment program, by Whitby Collegiate Institute, April 21, 1882.

speaking contest. The money was first awarded in 1916, and the Tamblyn Public Speaking prizes were presented until the

mid-1960s. The writer of this book competed in the Tamblyn contest while in Grade 9 at Henry Street High School in 1962.

In the 1880s, the coming of spring meant the election of a Dux (leader) of the boys and a May Queen by the Collegiate Institute students. These ceremonies were held on Arbor Day, when the Dux and May Queen planted trees on the school grounds. The Dux for 1887 was Hamar Greenwood (1870-1948), Whitby's most famous son.

Cricket was a popular sport in the 1880s because of the British origin of the families of the Collegiate Institute students. The school had a literary and a debating club, and the students presented entertainments in the Hopkins Music Hall at Brock and Colborne Streets where the fire hall is now. In 1927, a new brick addition was made to the school to provide three new classrooms and a gymnasium. This addition was opened on Dec. 2, 1927, by High School Inspector I. M. Levan, of the Ontario Department of Education. The old gymnasium of 1889 was demolished.

Although the Whitby Collegiate Institute received high praise from provincial inspectors in the 1880s, there were a few problems that had to be addressed. In 1890, the inspector stated that *"I am sorry to have to report that, owing to Mr. Waldron's defective hearing, his order is very poor and he fails*

generally to secure the attention of his classes. I am forced reluctantly to add that, owing to the same cause, he is not an efficient member of the staff. Most of the pupils can and do receive little benefit from his teaching". It was likely that Waldron, the science teacher, was not kept on staff in 1891, although the inspector's report for that year is missing and cannot be confirmed.

"PER ASPERA AD ALTA."

THE WHITBY COLLEGIATE INSTITUTE.

ESTABLISHED A.D. 1843.

Board of Education:

CHAIRMAN—JAS. McCLELLAN, ESQ.

JNO. E. FAREWELL, ESQ., LL.B., Q.C. A. M. ROSS, ESQ.
JNO. BALL DOW, ESQ., B.A. C. F. McGILLIVRAY, M.A., M.D.
JNO. FERGUSON, ESQ., CASTLE FOX, ESQ.
LYMAN T. BARCLAY, ESQ. JOHN BLOW, ESQ.
JAMES LONG, ESQ. JOHN BURNS, ESQ.
GEORGE PARKER, ESQ. FRED. HATCH, ESQ.

SECRETARY-TREASURER—D. ORMISTON, B.A.

PRINCIPAL—JNO. WAUGH, B. A., B. PAED.

Staff of Teachers.

JNO. WAUGH, B.A., B. PAED.,
  SPECIALIST IN CLASSICS.

G. H. HOGARTH, B.A.,
  SPECIALIST IN MATHEMATICS.

A. G. HENDERSON,
  SPECIALIST IN COMMERCIAL DEPT.

G. M. JONES, B.A.,
  SPECIALIST IN ENGLISH AND MODERNS.

W. A. DENT,
  SPECIALIST IN SCIENCE.

Brochure advertising the Whitby Collegiate Institute, 1896.

Gun Fight At Myrtle Station

The usually quiet community of Myrtle Station seemed more like the Wild West on Dec. 14, 1887, when a gun fight broke out between whiskey peddlers and two liquor act detectives. No one was able to tell how many shots were fired, but when the smoke cleared, one man had been shot three times. Fortunately for all concerned, he survived.

The sale and consumption of liquor was a social evil from earliest pioneer times in Whitby. As early as 1830, a Temperance Society was organized in the township to try to cope with drunkenness in the community. It was a common practice for liquor to be served at building projects such as barn raisings, sometimes with unfortunate results. When the Brooklin Flour Mill was constructed in 1848, and Trafalgar Castle in 1859-62, no liquor was allowed on the construction sites, thus preventing any serious accidents. The editor of The Chronicle complained in his paper that no one did anything to remove the body of a dead drunk from the roadside between Whitby and Oshawa. The hotels, as many as 10 in the Town of Whitby alone, served liquor at their bars, often to thirsty farmers who were waiting hours in the fall to unload their grain into boats at Whitby Harbour. George Keith (1838-1925) who worked as a clerk in Hamilton

The station house at Myrtle Station, where the gun-fight occurred.

and Roberts' general store in Whitby in 1858, recalled years later that there was a barrel of whiskey at the back of the store. Customers were invited to help themselves, free of charge. Saloons were a source of problems in downtown Whitby in the 1850s, and efforts were made by some residents to close them.

Local Temperance Societies urged the Provincial and later Federal Government to

pass laws to control the liquor traffic, but these laws were ineffectual and generally ignored. In 1878, the Canada Temperance Act (known as the Scott Act) was passed by the Federal Government, giving cities and counties the right to prohibit the retail sale of alcohol, if a majority of the citizens voted in favour. This act, however, did not prohibit consumption of alcohol. The hotel owners got around the law by renting their bars out to individuals who then served liquor. If the bar tenders were arrested, the hotel owners would say that they knew nothing of their activities because they were only renting out the bars. The bar tender, who leased the bar on a daily basis and brought in his own stock, would pay the fine and disappear, to be replaced by another daily tenant.

On July 16, 1885, 25 counties and 12 cities approved the Scott Act bylaw in local plebiscites. Ontario County voted 62 per cent in favour of prohibition, which came into effect on May 1, 1886. This figure was very misleading, for only 37 per cent of eligible voters cast their ballots. It was a case of a vocal minority imposing their will on a silent majority who liked their opportunity to drink.

Detectives were hired by the Government to enforce the Scott Act. Two of these detectives, based in Toronto were John S. Dennin and William C. McRae. McRae was an American sewing machine salesman who had failed in business and went into law enforcement. He was only 23 years old. Dennin and McRae visited hotels throughout Ontario County, taking note of where liquor was sold and who bought it. They proceeded to lay charges under the Scott Act, which caused a great stir in the community. The Scott Act

became a focus of threats and violence. In 1887, an average of 16 charges a week were heard in courts at Brooklin and Whitby.

On Dec. 14, 1887, Dennin and McRae had successfully prosecuted a number of individuals at Brooklin, and seeing that the mood of the community was ugly, decided to get out of town fast and take the train to Toronto from Myrtle Station. Word got as far as Port Perry that the detectives were on their way, and this caused a stir at the St. Charles Hotel, where George Brown leased the bar. Brown, along with Fred Corbin, owner of the Oriental Hotel and William Lattimore, leasee of the bar there, jumped into a buggy and proceeded to Myrtle Station to *"have it out"* with the detectives. A week earlier, both hotel owners had been charged by Dennin and McRae. They had been promised that the charges could be dropped if they paid enough money, but were afraid to, in case they were double-crossed. Brown and Lattimore had been drinking, and had armed themselves with revolvers. Thomas Trebell, another member of the party that proceeded to Myrtle Station, was armed with a large stick.

What happened when the drunken whiskey peddlers arrived at Myrtle Station was described by the Oshawa Vindicator as

"An Awful Scene."

"One of the most dramatic and lively scenes that ever occurred in these parts took place on the platform of the railway station at Myrtle at just exactly 7:09 on Wednesday evening," the Vindicator reported. *"At 6:30 on Wednesday evening, half a dozen or so persons were gathered in the little public room of the station, waiting for the up express for Toronto, which passes Myrtle at 7:12. These were Mr. J.A. Mulligan, President of the Toronto Branch of the Irish National League; an elderly and stout old lady; James Forrest, an old english farmer; W.C. McRae and J.S. Dennin, Scott Act detectives; Joseph Scott, the station agent and a Toronto World reporter. There were one or two loungers besides who were probably at the station merely out of curiosity.*

"Outside on the platform two men (Brown and Trebell) were walking up and down with measured pace. One of them was enveloped in a great coonskin coat. He was a large-sized man. The other was a small man, well dressed with an ordinary overcoat and a cloth cap. They seemed to be discussing some subject with considerable earnestness. They had not been at the station long, having arrived shortly before the reporter noticed them, in a buggy coming from the direction of Port Perry.

"Inside the station house McRae and

Dennin paced the floor nervously. McRae said on one or two occasions, 'Well I will sleep in Toronto tonight and not out in this God-forsaken country.' Both he and his companion seemed to be very anxious for the arrival of the express which was to carry them to the city. They were well-dressed men and both carried watches which they consulted every few minutes.

"Presently the small man who was pacing the platform came to the waiting-room door and beckoned the two Scott Act officers towards him. They responded and stepped outside. Then followed the scene. The little man caught Dennin who is a stout, well-built fellow of 27, by the lapel of the coat and said 'Come and take a walk with me.' This Dennin positively and peremptorily refused to do, and jerked himself loose of the other man's hold. Quick as a flash, two revolvers were drawn, one by each man. McRae, who was standing near by, also drew a revolver. There was a rapid clatter of exploding fire-arms, which much resembled the popping of a bunch of fire crackers. Just who fired the first shot, the writer, who was an eye-witness to the affair, is unable to say. Dennin and his antagonist began peppering at each other at close quarters. Then the antagonist (Brown) sank to the platform with three bullet holes in his body, two in the breast and on in the leg.

"Three or four men rushed from the back of the station, all with revolvers in the hands. Click, click, click, click went the weapons. Over a dozen shots were fired. and it was all over in less than three minutes. His supposed companions fled in the darkness behind the station. McRae and Dennin rushed into the waiting room with their smoking weapons in their hands. Dennin also carried the revolver of the man who had fallen, having wrestled it from his grasp. The little crowd outside didn't know which ways to turn or what to do. The station agent had locked his office and was nowhere visible. All attempts to get into his department proved futile. the affair was so sudden, so startling and so mysterious to the people in the waiting-room that they were paralyzed with fear.

"In the meantime the man in the coon-skin coat (Trebell) picked up the wounded man and carried him to the back of the station, and he sank down on a doorstep. He groaned heavily and gasped for breath. Then it became known he was George Brown, bar tender at the St. Charles Hotel in Port Perry... Then Mr. Coonskin held a lamp before the wounded man's face and said, 'Poor George.' Brown lay there still and breathing heavily and groaning.

" 'Go for a doctor,' shouted three or four people. No one seemed to know where a doctor was to be had. The nearest one was at Brooklin. Mr. Coonskin had a buggy tied to the platform but made no move toward summoning a doctor."

Considering the number of shots that were fired, the Vindicator reporter was amazed that only one person had been hit.

On Sunday, Dec. 19, 1887, William Lattimore, Thomas Trebell and Frederick Corbin were arrested, and eventually charged with conspiracy to attack the two detectives. Detectives Dennin and McRae were charged with causing bodily harm. The resulting court case was a confusing mess, for no one was able to determine how many shots were fired or by whom. The case was referred to the Spring Assizes at Whitby, where eventually it was thrown out for lack of evidence. Nobody was convicted, and the poor victim, George Brown, became a local hero in Port Perry.

The Day Brooklin Was Nearly Washed Away

Hurricane Hazel, in October 1954, is remembered by many Whitby residents as the worst storm in living memory. The storm of April, 1929 was just as severe, but the worst storm ever to devastate Whitby, centered on the village of Brooklin in June of 1890. At that time, Brooklin was a small community of businessmen and retired farmers with a population of about 800. Surrounded by rich farmland, it was a centre for milling in its early days, but by 1890 there were only two operating mills left in Brooklin, one run by John Robson (1859-1902) and the other by Peter Francis (1835-1910). The community's other major industry was a tannery operated by William J. Murray (1849-1932).

The hot humid days of June 1890 produced a pattern of unsettled weather, punctuated by violent thunderstorms. One of these storms passed over Brooklin on the night of June 3, filling the sky with brilliant flashes of lightning. After an unusually bright flash, flames were seen issuing from William J. Murray's tannery behind Robson's brick mill on Mill Street (now Cassels Road). Realizing that the tannery had been struck, the villagers formed a bucket brigade, for the village had no fire engine, and managed to confine the fire to the tannery building. But it was too late to save it from destruction.

The W.J. Murray Tannery is at the left of this picture of the Brooklin Mill, taken in the 1880s.

By morning, it was estimated that the fire had caused $20,000 damage, of which only $10,000 was covered by insurance. Twenty-five men had lost their jobs as a result of the fire. Creditors of the tannery were offered 40 per cent payment on what was owed to them, for that was all the company could pay. The W.J. Murray tannery, which had been constructed in 1854 by Moses Bartlett, was virtually wiped out physically and

financially by the fire. As it was one of Brooklin's largest industries, the loss was felt keenly by the villagers. Murray left Brooklin to set up another tannery in Toronto. He died at Woodville at the age of 83, poisoned by calcium cyanide while fumigating a mushroom farm.

The loss of the tannery was bad enough for Brooklin, but the worst devastation was yet to come. Two days later, on June 5,

1890 a cloudburst at The Ridges, north of the village, emptied gallons of water into the Lynde Creek, making it *"assume the proportions of a mighty river"*, according to The Toronto Globe. As the water overflowed the creek banks, bridges, mill dams and buildings were washed away in the flood.

By evening, six bridges and roads in Whitby Township had been washed out. Two of the three bridges in Brooklin were wiped out and the third left in an unsafe condition. Hill's sawmill in the 5th concession, south of Brooklin was swept away, as was nearly every mill dam in the township. The Whitby and Port Perry Railway between Whitby and Brooklin was washed out, cutting off all communication with the village by rail, and the C.P.R. telegraph line was down.

The Toronto Globe reported that Mr. Batty's barn and out buildings were swept away in the flood, Mills' tinshop was overturned and severe damage was done to Redman's furniture shop. One old resident many years later recalled seeing coffins from Redman's undertaking business floating down the creek.

William J. Murray and three assistants, working to clean up after the tannery fire, were swept downstream as they tried to rescue a number of horses. It was only by quick action of the villagers on the shore who tossed them ropes, that all were saved from drowning.

As if the physical damage of the June 5 storm was not enough, it was the night of a Provincial election and the storm played havoc with the voting. The ballots from the small hamlet of Alton in Pickering Township were never received, and many farmers who had intended to vote in the afternoon, never made it to the polls. John Dryden of Brooklin (1840-1909), the Liberal candidate who was to become Ontario's Minister of Agriculture after the election, defeated his opponent by only 145 votes, but because of the storm, the final tally was estimated to leave him only a dozen votes ahead. A big reception had been planned for Dryden on election night, his 50th birthday, but with all communication with Brooklin cut off, no one was able to attend. Dryden's home, Maple Shade Farm, is at the corner of Thickson and Columbus Roads. It was the custom of the farmers of Whitby Township to vote in the afternoon and journey to Whitby in the evening to participate in the election night festivities. There were no festivities on the night of June 5, 1890, for it had been raining for six hours and every road was washed out.

By morning, Whitby Township Reeve James R. Mathewson (1836-1897) estimated that the storm had caused $25,000 damage in his township alone. With severe flooding reported in Oshawa, Pickering and Bowmanville, it was estimated by The Globe of June 9 that total damage from the storm was close to a quarter of a million dollars. It would take weeks before road and railway links were restored to Brooklin and the damaged buildings repaired.

It is estimated that a storm of this magnitude occurs in the same area once each generation. Extensive studies have been undertaken in the last 40 years by the Central Lake Ontario Conservation Authority to minimize the effect of these sudden violent storms. Today, laws prevent construction of buildings on floodplain land.

A bill from the Brooklin Flour Mill, eight months before the storm of June 1890

Why William A. Holliday Worried While He Slept

In the 1890s, Brooklin merchant William A. Holliday (1876-1954) worried while he slept, if he could sleep at all. It was harvest season and he lay in his bed with $3,000 in cash under his pillow. Holliday feared he would be robbed, but he also knew he had to pay out at least $1,000 of that money the next day to farmers who were bringing their grain to market.

In those days, 100 years ago, when a school teacher was lucky to make an annual salary of $400, and good wages for dock workers at Whitby harbour were two dollars a day, one might wonder why Holliday was handling so much money. The reason was that he was in the grain trade, the most lucrative business in Whitby Township since the first settlers populated the community in the 1830s. Holliday had the very responsible position of paymaster for the Guy and Company of Oshawa which built a grain elevator at Brooklin in 1892.

When the farmers of Whitby Township brought their grain to the Brooklin elevator to be sold during the harvest season, they had to walk or drive uptown to Holliday's store to be paid. That store was in the yellow brick building beside the present Legion Hall in Brooklin. The Brooklin grain elevator held a very strategic place in the life of the village. It stood west of St. Thomas' Anglican Church on the Whitby,

The Brooklin grain elevator and railway station, looking south from Winchester Road, C. 1910.

Port Perry and Lindsay Railway, which was known locally as the *"Nip and Tuck"*. The railway was the chief means of transportation for grain from the northern farm lands to Whitby Harbour. The grain stored in the Brooklin elevator would be shipped by rail to the harbour where it would be transferred to schooners which shipped it to ports on the Great Lakes in Canada and the United States. The railway station for Brooklin, from 1895 to 1937 when it was destroyed by fire, was west of the elevator

William A. Holliday's shop, 58 Baldwin Street, was Brooklin's largest general store. The Whitby Township Hall was on the second floor until 1920, and the Beethoven Lodge, Independent Order of Oddfellows, was on the third floor. This picture was taken the time Mr. Holliday sold the store to William M. Lawrence in 1912.

and south of Winchester Road where Michael Kelly's is now. From the station platform, residents could watch wheat, bar-

ley, oats and peas being unloaded from farmers' waggons into the elevator.

The American McKinley Tariff Act placed tariffs on Canadian grain being shipped to the United States, starting in 1890, effectively killed the grain trade at Whitby Harbour. Even after the grain trade at the harbour had stopped, the Brooklin elevator continued to be a distribution centre for grain in Whitby Township. The Whitby, Port Perry and Lindsay Railway was closed in July 1941 after 70 years in business and the rails were torn up and sold as scrap metal for making munitions in the Second World War. With the railway gone, and grain no longer being shipped through Brooklin, the bottom part of the elevator became a coal shed for William S. Croxall (1875-1950) who owned it in the last years of its existence. It was demolished in 1950, the last of a complex of buildings that made Brooklin an important railway centre.

William A. Holliday gave up the general store in Brooklin in 1912 and moved to Toronto. In the 1920s and 1930s he returned to Whitby to operate a hardware store on Brock Street South. A man of many talents, he was the Brooklin reporter for the Whitby Chronicle in 1892 at the time he was handling vast sums of money. His columns were always signed *"W.A.H."* His father, Thomas Jackson Holliday (1839-

A bill from W. A. Holliday's store, December 31, 1912

1889) had moved to Brooklin from Coboconk in 1878 to operate the village's largest general store. After his early death at the age of 49, his son took over the business, and made a considerable amount of money.

Whitby Jail Was Not Escape-Proof

Whitby's original jail, located behind the Court House and Land Registry Office on Centre Street South, was built like a medieval dungeon. A massive stone building surrounded by a red brick wall, it was a formidable prison – but not escape-proof.

In November 1893, Sheriff John F. Paxton (1857-1936) issued a wanted poster for two convicts who escaped from the Whitby jail on the night of Nov. 29. Printed by the Gazette Steam print, this poster was placed in post offices throughout Ontario, but no record remains on whether the two men were apprehended.

Under the heading of $50.00 reward, the poster gave the following descriptions:

"John Kelly, alias Charles Symons, alias William Foster, alias John Leslie, is about 36 years of age, five feet eight inches in height, and weighs about 160 pounds, with reddish hair, bald in front. There is a small space in the front teeth of the upper jaw, a scar on the right hand, one on the left thumb and one on the index finger.

"John Burns or Byron is about 36 years of age, five feet seven inches in height, and weighs 155 pounds. He has dark hair, and short, flat, sharp pointed nose, high cheek bones, dark complexion, a scar on the right cheek, a figure of a crucifix on right arm, a cross and anchor on left arm, also several flags with eagle.

Whitby Jail looking from the Court House, c. 1940.

"The above convicts who were under sentence to the Kingston Penitentiary for seven and five years respectively for shop breaking, escaped from the Whitby Gaol on the night of Nov. 29, 1893. The above reward will be paid to any person giving such information as will lead to the recapture and return of one or both of the convicts."

The Whitby jail (or gaol as it was spelled 100 years ago) was constructed in 1853 of

$50.00 REWARD !

John Kelly, alias Charles Symmons, alias William Foster, alias John Leslie, is about 36 years of age, five feet eight inches in height, and weighs about 160 pounds, with reddish hair, bald in front. There is a small space in the front teeth of the upper jaw, a scar on the right hand, one on the left thumb and one on the index finger.

John Burns or Byron is about 36 years of age, five feet seven inches in height and weighs 155 pounds, he has dark hair, a short, flat, sharp pointed nose, high cheek bones, dark complexion, a scar on right cheek, a figure of a crucifix on right arm, of a cross and anchor on the left arm, also several flags with eagle.

The above convicts who were under sentence to the Kingston Penitentiary for seven and five years respectively for shop breaking, escaped from Whitby Gaol on the night of November 29th, 1893. The above reward will be paid to any person giving such information as will lead to the recapture and return of one or both of these convicts.

J. F. PAXTON,

SHERIFF, C. O.

GAZETTE STEAM PRINT, WHITBY.

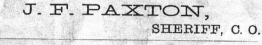

Sheriff Paxton's reward poster, November, 1893.

Queenston stone. It was in use until the present jail was constructed on Victoria Street in 1958, and was demolished in February, 1960.

The first report of an escape from the Whitby Jail was in the Whitby Chronicle of Nov. 7, 1872. It reported that the *"notorious Jackson"* and another man named William Smith, escaped through the cesspool adjacent to the toilets. Accomplices on the outside dug a hole a few feet under the jail wall, and as The Chronicle reported, *"the birds had flown."* These two prisoners, in jail for larceny, had complained to the governor, Walter Coulthard (1828-1908) that they were ill, and asked that their cells be left unlocked at night so they could get to the toilets.

Jackson was described as *"a native of Ireland, about 35 years, height five feet eight inches tall, hair light brown, with heavy beard and moustache, eyes sunken, and a scar on the right eyelid, was dressed in dark or light brown coat, grey vest, brown trousers with dark stripe down the seams, and new gaiter boots."*

A week later, Jackson and Smith were still at large and presumed to have headed for the United States. According to The Chronicle, *"the whole affair, to say the least of it, is a disgraceful bungle, and reflects most severely upon the energy, tact and ability of the authorities."*

An even more disgraceful set of circumstances occurred at the Whitby jail in the summer of 1907. Early in July of that year, two prisoners, one serving three months for assault and the other, six months for vagrancy, escaped from the jail and had 30 minutes' head start before they were discovered missing. The man on the assault charge had broke jail before. A month later, a 16-year-old awaiting sentence for theft, managed to escape, with the aid of a fellow prisoner. The teenager, James Wells, had a lengthy record for his age. He had been charged with stealing railway tickets at Sunderland, and after being given a second chance at freedom had stolen $18 from the Windsor Hotel in Whitby. These escapes and political pressure from the conservative Party, forced W.J. Davey, the jail governor, to resign in September 1907, and leave Canada for the United States.

Appointments of this nature were very politically oriented in the early part of this century. The Conservatives were after Davey's hide because he was a Liberal appointee as well as a poor jail keeper. The Toronto Globe, the leading Liberal paper in Ontario, stated on Sept. 12, 1907: *"No effort was made to conceal the fact that pressure was being brought to bear upon the powers that be to oust Sheriff Paxton and Governor Davey. It has been stated again and again by the more partisan workers that they would accomplish their purpose. So hot have the Conservatives made it for Davey that he has resigned."*

The new appointee as governor, John E. Schiller (1840-1921), a former hotel keeper in Toronto and Whitby, fared little better than his predecessor. In November, 1909, a prisoner on a work detail, picking apples, made off and was chased by the jail guard for two miles before he disappeared.

The Whitby jail was the site of only two executions in its 105-year existence. Archie McLaughlin, who murdered his wife and child so he could run off with another woman, was hanged in the jail yard in July, 1910. A resident of Uxbridge, he poisoned his wife and daughter and tried to cover up the crime by burning the house down. He was a poor arsonist and was caught. Dr. Horace Bascom (1863-1956), an Uxbridge doctor who was later a Whitby resident and Sheriff of Ontario County, discovered the poison in the bodies and charges of murder were laid against McLaughlin.

The other person executed was George Bilton, in December 1946, for killing a woman and her child in the woods east of Ajax. The writer of this book remembers being shown the trap door where this hanging occurred, when the jail was demolished in 1960.

OFFICIAL OPENING OF THE JAIL

at

WHITBY, ONTARIO

on

Thursday, June Nineteenth
One Thousand Nine Hundred and Fifty-Eight

Erected by

THE COUNTY OF ONTARIO

and

THE CITY OF OSHAWA

Program for the official opening of the new jail on Victoria Street, June 19, 1958. This jail, opened by the Hon. Ray Connell, Ontario Minister of Reform Institutions, is due to be closed within the next two years.

May Irwin, America's Greatest Comedienne, Was Born In Whitby

In the summer of 1896, a 34-year-old woman from Whitby shocked Victorian society and was denounced by the clergy when she received the first kiss ever shown on motion picture film. Her name was May Irwin, the star of the popular Broadway comedy *"The Widow Jones."* Thomas Edison, who was experimenting with motion pictures, asked her and her co-star, John C. Rice, to perform the kissing scene from *"The Widow Jones"* for his camera. The result was 50 feet of film of Irwin and Jones kissing each other – a film that later became known as the 50-foot kiss.

The spectacle of a couple kissing on film was too much for many prim and proper Victorians, although no one seemed to object to the scene on the stage. Some clergy called it scandalous, but the 50-foot kiss is now part of film history.

Making *"scandalous"* motion pictures was a far cry from Irwin's beginnings in Whitby, where she was born on June 27, 1862. Her father was Robert E. Campbell, son of Brooklin area pioneer John Campbell (1794-1876). Her mother was Sophronia Jane Draper, sister of Chester Draper (1823-1876) owner of Whitby Harbour. Although Robert Campbell's family was well connected, it did not receive any large amount of money from these wealthy relatives.

Georgina May Campbell, as Irwin was known in her youth, lived with her parents, one sister and three brothers, in a house rented from her uncle Chester Draper, at the corner of Byron and Elm streets where the Elm Street parking lot is now. The house was demolished in 1971. Some sources say she was born in this house while others say she only lived there. For part of her youth she lived on her grandfather John Campbell's farm on the sixth concession of Whitby. She often visited her rich uncle Chester Draper at his home, Burr Lodge, on Centre Street South at James Street.

Georgina Campbell was a happy plump young girl who used to run down the streets of Whitby, singing. She and her sister Adeline Flora Campbell (1859-1930) sang in the choir of All Saints' Anglican Church. The Campbell sisters often sang at popular entertainments in Whitby. They performed at the Mechanics' Institute Hall at Byron and Mary Streets where Pearson Lanes are now, the night before the building burned down on Nov. 27, 1873.

Life was a struggle for the Campbell family. The sisters were sent to St. Cecelia's Convent in Port Hope for further education when Georgina was 14 but suddenly her father's business failed and the family

May Irwin in 1913 Toronto Public Library photo)

May Irwin's childhood home, 105 Byron Street North, demolished in 1971.

such productions as *"The Widow Jones"*, *"The Swell Miss Fitzwell"*, *"Courted Into Court"*, *"Mrs. Black is Back"* and *"Belle of Bridgeport"*. When she later joined Charles Rohman, she was earning $2,500 a week and billed as *"undeniably the greatest farce actress in America."* By 1896, when *"The Kiss"* was filmed, she was the top comedienne in North America and one of the richest actresses in the country.

At the height of her stage career, May Irwin built a summer home in the Thousand Islands, near Clayton, New York, where she entertained her theatrical friends in grand style. The house contained six grand pianos and every guest room had twin beds and a bath. It was in May Irwin's summer home that Irving Berlin wrote his famous song *"Alexander's Ragtime Band."*

May Irwin was responsible for naming and popularizing Thousand Island salad dressing. On one trip to the Thousand Islands, Irwin was taken on a fishing trip by a local guide named George Lalonde, whose wife served a distinctive type of salad dressing. Irwin who was a fine cook and had written a cook book herself, took a fancy to this new salad dressing. It became a part of the menu at the Herald Hotel in Clayton, where Irwin and her husband often dined. She like the dressing so much that she named it *"Thousand*

was virtually penniless. In desperation, Mrs. Campbell sent her talented girls to Buffalo, New York, in 1876 to seek their fortune in the theatre because they were such good singers. The Buffalo theatre manager billed them as *"May and Flo Irwin"* because Campbell did not seem to him to be a good stage name. Therefore, they remained for the rest of their lives as May and Flo Irwin.

From 1877 to 1883, the *"Irwin Sisters"* were members of Tony Pastor's Theatre Company in New York City, until, at age 21, May Irwin joined Augustin Daly's *"Temple of Dramatic Theatre"* where she was soon stealing scenes from seasoned professionals such as John Drew and Otis Skinner. Under Daly, considered the greatest theatrical manager in the United States in the 1880s and 1890s, she starred in

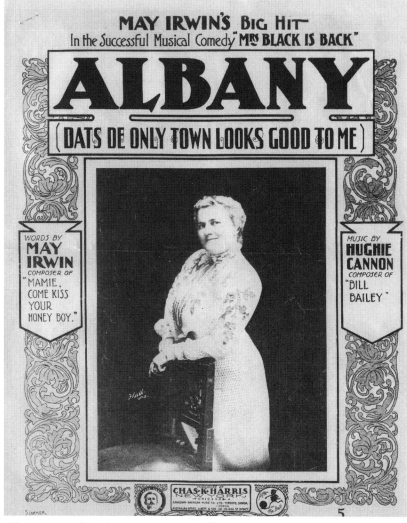

Sheet music for May Irwin's song "Albany, Dat's De Only Town Looks Good to Me," 1904.

Island Dressing" and gave the recipe to George C. Boldt, owner of the Waldorf Astoria Hotel in New York City. Boldt directed his world famous chef Oscar Tschirky to add it to the hotel's menu. The chef got the credit for introducing Thousand Island dressing, but it really began with May Irwin.

May Irwin lived in the Thousand Islands in the summer and New York City in the winter. Over the years she invested heavily in New York real estate, buying one or two lots in each block on Lexington Avenue from 43rd Street to the high fifties. In the spring of 1929, she sold all her property for as much as $670,000 a lot, escaping the stock market crash by only six months. While many financiers were ruined by the crash, she had millions of dollars in cash.

May Irwin visited her childhood home in Whitby only once, in 1886, 10 years after she left the County Town. In 1897, she was in Toronto, performing in *"The Swell Miss Fitzwell"* at the Grand Opera House. She was proud of her Canadian background and spoke of it fondly in an interview with the Toronto Daily Star in July 1930.

May Irwin was able to introduce many new facets to American entertainment. She was the first white woman to dance the Cakewalk on the New York stage, having learned it from the black hotel staff in the Thousand Islands. She introduced the popular *"Coon Songs"* of the 1890s and was one of the leaders in ragtime music. Her accomplishments as a *"coon shouter"* would not be acceptable in today's society, as the coon songs made fun of blacks. One of her most successful songs was *"May Irwin's Bully Song,"* which was issued in 1896 and she recorded it for Victor records in 1907. Only seven recordings were ever made by May Irwin, all in 1907. A copy of her recording of *"May Irwin's Frog Song"* is in the Town of Whitby Archives. May Irwin also introduced such famous songs of the *"gay nineties"* as *"After the*

Ball Is Over" and *"Ta-ra-ra-Boom-Der-e."*

May Irwin owned her own theatre in New York City for a while and raised money to start a national theatre in the United States. She was called upon to do a command performance for President Woodrow Wilson during the First World War. Wilson was so impressed with her that he named her *"Secretary of Laughter"* in his unofficial Cabinet. As early as 1902, she had considered retiring, but was still appearing on Broadway in 1925 at the age of 73 with Marie Dressler, another comedienne of the American stage who was born at Cobourg, Ontario.

May Irwin was married twice. After her first husband, Frederick W. Keller died, she married her manager, Kurt Eisfeldt. In her retirement years she raised horses at her farm at Clayton, New York. Today there is a museum to her memory in Clayton. May Irwin died at her home in New York City on Oct. 22, 1938, at the age of 76. At her request she was buried in a red satin dress.

Her sister, Flo Irwin died in 1930 at Los Angeles, California, at the age of 71. The two sisters went their separate ways early in their theatrical career. Flo Irwin, although an accomplished actress, never attained the fame of her sister. May Irwin was always proud of being a Canadian by birth, born near Toronto *"where they don't read Sunday papers."*

Front page of "May Irwin's Home Cooking," published in 1904

A Magnificent Gift From Mr. Massey

Hart A. Massey (1823-1896) was president of the largest farm implement manufacturing company in the world, and one of Canada's greatest philanthropists. It is said that he donated more than $300,000 to worthy causes during his lifetime. A staunch Methodist, he believed in the Methodist doctrine of giving something back to your community if you were a person of great wealth. Since the Ontario Ladies College (now Trafalgar Castle School) was a Methodist college, it qualified to receive some of the Massey money.

In 1895, the school had been trying for four years to raise $50,000 for a proposed addition. The college directors wanted to turn the school into a female university which would grant degrees on a level with the University of Toronto. The time was right for such a plan, but the school building was too small. In 1893, the Ontario Ladies' College had to reject applications from American students because there was no room for them. By the end of 1894, the directors had obtained subscriptions for $36,000, but were still $14,000 short of their goal.

It was at this point that Hart Massey entered the picture. On March 7, 1895, Massey informed the directors that he would donate $10,000 to complete the new addition, once the directors had raised $40,000. The grateful directors unanimously elected Hart Massey to the Board of the Ontario Ladies' College and announced that the addition would be named the *"Lillian Massey Hall"*, after

Lillian Frances Massey

Massey's only daughter. As a member of the Methodist Church, Massey would not allow cards, dancing, alcohol or tobacco in his home and restricted his daughter's social life so much that she did not marry until after he died.

Massey had already provided Toronto with Massey Music Hall and the Fred Victor Mission, and with his special interest in education, had made numerous gifts to Victoria College in Toronto, Albert College in Belleville, Alma College in St. Thomas and Methodist schools in Winnipeg and British Columbia.

Construction began immediately on a three-storey wing between the original Trafalgar Castle and *"The Cottage"*, the principal's residence. This addition was designed to include a dining room, a concert hall to seat 400 people, a kitchen and dormitories and baths on the upper floors.

On June 19, 1895, special trains brought a host of dignitaries from Toronto to attend the laying of the corner stone. George A. Cox, president of the Board of Directors, presented a silver trowel to Lillian Frances Massey, who assisted in spreading the mortar. Hart Massey, although aged and feeble, delivered an address to the large crowd. He compared the modern facilities of the Ontario Ladies' College with what female students had to contend with 50 years before, and stated: *"What a magnificent home these young lady students have."*

"Frances Hall", as the new building was eventually called, was completed during the summer and fall of 1895. On December 19, 1895, six months to the day

A tennis tournament at Frances Hall, May 25, 1903

after the corner stone was laid, Lillian Massey was again present for the official opening of Frances Hall. Frances Hall remains today much as it did when it was opened. The pipe organ, which once stood right of the stage in the concert hall, was dismantled in 1956 to provide parts for a new organ in Grace Chapel. The Loggia, an open arched passageway along the front, has been provided with storm windows so it can be used all year round. Otherwise, little has changed in more than 100 years.

Lillian Frances Massey's connection with Ontario Ladies' College did not end with the building of Frances Hall. On Sept. 1, 1902 she provided the necessary equipment to start a domestic science department at the school and sent a teacher every Saturday from her own domestic science training school in Toronto. Domestic science later became known as home economics in Ontario's high schools. The department at Whitby was later affiliated with the Lillian Massey Normal Training School of Household Science and Arts.

After Hart Massey's death at the age of 72 on February 20, 1896, Lillian Massey married John Treble, and died at Toronto in 1915. Her portrait still hangs in Frances Hall at Trafalgar Castle School. Although the Massey name was a household word in Canada a century ago, Canadians of today's generation remember best Hart Massey's grandsons, Vincent, who was Canada's Governor-General from 1952 to 1959, and Raymond, a noted stage and movie actor who played the part of Dr. Gillespie in the Dr. Kildare television series of the 1960s.

The original servant's wing of Trafalgar Castle was demolished to make way for the construction of Frances Hall. The Chronicle reported that the new hall could seat 400 people and had the same chairs as those Hart Massey had provided for Massey Hall in Toronto. Its acoustics were said to be admirable and the hall was lit throughout with electric lights. Massey Hall, still in use in Toronto, was opened a year before Frances Hall.

Albert Jackson's Political Career Started With A Knife Attack

In our grandparents' day Canadians took their politics very seriously. At election time, tempers flared, accusations were made and emotions ran high. In the municipal election of January 1897, a young Whitby resident, Albert W. Jackson (1870-1939) received a dramatic introduction to politics.

Albert and his brother Tom Jackson (1867-1906), who had won a seat on the town council a few days before, were walking along Brock Street when they were confronted by Ernie Gross (1859-1924) a hardware merchant whose store stood where Bayberry's shop is now. Gross, who did not like the outcome of the election, challenged Tom Jackson and called him a thief. Angry words were exchanged and a scuffle broke out on the sidewalk. In the midst of the struggle, Gross picked up a 13-inch carving knife and stabbed Albert Jackson in the face as he went to the aid of his brother. Jackson was not seriously injured, but the case went to court, with charges and counter-charges being laid by Gross and the Jacksons. A charge of assault against Gross was finally dismissed after three months before the magistrate.

Undeterred by the roughness of municipal politics, Albert Jackson decided to make politics his career. He was Whitby's second-longest serving politician, with 28 years on the Board of Education and Town Council. Tom Edwards holds the record with 36 years, and Heber Down (1889-1972) is third, with 21 years of service to

Albert W. Jackson

Whitby Town and Township. During those 28 years, Jackson was acclaimed to office 16 times and contested 12 elections. He only lost one election in that time, for the position of Reeve in 1929.

Jackson's political career started in 1901 as a member of the Whitby Board of Education, on which he served until 1904. In 1905-06 he was Reeve of Whitby, serving again in that position from 1909 to 1912, 1925 to 1928, 1930 to 1935 and 1938-1939. He served two terms as Mayor, 1907-08 and 1936-37. His non-elected positions included Collector of Customs from 1912 to 1921 and Town Clerk-Treasurer from 1921 to 1923.

While serving as Reeve in 1911-12, Jackson was responsible for negotiating with the Ontario Government for the establishment of the Ontario Hospital in Whitby. He carried out the delicate negotiations with the farmers whose lands were required for the 640-acre facility. He led several deputations to Queen's Park, where, on behalf of the Town of Whitby, he announced in 1912 that all the required lands were ready for purchase by the government.

As chairman of the Ontario County property committee he was active in planning additions to the Court House (now the Centennial Building) in 1910. In 1927, his fellow councillors chose him as Warden of Ontario County, a position similar to today's Regional Chairman.

Jackson was a keen student of

Members of the 34th Battalion of Militia boarding the Garden City at Whitby Harbour, 1909.

Parliamentary procedure and the provisions of municipal law. He was known to settle disputed points of law with facility and accuracy even though he was not a lawyer. A prominent worker for the Conservative Party in Whitby, Jackson could have been a candidate in any Federal or Provincial election, had he chosen to run.

In his business life, Jackson had a varied career, starting as a storekeeper in Port Whitby. He and his widowed mother operated the store that was taken over by Richard Goldring (1859-1945) in 1911. In the 1890s and early 1900s. Albert and his brother Tom operated a steamboat service from Toronto to Oshawa, Whitby and Newcastle. This prosperous business ended in tragedy in 1906 when both brothers contracted typhoid fever while refitting a steamer at Newcastle, and Tom Jackson died at the early age of 39. In later years, Albert Jackson was a real estate and insurance agent.

In the summer of 1900 the Jackson brothers found themselves in the middle of a *"boat war"* between the owner of their steamer, the Garden City, and the Oshawa Harbour Company. The Garden City was owned by Thomas Nihan, a Toronto man, who hired Tom Jackson as manager for his steamboat. The *"war"* started in 1897 when Nihan paid Oshawa Harbour Company $300 for docking rights. The following year, Jackson, then manager of a rival boat, secured docking privileges at Oshawa for $600. To settle the dispute, Nihan hired Jackson as his manager, combining the two men in the operation of the Garden City.

In the spring of 1900, Jackson secured docking privileges for his new boat, the Argyle at Oshawa Harbour for $600, forcing the Garden City out of the harbour. On a Friday morning in May, 1900, about 40 Oshawa citizens gathered at the harbour to ride the Garden City to Toronto, only to find a fence erected between them and the boat. The fence closed off the dock and was guarded by Oshawa's Chief Constable, wearing his official hat. Nihan, when he saw the barricade, headed uptown to see Oshawa's Mayor, Fred L. Fowke (1857-1939), who also happened to be harbour master. He offered Fowke five dollars to take down the barricade, but Fowke said he would charge Nihan $160 for two landings at the harbour. The plot thickens when it is realized that Fowke was also a provisional director of the company which owned the rival boat the Argyle. Although he always spoke against monopoly, it seemed he was forcing Nihan to pay top dollar for landing rights as long as the Argyle was in business.

While the dispute continued, the public had to take the train to Toronto or catch the Garden City at Whitby Harbour. No mention is made of the Argyle coming to their rescue. For a month, the situation remained a stalemate. The Argyle did not make an appearance and the owner of the Garden City did not want to put up $600 for landing rights at Oshawa. In an attempt to rescue himself from this awkward position, Nihan tried to lease the rights to a wagon service to take passengers and goods from Oshawa to Whitby Harbour where they could board the Garden City. Tom Jackson, meanwhile, advertised he would put another boat, the Columbian, into service from Oshawa in place of the missing Argyle. It too, never appeared.

By June 22, 1900 the *"boat war"* was over. Nihan purchased the docking rights at Oshawa Harbour from Jackson and promised to build a dock at the harbour as compensation to the harbour company. Finally, the citizens of Oshawa could travel to Toronto from their home port without having to go to Whitby.

Queen Victoria's Jubilee Was Compared To The Coming Of Christ

Just over 100 years ago, in June 1897, the British Empire celebrated the greatest event of the late 19th century – the Diamond Jubilee of the Queen Victoria's reign. The Whitby Chronicle stated: *"Next of the advent of Jesus Christ and His great salvation, the Diamond Jubilee of Good Queen Victoria is the most auspicious event in all history."* This may seem a great exaggeration, but to anyone of British nationality in 1897, there was nothing to compare with it.

Most people living had known no other monarch than Queen Victoria. She became Queen of the British Empire 60 years before, in 1837. No other monarch had reigned that long, anywhere in the world. She was 18 years old when she became Queen, was 78 at the time of her Diamond Jubilee, and was 81 when she died on January 22, 1901, having reigned for nearly 64 years.

Like all other communities in the British Empire, Whitby went all-out to celebrate Queen Victoria's Diamond Jubilee. The ceremonies began on June 20, 1897 with special thanksgiving services in the churches of the town. The Sons of England Lodge, formed 20 years previously, organized a Jubilee service in All Saints' Anglican Church, which was attended by the Town Council, the volunteer militia and all the fraternal societies of Whitby. The service

Brock Street looking south from Dundas Street at Queen Victoria's Diamond Jubilee, June 22, 1897.

started at 4 p.m. (the same time as a similar service in London, England) and as the bells in the tower rang, the congregation sang *"God Save the Queen."*

This service was only a prelude to Jubilee Day celebrations held on Tuesday, June 22, when a great parade marched through the town from the Collegiate Institute (now the site of Windsor Place seniors apartments at King and Colborne Streets) to the exhibition grounds. The exhibition grounds in 1897 were on the east side of Garden Street, opposite the site of Leslie McFarlane Public School. The parade started off with the firing of a 500-pound cannon at the exhibition grounds. This cannon continued to be fire regularly throughout the day. It was said to be heard for 25 miles and would shatter windows if set up too near homes.

The children of the town, led by a bugle band, marched through the main streets of Whitby, along with the militia, fraternal societies and other organizations. Mrs. Joshua Richardson (1833-1903), one of the oldest residents of Whitby, at the age of 64, played the part of Queen Victoria, as she was conveyed through the town in a special carriage. After the participants had marched onto the track at the exhibition grounds in front of the grandstand, Charles King (1837-1915), Warden of Ontario County, opened the official proceedings. King was owner of the King Brothers' Tannery which stood on Brock Street South where the No Frills Store is now. He could not seem to avoid bringing politics into his speech, suggesting that the Jubilee could be commemorated by building a home for the poor in Whitby. Ontario County did finally open a House of Refuge on High Street in 1903. The building is now apartments.

King was followed by William Ross, Reeve of Port Perry, who read Queen Victoria's Coronation oath from 1838, which was owned by the wife of one of the former county councillors. A speech outlining the life and deeds of Queen Victoria was delivered by John Dryden, MPP (1840-1909), who represented Ontario South in the Legislature and was Ontario's Minister of Agriculture. Dryden was owner of Maple Shade Farm, north-east of Brooklin. The official ceremonies concluded with Capt. Anson G. Henderson (1852-1928) of the 34th Battalion reading a telegram of greeting from Queen Victoria to her Canadian subjects. The program at the exhibition grounds continued with demonstrations of gymnastics and field exercises by the children of the town. The Boys' Brigades from St. John's Anglican Church, Port Whitby, and from Oshawa, presented a marching drill.

Each child who participated in the Jubilee festivities was presented with a flag and a souvenir handkerchief.

The program continued with a bicycle display on the track, with 25 entries decorated by their owners. Cyclists from Brooklin, Port Perry, Oshawa and Pickering, as well as from Whitby, entered and competed for prizes in men's and ladies' categories. There were also prizes of ten, six and four dollars for the rural schools making the best display in the parade. After the bicycle parade, the remainder of the afternoon was taken up with sports and games, including foot and bicycle races. The cannon boomed out a signal to halt the proceedings at 6:15 p.m. with several events uncompleted.

Decorated trains had brought hundreds of visitors to Whitby from Oshawa and the northern rural communities. Oshawa put off its Jubilee celebrations to July 1 in order not to conflict with Whitby's plans. To recover the $600 cost of the Jubilee celebration, admission to the exhibition grounds was 15 cents per man and 10 cents for ladies and children. The Ontario County Council contributed $50 toward the military parade, and the councillors were much in evidence at the event.

At 9 p.m., a crowd of 2,000 people marshalled in a field near the town to watch a bonfire arranged by the Sons of Scotland, Whitby Highland Club and the St. Andrew's Society of Whitby and Pickering. The 34th Regiment and the Citizens' Band provided the music for a parade of illuminated bicycles. As the bonfire of old boxes burst into flames, the people formed a circle around it and sang *"God Save the Queen"*, and *"Auld Lang Syne"*, followed by a fireworks display.

The main streets of Whitby were decorated as never before, in honour of the Jubilee. Evergreen trees were planted along Brock Street and flags hung from the buildings along the parade route. Photographs of the parade were taken by William E. O'Brien (1858-1925), Whitby's photographer, and were later published as post cards and in the 50th anniversary souvenir book of Ontario County in 1904. The decorations committee sold flags at wholesale prices at Andrew M. Ross's dry goods store on Brock Street South. Many homes in Whitby were also decorated for the Jubilee. Dr. Frank Warren's house where the medical centre is now on Dundas Street West, and the Court House (now the Centennial Building) were illuminated at night. The Royal Hotel, one of the town's most fashionable hotels, was also decorated.

The Whitby Chronicle reported that the roads were very dusty on Jubilee Day, but there were few cases of drunkenness at the celebrations. It was pointed out to all who cared to take note, that anyone attending the Queen's Jubilee would not live to see a Diamond Jubilee again in their lifetime. Since 1897 there have been only two Royal Jubilees, the Silver Jubilee for King George V in 1935 and Queen Elizabeth's Silver Jubilee in 1977. If Queen Elizabeth reigns for 60 years, her Diamond Jubilee would be in 2012, when she would be 86 years old.

Queen Victoria's Diamond Jubilee had special significance for one former Whitby resident, who was then living in Toronto.

Brock Street looking north from Dundas Street at Queen Victoria's Diamond Jubilee, June 22, 1897.

John Bengough (1819-1899) was born in St. Andrew's Fifeshire, Scotland, on May 23, 1819. He was always proud of the fact that he was born one day before Queen Victoria.

Bengough, who came to Whitby about 1853, was the father of John W. Bengough, (1851-1923), Canada's most famous 19th century political cartoonist, whose story is in another Chronicle in this book.

Rector Harris Showed How Not To Ring In The New Century

At midnight on Dec. 31, 1999, the residents of Whitby will celebrate the beginning of a new century and a new millennium. Although technically, the 21st century does not begin until Jan. 1, 2001, the celebrations will begin in the year 2000 with a special ceremony at Iroquois Park.

Rev. James H. Harris of St. Thomas' Anglican Church in Brooklin had his own ideas about ringing in the 20th century. He planned to ring the bell of his church on the stroke of midnight as January 1, 1900 began, and invited the residents of Brooklin to listen from the railway station site on the west side of Anderson street opposite the church. The rector wrapped his hand around the loop at the end of the bell rope at the appointed hour and pulled hard to ring the bell as loud as he could. It turned out, however, that he had pulled too hard, for the bell fell from its mooring in the tower to the lawn in front of the church. Rev. Harris, with his hand secured in the loop of the bell rope, was hauled up to the ceiling of the church by the weight of the falling bell. He let go, dropping to the floor, where he lay, seriously injured, until some of the parishioners found him. The bell, cast at Troy, New York, and installed in the church in 1873, had to be replaced. Fortunately, Rev. Mr. Harris recovered from his injuries.

This is only one incident in the colourful history of St. Thomas' Anglican Church. This picturesque white frame church, popular with artists and photographers, was built in 1869 from plans by the noted Toronto church architect Henry Langley (1836-1907). Thomas Lumsden (1827-1885) a local farmer, donated two acres of his land for a church and rectory in 1866. A building committee consisting of John D. Howden (1841-1927), Henry H. Spencer (1831-1894), Dr. Frank Warren (1850-1920), William H. Browne (1837-1894) and Peter Francis (1835-1910) was in charge of the church's construction.

Archbishop Derwyn T. Owen and Rev. John C. Clough, 1939.

St. Thomas' Anglican Church, Brooklin, with picket fence, Circa 1910.

Rev. James Mockridge of St. Paul's Anglican Church near Columbus was the driving force behind the construction of St. Thomas' Church. Until 1865, Brooklin was part of a parish which included Columbus, Ashburn, Manchester, Uxbridge and a number of other localities.

In 1874, a driving shed was built for the church and in 1879 a brick rectory was constructed east of the church. It was used until sold in 1951. A modern rectory was built south of the church in 1966.

St. Thomas', like many other small country churches, had high and low points in its history. In 1877, the rector's salary was cut to $100 a year and he had to contribute personally $25 towards that sum. In 1883, the foundation of the church shifted, and the plaster ceiling fell. Fortunately, there was no service at the time. The greatest crisis occurred in 1901, when a Mr. Pherrill used all the church funds to purchase a marble baptismal font. Since there was no money left after this was done, the wardens had to close the church for three years. This was not the only time St. Thomas' had to close. In the winter of 1917-18 during a severe coal shortage, the church was closed and its parishioners worshipped with the Presbyterians in a frame church where Mitchell Brothers' Building Supply store is now.

In 1904, when the church reopened after the font episode, it was decided to build a stone basement under the building. Rev. John Bennett-Anderson (1845-1923), the new rector, laid cement and did other manual labour along with the work crew. A year later, the interior of the church was lined with metal sheeting from the Pedlar People factory in Oshawa, at a cost of $65. It can still be seen on the walls and ceiling.

The high point in the history of St. Thomas' Church was the visit of the Archbishop of Toronto, Derwyn T. Owen, on Sept. 24, 1939, to dedicate a large selection of memorials. These included leaded glass windows donated by Mrs. John Moore (1877-1956) in memory of her husband, Dr. John J. Moore (1862-1937), a church warden for many years; an electric organ donated by Fred W. Browne (1870-1956) and a chancel screen designed by the noted Toronto architect Eric Arthur. The damask used to cover the front of the altar was specially woven for use in Westminster Abbey for the coronation of King George VI on May 12, 1937.

Besides things of beauty, there were practical additions made to the church. In 1882, a fence was constructed to keep cattle off the church lawn.

The first organ was installed in 1877 at a cost of $140, a large sum in those days. A concert was given in the old Masonic Hall to raise funds to pay for the organ, and one Sunday's collection went to the organ fund. In 1952, a full basement was put under the church for choir and Sunday School rooms. A portable classroom from Upper Canada College was attached to the back of the church in 1960 to provide a kitchen and more classroom space. In 1987 a new Memorial Hall was completed to give the small church adequate space for Sunday School and meeting rooms.

When St. Thomas' Church was built in 1869, its construction cost over $2,000. A number of entertainment evenings were presented, with admission at 25 cents, to raise funds to pay off the debt. In the church can be seen a marble plaque in memory of Thomas Lumsden, who provided the land in 1866. He died at St. Francis Xavier, Manitoba, in 1885. This time there was more money collected for the memorial than was needed, so the church's general fund received a boost from the remainder. The baptismal font, which nearly closed the church for good in 1901, is still in use today, nearly a century later, and the new church bell is rung safely every Sunday. It is expected it will be used to ring in the new millennium on Jan. 1, 2000, without any unfortunate incidents.

Whitby Was A Three-Industry Town

For the first 50 years of the 20th century, Whitby was sustained by only three manufacturing industries – a tannery, a buckle factory and a blanket factory. While Oshawa was always a manufacturing centre, Whitby was not. There were a number of small industries in the town in the 19th century, but by 1910, only three remained, all related to the horse and buggy trade. The popularity of the automobile spelled their end in the 1950s and 1960s.

The oldest of the three industries was the King Brothers' Tannery, founded by Joseph (1835-1930) and Charles (1837-1915) King. In April 1863, the King brothers, Jewish immigrants from Bohemia (now the Czech Republic) came to Whitby after a short stay in New York City, to establish a tannery where the No Frills plaza is now on Brock Street South. They selected Whitby as their site because of the harbour for shipping their products, and changed their family name of Koenig to King.

King Brothers' Tannery started with three employees and 12 vats which tanned fewer than 50 hides a month. By 1876, there were 40 employees doing about $100,000 worth of business in a year. In 1875, the tannery processed 500 hides and 12,000 calf skins. Many of the finished products were shipped to Britain and the United States. Leather produced by King's Tannery was used for

King Brothers' Tannery, during a parade in 1934. This is the only available photo of the tannery.

making harness and bridles for horses, soles for shoes, ladies' wear and industrial engine belts. In 1880, when there were 85 tanning vats, the tannery produced Spanish polished horse hides as a new line of business.

About 39 raw hides per day were processed through lime and other weaker solutions, where they remained for two to four months, according to the thickness of the leather. Heavy harness leather took five months to cure. After passing through vats, the hides were scoured and brought inside the tannery building where all the lime and dirt were rinsed out. Then they went to the curriers where the hides were made into finished leather goods. Bark from trees, required for the tanning process, amounting to 700 cords annually, was shipped after 1877 to Whitby from Victoria County on the Whitby, Port Perry and Lindsay Railway. Consumption of raw materials in one year amounted to 20 tons of gambia and sumac, 5,000 gallons of oil, 70 barrels of tallow, three carloads of lime, two tons of log wood, 1,800 pounds of copperas (a metallic chemical) and 2,000 pounds of soda.

The smell from the tannery was a constant source of annoyance to its neighbours. A popular rhyme recited by the school children of Whitby was:

"King's Tannery, proper noun, Stinks enough to knock you down. Indicative mood, past tense, Hang their cowhides on the fence."

Isabella Cormack, who lived on Green Street behind the tannery, tried unsuccessfully to sue the Kings because of the smell.

In 1883, Joseph King dissolved the partnership with his brother and moved to Toronto where he died in 1930 at the age of

The Buckle Factory in 1959.

94. Charles King brought two of his sons, Joseph (1869-1961) and Theodore (?-1965) into the business, with himself as president, Joseph as vice-president and Theodore as secretary. After their father's death, Joseph and Theodore carried on the business.

Additions to the tannery were made in 1888 and 1905. The number of employees reached 70 in 1890 and by 1905 the tannery was processing 300 hides a week. The increased use of the automobile after the First World War, spelled the end of King

Brothers' Tannery. The advent of plastics and the importation of leather from outside Canada also contributed to its demise. The tannery closed in November 1952 and was demolished in the summer of 1954. A Dominion store and plaza were built on the site the following year.

Whitby's second large industry was the buckle factory, founded in 1887 by Toronto industrialists George V. Martin and Samuel Trees (1838-1918). First known as the Martin Manufacturing Company, it stood on the site of the Price Chopper plaza on Brock Street South. Martin and Trees bought the old O'Donovan carriage factory, after receiving a bonus of $15,000 from the town council to come to Whitby. The cost of the site was $1,200. Some of the old carriage factory buildings were used by Martin and Trees and new ones were added over the intervening years. Martin moved to Whitby to manage the factory, while Trees remained in Toronto to handle the distribution side of the business. A number of skilled craftsmen were brought from Toronto, including the plant's first superintendent, Charles Barton (?-1932) and members of the Mowat family. Martin's daughter, Addie, was the first bookkeeper, and in 1889, the company hired George Whitelaw (1870-1964) as a travelling salesman. A Mr. Vancuran, foreman of the machine shop, came from a sim-

ilar factory in Buffalo, New York.

By April 1888, about 40 people were employed by the buckle factory, which made brass buckles for horse harness. In its first statement to the Town of Whitby, in May 1888, the Martin Manufacturing Company reported that it employed an average of 50 workers and paid $12,300 in wages, $2,300 more than what was required in the agreement with the town. The firm's only competition was the Skinner Company in Gananoque, which closed in the early 1900s, leaving the Whitby factory with a monopoly in the trade. Many Whitby families worked for two or three generations in the buckle factory, including the Mowats, Fallons, Bartons, Fegans, Andersons, Coffeys, Hartricks and Wilkinsons.

In October 1903, George V. Martin sold the factory to Fred Hatch (1861-1929) a former Whitby hardware store owner, and moved to Newark, New Jersey, because of ill health. The name remained Martin Manufacturing Company until it was changed to the Hatch Manufacturing Company in 1918. From 1906 to 1912, Fred Hatch hired Whitby builder Thomas G. Deverell (1860-1928) to construct new brick buildings for the buckle factory, until it covered almost an entire block of property. At the north-west corner of the property was the Hatch home, now the Montessori

School.

In 1906 the buckle factory reached a peak of 112 employees. One of those who started that year was 16-year-old Robin Nicholson who was one of the last three employees when the factory closed 58 years later. In the years leading up to the First World War, the gasoline engine began to replace the horse for transportation and farm machinery, but the war rejuvenated the company's sagging business. From 1914 to 1918 the plant was kept so busy with orders for Canada's cavalry and field artillery units, that it added a night shift and was in operation 24 hours a day. Before the war, the Canadian West had been a major market for the buckle factory but by the 1920s, only Quebec and the Maritimes were still in need of saddlery hardware products. Gasoline tractors had replaced the horse. These tractors were first shown in this area in 1916 at the International Plowing Match held on the R. J. Fleming farm (now Picov Downs) in what is now Ajax. As the market declined, a large number of employees were laid off and the remainder had their work week shortened.

In 1929, Fred Hatch died at the age of 67 and the buckle factory was purchased by Samuel L. Trees (1885-1957), son of the original founding partner Samuel Trees. Trees, who already owned a blanket factory in Whitby, left the management of the buckle factory to his brother James D. Trees (1877-1966). In 1930, he changed the name to Whitby Malleable Iron and Brass Company. While Canada suffered through the Depression of the 1930s, Whitby's buckle factory had a new lease on life. Because many people could not afford cars or even gasoline, the horse made a comeback. In the West, horses were hitched to cars known as *"Bennett Buggies"*, a slap at Prime Minister Richard B. Bennett, who was blamed by many for the ills of the Depression.

The buckle factory carried on through the Second World War and the 1950s, but finally closed its doors in May of 1964 after 76 years of operation. The last three employees, Robin Nicholson (1890-1970), Russell Bailey (1892-1967) and Gordon Noble (1902-1978) had the job of sorting and tagging the company's assets before they went on the auction block. On Oct. 14, 1964, crowds turned out to witness the auction of the contents of the buckle factory. Cecil Greenfield (1890-1966) who had worked at the factory for 55 years, said it was like seeing a relative laid away. In 1966, the buildings were demolished. The land remained vacant for nine years until 1975 when Gilbert Street was closed between Byron and Brock Streets and a Safeway

The Blanket Factory in 1912.

plaza built on the site. The Safeway store is now Price Chopper.

The third Whitby industry of the first 50 years of the 20th century was a horse blanket and collar factory called Samuel Trees

and Company. It was located on the east side of Brock Street, north of Mary Street where a small plaza stands today. The site had been occupied since 1854 by a foundry for making agricultural implements, under various owners. In 1909, with the death of the factory owner, William J. Clokey (1856-1909), the buildings were vacant.

In October 1909, the citizens of Whitby voted on a bylaw to provide municipal services and tax concessions to Samuel L. Trees of Toronto who expressed an interest in opening a horse blanket factory. In December, Trees moved into the factory, and three years later purchased the George Y. Smith mansion where the library now stands on Dundas Street West, as his home. Special machinery imported from England was installed in the factory and the first shipment of goods was made in February 1910. Trees built a two-storey brick addition to the factory the same year and brought workers from Toronto. During the First World War when horses were still used in warfare, the factory prospered, so much, in fact that Trees and his brothers presented a motor ambulance to the war effort in 1915.

Like the buckle factory, the Trees blanket factory had hard times in the 1920s and a new prosperity in the 1930s when people could not afford cars. In 1929, Trees purchased the buckle factory, so that he now owned two of Whitby's three leading industries. In October 1958, the Trees factory became the second of these industries to close. The factory remained vacant for four years, until it was demolished in 1962 to build an A and P store.

Whitby's industrial scene began to change after the Second World War, when an aggressive campaign was begun to attract small industries from Toronto. Among those acquired in 1946 and 1947 were the Natlie Knitting Mills, Empire Pant and Boys' Wear and the William J. Anderson Company which made jewellery boxes. In 1947, the town received a promise from the Dunlop Tire and Rubber Company to move its Toronto plant to Whitby. This was reconfirmed in 1953, and two years later the Dunlop plant opened in Whitby with 600 employees. This was the beginning of major industrial development in the 1950s and 1960s, culminating with the construction in 1964 of the Lake Ontario Steel plant, the town's largest employer. Whitby had suddenly entered the modern age.

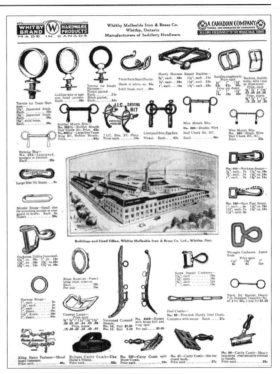

A page from Samuel Trees and Company's Summer 1932 catalogue, advertising Whitby Malleable Iron and Brass Co.

Heydenshore Park Was Once A Summer Resort

Heydenshore Park, with its beautiful frontage along Lake Ontario, is a popular public park today, but for 65 years it was a private summer resort of cottages owned by wealthy citizens of Whitby, Oshawa and Toronto. The idea of creating a lakefront park east of Whitby Harbour originated with Fred Howard Annes (1861-1940) in 1897 when he wrote a letter to The Whitby Chronicle outlining his proposal. The land proposed for the park was a 20-acre site owned since 1865 by Lawrence Heyden and his sister Barbara. Lawrence (1835-1906) and Barbara (1829-1916) were children of Lawrence Heyden Sr. (1804-1868), one of the *"Four Irishmen"* who settled in Whitby Township in 1821. In the 1820s, Lawrence Heyden Sr. kept a store in Whitby and later moved to Toronto where he was Clerk of the Crown and Peace. His children became very wealthy, and at her death, Barbara Heyden left an estate worth nearly half a million dollars. Besides the site of Heydenshore Park, the brother and sister owned the Jabez Lynde farm on Highway 2 at Lynde Creek.

After Annes's proposal for a lakefront park was made, the Town Council began to negotiate with Lawrence and Barbara Heyden, but with little result. In 1899, the Whitby Board of Trade (a forerunner of the Chamber of Commerce), asked the Town

Heydenshore Park looking east along the lakeshore in 1913.

Council to expropriate the Heyden property for a park. At the request of John B. Dow (1851-1910), president of the Board of Trade, a meeting was held in his office with Lawrence Heyden, who agreed to lease 20 acres of his property at a rent of $200 a year for 21 years. He also agreed to take stock in the amount of the first three years of rent. A joint stock company was formed with capital stock of $20,000, divided into 1,000 shares at $20 each. The provisional directors were: Lawrence Heyden, John B. Dow, James Rutledge (1842-1914), Lyman T. Barclay (1855-1925), Theodore A.

The original Heydenshore Park Pavilion (1901-1936).

McGillivray (1852-1925), Andrew M. Ross (1851-1936), William J.H. Richardson (1874-1953), Hugh M. Ross (1854-1923), Fred Hatch (1861-1929), Thomas G. Whitfield (1854-1928) and J.L. Madill. The first five directors, including Mr. Heyden, were lawyers.

The directors named their stock company *"The Whitby Street Railway and Park Company Limited."* Although the original intention was to link the park with the town by a street railway, the railway idea was abandoned as the automobile began to take over the roads. The park was named *"Heydenshore Park,"* after Lawrence and Barbara Heyden. By May, 1900 the park company's charter was granted by the Ontario Government. An experienced landscape gardener was hired to lay out the grounds and plant trees, and lots for cottages were leased. Among those who built cottages were: Fred Hatch, Dr. Charles F. McGillivray (1857-1944), William S. Gold (1864-1909), George Ross (1858-1936) and Thomas G. Whitfield of Whitby, and R.S. McLaughlin (1871-1972) of Oshawa.

Arrangements were also made with local and Toronto steamboat companies to bring passengers to and from Whitby Harbour so they could use Heydenshore Park.

Behind the row of cottages along the lakeshore, was an open public area for sports and games, in the centre of which was built a large frame pavilion for dances. The pavilion was built in 1901 with a covered dance floor reached by a flight of steps. Beneath the dance floor were refreshment booths. The architect for the pavilion was James M. Miller (?-1933) of Toronto. It measured 40 by 40 feet and cost $1,500 to construct. This pavilion stood until 1936 when it was demolished. The present Heydenshore Pavilion, built in 1971, is named after this building.

A special sports day was held on the August Civic Holiday at Heydenshore Park, and Toronto organizations such as the Danforth Business Men's Association held picnics in the park.

In 1901, Mathias W. Collins (1859-1933) a Whitby shoe store owner, purchased a small house in the northern part of the town and had it pulled to Heydenshore park by traction engines to be set up as his summer cottage. R.S. McLaughlin, who later became Chairman of General Motors of Canada in Oshawa had a cottage at Heydenshore Park, as well as his daughter,

The Mathias W. Collins cottage at Heydenshore Park, c. 1906.

Mrs. J.B. Pangman. McLaughlin presented the park with stone gates which were erected at the west end in 1929. These gates stood for 30 years until they were demolished to make way for a new water pump house in 1959.

In 1902, the Methodist Deaconesses built a home for underprivileged children at Heydenshore Park. Every summer children from the slums of Toronto were brought to Whitby to spend a week or two at the Methodist Fresh Air Home. A victim of the Depression, this home was closed and demolished after 1932.

During the First World War, the 182nd Battalion from Ontario County held a summer camp at Heydenshore Park in August 1916, to train its men for overseas service.

One of the leading promoters of Heydenshore Park was Fred Hatch. As the other directors of the Whitby Street Railway and Park Company died, Hatch acquired ownership of the park and passed it on to his sons Russell (1894-1958) and Clive (1888-1963). In 1965, the Whitby Public Utilities Commission purchased Heydenshore Park from Clive Hatch for $38,000 and demolished all but one of the cottages. The PUC bought the park in order to have land for future expansion of the water pumping station at the harbour, and provided the remainder of the land as a public park. In 1971, the PUC sold the park to the Town of Whitby. The present park consists of about 13 acres. In the 1970s the Kiwanis Club of Whitby adopted the park as a special project and over the years has provided picnic shelters, playground equipment and other facilities. Heydenshore Park was the site of trailer rallies by American tourists in the early 1970s and was one of the sites for events at the County town Carnival. In 1995 the Waterfront Trail was built through the park.

All that remains of the original buildings of Heydenshore park are a couple of sets of cement steps leading from the sites of former cottages to the beach.

Fred Howard Annes Was Whitby's Unappreciated Visionary

He was the founder of Heydenshore Park; he promoted the establishment of an airport at Whitby in the 1920s and predicted that one day Whitby and Oshawa would join together as one big city linked by railways to all parts of Canada. He was a visionary, far ahead of his time, who died in a poor-house, forgotten by the community he served for so many years.

Fred Howard Annes (1861-1940) was born into a significant family in Whitby's history. His grandfather, Ezra Annes (1796-1857) was the founder of the town's first Masonic Lodge in 1826 and served as Whitby's third mayor in 1857. He was the only mayor of the town to die in office, and the first to have a Masonic funeral. He is buried in St. John's Anglican Cemetery in Port Whitby, but no stone marks the site of his grave.

Fred's father, Henry Warren Annes (1824-1886) was a member of the Town Council in 1882-83 and 1885, but died at the age of 61 before he could complete the work of his municipal career.

Ezra Annes, born in Vermont, U.S.A. came to Whitby Township in 1818 and started working for a man named Losie who kept a store near Dundas and Euclid Streets. He married Losie's daughter, Maria, and purchased the block of land bounded by Dundas, Annes, Victoria and Henry Streets. At the corner of Dundas and Frances Streets, he built about 1836, a large stucco home, known at one time as *Clover Knolls.* This house was moved to Wellington Street in 1960 by Mr. and Mrs. Robert G. Langford, who had sold the Annes property for development. The Towne Plaza, with its A&P store, is on the site today.

Ezra Annes subdivided a portion of his property in the 19th century, but no development occurred until the 1950s, one hundred years after his death. Frances, Maria and Harriet Streets are named after his daughters, and Henry Street after his son, the father of Fred Howard Annes. Annes Street was named after Ezra.

Henry Warren Annes married on Jan. 26, 1859, Charlotte

Fred Howard Annes is in the lower right corner of this photograph of the 1913 Whitby Town Council, taken at The Village Inn, Oakville, during an inspection tour of sewage disposal plants.

Frances Howard (1831-1925), daughter of another early Whitby pioneer, Erastus Howard. They had three children, the first of whom died at the age of nine days. The other two were Fred Howard Annes and Maude Lillian Annes (1868-1940), neither of whom married. It was said that Fred Howard Annes was very much influenced by his mother, with whom he and his sister Maude lived most of their lives. When their mother died in 1925 at the age of 93, Fred was 64. Mrs. Henry Warren Annes was named honorary president of the County of Ontario Old Girls' Association when it was formed in 1904, because she was the oldest of the original pioneers of the town. The Old Girls' Association was an early version of today's service clubs. One of its major contributions to Whitby was the purchase of the site for the town's library at Byron and Dundas Streets in 1911. The library building is now Jim Flaherty's law office.

The citizens of Whitby considered the Annes family a rather eccentric lot, particularly Fred, with his grand ideas. The family home was then called *"Idylwild."* This, according to some people, was because the owner was *"idle and wild,"* and never did a day's work in his life. It is true that Fred Howard Annes had plenty of money and did not have to work, but he was an indus-

trious person nonetheless.

Fred Howard Annes emerged in the 1890s as a writer, promoter and visionary, who was either ignored or laughed at by some people in Whitby, but he was really a man ahead of his time. Little is known of him except through his writings, which were published in the Whitby, Oshawa and Toronto newspapers on various occasions.

In 1887, Annes was the editor of the Whitby Gazette, the rival to The Chronicle. In 1893 he was appointed as a representative of the Ontario Government at the Columbian Exposition in Chicago where he was influential in promoting the products of the province. For a number of years he was also a parliamentary reporter at Queen's Park. He was a constant writer of letters to newspapers, outlining his views on the future of the Whitby area and promoting development.

In 1897, it was Fred Howard Annes who approached the Whitby Town Council with a proposal to establish a summer resort at the harbour. His proposal resulted in the establishment of Heydenshore Park as a private resort of summer cottages east of Whitby Harbour, in 1900. The park remained as a summer resort until 1965 when it was purchased by the Public Utilities Commission and the cottages were demolished. It is now a public park main-

tained by the Town of Whitby and an important site along the Waterfront Trail.

In 1906, Annes wrote a letter to the Toronto World, outlining how the proposed Toronto and Eastern electric commuter railway would benefit Whitby by attracting Toronto businessmen to live in the town. The Toronto and Eastern was commenced in 1913 but never completed. It was not until the 1980s that Annes' vision of Whitby as a bedroom community for Toronto was achieved. In December 1988, the Go-Transit tracks were opened to Whitby, and subsequently to Oshawa.

In 1927, Annes wrote a nearly full-page article in the Oshawa Daily Times, extolling the virtues of Whitby as a site for an airport for planes and dirigibles, the lighter-than-air craft that were popular until the destruction of the *"Hindenburg"* 10 years later. Because the giant airships used hydrogen to lift them, this highly flammable gas was dangerous and could catch fire, as it did when the *"Hindenburg"* was attempting to land at Lakehurst, New Jersey, in 1937. Annes did much to promote the establishment of an airport at Whitby when it was learned that Camp Borden was going to relocate and establish an airport somewhere in southern Ontario. The 1927 airport proposal came to nothing, although a small airstrip was built on

The Annes homestead as it appeared before being moved to Wellington Street in 1960.

He wrote *"Whitby's Wonderful Transportation Endowment,"* for a special illustrated edition of *"The Gazette and Chronicle"* in June 1913, and the commercial and industrial edition of the Ontario Reformer, Oshawa's newspaper, in 1916. He is undoubtedly the author of the illustrated promotion book, *"Whitby, The Best Residential Town Near Toronto,"* issued by the Town Council in 1914. By the 1920s Annes was predicting that Whitby and Oshawa would join together one day as a single community. It was proposed again by Oshawa in 1970 at the time of the Oshawa Area Planning and Development Study (OAPADS), and is now under discussion in the late 1990s as the Provincial Government is restructuring municipalities of the Greater Toronto Area. Whitby citizens have never supported amalgamation with Oshawa. In 1970, someone placed a mock tomb stone at Dundas and Green Streets bearing the inscription: *"Here lie Oshawa's plans to amalgamate with Whitby; May they rest in peace."* In 1997, the Town of Whitby polled its residents on amalgamation and found 97 percent of them opposed to joining Oshawa. The issue is expected to continue as a controversial topic: as the next municipal election approaches in the year 2000.

Following the family tradition, Fred

the site of Lake Ontario Steel in 1941 for transferring goods during the Second World War. It was an alternate site to the Oshawa Airport, established in 1943.

The Whitby Town Council made use of Annes' talents on a number of occasions.

The Ontario County House of Refuge (now Heritage Estates), 300 High Street, where Fred and Maude Annes died 11 days apart in 1940, The House of Refuge was replaced by Fairview Lodge in December, 1951.

as president of the Whitby Women's Institute in 1927-28. By the 1930s, old and unable to care for themselves, they were placed in the Ontario County House of Refuge (now High Street Manor behind Fairview Lodge) where they died 11 days apart, Maude on Nov. 28, and Fred on Dec. 9, 1940. The last of their noted family, they were almost forgotten by the people of Whitby when they died. The Annes house was filled from floor to ceiling with historical documents, papers and photographs. Everything was sold at one of the largest public auctions ever held in Whitby. What was not destroyed went for rock-bottom prices, a sad end to an illustrious family. It is even more unfortunate to note that when Fred and Maude Annes died, officials at the House of Refuge got Maude's birth date wrong on her death certificate and did not even know Fred's birth date. According to The Whitby Chronicle he was born on Aug. 28, 1861, and would have been 79 years old at the time of his death.

Howard Annes served on the Whitby Town Council from 1902 to 1904, 1907 to 1908,1913, 1916 and finally in 1919. He was the third generation of his family to do so. Pictures of Fred Howard Annes are difficult to find. He appears in the Town Council photograph of 1913, which accompanies this Chronicle, and his portrait was printed in the Toronto Saturday Globe in 1905.

As the years went by, Fred and Maude Annes withdrew from public life. Maude was active in theatrical groups in Whitby and the Old Girls' Association, and served

The Day When Bullets Flew Through Downtown Whitby

On Sunday, June 9, 1901, Whitby's citizens ran for cover as bullets flew through the downtown. A projectile shattered the plate glass window of John Saunders' boot and shoe shop, and Rev. John Abraham (1843-1926) minister of St. Andrew's Presbyterian Church, was among those wounded that day. The cause of all this excitement and danger was not a gun fight at the O.K. Corral. It was one of the biggest fires in Whitby's history, in a hardware store filled with gunpowder and boxes of ammunition. As the flames reached these hazardous items, there were explosions within the burning store, and bullets flew in all directions across Brock Street.

The burning building was the Gross and Granger hardware store on the west side of Brock Street where Bayberry's store is today. When it was built, 42 years previously, the Gross and Granger building was one of the finest business blocks in downtown Whitby. It was constructed in 1859 by James Wallace (1814-1882), a local contractor and entrepreneur who had served as Whitby's second mayor, three years previously. Among his accomplishments was the building of the Ontario, County Court House, now the Centennial Building.

In 1858, Wallace founded the Whitby Highland Rifle Company, a forerunner of today's Ontario Regiment. He lived at Burr

A stream of water is being sent through the windows of the Gross and Granger building, at left, during the fire of June 9, 1901.

Lodge on Centre Street South, one of the largest mansions in Whitby, which still stands as an apartment building, north of James Street.

Wallace's Block, as the Gross and Granger store was originally called, was a three-storey building, with a front of white brick and the back and sides of red brick. The

Semi-Weekly Chronicle, Whitby' newspaper in 1859, stated there was cast iron work around each of the windows in the same style as the Toronto Masonic Hall, built in 1857 on Toronto Street and demolished 100 years later. The Wallace Block consisted of two stores on the ground floor and offices on the second and third floors. The

A bill from Gross and Granger's hardware store, 1882.

first occupants of the ground floor were the hardware store of J.S.Donaldson (1830-1918) and the Bank of Montreal, Whitby's first bank. Because one of the stores was occupied by a bank, the building was equipped with large vaults for storing valuables.

In the 1870s, the hardware store was operated by Gross and MacNachtan, followed in the 1880s by Gross and Granger, the partners being George Conrad Gross (1807-1893) and William Granger (1848-1914). William Granger was married to Annie Laura Gross (1850-1893), a daughter of his senior partner. George Conrad Gross was German by birth, but had lived in England before emigrating to New York City in the 1840s. He settled in Whitby in 1859. In 1883 he built the large castle-like house at Byron and Colborne streets, now occupied by Jerry and Judy Moskaluk. Following his father's death in 1893, George Ernest Gross (1859-1924) took over the store.

From 1860 to 1867, Composite Masonic Lodge met in rooms on the third floor of Wallace's Block. James Wallace, a leading member of the lodge, offered the rooms at a good rental fee of $90 a year. The first meeting in the new building as held on March 1, 1860. In 1867, a better rental offer was made and the lodge moved to the

Lowes and Powell building at Brock and Dundas streets where the bank of Commerce is today. The Lowes and Powell building was demolished in 1964.

The dramatic events of June 9, 1901 began at 5 a.m. when William Dent and George Ernest Gross, who lived in the rooms above the hardware store, smelled smoke. The alarm was raised and the Merryweather steam fire engine was soon on the scene, shooting two streams of water into the burning building. It was to continue fighting the fire for three hours, aided by a volunteer bucket brigade that was stationed on the roofs of nearby stores and the Queen's Hotel (now the Corner Store) at Brock and Colborne Streets.

A piano and most of the furnishings of Gross's rooms were removed safely, as well as equipment from Dr. Woodrow's dentistry office on the second floor, and much of the hardware stock. When the flames reached the boxes of cartridges and gunpowder at the back of the hardware store, the flying bullets sent people running in all directions. For half an hour, it was impossible to get near the burning building because of the bullets and explosions. Several people were wounded by the bullets, but fortunately, there were no serious injuries.

With no way of fighting the fire, Mayor Andrew M. Ross (1851-1936) called

Oshawa Mayor Fred L. Fowke for help. The Oshawa Fire Brigade arrived as soon as it could, but by that time the Gross and Granger hardware store was a smoking ruin. The massive three-storey building was gutted, with only the front and side walls left standing. The back wall had collapsed. The Toronto Globe, which reported extensively on the fire, estimated the loss on the building as $6,000, insured for only $3,000; and the loss on Gross and Granger's stock was $12,000, insured for $4,000.

The story of the Gross and Granger fire did not end on June 9, 1901. More incidents were to come. By October 1901, the blackened walls of the old building were still standing, so the Town Council asked its solicitor to take steps to have them removed. In November, Lyman T. Barclay (1855-1925), a local lawyer, offered to undertake the rebuilding of the Gross and Granger store, which he estimated would cost him $3,000. William Westlake (1847-1916), a Whitby contractor, was ready to undertake the job, but nothing was done. The walls remained standing until July 7, 1902, when they crashed down on the neighbouring wooden shops of jeweller Arthur Gilpin (?-1930) and barber James Worfolk (1862-1926). Mrs. Worfolk was upstairs in her husband's shop when the walls fell. She barely had time to dive under

a table to save herself. Mrs. Worfolk was pregnant at the time. It was very fortunate that she did not lose her baby from the shock of nearly being killed by falling bricks. Considerable damage was done to the barber shop, where the Chamber of Commerce building is now, but she was not injured. The baby, Hazel J. Worfolk (1902-1982) was born a month later on Aug. 3, 1902, and lived to be nearly 80 years old. A well-known Whitby resident who worked in the Land Registry Office for nearly 50 years, she often told the story of how she almost did not come into the world because of a falling building.

By the third week of July, 1902, the remainder of the brick walls of the Gross and Granger building were removed and the story of one of Whitby's oldest downtown blocks came to an end. Within four years, the building now occupied by Bayberry's and the former Maple Leaf Billiards, was constructed on the site by Thomas Jackson (1867-1906).

The photograph of the Gross and granger fire, accompanying this chronicle, was taken by Newton Johns who travelled from Oshawa to Whitby on a bicycle when he heard news of the fire.

These Cannons Made A Round Trip In 87 Years

Whitby teamster Joseph Heard (1860-1941) probably wished he had never received a call from Ontario County Clerk John E. Farewell to make a delivery to the Court House early in 1902. Col. Farewell made a most unusual request – to transport two cannons from the uptown railway station at Dundas and Hickory Streets, upon their arrival by train from the Citadel at Halifax, Nova Scotia. Col. Farewell, commanding officer of the 34th Regiment (now the Ontario Regiment) had learned in November 1901 that the military authorities at the Citadel were disposing of surplus cannons and he thought a pair of them would look impressive in front of the Court House at Whitby.

The cannons, officially known as seven-inch RML (rifled muzzle-loading) guns, were manufactured at the Royal Arsenal at Woolwich, England, in 1866 and shipped to Halifax to become part of Canada's east coast defences. Since 1879, they were part of the armament at the Citadel, a massive fort on a hill in the centre of the city. After Col. Farewell received permission from the chief ordinance officer at the Citadel to receive the cannons on behalf of the County of Ontario, they were taken to the Intercolonial Railway station at Halifax. The contractor who moved them

Members of the Ontario County Council of 1902 posing on one of the cannons in front of the old Court House

from the Citadel estimated it would cost him $32 to take them by wagon with teams of horses, but had to charge $46.85 because of the difficulty of the job. Each

of the two cannons weighed seven tons and the undercarriages weighed an additional seven tons each. One of the contractor's wagons was badly damaged by the weight of the guns.

When the guns arrived at the Whitby station, they waited for a week before unloading because the County Council could not find a contractor willing to move them. Bets were taken by local citizens that they would never reach the Court House. The job was finally accepted by Joseph Heard and his sons, Bill, Dick and Harold who for many years kept a livery stable where the Baby Shack store is now on Brock Street North, and later a garage at the corner of Brock and Elm Streets.

The Heards placed the cannons and carriages, one at a time, on wooden beams laid between two wagons, each wagon being pulled by two teams of horses. The wagon wheels cut deep ruts into the dirt road on the way to the Court House and pushed cedar posts on a sidewalk at the four corners more than a foot into the ground. When the cannons arrived at the Court House, a stump-pulling machine was used to hoist them onto concrete bases made by stone mason John Smith (1854-1912).

The Heards first attached the stump puller with wires to the Court House wall, but the County Councillors, fearing it would pull the bricks out, ordered the machine to be connected to a row of

One of the cannons being swung into position for the trip to Halifax, July, 1989.

maple trees on the lawn. It took two weeks and much effort to get the cannons in place. Joseph Heard was paid $80 for his work, $12 more than his original estimate. At one point he had even considered abandoning the job and taking a financial loss because of the difficulty of moving 28 tons of solid steel. When the work was finally done, the County Council called for a detailed report on the cannon project and its costs. Like Joseph Heard, the councillors probably wished they had never seen the cannons.

For 62 years, the cannons reposed on each side of the walk leading to the Court House (now the Whitby Centennial Building). Local children, including the author of this book, climbed over the cannons, playing war games, and on one occasion, when a witness was found to be missing from the Court Room, he was discovered asleep under one of the cannons. Birds nested in the muzzles of the guns and the members of the County Council posed on them for their official photographs.

In March 1942, Ontario County and Whitby almost lost the guns when the Whitby War Effort Committee proposed that they be melted down for munitions during the Second World War. A deputation of Whitby citizens appeared before the County Council to ask for the guns for scrap, but the Council vetoed this proposal, saving the guns from the fate that met many metal relics of olden times during the war. A German gun accepted as a war prize by the Whitby Great War Veterans' Association in 1918 and placed in front of the Armories on Dundas Street East beside the Cenotaph, was likely sacrificed to the scrap drive.

When the new Ontario County Court House was built on Rossland Road in 1964, the old Court House on Centre Street was abandoned by the county and its fate was uncertain. On June 16, 1964, the cannons were loaded on a flatbed truck and taken to the new building. They were hoisted into place by a crane in a matter of minutes, without any of the fuss and trouble experienced in 1902. It took only four hours instead of two weeks to get the job done. The cannons were placed in a small landscaped garden on the front lawn of the new Court House, where they remained for the next 25 years.

In the 1980s, the Federal Government announced a plan for restoration of the Halifax Citadel, the most visited government tourist attraction in Canada. Part of the plans involved placing the cannons back on the ramparts from which they had been removed at the turn of the century. One of the problems with this plan was that none of the carriages for the cannons remaining at the Citadel had survived. The only cannons complete with carriages that could be found were at the Whitby Court House. The Federal Government approached the Region of Durham, successor to the County of Ontario, about returning the cannons to Halifax, but the Regional Council declined the request. A few years later, a citizens committee in Halifax, called The Friends of the Citadel, made another request to the Region of Durham for return of the guns. In December 1988, the Regional Council agreed unanimously to the group's request, and arrangements were made to send the cannons back to Halifax.

At a ceremony on the Court House Lawn on July 8, 1989, Durham Regional Chairman Gary Herrema officially turned over the cannons to Major Tom Bauld, chairman of the Halifax Citadel Foundation. The Ontario Regiment, of which Col. Farewell was once commanding officer, formed an honour guard. Whitby Mayor Bob Attersley welcomed Mayor Ron Wallace of Halifax and special recognition was given to James L. *"Bud"* Heard, whose father Dick and grandfather Joseph had moved the cannons to the original Court House in 1902. Peter Cox the Halifax Town Crier and a Halifax piper from the 78th Highlanders, took part in the ceremony. The Halifax officials expressed their thanks to the Region of Durham, for it would cost only $70,000 to move the real cannons back to the east coast city, instead of spending $250,000 to build replicas. It was also noted that Peter Cox was a native of Woolwich, where the guns were made.

A few days after the ceremony, the guns were loaded on flatbed trucks for the six-

The official party at the send-off for the cannons, at Whitby, July 8, 1989.

Mayor Wallace lifted a Union Jack flag to unveil the cannons, back in their place on the ramparts after 87 years. In appreciation of the Region of Durham's gift, Mayor Wallace presented Herrema with a certificate naming him the first Honourary Town Mayor of Halifax, and he, in turn, presented the mayor with a framed colour photograph of the cannons in front of the Durham Region headquarters in Whitby. Major Bauld presented Don Evans, Chief Administrative Officer of Durham Region, with a certificate naming him an Honorary Lieutenant–Colonel of the 78th Highlanders.

The fanfare continued after dark, featuring a precision drill by the 78th Highlanders, Scottish dances and a march-past by the Halifax Police Pipe and Drum Band. The rousing finale featured a selection from the 1812 Overture by the Naval Reserve National Band, punctuated by fireworks and the recorded sound of cannon fire. A huge sign, constructed of blazing fireworks sparkling in the night sky, read: *"Thank You Durham."* In exchange for the cannons, the City of Halifax presented the Region of Durham with an anchor from a modern decommissioned war ship, which can be seen on the Lions Club promenade at Whitby Harbour.

day *"Cannonball Run"* to Halifax where they received a police escort into the city. On July 19, 1989, a fanfare to celebrate the return of the cannons was held at the Halifax Citadel. About 500 people assembled to witness a two-hour military spectacle of stirring music and pageantry. Following a volley of rifle fire by students dressed as members of the 78th Highlanders which were stationed at the Citadel more than a century ago, Durham Region Chairman Herrema and Halifax

Whitby's Fresh Air Home Was A Refuge For City Children

For more than 30 years, the underprivileged children of Toronto were able to enjoy a week's holiday on the shores of Lake Ontario, at Whitby, thanks to the Deaconesses of the Methodist (now United) Church. As early as 1887, the Deaconesses began a program to send children from the poorest parts of Toronto to farm homes in the country. By the turn of the 20th century plans were under way to build a permanent home for these youngsters.

A perfect spot for a fresh air home was Heydenshore Park, which was incorporated by the Whitby Street Railway and Park Company as a summer resort in 1900. In July, 1901, the Park Company offered two lots on the lakeshore at Heydenshore Park to the Methodist Deaconesses. The site was where the most recent portion of Whitby's water filtration plant was built in 1976-78. On May 1, 1902, Park Directors John Ball Dow (1851-1910), Hugh Ross (1854-1923) and Lyman T. Barclay (1855-1925) met Miss E. Jean Scott, superintendent of the Toronto Methodist Deaconess' Home and Walter Seldon at the Whitby station and escorted them to the park where they staked out the site of the home. A contract was let to a Mr. Young for $4,000 to build a long one-and-a-half storey frame building with a verandah on all four sides, facing Lake Ontario. The building was designed to

The Methodist Deaconess's Fresh Air Home, as it appeared in 1905.

accommodate 70 children and staff. The Deaconesses had brought 250 children to Heydenshore Park free of charge, on the steamers Garden City and Argyle in the summer of 1901, for a week's stay in Whitby. For a cost of two dollars, a child could spend a week at the Deaconess's camp.

Saturday, July 5, 1902 was selected a the date for the official opening of the Fresh Air Home. Following a torrential downpour, a rainbow appeared in the sky, as a good omen for the future of the new home. Once the rain had stopped, Rev. Dr. Parker, chairman of the Deaconess's Board, officially opened the building, followed by speeches by Whitby Mayor Andrew M. Ross (1851-1936), Rev. Vernon H. Emory (1853-1920), minister of the Whitby Methodist Tabernacle and Fred Howard Annes (1861-1940), the founder of Heydenshore Park. Also speaking was Rev. Dr. Sparling, pastor of Metropolitan Methodist Church,

Children from the Fresh Air Home bathing in Lake Ontario, 1916.

during July and August, 500 poor children from Toronto spent a week at the home, and in September, 70 poor women and their babies stayed there. The final cost of the construction of the Fresh Air Home and its furnishings was $5,280. *"A doctor accompanies each party and his services are much in demand, in bandaging wounded fingers and sometimes treating more serious disorders,"* the annual report stated.

The work of the Deaconesses continued year after year, with some of the financing being provided by the Toronto Daily Star's Fresh Air Fund. In 1918, it was reported that 193 children attended the home. All went well until the onset of the great Depression of the 1930s, when funds were increasingly hard to come by. There was talk of closing the Fresh Air Home in 1932, and shortly afterwards it shut its doors for good and was demolished. There are still people living today who attended the Methodist Fresh Air Home at Whitby and have happy memories of pleasant days there.

In 1905 the Toronto Globe reported that the children "sit down to a well-ordered table three times a day, and supplied with nourishing, well cooked food. Here too, they put into practice the housekeeping lessons they have been taught during the year, and take their turns in washing dishes and making beds."

Toronto. Refreshments were served in the spacious dining room overlooking a stone beach which was part of the property provided for the home by the Whitby Street Railway and Park Company.

The young children brought by boat from Toronto were taught housework, sewing, prayers and other things felt useful to their future lives. Swimming in the lake was an important part of the program. It was noted that *"any little child of whatever denomination or race, Jew or Gentile, black or white,"* was eligible to stay at the home in Whitby. The first annual report, for 1902 stated that

The House of Refuge — A Last Resort For The Old And The Poor

Located at 300 High Street behind Fairview Lodge, is a large brick apartment building known in recent years as Heritage Estates and High Street Manor. Today it contains modern apartments, but not so many years ago it was a home for the old, the poor and the destitute of Ontario County. Known as the House of Refuge, it was the last place where anyone would want to spend his or her final days.

In the mid 19th century, counties in Ontario were urged to build Houses of Refuge for their disadvantaged citizens. It took nearly 50 years for one to be built in Ontario County, of which Whitby was the County Town. Discussions began in the County Council as early as 1857, but it was not until 1899 that a vote was finally taken to proceed with construction. The high cost of the project prevented the Council from voting in favour of it for so many years. On Aug. 21, 1899 a vote of the ratepayers of the county passed a proposition to construct a House of Refuge at a cost of $25,000, by 35 votes.

In 1901 a site was chosen on the old Cochrane farm at Whitby for a House of Refuge and Industrial Farm, where able-bodied residents would grow crops to feed the inmates of the home. On Nov. 13, 1901, the County Council accepted the tender of Thomas Deverell (1860-1928) of Whitby for construction of the House of Refuge. The cost included $3,113.50 for the site, $850 for a

Ontario County House of Refuge in 1906.

barn, $900 for outbuildings and $18,040 for the House of Refuge building. Additional costs included $200 for digging a well, $600 for architect's fees, $562 for beds and bedding, for a total cost of $25,467.66. Of that amount $21,550 was to be paid by the County of Ontario over 20 years, and $4,000 by the Ontario Government. The architect was George Martell Miller (?-1933) of

Toronto, who also designed Frances Hall at the Ontario Ladies' College (now Trafalgar Castle School).

By April, 1902, the foundation was nearly completed and the barn almost finished. Feb. 11, 1903 was a gala day for the county as Col. J.E. Farewell (1840-1923), county clerk and solicitor, acted as master of ceremonies for the official opening, presided over by Ontario

County Warden William Bloomfield of Mara Township.

In June of 1903, Robert L. Huggard (1837-1917), a Whitby nurseryman, planted about 1,000 trees and berry bushes on the 50-acre House of Refuge lands, to add to the 600 already planted by John E. Schiller, the superintendent. In February, 1904, the Commissioners of the new House of Refuge made their first annual report to the Ontario County Council. They recommended that fire hoses and water tanks be provided, as the new building had no fire protection. In 1906, a motion was passed to purchase a burial plot for indigent residents in Union Cemetery at Oshawa. A second plot was later provided in Groveside Cemetery, south of Brooklin. The saying *"buried along with her name"* was a reality, for the residents of the House of Refuge. Before 1958, there were no markers for those buried in the House of Refuge plots.

In 1907 John F. Lavery (1854-1943) succeeded John E. Schiller (1840-1921) as superintendent of the House of Refuge. Lavery, a former veterinarian from Sunderland, got the job as a political appointment.

The Toronto Globe reported on Jan. 31, 1911 that a man named Samuel Laughn of Uxbridge, died at the house of Refuge at the age of 108. He was likely the oldest person to ever live there.

By the 1940s, the Ontario County House of Refuge was considered antiquated and in need of being replaced. After several years of debate by the County Council, it was decided in 1949 to build a modern home for the aged, which was completed in December of 1951. As Fairview Lodge, it was one of the most modern such homes during the post-war years, a showpiece for the county.

When Fairview Lodge was completed, the old county home was put up for sale by tender. At that time it housed 96 residents, plus staff. On the top floor were seven rooms, on the second floor there were 13 bedrooms and five bathrooms and on the ground floor there were seven bedrooms, two dining rooms, a dispensary, two bathrooms and a kitchen. Five rooms in the basement were used as living quarters, in addition to a heating plant, laundry and large utility room.

In May of 1952, the House of Refuge was sold to Helen Chatterton of Oshawa for $15,000 and was converted into apartments. It almost became a general hospital for Whitby. Dr. Joseph O. Ruddy (1900-1969) and a number of citizens of Whitby made an offer to buy it for a hospital but the deal with the county fell through. Whitby was not to get a general hospital until the end of 1969, after 20 years of work by Dr. Ruddy.

In the 1950s, the County of Ontario sold the Industrial Farm lands to contractors who built subdivisions. Some of the streets were named after County politicians. Warden Wilson Avenue was named after Garnet Wilson of Cannington, the Ontario County Warden of 1954. Giffard Street (spelled incorrectly) was named after Lyman Gifford, County Warden of 1938 and a former mayor of Oshawa. Lee Avenue was named after Whitby Reeve Kenneth Lee (1910-1969).

For 20 years, 1952 to 1972, the old House of Refuge was an apartment building. By the late 1960s it was the subject of a number of inquiries by the Town Council, which considered it to be a fire hazard. The council's worries proved to be valid, for on Sept. 28, 1972, a fire broke out in the attic, causing $18,000 damage. The Town Council closed the building, but a year later it was purchased by Steve Agh of Toronto who converted it into luxury apartments. Bricks from the old General Motors north plant in Oshawa, which dated from the same time as the House of Refuge, were used to make repairs and renovations. The old General Motors plant was being demolished to build McLaughlin Square.

By 1977, the renovation of 300 High Street was completed, and since that time the old building has had a new lease on life as modern apartments. It is a good example of how old buildings can find a new use if there is enough money and imagination to make it happen.

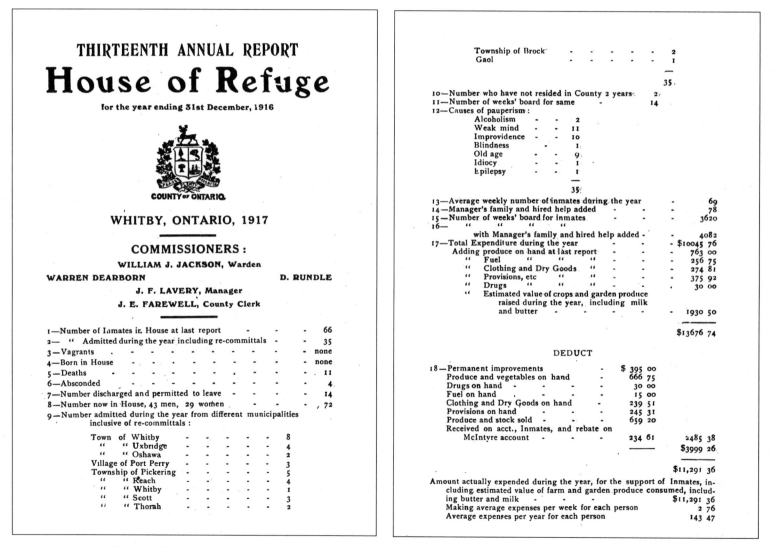

THIRTEENTH ANNUAL REPORT

House of Refuge

for the year ending 31st December, 1916

COUNTY OF ONTARIO

WHITBY, ONTARIO, 1917

COMMISSIONERS :

WILLIAM J. JACKSON, Warden

WARREN DEARBORN   **D. RUNDLE**

J. F. LAVERY, Manager

J. E. FAREWELL, County Clerk

1—Number of Inmates in House at last report	-	66
2— " Admitted during the year including re-committals	-	35
3—Vagrants	-	none
4—Born in House	-	none
5—Deaths	-	11
6—Absconded	-	4
7—Number discharged and permitted to leave	-	14
8—Number now in House, 43 men, 29 women	-	72

9—Number admitted during the year from different municipalities inclusive of re-committals :

Town of Whitby	8
" " Uxbridge	4
" " Oshawa	2
Village of Port Perry	3
Township of Pickering	5
" " Reach	4
" " Whitby	1
" " Scott	3
" " Thorah	2
Township of Brock	2
Gaol	1
	35

10—Number who have not resided in County 2 years	2	
11—Number of weeks' board for same	14	

12—Causes of pauperism :

Alcoholism	2
Weak mind	11
Improvidence	10
Blindness	1
Old age	9
Idiocy	1
Epilepsy	1
	35

13—Average weekly number of inmates during the year	-	69
14—Manager's family and hired help added	-	78
15—Number of weeks' board for inmates	-	3620
16— " " " " with Manager's family and hired help added	-	4082
17—Total Expenditure during the year	-	$10045 76
Adding produce on hand at last report	-	763 00
" Fuel " " "	-	256 75
" Clothing and Dry Goods "	-	274 81
" Provisions, etc " "	-	375 92
" Drugs " " "	-	30 00
" Estimated value of crops and garden produce raised during the year, including milk and butter	-	1930 50
		$13676 74

DEDUCT

18—Permanent improvements	-	$ 395 00	
Produce and vegetables on hand	-	666 75	
Drugs on hand	-	30 00	
Fuel on hand	-	15 00	
Clothing and Dry Goods on hand	-	239 51	
Provisions on hand	-	245 31	
Produce and stock sold	-	659 20	
Received on acct., Inmates, and rebate on McIntyre account	-	234 61	2485 38
			$3999 26
			$11,291 36

Amount actually expended during the year, for the support of Inmates, including estimated value of farm and garden produce consumed, including butter and milk	-	$11,291 36
Making average expenses per week for each person		2 76
Average expenses per year for each person		143 47

Annual Report of House of Refuge, 1917.

The amount expended on the House and Farm account is as follows :

Hired Labor for Farm and House $1370 55
Stock and Farm - - 233 02
Manager, Matron and Inspector - 1100 08
Physician's Salary and Medicine - 376 22
Books and Stationery - . 4 25
Improvements on Buildings, and
    Furnishings and Clothing - 1840 47
Provisions, Fuel, Light and Water 4000 69
Incidentals, Commissioner's fees,
    Burials and Insurance - 661 73
Sending Inmates to Home and Friends 63 75
Permanent Improvements - 395 00

                        $10045 76

Expense per week per inmate deducting farm and garden
    produce, and milk and butter consumed   2 58
Ditto for each person   2 29
Expense per week for each inmate in house adding produce
    consumed, and interest on investment ($25,000 at 4%)   3 39
Ditto for each person - -   3 00

CROPS RAISED

40 Tons Hay   @   10 00   400 00
75 bus wheat   1 70   131 50
300 Bus. Oats   65   200 00
180 " Barley   1 00   180 00
8 Acres Corn Fodder   160 00
50 Bags Potatoes   2 00   100 00
360 bus. Mangolds   16   54 00
100 bus. Turnips   25   25 00
Fruit   40 00
Vegetables   75 00
Milk   400 00
Fowl   50 00
Eggs   80 00
1 Hog, 175 lbs.   16   28 00
1 Calf, killed and consumed in house   7 00

                        $1,930 50

FARM STOCK AND PRODUCE SOLD

8 Hogs 157 85
1 Cow 65 00
2 Hogs 49 20
1 Cow 80 15
Oats and Buckwheat............... 56 90
1 Calf 5 00
1 Calf 5 00
Hay 10 65
5 Hogs 130 40
1 Calf 5 00
1 Cow 93 75

                    $658 90

STOCK ON HAND

2 horses 300 00
6 cows...................... 480 00
3 young cattle 150 00
2 calves 25 00
2 hogs 60 00
60 fowl...................... 110 00

                    $1125 00

IMPLEMENTS

1 Binder (Massey-Harris)   3 Wheelbarrows
1 Mower (Massey-Harris)   1 Pulper (Massey-Harris)
1 Seed drill (Coulthard & Scott)   Rakes, Forks, etc.
1 Cultivator (Massey-Harris)   1 Garden Cultivator and attachment
1 Wagon (Chatham)   1 Fanning Mill
1 Wagon Rack   1 Roller
1 Corn Cultivator (Cockshutt)   1 Horse Rake
1 Scuffler   1 Spraying Outfit
2 Plows (Wilkinson)   1 Gang plow
1 Set Harrows   1 Set Sleighs
2 Sets Harness (1 good)   2 Lawn Mowers

The following table shows the number admitted each month during the year ending December 31st, 1916, exclusive of re-commitals, age when admitted and sex—

Month	Total	Maie	Female	From 30 to 60	Over 60
January.........	4	4		1	3
February........	2	2		1	1
March	2	1	1		2
April	4	2	2		4
May............	3	1	2	1	2
June...........	2	1	1		2
July...........	3	2	1		3
August					
September........	3	2	1		3
October.........					
November.	2	2			2
December.......	3	3			3
Totals	28	20	8	3	25

The Misguided Philanthropy of Mrs. Gold

In November 1903, the citizens of Whitby were shocked to discover that one of the richest and most respected women in the town had borrowed nearly $17,000 from her neighbours over a period of 20 years, and given all the money to charity. When the story appeared in the Toronto Globe, a closely guarded secret was revealed. Even her husband and son did not know what she had done. She owed thousands of dollars in interest to people from whom she had borrowed money to give to the poor of Whitby and a number of religious organizations.

The woman in question was Mrs. Matthew Gold (1842-1926) who lived in a large brick house at the corner of Byron and Dunlop Streets, now a Montessori School. Mrs. Gold had led a privileged life for many years. A daughter of a wealthy landowner in the Almonds area of Whitby, David L. Reed (1803-1887), she received a legacy of $20,000 and a large farm on his death. In 1885, Mrs. Gold and her husband, Rev. Matthew Gold, purchased the former home of Sheriff Nelson G. Reynolds at Byron and Dunlop Streets and lived in style, although, Mrs. Gold did not spend much money on her own needs.

It was the fate of the less fortunate people of Whitby that occupied Mrs. Gold's mind. It was not long before she had given away

This house, pictured in 1973, had to be sold to pay Mrs. Matthew Gold's debts, in 1903.

the $20,000 she had received from her father's estate, and mortgaged her home and the farm, all to provide money for the poor and destitute. But it did not stop there. After her fortune was gone, she began to borrow money from local businessmen and her friends around town to continue her philanthropy. Each person was told that he was the only one she was approaching for loans, and that the loan was to be their private secret. The interest on these loans soon mounted up. In desperation, Mrs. Gold mortgaged her farm, worth $4,500, to within $1,000 of its value, and mortgaged her fine home for $1,500.

When the bubble burst, and Mrs. Gold was found out, she was $17,000 in debt and owed money to a large number of the citizens of Whitby. About 20 creditors met in the office of Whitby lawyer John B. Dow (1851-1910) to find out how they could recover their life savings from Mrs. Gold. These included local merchants, retired farmers and even some of her relatives, all of whom had been unaware of the financial losses they were likely to face, now that Mrs. Gold's philanthropy had been exposed.

Mrs. Gold's husband and her son William S. Gold (1864-1909) were determined to come to her rescue, but could only offer 50 cents on the dollar, after contributing $6,000 from their own funds and selling all of Mrs. Gold's real estate. The creditors were not happy with the proposed settlement, but realized they were lucky to get back what they did. The beautiful brick residence which had been Rev. and Mrs. Gold's home for 18 years, was sold to Fred Hatch, the new owner of the buckle factory, which occupied most of the same block. In the 1970s it was known as the Hatch House restaurant.

Following the settlement of Mrs. Gold's finances, she and her husband went their separate ways. She moved to Toronto, where she died on Sept. 25, 1926, at the age of 84. He returned to his home in Somerset, England, to resume his work as a preacher. Both local and Toronto newspapers reported extensively on Mrs. Gold's affairs,

and commented editorially on the psychological aspects of this strange woman who had fooled everybody for 20 years.

If one is surprised at the behaviour of Mrs. Gold, her husband had his own claim to fame. When he died at Luckwell Bridge, Somerset, England, on Oct. 19, 1938, at the age of 103, he was said to be the Great Britain's oldest minister. He had been a Baptist preacher for more than 80 years. Rev. Gold was born at Winsford, Somerset, England, on Feb. 28, 1835. Until he was 20, he worked on his father's farm, and then sailed to Canada, where he became a teacher in the Almonds school at the border between Whitby and Pickering Townships. He then studied to be a minister, and was in charge of churches at Whitevale and Lindsay. In 1859, he married his wife, whom he had met while teaching at Almonds. Before returning permanently to England, he acted as a supply minister, and superintendent of Missions in Manitoba, Saskatchewan and Alberta.

Rev. Gold made more than 20 trips back to England before he returned to stay after he and his wife separated. He learned to ride a bicycle at the age of 60 and continued to ride until he was 93. On his 100th birthday the church bells were rung at his birthplace and a public tea was held at Winsford. At the age of 102 he could still walk a mile every day, using a walking stick he made himself. He was a noted cricket player, still participating in the game at the age of 80.

FORMER WHITBY MINISTER NOW 102 YEARS OLD

Rev. Matthew Gold, Who Left Here 30 Years Ago, Resides in England

Of interest to Whitby people was a recent English news despatch to the effect that Rev. Matthew Gold, England's oldest minister, has passed his 102nd birthday at Minehead. Whitby's older residents will remember Mr. Gold as a citizen of this town for many years. While here he was not in a pastorate, having retired from the active Baptist ministry some years previously. At that time however he did considerable local preaching. Almost 30 years ago he returned to England, the land of his birth and has been preaching there more or less regularly ever since. His wife and son died here some years ago but several grandchildren still live in Toronto.

Rev. Matthew Gold's 102nd birthday as reported by the Whitby Gazette and Chonicle, March, 1937

Mrs. Richard Hopper Lived In Three Centuries

On Nov. 21, 1903, there died in Oshawa, a lady whom the Toronto Sunday World described as *"the oldest woman in Canada"*. Her obituary was front page news and her life story filled three columns of the paper. Mrs. Richard Hopper (1800-1903), who had lived in Whitby and Oshawa for 50 years, died at the home of her son, Thomas, at the age of 103 years, seven months and 27 days. Today it is fairly common for people to live well into their '90s, but it is still unusual for a person to live to the age of 103. The oldest person known to have lived a long time in Whitby, Clara May Colwill (1884-1991) lived to 106 years, 6 months and 27 days. Fairview Lodge has residents who have lived to more than 107 years, although they have only been Whitby residents since entering that home. In 1903, to reach the century mark was a considerable accomplishment, for very few people even lived to the age of 90. To live to 103 was practically impossible to comprehend then.

"Grandma Hopper," as she was affectionately known, lived a remarkable life by any standards. She was born on March 25, 1800 in the tiny village of Hartland, Devonshire, England. Her maiden name was Mary Shaddick. She had the almost unique distinction of having lived in three centuries, for the 18th century ended at the end of 1800 and the 19th at the end of 1900. The 20th century began on Jan. 1, 1901. With the current century and millennium drawing to a close, it will be interesting to see how many Canadian residents will have lived in three centuries this time.

Mrs. Hopper often told of seeing bonfires lit on the coast of the English Channel in early 1806 when news reached England that Horatio Nelson had won the Battle of Trafalgar. She was then six years old. She had vivid memories of the time of the Battle of Waterloo in 1815, the Great Comet of 1811 and England's worst snow storm in 1813. She lived through the reigns of five English sovereigns, from King George III to King Edward VII. When the new gold and silver coinage was established in Britain in the mid

Mrs. Richard Hopper at the age of 100, March 25, 1900.

19th century, she was personally presented with one of the new shillings by Queen Victoria. This keepsake she treasured for the rest of her life.

In 1819, at the age of 19, Mary Shaddick married Richard Hopper (1799-1885) and had a family of nine children, three of whom were still living at the time of her death, the oldest being 84 years old. Mrs. Hopper left 142 living descendants at the time of her death in 1903, consisting of three children, 52 grandchildren, 55 great-grandchildren and 12 great-great-grandchildren, the youngest being three months old. Anyone preparing a family tree would have quite a job to record all her descendants to the present day. Some are still living in Whitby and Oshawa.

In 1853, Mr. and Mrs. Richard Hopper and two sons, Richard Jr. (1827-1889) and John (1830-1901) left England for Canada, landing at Quebec after an ocean voyage lasting seven weeks. They decided to settle in Whitby, where Richard Sr. was a farmer near Lynde Creek. Richard Jr. was a teamster and John was a caretaker of the Whitby Town Hall. After living a married life of 66 years, Mrs. Hopper was widowed in 1885 at the age of 84. After living more than 30 years in Whitby, she decided to move in with her son Thomas (1838-1907) in Oshawa.

Five generations of the Hopper family, March 25, 1900. Mrs. Richard Hopper is at left, on her 100th birthday. The other members of the family are unidentified.

Mrs. Hopper possessed all her faculties up to the time of her death, although her eyesight was failing. Up until two days before her death she still made her own bed and assisted in the housekeeping. On the eve of her 98th birthday in 1898, Mrs. Hopper composed the following verses, which were printed in her obituary in the Toronto Sunday World of Nov. 29, 1903:

My life is swimming along,
I will soon reach the shore.
Then I will be in Heaven,
Where I shall die no more.
Farewell to Whitby chapel,
and the friends I love so well
Soon I shall be called to leave you
And bid you now farewell
I hope you'll all prove faithful
And try to meet me there,
Then I will come to greet you
And all my joys you'll share.
Then you and I with joy
Will meet our friends together
To praise the Lord and God most high
Forever and forever
Then shall we sing and shout and tell
That Jesus hath done all things well.

It is of interest to note that there are still people in the Whitby-Oshawa area who were alive when Mrs. Hopper died in 1903. If they are old enough to appreciate that fact, they might have actually met a woman who was born nearly 200 years ago in the 18th century, for whom the far distant past was a living reality.

Whitby's Greatest Celebration - The Ontario County Jubilee of 1904

Whitby has seen many celebrations in its history, but one of the grandest ever was the four-day commemoration of the 50th anniversary of the founding of Ontario County. From July 1 to 4, 1904, the Ontario County Jubilee and Old Boys' Reunion drew hundreds of former residents back to the old County Town to celebrate and meet old friends. Old Boys' Reunions were popular events in the early 1900s, as many young men in the previous 25 years had left the small towns and villages of their birth to seek their fortunes in the big cities. It was a welcome idea for them to return to their old homes for a reunion. Brooklin had staged a highly successful Old Boys' Reunion on the May 24th weekend in 1903, so now it was the Town of Whitby's turn.

Planning for the Ontario County Jubilee and Old Boys' Reunion began in January 1904 with a meeting between the Town Council and the Whitby Board of Trade. The enthusiasm was evident enough to form a Jubilee and Old Boys' Association on Feb. 22. County Judges, MPs and MPPs were named as honorary presidents and the head of each municipality in the county outside Whitby was an honorary vice-president. John Vipond (1849-1926) of Brooklin, Warden of Ontario County, was elected president of the association, while Whitby Mayor E.R. Blow (1860-1930) and Charles King (1837-1915) of the Board of Trade were vice-presidents. Fred Howard Annes (1861-1940) Whitby's visionary who first suggested the reunion, and lawyer Arthur E. Christian (1871-1931) were secretaries, Another lawyer, James Rutledge (1842-1914) was treasurer.

Whitby Old Boys in Toronto formed an executive also, at a meeting in the King Edward Hotel, with Col. John A. McGillivray (1852-1911) as president.

On July 1, 1904, the opening day of the reunion, the streets of Whitby were decorated with mottoes, evergreens, bunting, flags and Chinese lanterns. Young boys ran through the streets setting off firecrackers. The Whitby Citizens' Band, dressed in their new uniforms, met the trains from the north and west, at the railway stations and escorted the visitors into town. About 1,000 people came by train from Toronto. The band had just started to lead them in a procession from the new Whitby Junction Station (now Whitby Arts Station Gallery) to the downtown, when rain came pouring down. The Whitby Gazette commented that *as a consequence, the procession was not a success.* Rain was to be a problem throughout the four-day Jubilee.

Festivities began, despite the rain, with a reception in the old town hall at Brock and Colborne Streets where the fire hall is now. Mayor Blow read an address of welcome, responded to by William Ross, MP, on behalf of the Old Boys. He was followed by George H. Ham (1847-1926) an old Whitby boy who was public relations director for the Canadian Pacific railway and was known as *"The Mark Twain of Canada."* Ham talked about his school days in the 1850s when teachers gave boys a caning if they misbehaved.

W.H. Hoyle, MPP, recalled how Ontario's Lieutenant Governor Oliver Mowat (1820-1903) had started his political career in Ontario County. T.N. Gibbs (1821-1883) of Oshawa had been a member of Sir John A. Macdonald's Cabinet and the Ontario Minister of Agriculture and Deputy Minister of Education were Ontario County Men. The Minister of Agriculture was John Dryden (1840-1909) of Brooklin. Other speakers included Robert M. Thornton (1841-1913), a son of Rev. Dr. Robert Thornton (1806-1875) the founder of the Presbyterian Church in Whitby; George H. Robinson (1844-1921) a former head master of the Whitby Collegiate Institute, and the president of the Brock Old Boys' Association.

The afternoon of July 1 was devoted to sports and games at the exhibition grounds located at the north-east corner of Dundas and Garden Streets where a new housing development was built in 1998. In the evening there was a home-comers' reception hosted by the ladies' of the town at the town hall, followed by a free concert by the Old Boys and Girls. Encores were called for many times, but the chairman, Col. J.E. Farewell (1840-1923) kept the strict rule of no encores, as the Toronto people had to catch a train home at 11 p.m.

The second day of the Jubilee, Saturday, July 2, 1904, was devoted to the history of Whitby and Ontario County. The County Council marked the 50th anniversary of the founding of the county with ceremonies in the court house (now the Whitby Centennial Building). A few people who had witnessed the laying of the corner stone 51 years earlier were introduced. One of these old residents was Mrs. Robert J. Gunn (1821-1911) who sat on a jury in a mock trial at the opening of the court house in April 1854.

John Ball Dow (1851-1910) a Whitby lawyer, read the history of the founding of Ontario County from "*The Life and*

The Whitby Citizens' Band in front of Arthur Allin's Drug Store (now Van Belle Flowers) at the Ontario County Jubilee, 1904. From left to right are: Arthur Allin (band manager), Arthur Hopper, Roy Winn, Charles Scott (in bowler hat), George Laval, William Toms, John Mowat, Robert Nicholson, "Baldy" Wilkinson, Joseph Thompson, unidentified, William Ellis, Edwin W. Evans (band master), Samuel Mowat, Albert Toms, Leo Smith, Frank Bryan, James Woodward, Arthur Nicholson.

Times of Joseph Gould," written by Whitby Chronicle editor William H. Higgins (1830-1904). The morning was devoted to many speeches reminiscent of the old days of Whitby from the time when Peter Perry first advocated the separation of Ontario County from the old County of York, in the 1840s.

After the ceremonies in the court house, the Old Boys and Girls moved on to the Collegiate Institute gymnasium at the corner of Centre and Colborne Streets where the Windsor Place seniors' apartments are today. This wooden building was constructed in 1889 and demolished in 1927. Here they viewed an historical display set up by Col. Farewell. A portrait gallery of famous Ontario County men, military relics dating back to the Rebellion of 1837 and pioneer artifacts were shown.

The afternoon was again devoted to sports at the athletic grounds (now Rotary Centennial Park) featuring a lacrosse match between two Oshawa teams. Once again, rain played havoc with the arrangements as spectators dashed for cover. A promenade concert and fireworks on the grounds of the Ontario Ladies' College (now Trafalgar Castle School) was held in the evening. One man was severely injured when a rocket exploded in his hand, but otherwise the event was enjoyed by all.

Sunday, July 3, saw the town's churches filled to capacity as former pastors preached sermons to their respective congregations. In the afternoon there was a

Whitby's first picture post card, a souvenir of the Ontario County Jubilee and Old Boys' Reunion, July 1-4, 1904.

memorial service conducted by the fraternal societies of the town on the Ontario Ladies' College grounds. A massive parade, led by the Whitby Citizens' Band and Composite Lodge of the Masons, wound its way through the town to the college.

The last day of the Ontario County

Jubilee, July 4, saw the 48th Highlanders' Band from Toronto arrive in town and march up Brock Street to play in front of each of the town's hotels. The afternoon of July 4 was declared a public holiday by Mayor Blow as the citizens and visitors moved to Heydenshore Park at the lake for more games and sports. This was the first time the park, only four years old, had been used for a major event. It had been established as a private resort with cottages in 1900. The heavy waves on Lake Ontario prevented the aquatic sports from being held, but a football tournament was won by Pickering. The 48th Highlanders provided a concert in the original Heydenshore Pavilion, an open-air dance hall. As the proceedings were nearing a close, the rain came down again, and everyone scattered for shelter.

The last event of the Jubilee was a band concert in the town hall by the 48th Highlanders, which included Scottish dancing and a *"chalk talk"* by Whitby's famous cartoonist John W. Bengough (1851-1923). The highlight of the evening was the performance of the *"Government House Waltz,"* written by the wife of the rector of All Saints' Anglican Church, Mrs. A. H. Wright.

The Ontario County Jubilee and Old Boys' Reunion ended on July 4, 1904,

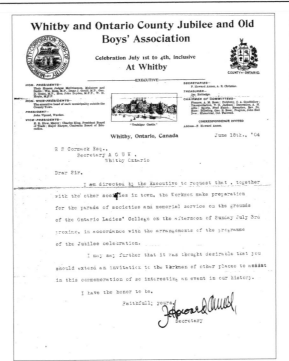

but it left some lasting benefits to the town of Whitby. The women of the town formed the Ontario County Old Girls' Association, a forerunner of today's service clubs, which carried out many bene-

ficial deeds for the town for 25 years. The Old Girls' Association was responsible for purchasing the land at Dundas and Byron Streets for the Carnegie Public Library in 1911 and maintained the library property for many years. The *"Old Girls"* celebrated their 25th anniversary in 1929, but disbanded shortly after, as the old members had nearly all died and no younger descendants of the pioneers had joined the organization.

The *"Old Boys"* did not fare so well, for their association did not continue as the *"Old Girls"* had done. There was a proposal to reorganize the Old Boys in 1921, but nothing was done. There would not be another Old Boys' Reunion in Whitby until the town's Centennial in 1955. The last such celebration was Whitby's Homecoming Year in 1973, held in conjunction with the County Town Carnival. The only known photograph of the Ontario County Jubilee and Old Boys' Reunion is one of the Citizens' Band standing in front of Arthur Allin's Drug Store. In the background can be seen a banner which reads *"Old Boys Register Here."* Perhaps few pictures were taken because of the rain. In the Whitby archives are some pins worn by old boys at the reunion, and Whitby's first picture post card, issued as a reunion souvenir.

The Promotion of Whitby – 1907 Style

Promotion of Whitby as a good place to *"live, work and play"* did not start with former Mayor Bob Attersley and the town council of the 1980s. As early as 1907, the town was promoted through a little booklet entitled *"Whitby, The Beautiful, Healthful County Town of Ontario County."* Published by the Whitby Board of Trade (a forerunner of the Chamber of Commerce), this booklet featured a description of the town, photographs of its various landmarks and advertisements for local businesses.

The Board of Trade was incorporated in 1899, with lawyer John Ball Dow (1851-1910) as president. In 1907, Dr. Wellington Adams (1848-1918), a local dentist, was president and Dr. John Waugh (1861-1924), the public school inspector, was secretary. The Mayor of Whitby, who was the driving force behind the publication of the promotional booklet, was Albert W. Jackson (1870-1939).

The following is the complete text of the booklet, telling the world of Whitby's virtues in 1907:

"The beautiful Town of Whitby is situated 28 miles east of the Queen City of Toronto and enjoys the reputation of being patronized by many distinguished visitors."

"The most interesting thought of mankind is Home. The most beautiful and Home Section of Ontario is Whitby.

"This famous old county town is situated on a large and finely sheltered bay on the north shore of Lake Ontario. At the water front is Heydenshore Park, with its inviting cottages and spacious camping grounds.

"Here also is located the Children's Fresh Air Home, where hundreds of little ones enjoy the cool lake breezes during the warm summer days. For the accommodation of picnic parties, the Park Committee have provided a band stand and lunch counter, also tables and seating accommodation, offering an enjoyable outing to parties from the city on a Saturday afternoon, when the steamer (which makes three trips a week from Whitby to Toronto) runs a special trip from Toronto to Whitby, leaving at 2 p.m. and returning in the evening.

"As a residential town, Whitby is unsurpassed. Not only is it picturesque, but healthful. We will mention some of the advantages residents are enjoying, and yet there is room for many more people who may desire to make their homes on this favoured spot. It is accessible to the city by boat and train. The beautiful shaded streets – no town in the Dominion has been more favoured by nature than Whitby. The shade trees are maples. The people are cultured and refined. Handsome churches – Anglican, Methodist, Catholic, Baptist and Presbyterian. A public library with a large stock of volumes. The people enjoy pure air. The streets are paved and equipped with electric

lighting. We offer educational advantages second to none. Good phone service and waterworks. The residents invite all good people to make their home here and partake of the many advantages and comforts offered by beautiful Whitby.

"The busy city man may reside here with his family, direct the education of sons and daughters, go to the city by suburban train service each morning at a nominal rate, returning at eventide.

"Educational Advantages – The Collegiate Institute has given practical results. Here many leading men of the day have built the foundation of success under its able and indefatigable principal. Henry Street is where training commenced. Whitby Model School, the Ontario Ladies' College and Ontario Conservatory of Music and Art – the largest and best equipped college for women in Canada. Palatial buildings, beautiful grounds, steam heating. A beautiful home of Christian culture. A progressive institution offering highest facilities for the study of Literature, Music, Art, Oratory, Commercial and Domestic Science. Here also the successful Summer School is held.

"The College course of lectures and concerts, which are open to the public, in addition to visiting companies to the town during the winter months, affords an opportunity for pleasant and profitable entertainment to lovers of music and literature.

A bird's eye view of Whitby in 1907, looking south-east from the old water tower at Dundas and Euclid Streets, which was built in 1904 and demolished in 1950. At left is the spire of All Saints' Anglican Church and right the steeples of the Methodist Tabernacle (now St. Mark's United Church).

"*Auto-car tourists make Whitby a favourite resort for an ideal afternoon outing from the city. With good broad roadway and picturesque landscape, the business man would find it a pleasant run to and fro to office or warehouse.*

"*The Armories, headquarters of the 34th Battalion, with adjoining band stand, is near the business centre of the town. The band furnishes open air concerts throughout the summer.*

"*Ontario is justly celebrated for its apples. Of the fifty or sixty million bushels produced in the Province during the year, none are more celebrated for flavour and keeping quality than those grown in the Whitby district, and are exported to Great Britain in large quantities.*

Whitby had a population of about 2,500 in 1907. It was a quiet residential town of retired farmers, county officials and down-town merchants who would stay open until midnight on Saturday nights to accommodate the farmers from the surrounding township. The only major industries (not mentioned in the promotion book) were the King Brothers' Tannery (now the site of the No Frills Store), The Farmers' Co-operative Manufacturing Company which made agricultural implements (now site of Coffee Time Donuts) and the Martin Manufacturing Company, the buckle factory (now site of Price Chopper). All these factories were on Brock Street.

In 1907, Whitby portrayed itself as a friendly town. At the bottom of the page listing the community's churches, were the words "*Strangers Welcome.*"

Over the years, Whitby has produced many more promotional booklets. In 1914, under Mayor James E. Willis, the Town Council produced an illustrated booklet, "Whitby, The Best Residential Town Near Toronto." There was no further promotional activity until a small pamphlet was issued in 1941, entitled: "The Town of Whitby Invites You To Consider These Pertinent Facts." In the 1950s and 1960s, a number of brochures were printed by the Whitby Industrial Commission, depicting the town as a good location for industry. Since 1984, Whitby has had its own marketing department.

Selecting The *"Ideal Woman"*

One of the oldest traditions, carried on in Whitby for more than 90 years, is the May Court Festival at Trafalgar Castle School, formerly the Ontario Ladies' College. Since 1907, the students of the school have elected a May Queen and celebrated the coming of spring with dances, gymnastics and a May Pole dance.

The May Day celebration goes back to pagan times as a festival to welcome spring. May Day may be a later version of the ancient Roman Floralia celebration. In England and most of Europe, it was popular during the Middle Ages. At the time of Henry VIII, dramatic characters took part in elaborate spectaculars, with characters already popular in the 15th and 16th centuries, such as Robin Hood, Jack in the Green and Morris dancers. The Morris dancers usually ended with a May Pole dance around a sacred tree. The going out and picking of flowers and branches and bringing them home was the symbolic act of bringing in the May — bringing new life and spring into the village. Gradually the May Day festivals died out, often because the May Pole was left standing all year, and superstitions evolved that the girl chosen as May Queen would not live another full year.

In the 1880s, the British writer John Ruskin (1819-1900) started a movement

The May Pole Dance at the First May Court Festival, May 24, 1907.

to revive such ancient customs as the May Court Festival in English schools. In Canada, Lady Aberdeen, wife of Canada's Governor-General from 1893 to 1898, carried on Ruskin's work. When she, her husband and daughter, Lady Marjorie Gordon, visited the Ontario Ladies'

College on Oct. 19, 1898, she spoke of how she had started a May Court Festival at the Ottawa Ladies' College. Lady Marjorie Gordon read a code of ethics written by the Ottawa May Queen and suggested that such a festival could be commenced at the Ontario Ladies'

The first May Queen, Anna Harley and her attendants, May 24, 1907.

resent the *"ideal woman"*. For many years this was the subject of speeches by guests of honour at the May Court Festivals. What actually represented the *"ideal woman"* was not easy to define. Only the speech of Canon Henry Cody, rector of St. Paul's Anglican Church in Toronto, delivered on May 24, 1912, appears to have survived, to give an insight into the character of the *"ideal woman"*. In this speech, Canon Cody referred to Queen Victoria and the Virgin Mary as examples of the ideal woman. He cited three important virtues: inwardness of character, submissiveness and self-sacrifice as traits of an *"ideal woman"*. In his summary, he urged the Ontario Ladies' College students to *"seek to elect the girl who combines good judgment with a warm and sympathetic heart; who has grace of carriage and charm of manner; who possesses the inestimable gift of tact, the very bloom on the fruit of unselfishness and sympathy; who can see the humorous side of things, or at least who will aim to cultivate the virtue of cheerfulness; who tries to see life from the viewpoint of others; who ardently loves her country; who reverences her conscience and makes service her standard of greatness; who in a word, is both womanly and Christian."*

In the early days of the May Court Festival, a system of coloured cards representing studentship, deportment and other qualities were issued to rate the candidates for May Queen. Blue cards indicated poor candidates, white for medium, pink and white for medium to good, pink for good, red for very good and purple for excellent. Originally, the student body voted for the May Queen only a few hours before the ceremony. Now the selection is made several days before. At one May Court Festival, there was a tie between two students, so the principal of the school had to cast the deciding vote.

The first May Court Festival at the Ontario Ladies' College was held on Victoria Day, May 24, 1907. Ontario County Senior Judge Neil McCrimmon (1858-1911) read the address on *"The*

College. In support of this proposal, she wrote an article on the 1899 May Court Festival at Whitelands School in England, for the June 1902 edition of *"Vox Collegii"*, the Ontario Ladies' College school magazine.

It was not, however, until 1907, that a May Court Club was founded in Whitby. The first May Court Festival was held on May 24, Victoria Day, rather than the traditional May 1, and remained on May 24, for many years. Now it is usually held in the last two weeks of May. The May Queen was supposed to rep-

Ideal Woman", tracing the history of May Court Festivals from pagan Rome through modern English history. A dozen ballots had to be cast before a May Queen was selected. The winner was Anna Harley (1888-1971) of Brantford, an 18-year-old senior student. In 1913, Miss Harley married R. Gordon Grobb, a purchasing agent with Massey Harris farm implement company, and they returned to Whitby after her husband's retirement in 1937. After Mrs. Grobb's death, her daughter, Mrs. J. W. Anderson, for many years presented a Bible in her mother's memory to subsequent May Queens.

Following the coronation, which for many years was on the steps of the Loggia beside the 1895 cornerstone of Frances Hall, there was a display of gymnastics and the traditional Maypole dance by the students. In the early days, the ceremonies on the College lawn were followed by a hay rack ride to Corbett's Point (now Thickson's Point) at the foot of Thickson Road, for a picnic and fireworks display.

Rain was always a concern to the students when the May Court Festival day arrived. There have been few rainy days in the history of the occasion, the first being in 1914. The first Whitby student to be elected May Queen was Olive Holliday (1882-1980), later Mrs. George F. Denyes

in that rainy year of 1914. Well into her '90s when she was living at Fairview Lodge, she would visit her old school for each May Day. Mrs. Denyes was the first May Queen to wear the May Queen's pin, in the shape of a crown containing a gold nugget from the Yukon, a gift from the 1912 May Queen, Meda Watt. For years it was presented to each succeeding May Queen.

Starting in 1917, the Trafalgar Daughters, an early alumnae association, provided a pin which each May Queen could keep as a souvenir of her election. It replaced a pennant, which was formerly the only souvenir the May Queen received to represent the honour she had been awarded by her fellow students.

In the early years, the May Court Club did more than arrange the May Court Festival. The members raised money for charities such as a hospital in China, and patriotic purposes during the First World War. The 1921 May Court Festival was of special significance for two reasons: first that the May Queen, Cort Reynolds, was a granddaughter of Sheriff Nelson G. Reynolds who built Trafalgar Castle; and secondly, it was the last time Rev. Dr. John J. Hare (1847-1922) was able to attend. Principal for 41 years, from the school's founding in 1874 to his retirement in

1915, he had the honour of delivering the address on *"The Ideal Woman"*.

During the 1930s, Rev. Dr. Charles R. Carscallen (1878-1968), the principal, filmed the May Court Festivals with a movie camera given to him by the students. In 1937, the school yearbook was dedicated to all former May Queens. A large panel in the main hall lists the names of all the school's May Queens, starting in 1907. May Day also had its incidents of beauty and humour. After the queen of 1934 was crowned, a white butterfly settled on the crown and poised there for a moment — a sign of good luck. In 1937, as the queen descended from the throne, a black kitten paused at her feet and crossed her path — a sign of bad luck?

Starting in 1954, the May Queen was crowned in the afternoon instead of the morning, so that guests who had to travel long distances, could arrive in time for the ceremonies.

In recent years, the May Court Festival has been revised and modernized, but the essence of the event is still there after nearly a century.

A Salute To Whitby's Olympians

For a small Ontario town, Whitby has had more than its share of Olympians. In all, 16 Whitby sports figures have participated in the Summer or Winter Olympics, since 1908.

Whitby's first Olympians were Louis J. Sebert (1886-1942) and William B. Goldsbro (1884-1937), both of whom participated in track events in the 1908 Summer Olympics at London, England. Although both were Toronto residents when they competed, Sebert was born in Whitby and Goldsbro in Brooklin.

Louis Sebert was the son of Oliver Sebert, a champion lacrosse player of the 19th century who was a member of the Oshawa Maple Leafs who won the Canadian Lacrosse Championship in 1878. Early in his life he moved to Brooklin where his father was owner of the Brooklin House hotel, now the headquarters of Royal Canadian Legion Branch 152. While attending the University of Toronto, from which he graduated in medicine in 1912, Louis Sebert excelled in track athletics and at the time of his death was a member of the University's athletic board.

While at the Whitby Collegiate Institute, he won the Langevin Cup for the school's athletic championship, three times, in 1903-05. He was the first student to achieve this feat. In his honour the cup was renamed the Langevin-Sebert Cup. After his graduation from the University of Toronto, Sebert served in the Royal Canadian Medical Corps in France during the First World War. After the war he began a career in opthamology (treating diseases of the eye) and served at the Toronto Sick Children's Hospital, St. Joseph's and St. Michael's Hospitals.

William Goldsbro was the son of a Brooklin shoemaker who had a shop where the Bank of Commerce is now, on Baldwin Street. He moved to Toronto where he joined the YMCA and gained a reputation as a marathon runner. In 1912 he joined the advertising staff of the Evening Telegram, being advertising manager at the time of his death 25 years after.

Louis J. Sebert, Whitby-born track representative at the 1908 Summer Olympics.

Neither Sebert or Goldsbro won medals at the 1908 Olympics. It was a long time, 52 years to be exact, before another set of Whitby athletes competed in the Olympic Games.

At the 1960 Winter Olympics at Squaw Valley, California, five members of the Whitby Dunlops, 1958 World Hockey Champions, participated as members of Canada's Olympic team, the Kitchener-Waterloo Dutchmen. The Dunnies' manager Wren Blair was the coordinator of the 1960 Olympic hockey team. The four former Dunnies players were: Bob Attersley, centre; Fred Etcher, left wing; George Samolenko, right wing and Harry Sinden, defence.

The 1960 Olympic hockey tournament was a tough series for the Canadian team which outshot the United States team 51-17, but lost the Gold Medal to the Americans 2-1 in the final game. The Canadians had to settle for the silver medal. It was especially frustrating for the star centre, Bob Attersley, who hit the crossbar three times, but could not get the puck into the net during the final game.

Wren Blair went on to a long hockey career which included coaching the Minnesota North Stars, a part ownership of the Pittsburgh Penguins, and director of personnel for the Los Angeles Kings. Harry Sinden coached the famous 1972 Team Canada to victory over the Russians in one of the most exciting series in hockey history. Bob Attersley returned to Whitby where he built up a successful tire business and served as Mayor from 1980 to 1991, the longest term in the town's history.

Whitby's greatest Olympic achievement was by swimmer Anne Ottenbrite at the 1984 Summer Olympics at Los Angeles, California. She won a gold medal for the 200-metre breaststroke, the first swimming gold medal won by a Canadian since the modern Olympics began at Athens, Greece in 1896. She went on to win the silver medal in the 100-metre breaststroke and a bronze medal as a member of Canada's individual medley relay team.

Olympic Gold Medalist Anne Ottenbrite riding in a parade in her honour on Aug. 25, 1984.

On Aug. 25, 1984, Whitby declared *"Anne Ottenbrite Day,"* for the town's *"Golden Girl."* She rode in a massive parade, was granted the freedom of the town and the swimming pool at Iroquois Park was named after her. It was especially appropriate that these honours were presented by another Whitby Olympian, Mayor Bob Attersley.

Ottenbrite almost failed to compete in the Olympics. Just weeks before the Canadian Olympic Trials she dislocated her knee. She missed the trials, but on the advice of an Olympic team doctor, she was able to compete. It was a close call. As a result of her Olympic victories, she was named Canada's female athlete of the year for 1983-84, named to the Order of Canada in 1985, inducted into the Ontario Swimming Hall of Fame in 1990, and in 1994 entered Canada's Sports Hall of Fame. Ottenbrite is now married and is a swimming coach at the University of Guelph.

Whitby was also represented at the 1984 Summer Olympics by Glenn Beauchamp, who competed in Judo and returned to compete again in the 1988 Summer Olympics in Seoul, South Korea.

Five Whitby residents competed in the Seoul Olympics: Glenn Beauchamp in judo, Christina McDonald and Lori Strong in gymnastics, Terry Paul in rowing and Lori Melien, who won a bronze medal in swimming. Lori Strong returned to compete in the 1992 Summer Olympics at Barcelona, Spain.

Three graduates of Whitby's Minor Hockey Association, Joe Nieuwendyk, Keith Primeau and Adam Foote were members of Canada's Olympic hockey team at the 1998 Winter Olympics at Nagano, Japan. This was the first time that professional players from the National Hockey League were permitted to play on a Canadian Olympic team. Joe Nieuwendyk was a member of the Dallas Stars, Keith Primeau of the Carolina Hurricanes and Adam Foote of the Colorado Avalanche. All three were sent large greeting cards signed by Whitby residents, wishing the best in the tournament. Unfortunately, Canada did not win a medal in 1998, although hockey has always been considered our national sport.

Joe Nieuwendyk gained further fame in 1999 when he was a member of the National Hockey league team the Dallas Stars, which won the Stanley Cup. Nieuwendyk received the Conn Smythe Trophy as the most valuable player of the playoff series. On July 23, 1999, he brought the Stanley Cup to Whitby for the first time and signed autographs at a reception at Iroquois Park.

Anne Ottenbrite with Royal Canadian Legion Branch 112 members at the raising of the Olympic and Canadian flags at Iroquois Park Arena, August 25, 1984. On "Anne Ottenbrite Day" the swimmer was given the Freedom of the Town of Whitby, the youngest person to receive this honour. Whitby swimming pool was also named after her.

When the Tories of Myrtle Fought the Grits of Myrtle Station

The ancient principle of separation of Church and State seemed to be forgotten briefly in 1908 when the communities of Myrtle and Myrtle Station fought over the building of a new church. The Methodist community was called a house divided against itself, with various factions writing letters to the Toronto Globe, each refuting the claims of the other. Although the dispute was over the location of a new church, the Conservatives of Myrtle found themselves pitted against the Liberals of Myrtle Station.

The problem began when the board of trustees of the Methodist Church at Myrtle decided the old frame church there could not be repaired any more, and with two members absent, voted to sell the building to John Bright (1865-1917), a resident of Myrtle Station. The church had been constructed in 1857 by the Methodist Episcopal congregation of Rev. Gardner Wells (1807-1883). It was located on the east side of Highway 12 where Willi's Car Care is located. The stones in the old church cemetery can still be seen behind the garage.

With the church now owned by John Bright, who proceeded to pull it by teams of horses to Myrtle Station, the board of trustees was faced with finding a new site on which to build a modern church. When differing factions wanted the new church at either Myrtle or Myrtle Station, only a mile apart, John Carmichael (1834-1908) offered a site midway between the two communities as a compromise, but died before a deal could be made with the trustees.

The *"sturdy farmers"* of Myrtle intervened to prevent Carmichael's sons from selling the land to the board, while the minister, Rev. Edwy E. Howard (1843-1922) made a private deal with John Bright for a piece of land at Myrtle Station. Rev. Howard felt pressured to take action because the bricks for the new church were already at the railway depot at Myrtle Station when John Carmichael died. His action of purchasing Bright's land split the congregation, with about 15 parishioners worshipping with Rev. Howard at Myrtle Station and about 32 taking over the Temperance Hall at Myrtle and hiring a minister from Toronto. The Temperance Hall, across the road from the site of the old church, was demolished in 1978.

It was alleged that politics played a part in the matter because Peter Christie, the Conservative member of Parliament for South Ontario, was asked to lay the corner stone for the new church at Myrtle Station on Aug. 27, 1908. Rev. Howard stoutly denied that Christie had been selected to lay the stone because he was a Conservative. He had been asked to do the honours because he was the local Member of Parliament.

Other allegations were tossed out at the Myrtle Station faction. John Bright, it was said, was not even a member of the Methodist Church. He was an Anglican, if he belonged to any church at all, said the Myrtle faction. The Myrtle farmers were also annoyed that the Myrtle Station church had the support of the hotel keeper there, feeling that alcohol and religion did not mix. The *"kickers"*, as the Myrtle faction were called, expressed their determination never to join the Myrtle Station church, even though it was opened for worship early in 1909.

Charges and counter charges were printed in The Globe, Toronto's leading Liberal newspaper, which first published a story on Oct. 31, 1908, headlined *"Trouble at Myrtle"*. Rev. Howard described charges that his flock had deserted him as *"utter nonsense"*, and blamed The Globe for trying to make a political issue out of the situation. Meanwhile, three trustees for the Myrtle faction took issue with Rev. Howard's statements, accusing him of acting on his own in building the church at Myrtle Station without the backing of the board of trustees. How long it took for tempers to calm down and the two congregations to reunite, is not known, but by 1943 when James Beacock

Myrtle Methodist (now United) Church when it opened in 1909.

The old Myrtle Methodist Episcopal Church as Elmer Cooke's garage, 1975.

(1861-1943), the last of the original trustees of 1908, died, there was finally peace in the Myrtle community.

The Myrtle United Church, as the church is now called, was built at a cost of $4,000, by John Stovin of Port Perry. Rev. Dr. Carman, General Superintendent of the Methodist Church of Canada, dedicated the church on Jan. 31, 1909. There was no hint of the simmering dispute in the press reports of the opening. No adverse comment appeared when former Member of Parliament William Smith (another Conservative) was asked to chair the meeting the following day to raise the remainder of the money needed to complete the church. One of the features of the day was an auction sale of an autographed quilt made by the ladies of the church. George Pepper of Toronto purchased it for $22.50 and presented it to the minister's wife, Mrs. Howard. On Oct. 2, 1977, nearly 70 years later, Mary Howard, daughter of Rev. Edwy E. Howard, the first pastor, presented the quilt back to Myrtle United Church. Bearing the signatures of many citizens of the Myrtle community and the Whitby Township Council, it is now kept at the church. In light of the raging controversy of 1908, it would be interesting to see who did not sign the quilt.

The old wooden Methodist Church which was moved to Myrtle Station in 1908, has an interesting history. There were complaints that John Bright let it sit on the road between Myrtle and Myrtle Station for some time before he relocated it to the east side of Highway 12 at Myrtle Station. In 1920 it was moved to the west side of the road, north of the C.P.R. tracks, where it became a service station operated by Elmer Cooke (1895-1977). Cooke operated the service station for British American and Gulf Oil Companies for 57 years, being Ontario's oldest service station operator when he died at the age of 81. The Cooke garage was demolished in 1980. A variety store called *"The Whistle Stop"* now stands on the site.

Whitby's First Movie Theatre Was A Gem

When the first movie theatre in Whitby opened in September 1909, it was so popular that its patrons did not want to leave after the show was finished. R.S. McQuaid, manager of the Gem Theatre, located on Brock Street, south of the fire hall, had a real problem on his opening night. He had a captivated audience sitting on kitchen chairs inside while there was a lineup of eager patrons waiting outside the door for the second show.

Those who attended the first show sat through the movie, but when it was finished, no one got up to leave. McQuaid, a little frustrated at how to handle the situation, stepped out in front of the screen and thanked the audience for coming. Still no one left. McQuaid ran the show a second time, and still nobody left. He finally had to stop the projector and tell his audience that the show was really over.

Word soon spread that the modern miracle of moving pictures had come to Whitby. McQuaid's assistants were projectionist Cecil Greenfield (1890-1966) and Harry Pomeroy, a singer and pianist. Those were the days of silent films when live music was provided on the violin or piano. Movies were not the only attraction. Between the films, which lasted about 10 to 15 minutes, Pomeroy would sing popular songs of the day and Greenfield would play selections on the violin.

When the Gem Theatre opened in

Harry Pomery, R.S. McQuaid and Cecil Greenfield in front of the original Gem Theatre, 1909.

September 1909, the price of admission was five cents, but by December the price had risen to 10 cents for adults and five cents for children. It was common practice to have as many as five films showing on one night.

These were advertised on large signs outside the theatre and on handbills distributed throughout the town. The sign in the accompanying photograph reads: *"To-Night's Program (By Request): Two Large Fires in New*

York City, also two new ones, subjects later. Song: Pal of Mine. This Fire Picture will not be shown again. Come in and see it."

A handbill in the Town of Whitby Archives advertises a *"special extra double program"* for Wednesday, December 8, 1909. *"The program for tonight will be an exceptional good one,"* it states rather ungrammatically. *"Our special picture will be Maryland in 1777, a story of the American and English War. It will no doubt prove to be one of the best pictures ever shown here. You cannot afford to miss this."*

The Gem Theatre lasted only a few months. In 1910, a second movie theatre opened in the old Whitby Chronicle Building, north of the Royal Hotel. Owned by the proprietor of the hotel, John H. Perrin, it was called the Royal Theatre. The Royal Theatre went through several ownerships until it was purchased by John Strathy and William G. Goodman (1897-1979) of Toronto, who changed the name to Brock Theatre. In 1938, they built a new Brock Theatre where Classy Q's is now, which many Whitby residents will remember. It was sold in 1971 and remodelled into a sports bar in 1990.

By a strange coincidence, the building occupied by the original Gem Theatre is now a jewellery store called *"Gems."*

One of the features of the year at the Brock Theatre was free movies at Christmas, offered by Messrs. Goodman and Strathy. In the 1930s and 1940s, admission to the theatre was 10 cents.

One of the few people in Whitby who took home movies in the 1930s was Norman Irwin (1903-1983), owner of Red Wing Orchards, west of the town on Highway 2. One of his films, made in 1936, and now in the Archives of Ontario, showed each member of the Whitby Rotary Club, taken at the club's meeting place, the Whitby House Hotel. One member of the club who was not present in 1936, was filmed 10 years later, and his picture was spliced into the film. He was Samuel Trees. (1885-1957).

WEDNESDAY NIGHT
DECEMBER 8th - 1909

SPECIAL EXTRA
DOUBLE PROGRAM
WHERE?
GEM THEATRE

The program for to-night will be an exceptional good one. Our special picture will be "Maryland in 1777", a story of the American and English war. It will no doubt prove to be one of the best pictures ever shown here, you cannot afford to miss this.

"My Wife's Gone to the Country", is another special picture which is full of bright, sparkling comedy. This picture is a brand new one and is considered one of the greatest hits in film subjects of the season.

"A Marriage of Convenience", is another good subject that will no doubt prove to be a valuable number on to-nights program.

"A Tax on Bachelors", is another comedy subject and will make you laugh sure. It is one of the best comedy numbers. Don't miss this extra good program or you will sure miss a treat.

The song is one of Ted Snyder's publications entitled "It's the Pretty Things You Say". It is a very pretty number and will be beautifully illustrated

Special violin selection by Mr. C. Greenfield.

PROGRAM:

1. Picture—" Maryland in 1777."
2. Picture—" My Wife's Gone to the Country."
3. Song—" It's the Pretty Things You Say."
   Published by Ted Snyder Sung by Harry Pomeroy.
4. Picture—" Marriage of Convenience."
5. Picture—" Tax on Bachelors."

STAFF:

R. S. McQUAID - - - - - Manager
C. GREENFIELD - - - - Operator
H. POMEROY - - - Singer and Pianist

ADMISSION—Adults, 10c ; Children, 5c.

Gazette-Chronicle Print

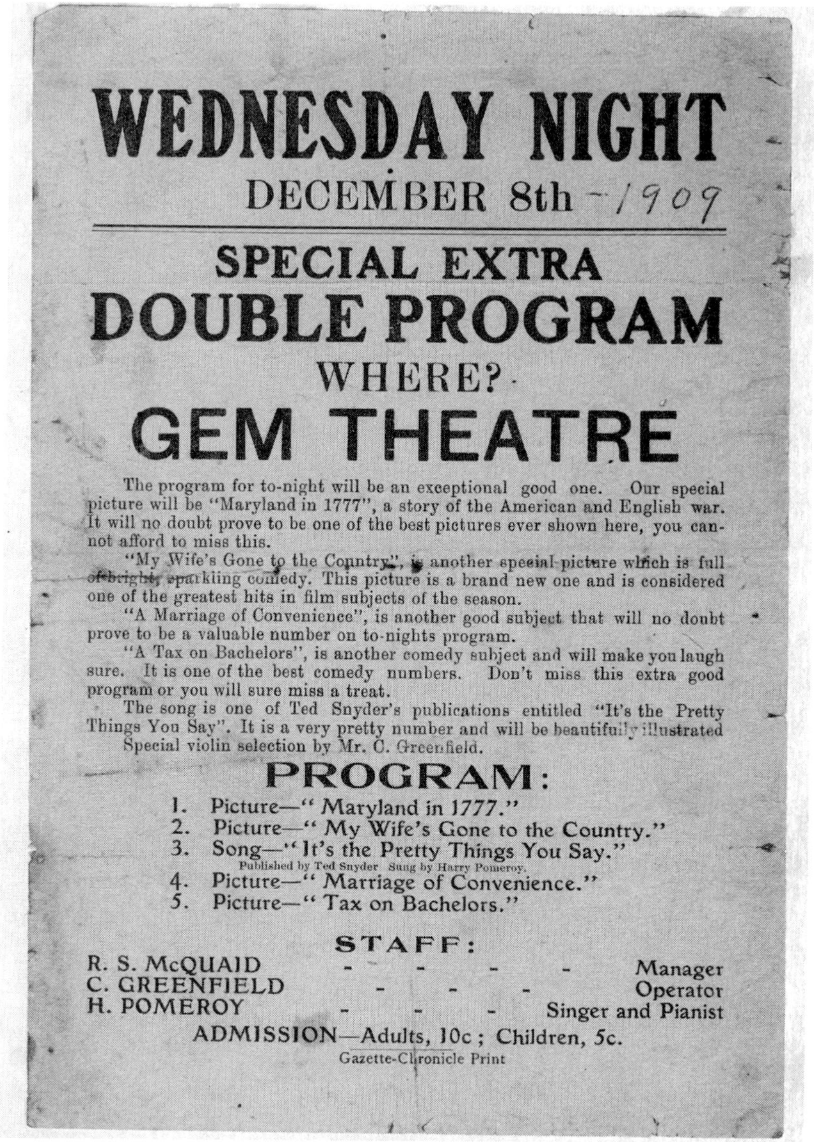

A handbill for the Gem Theatre's program of December 8, 1909.

How The Devil Got Into Devil's Den

In the middle of the Heber Down Conservation Area, along the nature trail is a valley known for more than a century as Devil's Den. Two boys playing pranks on their friends were responsible for the name, but they almost did not live to tell about it.

At Devil's Den the valley of the Lynde Creek plunges 94 feet into a densely wooded area which more than 100 years ago was filled with a pine forest. In the 1880's, this was a wild piece of country, a good place for young farmers' sons to play when they had nothing else to do. The popular sport in those days was to give stump speeches like the politicians. A boy would go into the woods and stand on an old stump where he made a speech to his friends.

Two local boys who were bored with stump speaking, Jim Delong and Albert Lynde, decided they would put a scare into their friends one night. Jim could yelp like a wildcat, enough to scare anyone. Albert was good with a knife, so he cut a wildcat's foot from a potato and planted footprints in the sand throughout the valley. When some unsuspecting boys were in the midst of a stump speech, Jim, hiding in the bush not far away, would let out a blood-curdling cry of a wildcat. Albert would rush up to the terrified boys, tell them there was a wildcat in the woods, and lead them away from Jim's hiding place.

A track crew posing on the completed Devil's Den bridge, May, 1910.

The frequent cries of the wildcat and the many sightings of footprints in the valley caused the area farmers considerable anxiety. With a wildcat on the loose, they feared that somebody could get hurt. A few weeks after the wildcat cries were reported, the farmers brought in two professional cat hunters from Uxbridge to track it down and

Devil's Den, looking east during the construction of the Canadian Northern Railway trestle, January, 1910.

kill it. Unaware of the hunters, Jim and Albert continued to play they game in the valley. On one occasion the hunters, armed with their shotguns, walked right over a log where Jim was hiding. He saw the gun and heard the talking about killing the wildcat.

That night, Jim Delong and Albert Lynde had a conference after going home. They realised that the wildcat game had got out of hand and they had better stop it now. Never again did they play wildcat in the val-

ley, and kept the secret to themselves. Well, almost. Albert Lynde told his nephew Keith Lynde (1900-1984) about the wildcat, and Keith told the author of this book.

The terrified farmers, however, thought the cries of the wildcat sounded like the screams of the Devil – thus the name Devil's Den was applied to the valley of the Lynde Creek in the 5th concession of Whitby Township.

Devil's Den however, continued to throw

a scare into the local farmers.

During the winter and spring of 1910, the Canadian Northern Railway was built through Whitby Township, passing through Devil's Den. The contracting firm of Mackenzie and Mann hired many local labours to build a steel railway trestle 735 feet long and 94 feet high across the den. The soil was cut from under the frozen banks of Devil's Den by hand, so the concrete abutments could be sunk 25 feet into the ground. A shovel used by the workers was unearthed by Eugene Lynde (1936-1969) more than 50 years later, 15 feet underground near one of these concrete footings.

Alfred and Jim Lynde were among the labourers who mixed cement by hand on a 16-foot square platform known as a sweat board. The gravel for the cement was heated by a Spencer steam engine after it had been hauled a distance of five miles by a team of horses. The 40 to 45 labourers lived in a tent camp south of the construction site throughout the winter of 1910. Wages were 25 cents an hour for the construction workers. The drivers of the teams which hauled the waggons of gravel were paid five dollars a day, while Charlie Lynde, the water boy, got 50 cents a day for bringing the thirsty men water from a nearby spring.

The railway trestle was finished on May

24, 1910. Two trains a day carried milk and vegetables along the railway. Stations were located at Greenwood in Pickering Township (Greenburn Station), the side road west of Coronation Road (called Kinsdale) and east of Highway 12 (called Brinllook). The last station was a rewording of "Brooklin".

During the First World War, troop trains made regular runs on the Canadian Northern Railway. There was quite an uproar in the community when a section foreman found a logging chain tied around the rails on the Devil's Den bridge shortly before a troop train was due to cross it. With sabotage suspected, two armed guards were stationed at each end of the bridge for the duration of the war.

During the 1920s when prohibition was enforced in Ontario, moonshiners shipped bottles of contraband liquor in crates of vegetables along the railway.

By the time of the Depression in the 1930s, the Canadian Northern Railway ceased operation and the tracks were removed. The giant trestle over Devil's Den was dismantled. All that remains today are several concrete footings in the valley and the large abutments at each side of Devil's Den. The western abutment is a lookout near the site of the Heber Down Conservation area trailer park.

The Devil's Den bridge, looking from the bottom of the valley, 1922.

Since 1966, Devil's Den has been a part of a conservation area, named after Brooklin farmer Heber Down (1889-1972) who provided some of its land. And the only screams in Devil's Den today are the children's laughter and not real or imagined wildcats.

Whitby's Greatest Loss Was the Old Post Office

Ask any Whitby resident who lived here before 1960 what was the town's greatest loss, he will likely say it was the demolition of the old post office. The post office, which stood for 50 years at the corner of Brock and Dundas Streets where the Bank of Montreal was located, was truly a landmark. Before it was demolished in May 1959, it was the place where the townsfolk gathered on its stone steps to pass the time of day. Whitby residents set their watches by its tower clock, and everyone came there at some time of the day to pick up their mail, for there was no mail delivery in Whitby until 1959.

During the early 1900s the Federal Government built a series of new post offices throughout Canada. The Whitby Town Council petitioned the Government for a new post office in May, 1903, for it realized that the old post office, in the McMillan Block on Brock Street North (now Go Natural Foods) was totally inadequate. In November 1907 the Government agreed to purchase from lawyer Lyman T. Barclay (1855-1925) the lot at Brock and Dundas Streets where the old Albion hotel stood. Cost of the lot was $5,000. Through the efforts of Fred L. Fowke, M.P. of Oshawa (1857-1939) the Whitby post office was to be built of the finest red and grey sandstone from the quarries at Indianstown, New Brunswick.

Gay and Son of Oshawa were the contractors who built the post office. Construction began early in 1909 and the building was completed by September, 1910. There was no official opening for the post office. The keys were turned over to the postmaster, John D. Howden (1841-1927) on Sept. 23, and Alex Whitelaw (1840-1929), the first caretaker, moved into his residence on the third floor. Whitelaw had only one arm, as a result of an accident, but was still able to carry out his duties, which included winding the tower clock every eight days.

The ground floor housed the town's post office and the receiving room of the customs department which was located in Whitby

The Whitby Post Office decorated for the Coronation of King George V, June, 1911.

until it moved to Oshawa in 1935. The second floor contained the customs office and the office of Inland Revenue.

Since there was no mail delivery, residents came daily to the post office to collect their mail from a series of 657 boxes and 41 drawers.

The main entrance was through two doors at the base of the clock tower, leading into a lobby lined with oak panelling and plate glass windows. The boxes were made of brass and each window or wicket was trimmed with brass and bore a name plate. An oak-topped writing desk stood in the public lobby and there was a drop letter box on the Brock Street side of the building for mail being sent within Whitby. The post office was lighted by electricity and heated by a hot water furnace, boasting all the modern conveniences of its time.

When the post office opened in 1910, postage for a letter was three cents and a post card, one cent. All mail was cancelled by hand at a rate of 30 to 40 letters per minute, until a mechanical canceller was installed in 1930 which could mark 350 letters per minute.

The most prominent feature of the Whitby Post Office was its clock tower, with four faces and a mechanism which struck the hours, quarter-hours and half-hours. The clock was made in England and

Postmaster John D. Howden at his desk shortly after the post office opened in 1910.

installed in the tower by Phillip Taylor (1831-1911), a Whitby Jeweller. Taylor first set the clock going on his 80th birthday, Jan. 20, 1911. He charged $1,500 to install the clock. It took 800 pounds of weight to power the six-foot, 80-pound pendulum which drove the clock. Once a week, the one-armed caretaker, Alex Whitelaw had to wind the clock with a big crank like those used to start early automobiles. Only three caretakers staffed the post office and wound the clock – Alex Whitelaw, John Ard (1854-

1931) and Bill Ashton (1896-1980).

When the old post office was closed in 1956 and the new building opened at Dundas and Perry Streets, there was much comment on what would happen to the old clock. On Aug. 9, 1956, it stopped at 8:43 p.m., and Bill Ashton had instructions from the Federal Department of Public Works not to rewind it. The Daily Times-Gazette, Whitby and Oshawa's newspaper published a tribute to the clock signed by *"The Observer"*, who noted that *"it was not a member of a union but was continuously on strike."* Another observer noted three weeks after the clock had stopped, that its hands had advanced by two minutes, and a few days later by five minutes. This was considered quite a feat by a clock that had not been wound for a month.

By mid-September 1956, the town council was debating how the clock could be kept going for the benefit of the many people who relied on it to know the time.

A letter was sent to the Department of Public Works asking that Bill Ashton be permitted to keep the clock running. Time finally ran out for the old post office in 1959 as the wreckers took over. The clock was offered to the town as a relic for a museum but Mayor Harry Jermyn said it was not an antique for it was only 48 years old, and the town had no museum. In the

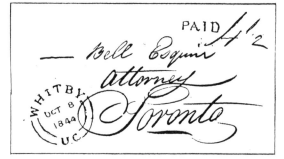

A letter from the Whitby post office, mailed October 8, 1844

nick of time, the clock was rescued by Percy Nicholls who purchased the entire works for $15. He had a sentimental attachment for the clock for it had kept him on time for work for 16 years. It took six hours to dismantle the works piece by piece with wrenches. A partition had to be removed to get at the 24 lead weights attached to the wires that drove the mechanism. It was noted that if the clock was reassembled, it would require a room six feet square and 15 feet high to accommodate it. The works and one face of the clock were owned until recently by Earl Pascoe, a life-long Whitby resident, who has displayed it many times on Heritage Day on its original site in the Bank of Montreal building.

The author of this book, like many Whitby residents, has fond memories of the old post office. On his first day in Whitby in 1955, after moving from Toronto, he was sent to the post office to pick up the mail from the General Delivery wicket. Four years later, at the age of 11, when the post office was being demolished, he picked up the smallest stone he could find and tried to carry it home as a souvenir. He only got as far as the United Church, before he had to call his parents to come and pick up the stone in the car. When they got it home, they weighed it on the bathroom scale and discovered that it weighed 37 pounds. The stone now reposes in the author's garden.

Whitby Postmasters

Post Office Opened, April, 1824

1824 -	Johan Borlase Warren
- 1834	J. S. Herrmans
1839 - 1861	Alexander McPherson
1862 - 1866	David Smith
1867 - 1869	Francis Keller
1869 - 1882	Robert Hervey Lawder
1882 - 1885	Charles Nourse
1885 - 1924	John Dundas Howden
1924 - 1944	Gordon Bennett Whitfield
1944 - 1946	Mrs Carla Ledora Cowieson (acting)
1946 - 1947	Elizabeth Ferne Nichols (acting)
1947 - 1963	Wilson Henry Brown
1963 - 1972	Lawrence William Hall

Post Office became a sub-station of Oshawa, April, 1972

Our GO-Transit Service Is Nothing New

On Dec. 4, 1988, the first GO-Transit train arrived at Whitby, bringing commuter rail service to Toronto for the first time. It is little known today that such a service was first proposed more than 90 years ago, and almost became a reality after the First World War. If it had not been for a lack of money, and a few stubborn politicians, Whitby's place as a commuter bedroom community for Toronto would have been established long ago and we would have seen the growth of the 1980s taking place in the 1920s.

Electric commuter railways between Toronto and outlying communities were the concept of Sir Adam Beck, the founder of Ontario Hydro in 1906. Quick access to Toronto would allow city residents to live in quiet suburban towns and commute to work, and the products from the outlying communities could be shipped quickly and easily to markets in Toronto. In a time when the automobile was in its infancy and unpaved roads were turned into muddy quagmires in the spring and fall, a system of electric railways seemed a cheap and beneficial way of linking communities in Southern Ontario.

At the urging of Sir Adam Beck, the Federal Government Incorporated the Toronto and Eastern Railway on April 12, 1910 to build and operate a railway easterly

Mayor Richard N. Bassett driving the first spike for the Toronto and eastern Railway in 1923. Railway Manager E.W. Oliver holds the nickel-plated spike.

from Toronto through Pickering, Whitby, Oshawa and Bowmanville, with a final terminus at Cobourg. Plans were also made to extend railways to Peterborough, Markham, Stouffville, Uxbridge and Lindsay. It was expected it would take five years to complete the line.

The Toronto and Eastern Railway was a project of the Canadian Northern Railway

which was building a line from Toronto north of Whitby and Oshawa in 1910. Originally, Whitby and Oshawa opposed construction of the Canadian Northern, but gave permission when assured that an electric line would be built through these lakefront communities. The Canadian Northern, now long gone, ran south of Brooklin, through the Heber Down Conservation area. The abutments for the trestle across Lynde Creek can still be seen at Devil's Den.

In July 1910, the Toronto and Eastern was surveyed from Cherrywood in Pickering Township to Bowmanville, a distance of 23½ miles, and was approved by the Minister of Railways in Ottawa. Approval for the route from Pickering to Toronto was granted in 1912. The route was to run parallel to the Kingston Road (Highway 2), and follow Mary Street through Whitby, Bond Street through Oshawa, and Wellington Street through Bowmanville. Mackenzie and Mann (who were also partners in the Canadian Northern) were the contractors for the Toronto and Eastern. Grading for the right-of-way through Whitby began in the summer of 1913. By the following summer the rails had been laid through the town.

Construction along Mary Street was not without its problems. A number of home

A work train removing the rails from the Toronto and Eastern at Red Wing Orchards in 1927.

owners along the street did not want their lawns and sidewalks torn up to make room for the railway. Therefore, part of the road allowance was used, making the remainder of Mary Street very narrow.

One of the worst sink holes on the line was where Mary Street crossed Ash Creek. In building a bridge over the creek, the contractor had to sink piles more than 40 feet into the mud to find solid ground.

When the First World War broke out on Aug. 4, 1914, the tracks had been laid from Bowmanville to Lynde Creek in Whitby, a distance of 14½ miles. Work trains took ties and rails along the completed part of the line but no passenger or freight service had begun. Also, no work had been done to electrify the line.

The First World War brought construction on the Toronto and Eastern to a halt. The labourers were needed for the army and the money being spent on the railway was diverted to war production. Another reason for halting construction was a plan by Ontario Hydro to build its own radial line in the area.

When the war ended in 1918, there was agitation in the lakefront communities to resume construction. The Canadian Northern was granted the right to full ownership of the railway in 1918, but all efforts to get the project going again, ended in a lot of talk and no action. Public meetings were held frequently in Whitby, Oshawa and Bowmanville in 1918 and 1919 to urge that work begin as soon as possible to complete the Toronto and Eastern. Real estate dealers had made several significant sales of large homes in Whitby and Brooklin with the promise that they soon would be linked by rail to Toronto.

In 1923, the Toronto and Eastern was taken over by the federally-operated Canadian National Railway. With new ownership, work finally began to repair the neglect of eight years. Fourteen rotting trestles were rebuilt. Whitby Mayor Richard N. Bassett (1880-1940) was called upon to drive the first spike to mark commencement of construction.

There is some indication that the Canadian National had no intention of completing the Toronto and Eastern. No work was done to electrify the existing line

The first GO-Transit train coming into Whitby station, December 4, 1988.

and nothing was done to build the link between Pickering Village and Scarborough. It was said that William H. Moore (1872-1960), a future Liberal member of the federal government, would not sell his land at Dunbarton to the railway, thus preventing completion of the link to Toronto. Accusations were also made that the Canadian National was trying to improve its public image by completing the Toronto and Eastern, while planning to shut down the Canadian Northern. By July 1924, after a year of half-hearted work, the construction crews left the Toronto and Eastern again.

A year later, the president of the Canadian National toured the line by automobile and came to the conclusion that the line would be abandoned permanently. The Oshawa Railway company had electrified about 2,000 feet of track between Oshawa Boulevard and Mary Street for improvement of switching facilities to the growing General Motors plant, but this was the only work completed.

During the summer of 1927, Canadian National work crews removed all the rails and ties from the Toronto and Eastern Railway and let the right-of-way go to seed.

One of the reasons cited for the demise of the Toronto and Eastern Railway was the increased use of the automobile in the 1920s. Roads were now being paved (Brock and Dundas Streets were paved in 1921) and more people were using cars than would likely use an electric railway, the officials stated. Between 1921 and 1923, Brock and Dundas Streets became Provincial Highways. Many tourist stops were established along Highway 2 in Whitby because the town was a day's drive from Toronto. However, the day of electric commuter railways was over before it had even begun. Although all evidence of the Toronto and Eastern right-of-way has disappeared along Mary Street, embankments and depressions in the ground could still be seen in the fields north of Highway 2 between Whitby and Oshawa in the 1960s, before they were wiped out by commercial development.

The establishment of a commuter railway from Toronto was finally realized in 1967 when GO-Transit rail service was started from Toronto to Pickering. Bus service from Pickering to Whitby started in 1970, while rail service to Whitby was completed 11 years ago. Even though there is finally a commuter rail link between Whitby and Toronto, it can only operate full service during rush hours because of funding cutbacks. Today, as it was 75 years ago, money was the determining factor in providing government services.

When Canada's Horsemen Came To Whitby

For two years, 1913 and 1914, Whitby was a mecca for horse enthusiasts, as it presented its first horse shows. The town park, now Rotary Centennial Park, was the site of a magnificent spectacle organized by Thomas Cussion, proprietor of the Royal Hotel and manager of Meadowbrook Farms, owned by Sir Henry Pellatt (1859-1939). Pellatt, who was building Casa Loma as his palatial home in Toronto, had purchased the farm in Pickering Township (now Ajax) a few years previously. The farm still carries on Pellatt's tradition of horse breeding as Picov's Horseman Centre.

One wonders if Sir Henry had more than a little influence in setting up the Whitby Horse Show, for he won most of the prizes. Sir Henry's *"Lord Kitchener"*, described as *"the finest horse in Canada"* and *"Casa Loma Squire"* and *"Casa Loma Lad"* were among the prize winners. He was also Honorary President of the show.

In May 1913, a Whitby Horse Show Association was formed, with Fred Hatch as president; Thomas Cussion, vice-president; Albert W. Jackson, secretary and Samuel Trees, treasurer. These men were among the wealthiest citizens of the town. Fred Hatch (1861-1929) was the owner of the buckle factory, and Samuel Trees (1885-1957) owned the blanket factory, two of Whitby's three large industries. The buckle

A view of the 1913 Horse Show looking from the north end of the Town Park.

factory was where the Price Chopper plaza is now on Brock Street South, and the blanket factory was on Brock Street North where Coffee Time Donuts is located.

The Town Council authorized a grant of $250 for the horse show. Work began immediately to prepare the town park for the big event. Seventy loads of earth were dumped to level up uneven spots and a 500 seat grandstand was erected around a show ring. In the north end of the park, space was provided for parking automobiles at 50 cents each. Admission to the grounds and carriage parking cost 25 cents.

The Whitby Horse Show of 1913 opened on July 15 and ran for two days. Prizes

WHITBY HORSE SHOW

$2,000 IN PRIZES

TUESDAY and WEDNESDAY, JULY 15th and 16th, 1913

Prize List and Programmes will be out in a few days

Whitby's Horse Show bids fair to be the Biggest Event in the History of the County
Entries coming in from all parts of the Province.

Reduced Rates on all Railroads

FRED HATCH,
President.

T. CUSSION,
Vice-President.

ALBERT W. JACKSON,
Secretary.

Advertisement for the 1913 show published in the Whitby Gazette and Chronicle.

included $2,000 in cash and a number of silver cups. More than 40 classes were open for competition, including jumpers, horses in harness, ponies and draught horses. An entrance gate of evergreens decorated with the show colours, purple and gold, was erected at the park, which was surrounded by a high fence of buckram. Inside the

fence were the grandstand with 17 private boxes, the judges' stand and a bandstand, all decorated in purple and gold.

More than 2,000 people, many from out of town, jammed the park to see their favourite horses. Among the distinguished guests were W.E.N. Sinclair (1873-1947), M.P.P. for South Ontario; R.S. McLaughlin

(1871-1972), president of the McLaughlin Carriage Company in Oshawa; Senator Robert Beith of Bowmanville; ex-M.P. Peter Christie and Col. J.F. Grierson of Oshawa.

After the show, a lawn party was held at The Grange, at Mary and Pine Streets, the summer home of J.B. Laidlaw (1866-1953), president of the Norwich Union Insurance Company. The Grange, later owned by F.L. Beecroft (1868-1963), was demolished in 1976 and apartments built on the site.

The second annual Whitby Horse Show was held from Aug. 12 to 14, 1914. The Association made an unsuccessful bid to have a permanent grandstand erected in the park. It asked for $500 for this project and received only $250. The 1914 show was bigger than the one the previous year. The number of classes was increased to 60 and prize money to $3,500.

The show received another boost from the presence of the famous hunters and jumpers owned by the Hon. Clifford Sifton, a noted horse breeder and member of Sir Wilfrid Laurier's government. Thirteen Sifton horses competed in a field of 27, three receiving prizes.

An indication of the success of the 1914 show was the private boxes in the grandstand which were increased to 50 from the 17 in the 1913 show. Because of the

The Whitby Horse Show Committee, 1914. Back row, left to right: Edward D. Warren, unidentified, Mayor James E. Willis, George Whitelaw, Albert W. Jackson, Arthur T. Lawler, Thomas Cussion, unidentified, James Rutledge, unidentified, Fred Hatch, unidentified. The two men in front are unidentified.

town.

The Gazette and Chronicle reported that the horse show *"surpassed the average fall fair in interest and attraction, and was a hundred times more valuable as an advertising feature to the Town of Whitby."* It was estimated that as many as 5,000 people attended the three-day 1914 show.

With the future of the Whitby Horse Show appearing so bright, it looked as if it would put Whitby on the map. But this was not to be. A week before the 1914 show opened, the First World War began. By 1915, there were more serious matters to deal with than showing horses and there was not the money or the personnel to continue the project which had began so successfully two years before. There were no further horse shows held in Whitby. A few relics of the Whitby Horse Shows are in the Whitby Archives, including a 1914 program and 1913 letterhead, as well as a few photographs. But what happened to all those silver cups?

Whitby could have become as famous for its horse shows as Cobourg in the early part of this century, were it not for the First World War. With the end of the Whitby Horse Show, Thomas Cussion, its founder, left town, and nothing further is known about him.

increased size of the 1914 show, the stabling at Whitby's hotels could not accommodate all the horses which were on hand to compete. To make room for the extra horses, the new Burns Arena at Green and Gilbert Streets was converted into a horse barn, providing 75 stalls. The liquor store stands on the site today. Another sign of success was that in 1914 there were 350 entries, compared to 175 in 1913. The Whitby Horse Show was well on its way to becoming a feature tourist attraction for the

Whitby A Leader In Mental Health Care For 80 Years

One of the most significant announcements made by the Government of Ontario, affecting the Town of Whitby, occurred on Feb. 17, 1912 when it was announced that an *"asylum"* would be built in the town. Although the name has changed over the years, from Ontario Hospital, to Whitby Psychiatric Hospital, to Whitby Mental Health Centre, this facility has been an integral part of Whitby's life for more than 80 years.

"Province to build asylum near Whitby" read the front-page headline in the Toronto Globe, the leading newspaper in Canada in 1912. The Globe announced that *"one of the most thoroughly equipped asylums for the insane on the continent"* was to be constructed on a parcel of land nearly a mile square, consisting of 624 acres. Much more land than was required by the hospital buildings was purchased, for the Government planned to make the hospital self-sustaining, with a farm to provide food and milk for the patients. The farm would not only provide food, but would also provide outdoor therapy and exercise. The hospital farm was an integral part of the operation until it was closed in 1969.

One reason the hospital came to Whitby was that in 1911, the site of the old mental hospital at 999 Queen Street in Toronto was sold to the Grand Trunk Railway and the

Travelling derrick used to build the Ontario Hospital in 1913. Standing in front are Harry "Pud" Watson and John Ridgley.

Massey-Harris Manufacturing Company which made farm implements. The Whitby hospital was to replace Queen Street hospital and still be within easy distance of Toronto, but the Toronto facility never did close. The

original building dating from 1846 was replaced by a new hospital 130 years later.

Throughout 1911, the Ontario Government had been considering several sites for a new hospital, with Whitby being the most favoured one. However, one man almost prevented the hospital from coming to Whitby. He was John Smith (1841-1912), the owner of *"Bayside"*, the largest of the farms the Ontario Government wanted. Bayside was located on the west side of Whitby Harbour. First settled by William Gordon (1797-1876), in 1838, it had been owned by the Smith family since 1887. The Provincial Government badly wanted Smith's farm as the site for the hospital buildings, but he would not sell under any circumstances. Just when it seemed that the project might be abandoned, John Smith died at the age of 70 on Jan. 18, 1912. Thirty days later the Government announced that all negotiations for the hospital site had been completed. The Town of Whitby was represented by Albert W. Jackson (1870-1939), the town Reeve, a veteran politician who was very instrumental in negotiating for the land owned by the farmers on the lakeshore. Jackson also negotiated with the province and the Whitby Water and Light Commission to provide cheap water and electric power for the hospital, at special rates charged only to industries. The agreement he worked out was for seven cents per 100 gallons of water and six cents per 1,000 watts of electricity. The availability of cheap water and light was a major factor in determining the Whitby site for the

Carpenters in front of one of the hospital cottages during construction, 1914.

hospital.

The initial announcement stated that the hospital would be built according to the plan of the great Centre Islay Asylum at Long Island, New York, but there were also European influences in the buildings. The Whitby hospital was one of the first mental hospitals in the world to be built with a system of cottages rather than a single building. This new approach to mental illness was to

Callisthenics on the Mitchell Farm, May 26, 1916.

way to Oshawa. The military review was considered a great success from several points of view. It proved that Whitby supported a county battalion even though many men had already gone overseas, and provided an opportunity for the men to experience battle conditions before a friendly home crowd. The 116th Battalion was so successful that recruiting began almost immediately for a second Battalion, the 182nd.

A few months later, many of these young men perished in the real battles of the First World War in France. Col. Sam Sharpe was so devastated by the loss of his men that he committed suicide by jumping out a hotel window in Montreal, shortly after his return in 1918.

bition of physical drill under the leadership of Sgt. *"Billy Hole."* At the conclusion of the review, the soldiers marched through the town, passing a reviewing stand on which were Mayor Frank Warren (1850-1920), Col. Michael O'Donovan (1834-1918), Col. John E. Farewell (1840-1923) and Major William Smith MP (1847-1931). Cols. O'Donovan and Farewell were veterans of the Canadian forces which repelled the Fenian Raids at Fort Erie in 1866. The home of Fred Howard Annes (1861-1940)

where the A&P Plaza now stands at Dundas and Frances Streets, was opened to the soldiers so they could be served refreshments by the ladies of Whitby. Two parallel columns of men entered the estate from the west, were served under a marquee on the front lawn, and continued on their march through the town.

Col. Sharpe drew the men to attention and officially thanked the ladies for their hospitality. The battalion gave three rousing cheers and a *"tiger"* and proceeded on its

A receipt for a contribution of $10.00 from George W. Dryden to the Whitby Patriotic Fund, October 2, 1915

293

The Bay School was Plagued by Financial Problems

Schools are expensive, so it was not surprising that the Town of Whitby ran into financial problems when it began construction of a new school at Port Whitby in 1915. The First World War was already beginning to drain the Canadian economy and labour was scarce. The land title for the Brock Street School records 16 mechanics' liens issued on the property in 1915-16 by contractors who had not been paid.

As one of the oldest parts of the Town of Whitby, Port Whitby, also known as *"The Bay"* has been a site of a school since pioneer times. As early as 1837 there was a log school house on Victoria Street, east of St. John's Anglican Church, where the parishioners' parking lot is today. While the church was being constructed, the Anglicans shared the school with the Methodists, but they could not get along, even on a Sunday. The Anglicans therefore moved their services to the home of John Welsh (1810-1859) until St. John's was opened in July, 1846.

Port Whitby's second school was a one-storey brick building constructed on Dufferin Street, back from the road in 1851. It still stands behind the old Brock Street School. It was in this building that the first meetings of the Provisional Council of the County of Ontario were held in 1852. The old school house served until 1916 when it was replaced by the Brock Street School and sold to Hugh Ross

The new Brock Street Public School as it was at the time of opening in 1916.

(1854-1923) for use as residence, at $560. Its address today is 1516 Dufferin Street.

By 1915, the Whitby Board of Education and the Town Council realized that the old Dufferin Street School was antiquated. It had no washrooms, and the wind in the winter blew fiercely through cracks in the walls.

On May 2, 1915, Frances E. Woodhouse (1851-1933) sold a tract of land at the corner of Brock and Victoria Streets as a site for a new school. She was the eldest daughter of John Woodhouse (1816-1888), principal of the old

Bay School for 30 years. Eleven days later, tenders were called by W. Grayson Brown, an architect from Hamilton, for construction of the new Bay School and renovations to the High School on Colborne Street West, now the site of a senior citizens' apartment building. By June, 1915, the excavation for the basement was completed but then the money had ran out. The Board of Education had to ask the Town Council for an additional $8,000 to complete the two schools.

Some of the contractors who issued leins on

Brock Street School, Room 2, April 10, 1923.

pupils did not go on to high school in 1916.

The second principal at the new Bay School, from 1918 to 1930, was Margaret W. Kennedy (1898-1988). She left Whitby in 1930 to teach in Toronto and became the first woman principal in the Toronto School system. After retiring from teaching in 1963, she obtained a law degree from the University of Toronto. Miss Kennedy returned to Whitby where she served on the cemetery board of St. John's Anglican Church, and was president of the Whitby Historical Society.

Another Brock Street School principal was Harry W. Jermyn, who served as Whitby's mayor in the 1950s. After two years at Brock Street School, 1930-32, he became principal of the Dundas Street (now Florence M. Heard) School.

By 1969, the old Brock Street School had outlived its usefulness. There were only 70 pupils attending the school, as the number of young people residing in Port Whitby had decreased. Since the Board of Education required 250 pupils to build the new school, it was decided to close Brock Street School, which did not have a gymnasium or a library. The students were bused to Kathleen Rowe and other schools.

In September, 1998, the old Brock Street School was demolished after standing empty for 29 years. Present plans call for the erection a fire hall on its site.

the new Bay School because they had not been paid, were Thomas G. Deverell, for the mason work; Joseph Heard, who transported the building materials to the construction site; Clarence M. Stevens, who did the electrical work; Pease Foundry Company of Toronto, which provided the furnace and Aikenhead Hardware, of Toronto. Leins were also issued by the Oshawa Brick Company, and Georgian Bay Book Mills who provided the school with its text books. Since the Board of Education could not afford new desks for the Bay School, old desks were taken from the high school.

In spite of the financial problems, the Brock Street School officially opened on May 1, 1916. It was a two-room school with 40 students per class room. W.A. Henderson, the last teacher at the old Dufferin Street School, was the principal. There was little ceremony at the opening of the new school because of wartime conditions. On the first day of classes, the chairman of the Board of Education made a short speech to the students, expressing the hope that they would take care of the school property and improve every moment of time at school since 90 per cent of public school

The Whole Town Turned out for the Mule Train Wreck

One of the most photographed events in Whitby's history was the mule train wreck of 1916. The whole town turned out to take pictures and collect souvenirs from a wreck that should have never happened. The Town of Whitby Archives has 14 photographs of the mule train wreck, two of which are in the Ontario Archives. For many years the pictures in the Ontario Archives were wrongly identified, until the author of this book was able to confirm that they were the Whitby mule train wreck.

At 4:30 a.m. on Nov. 2, 1916, a train of nine cars and an engine was proceeding east on the Canadian Pacific Railway tracks through Whitby. About a half-mile east of Brock Street, the train approached the junction with the Whitby, Port Perry and Lindsay Railway near Garden Street. The train was loaded with mules bound for Montreal to be shipped overseas as pack animals for the First World War. At the junction stood a switching tower, where the man on duty was supposed to give a signal for the train to stop or proceed. He gave the signal to proceed, but instead of opening the derailing switch on the Whitby and Port Perry line as a safely measure, he opened the derailing switch on the C.P.R. line.

As a result, the train shot off the tracks. A protecting rail kept the engine from plunging off the roadbed, but the car behind the tender turned over on its side and plowed up the

Whitby citizens inspecting the mule train wreck, on the morning of November 2, 1916.

track for some distance. The car behind the tender jumped the track also, but it did not turn over. The remaining eight cars stacked up behind, like the cars of a model train set. Three cars swung at right angles to the track, another turned a summersault, and another lay with one end up in the air. Part of the wreck straddled a ditch and a farmer's wire fence.

The train contained 180 mules, 20 to a car. When the train went off the tracks, these poor beasts were tossed around in the cars and piled on top of each other. Some broke out through holes in the smashed cars. Remarkably few were killed by the impact of the crash, but many were so badly injured that they had to be destroyed.

With each mule valued at $97, the total loss in animals was estimated at $1,500. About 150 were killed or had to be destroyed. By daylight, most Whitby residents had heard of the mule train wreck and went to have a look. They posed for pictures on the locomotive and watched as the a C.P.R. railway crane from Toronto was used to clean up the mess. Carcasses of dead mules lay by the track close to the wreck, while those that had survived wandered about the scene of the crash. It was 3 o'clock the day after the accident that the tracks were finally cleared. The unfortunate switchman who was responsible for the wreck was know for many years afterwards as "mule killer".

Tom Thomson Learned His Art From Whitby's Florence McGillivray

Not long before his untimely death by drowning in 1917, Canada's most famous artist, Tom Thomson, was visited in his studio by Florence McGillivray, one of our country's most noted women artists. Thomson's friend Mark Robinson, a ranger at Algonquin Park, recorded that *she gave him a few valuable hints from her long experience in art.*

Although Florence McGillivray had gained an outstanding reputation as one of the best women water-colourists in Canada, her name is not so familiar in art circles today. Florence H. McGillivray was born on March 1, 1864 at Burnside Farm in Whitby Township near Audley, a daughter of George McGillivray and Caroline A. Fothergill. The site of the farm is now the corner of Taunton and Lakeridge Roads, on the border between Whitby and Ajax.

Her artistic talent came naturally, for her grandfather was Charles Fothergill (1782-1840), editor of the first Canadian Almanac, and an artist of considerable merit. A naturalist, he painted many watercolour pictures of Canadian birds which are now housed at the Royal Ontario Museum in Toronto. Charles Fothergill was the Canadian equivalent of the famed American naturalist John James Audubon.

In 1870, when Florence was six years old, her family moved to *Inverlynn,* a large

Florence McGillivray at the time she was an art teacher at the Ontario Ladies' College, 1906.

brick home at the corner of Raglan and Giffard Streets in the Town of Whitby. Still owned by descendants of George McGillivray, this is the last of the old estates of Whitby. In 1971 the house was used for the filming of Mazo de la Roche's

"Whiteoaks of Jalna," by the Canadian Broadcasting Corporation.

At the age of seventeen in 1881, Florence McGillivray won two first prizes at the Bowmanville Fair for her watercolour paintings. Five years later, she offered classes in oils, watercolours and china painting at the women's Christian Temperance Union free reading rooms in Whitby.

She received her initial art training at the Central Ontario School of Art and the Toronto Art School from such well-known artists of the day as William Cruikshanks, F.M. Bell-Smith, J.W.L. Forster, Lucius O'Brien and F. McGillivray Knowles. For many years in the early 1900's, Florence McGillivray was an art teacher at the Ontario Ladies' College in Whitby (now known as Trafalgar Castle School), working closely with F. McGillivray Knowles, a visiting art critic at the school. Lucius O'Brien, who was one of her teachers, was art director at the Ontario Ladies' College in the 1890's. A large oil painting of Venetian gondolas, painted by Florence McGillivray, hangs in the common room at Trafalgar Castle School. Miss McGillivray acted also as an art critic at Pickering College, located in Pickering Village (now part of Ajax) until the college burned down in December 1905 and was rebuilt at Newmarket.

In her vacation time, Florence

McGillivray travelled extensively in Canada and the British West Indies, painting wherever she went. Accompanying this Chronicle is a sketch she made of a moonlit night in Jamaica.

In 1913, Miss McGillivray went to Paris where she studied under Simon and Menard. She exhibited a painting of a French nun, entitled *"Contentment,"* at the Salon des Beaux Arts that year, and was elected president of International Art Union, which was disbanded a few years later during the First World War. Miss McGillivray's subsequent work showed the influence of the French impressionism which she learned at that time.

On her return from Europe, she settled in Ottawa with her sister, Mrs. David MacLaren (1850-1940), but continued to travel, painting in Labrador, Newfoundland, the Canadian West and the New England States. Florence McGillivray was elected a member of the Ontario Society of Artists and the Society of Women Painters and Sculptors of New York in 1917. In 1925, she became an associate of the Royal Canadian Academy and was a member of the Canadian Water Colour Painters Society.

Two Florence McGillivray paintings were exhibited at the Royal Canadian Academy's Toronto exhibition in 1914, one of which was purchased by the National Gallery in Ottawa. At the time of her death, 24 years later, the National Gallery possessed four of her paintings, two of the Labrador coast; one painted in Whitby, known as *"The Sentinals,"* and a fourth being a snow scene. Florence McGillivray was painting her best work at the time the Group of Seven was revolutionizing Canadian art. Although Tom Thomson died before the Group of Seven was formed in 1920, he led the way in the development of their style of painting Canada's northern forests. Thomson's father, John Thomson (1840-1930) was born in Whitby and attended the Whitby Grammar School. Tom Thomson was born in 1877 on a farm near Claremont, west of Whitby in Pickering Township.

A moonlit night in Jamaica, a sketch by Florence McGillivray.

After many years in Ottawa, Florence McGillivray retired to Toronto in the 1930's, where she became actively interested in the formation of a pioneer museum at the Guild of All Arts (now the Guild Inn) in Scarborough. Fifty years later, the wife of Spencer Clark, founder of the Guild of All Arts, used a painting of sailing vessels at Whitby harbour by Florence McGillivray on her Christmas cards. The Guild Inn today is the scene of a garden decorated with stone work from many of Toronto's demolished 19th century buildings.

Florence McGillivray died at Toronto on May 7, 1938, prior to the opening of the Guild museum, and her funeral was held from the old family home, "Inverlynn," at Whitby. She is buried in the McGillivray family plot in Union Cemetery, Oshawa.

Today, Florence McGillivray's work is not as well known or recognized as it was 80 years ago. One Whitby resident tells the story of attending a sale at an old farm home in Kitchener a few years ago and recognizing a watercolour painting of a moonlight scene by Florence McGillivray. The painting was lying on a table with a pile of other pictures. The Whitby resident offered $20 for the picture and was told by the young man who had bought the house that she could have it for $18. She handed him a $20 bill and proceeded to leave with the picture. Suddenly, the young man called her back, but it was not because he recognized the value of the painting. He wanted to give the customer her $2 change. The painting was framed in Berlin (Kitchener's name before 1916 when the First World War changed Canada's attitude towards German names), and was inscribed on the back: *"For the Briethaupts."* Members of the Briethaupt family attended the Ontario Ladies' College when Florence McGillivray was an art teacher there. Louis O. Briethaupt visited the Commencement exercises at the school in 1955 when he was Lieutenant-Governor of Ontario. The moonlight painting which was obtained for only $18, was worth at least $200, when the Whitby resident purchased it about 20 years ago. It would not have even attracted her attention, had it not been for the first retrospective exhibition of Florence McGillivray's paintings, held at the Whitby Arts Station Gallery when it opened in 1970. This exhibition at the Station Gallery gave Whitby citizens the first opportunity in more than 50 years to view the work of this hometown artist.

Besides the painting of the gondolas at Trafalgar Castle School there is a Florence McGillivray painting of fishing boats at the Whitby Public Library, which she presented to the Library in 1937. Some of her paintings have a particular historic value. One canvas depicts the Cascades on the Gatineau River near Ottawa. These Cascades disappeared many years ago when a power dam was constructed on the river. *"The Cascades"* and another picture of a covered bridge in Quebec were selected in the late 1960's to be part of a government-sponsored exhibition which was sent across Canada.

WHITBY ARTS INCORPORATED

presents

Florence McGillivray
Retrospective

EXHIBITION

at

"THE STATION"
CORNER HENRY AND VICTORIA STREETS

October 4th - October 18th,
1970

WEEKENDS ONLY

Program for Florence McGillivray Retrospective Exhibition, The Station Gallery, 1970

A Soldier's Letters Reveal War's Human Tragedy

Six faded and tattered letters in the Town of Whitby Archives, written by Cullen Perry (1893-1918), grandson of Whitby's founder Peter Perry, offer a poignant insight into life during the First World War. Cullen Perry had one of the longest records of service among Whitby's men who served in the war, and eventually, like so many, paid the supreme sacrifice.

He enlisted in the Queen's Own Rifles of Canada on Aug. 12, 1914, about the time of his 21st birthday. The war had begun only eight days previously. Cullen was the son of John Ham Perry (1827-1896) from his second marriage, at the age of 61. He started a career in banking at Cobourg in 1910. At the outbreak of war he was working at the Toronto branch of the Sterling Bank.

Perry went to Europe with the First Canadian Contingent and saw plenty of action. He was slightly wounded at the Battle of St. Julien with a spent bullet, but took part in the battle until its close. In 1916 he was struck in the face with an explosive when in charge of a bombing party in No Man's Land. He was brought back to the British lines by a Sergeant who crawled out under heavy fire to save him after the German flares died down. He returned home for a month in July 1916, but went back to the battlefields of Europe

and was wounded at the Battle of Vimy Ridge on April 9, 1917.

After his recovery from that wound, Perry decided to join the Royal Flying Corps, a much more dangerous profession, for the

Cullen Perry

life expectancy of a pilot on the Western front was six days. His training took him to Alexandria, Egypt where the letters begin.

The first letter, dated Aug. 22, 1917, at Reading, England, states: *"My Dear Mother: I was so glad to get your lovely birthday letter and the socks, handkerchiefs and cigarettes. I*

am especially glad of the socks. I came up here from Dover, Sunday. Am on a course. This is where John (his older brother) *was a few weeks ago on his pioneer course, but my course is for the Flying Corps, and I will be at it for several months. I won't be going to France again till next year and I am very glad. We have very long hours here, first parade from six to seven in the morning, then nine to 12 and two to five, so you see there isn't much time when there is a lot of study to do at night. I had a letter today from the friends I stayed with at Anglesey this summer. They just got a telegram from the War Office saying one of their sons who is a Doctor in France has been gassed. It's a terrible thing, you know, mother, and affects the heart, lungs and throat."*

In his next letter, dated Oct. 23, 1917, from *"France, near Italy"*, Perry describes his train trip on the way to Egypt.

"I do hope, Mother Dear, you're not worrying about me, as I am really quite as safe as you are at home," he said.

From Egypt, he wrote on Nov. 6, 1917: *"I wrote last just before sailing from Italy. We arrived at Alexandria two days ago and had a very pleasant trip across. No submarines, thank goodness. I expect the same crowd of boys are around Whitby, with no thoughts of joining the Army. They will be no use as soldiers, even if conscription does pass."*

Describing the thrill of flying, Perry wrote

on Nov. 18, 1917: *"It's lovely in the early morning flying over the Mediterranean before the sun comes up and the sun rise is really beautiful when you're 4,000 feet up."*

A week later, he commented that he had received no mail and wondered *"perhaps the submarines got the first lot from England."* Once he received news from home, he told his mother on Dec. 2, 1917: *"I feel so sorry for the parents of the dear boys who have been killed, and please mother, tell them so for me. I'd write Mr. Rice but you didn't mention which of the boys it is, and young Long, really, I don't know how to spell his name. It's one of those extraordinary names like Mine-Lollie, or something like that."* The men he was referring to were Arleigh Rice and Laurier Long.

In his letter, Perry went on to mention how the men back home *"must be a bit nervous about conscription"* and told his mother he had several good job offers for after the war.

"My old friend Miller who came out here with me two years ago is finished as far as the army is concerned. He was shot in the lung, you know, and has had five or six operations."

In the last letter, dated Dec. 18, 1917, Cullen Perry commented on the death of more of his friends.

"I saw in the London papers that Bob Dow has been killed. Am writing Gladys Greenwood today. She must feel it very much, as I am sure she liked Bob better than anybody."*

Bob Dow (1883-1917) was a son of John Ball Dow, a noted Whitby lawyer. Gladys Greenwood (1886-1966), a sister of Whitby's most famous son, Hamar Greenwood, moved to England and married the Hon. Simon Rodney.

"I haven't seen a speck of news, Mother, since last writing," Perry continued. *"I haven't done a thing since, except read, sleep and eat. I expect it's awfully cold at home now, and Saturday is probably the big Xmas fair. It seems years and years since I was home for Xmas fair and it probably is a good many, for before the war we only got home Xmas eve."*

His last comments are on the Halifax explosion of Dec. 6, 1917 when a munitions ship was struck by another ship in the harbour. The explosion destroyed much of the city.

"What a terrible disaster at Halifax. The suspense of the soldiers in France from their waiting for news of their relatives must be awful."

On Feb. 3, 1918, Cullen Perry's luck ran out. After being wounded three times in France and flying so many times in England and Egypt, he was killed in a plane crash at Alexandria. It is believed that he fainted while flying and lost control of his plane. He was pulled from the wreckage alive, but died in hospital four hours later from a fractured skull. He was buried in the Chatley Cemetery in Alexandria and a picture of his grave was sent to his mother. A friend in the Royal Flying Corps said of Cullen Perry: *"Everywhere he was loved and admired. His Commanding Officer told me he was utterly fearless and one of the best fellows ever at Aboukir."*

Mrs. Perry received a note of condolence from King George V and Queen Mary, but nothing could replace her youngest son. His older brother John. H. Perry (1892-1976) survived the war, and served in England in the Second World War.

On Jan. 11, 1920, a brass tablet was unveiled in All Saints' Anglican Church in memory of Cullen Perry, as his brothers, John and Peter looked on. Still visible on west wall of the church, it reads: *"In loving memory of Cullen Hay Perry, Royal Fusiliers and Royal Flying Corps, died February 1918, aged 24 years, Alexandria, Egypt."*

John Ham Perry was manager of the Dominion Bank in Whitby from 1926 until the Second World War broke out in 1939, when he again enlisted. After the war he returned to Canada and was appointed to the Head office of the bank in Toronto. He moved to Toronto, ending more than 110 years of residence by the Perry family in Whitby.

Wounded Soldiers Made Their Home At Whitby During The First World War

During the terrible years of the First World War, Whitby played a prominent part in the rehabilitation of wounded soldiers. From February 1917 to October 1919, as many as 1,500 soldiers, fresh from the battlefields of Europe, were housed at the Ontario Hospital, later the Whitby Psychiatric Hospital. When the war broke out in August 1914, construction was well under way on what was to be one of the most modern hospitals for the mentally ill in North America. Most of the buildings of the hospital at Whitby were completed by the summer of 1916, and some patients were moved in from Orillia and Toronto. With the casualties of the war mounting alarmingly, the Federal Government was in desperate need of facilities for rehabilitation of those who had survived, but were injured in body and mind. Since the Whitby Hospital was new and largely unoccupied, it was the ideal place for a Military Convalescent Hospital, managed by the Solders' Aid Commission.

In February 1917, the psychiatric patients were moved to Orillia and replaced by 500 wounded soldiers. On Feb. 15, 50 soldiers from the Spadina and College Street Convalescent Hospitals in Toronto were taken in a special rail car to Whitby. Eight cottages, which could hold 60 men each, were prepared for the first of the soldiers to

Soldiers at a garden party at the home of George W. Dryden, 400 St. John Street West, July 28, 1917.

arrive. Twenty-two *"stretcher cases"* arrived from Montreal in March, along with 70 amputees. Many of the soldiers at the hospital had lost arms or legs in battle. Programs in vocational training were provided, including a carpenters' shop and motor

mechanics' shop.

Some of the first official visitors to the hospital at Whitby were John B. Laidlaw (1866-1953), vice-chairman of the Soldiers' Aid Commission and W. W. Nichol, vocational officer for Ontario. Laidlaw kept a

Physical training at the Military Convalescent Hospital, 1917.

the downtown and the hospital, if they wanted business trade from the soldiers who were able to leave the hospital on day passes. Otherwise, the soldiers would go to Oshawa by train to shop. Various attempts were made to provide transportation into the town for the soldiers. One soldier-patient set up his own jitney service, charging 25 cents for a one-way trip in a Model T Ford. Joseph Heard (1860-1941) provided a taxi service and motor bus for the soldiers.

As many as 250 passengers a day would ride the train from Toronto to visit the patients in the Whitby hospital. To make their journey easier, a railway siding was constructed from the Whitby Junction station at the foot of Byron Street, to the hospital grounds. This station, which stood near the east end of the present GO-Transit platform, was moved to the corner of Henry and Victoria Streets in 1970 and converted into an art gallery. The private railway which served the hospital was a makeshift operation reminiscent of the *"Toonerville Trolley"*. The locomotive was an old shunting engine and the passenger car was a converted Toronto street car. The street car was brought to Whitby on the Canadian Pacific Railway, put on skids, and towed by horses, over the snow to the hospital.

One of the integral parts of the hospital

summer home in Whitby, called *"The Grange"*, at the corner of Mary and Pine Streets. This and many other Whitby homes were opened to the soldier-patients for garden parties during the war.

Among the vocational opportunities at the hospital in addition to carpentry and motor mechanics, were shorthand, typing, bookkeeping, and academic courses designed to enable the soldiers to return to civilian life with a trade or skill which would lead to employment.

The presence of 1,500 soldiers in Whitby when the hospital reached its capacity, had several important effects on the Town of Whitby. Transportation was one of the most significant factors. The citizens of Whitby were advised to set up a bus system between

was the amusement hall, built specially for the soldiers. In May 1917, work commenced on the construction of the *"rec hall"* which could seat 1,200 people. It provided a stage for live and motion picture shows upstairs, while downstairs there were a canteen and bowling alley. These facilities were used by the patients at the Whitby Psychiatric Hospital until the new Whitby Mental Health Centre opened in September 1996. On Aug. 31, 1917, Canada's Governor-General, the Duke of Devonshire, paid a visit to the hospital and officially opened the recreation hall. It was the first of two visits he made to the hospital.

The soldier-patients published their own newspaper, *"The Soft Diet"*, a mixture of news, jokes and comments on life at the hospital. Unfortunately, not one of these papers is known to have survived to this day.

A number of soldiers and nurses were specially trained to give massage treatments to the amputees. Young women students from Toronto also volunteered to do this important work, which was photographed by the Toronto Star Weekly.

In February, 1918, a year after the soldiers moved into the hospital, it was announced that room would be made available for as many as 2,500 soldiers, through the addition of tents during the summer months.

Construction of the Recreation Hall, 1917.

Two months later, the Whitby Hospital was the first to provide garden plots for its patients. Plans for allotments were drawn by the drafting class at the hospital, and the farm tractor class did the cultivating. W. W. Nichol of the Soldier's Aid Commission reported:

"We are adding to the value and scope of the school by the addition of a one-acre school garden, divided into small individual plots. The ground has been prepared and arrangements made and the Department of Agriculture has provided us with a number of expert speakers, the first of whom speaks in the hospital on April 8th. Every department of the school will help in making this new department a success.

In connection with our manual training shop we intend to have a small plot on which will be erected models of buildings, such as tool sheds, chicken coops and other small buildings used in connection with truck gardening. The commercial class will teach the men elementary bookkeeping necessary in successful marketing of produce and some of the general periods of the general information class will be given over to lectures having a special bearing on agricultural work."

The soldiers at the Military Convalescent Hospital received many gifts from the citizens of Whitby and the surrounding area. The ladies of the Soldiers' Comforts Club provided benches for the patients in downtown Whitby, and the citizens of Port Perry furnished a room in one of the cottages. J. W. Alexander of Bowmanville provided an organ for the recreation hall as a Christmas present in 1918. A number of Toronto theatrical troupes presented entertainments in the hall. The Garrick Club of Toronto presented a play called *"The Passport"*, before a mixed crowd of soldier-patients and residents of the Town of Whitby. Weekly dances were also held in the *"rec hall"*. The soldiers even had their own hockey team, coached by a blind patient, Sergeant Graham.

In March 1919, a massive barn was begun at the north end of the hospital property, at

The train to the Military Convalescent Hospital, 1918.

the corner of the Farm Road and Victoria Street. It served the Ontario Hospital farm for 50 years until the farm was closed in 1969. The great barn burned down on Nov. 4, 1976, the loss including all the wooden forms that were made to shape the concrete walls of the Whitby General Hospital in 1968. These forms which were saved for the time when an addition could be made to the hospital, were stored in the barn, along with a large quantity of surplus outdated furniture from the Psychiatric Hospital.

While Whitby provided much assistance to the hospital during its three years of operation, staff of the hospital gave something back to the town as well. Bennett McGowan, the chief accountant, was responsible for founding the Vimy Ridge Loyal Orange Lodge in Whitby, in 1917. This lodge operated for about 50 years, with many local citizens being members. Vimy Ridge Lodge hosted one of the last big Orangeman's Day parades at Whitby on July 12, 1937, which was attended by numerous lodges in the district. McGowan returned home in Ireland in January 1919, to get married.

A few of the soldiers who lived at the hospital decided to stay in Whitby after the military authorities turned it back to the Ontario Government. One of these soldiers was Harold W. Boys (1897-1993) who opened a garage on Dundas Street, west of the Four Corners. From 1931 to 1965 he was the engineer for the Whitby Volunteer Fire Department, responsible for maintaining and servicing all the town's fire trucks.

During the summer of 1919, many of the soldiers at Whitby were transferred to other hospitals, such as St. Andrew's at Rosedale Heights in Toronto. When they were told in the early spring that they would be leaving, many of the soldiers did not want to go, because they enjoyed fishing, bathing and boating in Lake Ontario at Whitby. They had endured a long cold winter, and now they were forced to move just as the good summer weather was coming, they said. However, the Ontario Government had asked for the return of the hospital buildings after the close of the war, and this was carried out on Oct. 23, 1919 when the first psychiatric patients were moved back to the Whitby Hospital.

Life at the Military Convalescent Hospital was very well documented by photographs, for there were no restrictions on the use of cameras as there are in a psychiatric hospital. No one is allowed to photograph mental patients. A set of at least 26 photo post cards of activities at the military hospital in 1917 and 1918 is in the Town of Whitby Archives, as well as numerous snapshots taken by Whitby citizens. One photo of a group of soldiers has the face of one of the soldiers scratched out with a pen. It was learned from another undamaged copy of the same photo that this particular soldier was thumbing his nose at the camera.

Soldiers and a nurse on the front steps of one of the cottages at the Military Hospital, 1917. As many as 1,500 wounded soldiers lived at the hospital, which was taken over from the Ontario Government by the Federal Soldiers' Aid Commission from 1917 to 1919.

The House That Wasyl Hunka Built

Of the thousands of wounded soldiers who were treated at Whitby's Military Convalescent Hospital during the First World War, one man became something of a celebrity. An account of his achievements at the hospital was printed in the Toronto Star Weekly, his picture appeared on post cards issued by the hospital, and even the Governor-General of Canada took an interest in what he was doing.

From February 1917 to October 1919, the buildings at the Ontario Hospital (later Whitby Psychiatric Hospital) were used by the Federal Government as a rehabilitation hospital for wounded soldiers. As many as 2,000 men at one time were treated in this facility. Free education was offered to any men who wished it. A vocational school was established to teach carpentry and other skills, so the men could find a trade when they were released from the hospital.

In May 1918, there arrived a man named Wasyl Hunka (1888-1961), a Russian who had served with the Canadian Expeditionary Force. When he came to Whitby, Hunka could not speak a word of English. In his far-off home in Wolenski Huberne, education was a privilege offered only to the barons' and the lords' sons. The peasants laboured all day in the fields and had no opportunity to improve themselves.

Hunka was a determined man with plenty

Wasyl Hunka posed proudly with his model house in this post card view taken in 1918.

of initiative, who eagerly accepted the hospital's offer to take courses in English. Within five months, he was able to read and write English easily and enjoyed reading *"Robinson Crusoe."* Not satisfied with stopping there, Hunka enrolled in the hospital's manual

training and building construction classes, where he was first taught how to build the framework of a house wall. He went on to learn how to construct corners, joists, window frames and door frames.

Once he had learned the basics of building construction, Hunka decided to build a model house, using the skills he had learned at the hospital. The result was a perfectly executed wooden model, six feet high, three feet wide and five feet long, weighing more than 400 pounds. The Star Weekly, in a feature article in August 1918, commented that the house was *"not a mere shell, but a perfect piece of construction, following in every detail the actual construction of a first-class frame dwelling. The mixed architecture is intentional, designed with the idea of giving the builder a knowledge of the various forms which might be used."*

The interior of Hunka's house was just as carefully constructed as the exterior. Stairs, accurately modelled, connected the upper and lower floors, every room was completely furnished, and the house was lit by electricity. When he started building the model, Hunka knew nothing of house construction, but, by following drawings on paper which were provided for him, he was able to make all the delicate parts required and place them together, including all the miniature furnishings.

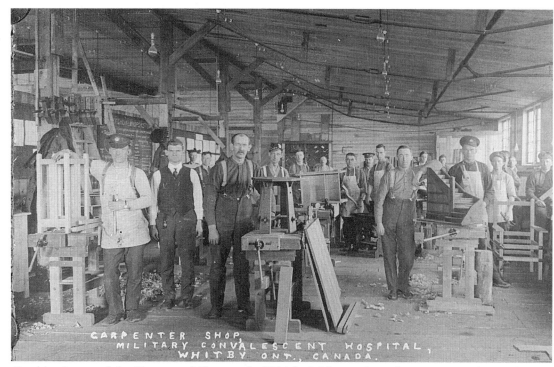

In this picture of the Carpenters' Shop at the Whitby Military Convalescent Hospital, Wasyl Hunka (wearing a military cap) is standing at right with the staircase for his model home.

a picture of the interior of the carpenters' shop. The hospital made 26 photo-post cards for use by the soldiers in 1918. Today, they are among the best records we have of life at a military hospital in the First World War.

After he was discharged from the Military Convalescent Hospital in 1918, Hunka settled in Oshawa, where he remained the rest of his life, living in a house at 420 Dunkirk Street. The story of Wasyl Hunka, who changed his name to William after he left the hospital, came to a tragic end on September 15, 1961. At the age of 73, and nearly blind, he was struck by a car and killed, when he tried to cross Highway 401 on foot between Ritson Road and Bloor Street. He is buried in the Soldiers' Plot at Oshawa Union Cemetery.

Wasyl Hunka was one of several thousand soldiers who passed through the Whitby Military Hospital from 1917 to 1919, but was one of very few who received national publicity. Most of the soldiers either recovered at the hospital or were shipped to other military hospitals. A few stayed in the Whitby area and went into business here, but most eventually went back home.

The buildings where Wasyl Hunka lived and worked are soon to be demolished, although a few are likely to be saved. Among those which may be spared from demolition is the recreation hall, built in 1917.

When Canada's Governor-General, the Duke of Devonshire, visited the hospital in 1918, he was introduced to Hunka, and expressed an interest in purchasing the house when it was completed. Unfortunately, the Governor-General did not purchase the house. It stood on the porch of one of the cottages at the hospital until the soldiers left, and for many years remained at Hunka's new home in Oshawa. Its ultimate fate is unknown.

A photograph of Hunka standing beside his model house was printed on a post card issued by the hospital, and he also appears in

CARPENTER SHOP,
MILITARY CONVALESCENT HOSPITAL,
WHITBY ONT., CANADA.

In 1918 They Cut Down The Shade Trees For Fuel

Whitby citizens faced one of the town's worst crises in the early months of 1918, as a result of the First World War. A severe coal shortage coupled with one of the coldest winters on record disrupted daily life and added to the miseries brought on by the war. For days and sometimes weeks, there was no coal to heat the homes of Whitby, when the temperature dropped to a record 30 degrees below zero, Fahrenheit. For the first time in its history the Whitby Public Library had to close its doors because there was no coal to heat the building. Those who had coal were required to share it with their neighbours who had none.

The Town Council, early in 1918, established a fuel committee to oversee the distribution of coal when it did arrive by boat at the harbour, for there was not enough to satisfy everyone's needs. In early February, with no coal having come into town for several days, the Town Council had to make a desperate decision. The Council asked the streets committee to work out a plan for cutting down some of the shade trees on the streets for fuel. Maple trees that had stood for more than 60 years had to be sacrificed, because the streets committee believed that if enough were cut down, there would be a supply of good firewood which would last until the next coal shipment arrived.

On Feb. 12, after three days without any

Ice at Whitby Harbour in the Winter of 1918.

fuel, the town's factories, the King Brothers' Tannery, Samuel Trees' blanket factory, and Fred Hatch's buckle factory were closed, so their employees could cut down trees select-ed by the streets committee. On March 1, the town's schools, which had been closed for two weeks, because of the lack of coal were reopened. The crisis eased for a while,

Another view, of the pump house and Heydenshore Park, in the winter of 1918. It is not recorded if the coal supply for the water pumping station ran out.

coal. A carload of 30 tons had arrived, but the fuel committee still had to limit two tons to each customer. Customers had to pay $10.50 in advance for the coal and wait for it to arrive. There was no guarantee when the next load would arrive. Mayor Ernest Harper (1867-1944) and the council's fuel clerk, Edith Connor (?-1946) were in charge of distributing the coal.

At Whitby Harbour an ice cutting machine was at work, carving 4,000 blocks of ice out of the bay for storage at the Military Convalescent Hospital (now Whitby Mental Health Centre). The blocks were one foot wide and two feet thick. Even the oldest inhabitants could not remember ice that thick in Whitby Harbour. The ice harvest was carried out at the end of the west pier leading from the hospital grounds. The blocks were transported to a large ice house beside the hospital's power station which was demolished about 20 years ago. In the summer the ice was used in ice boxes, the forerunner of the modern refrigerator. Thus, the bitter winter of 1918 had produced one lasting benefit. It is not recorded, however, how many trees were cut down and if they were replaced.

Whitby has not suffered a fuel crisis since that bitter winter of 1918. With today's nuclear plants and natural gas, it is not likely to happen again.

as the citizens were able to receive lots of one ton of coal each, under the supervision of the fuel committee. It was not long, however, before the crisis intensified.

With another shortage to endure, between 40 and 50 citizens lined up in front of the town hall at Brock and Colborne Streets and *"fairly fought"* for a chance to get some

Whitby Fared Better Than Most Communities In The 1918 'flu Epidemic

Just as the First World War was coming to an end, the world was ravaged by the great Spanish Influenza epidemic of 1918. Although it is not realized by many today, there were more deaths in the three-month 'flu epidemic than the entire war. The combined disasters killed more than 12 million people. In Toronto, more than 900 lives were lost from the 'flu from October to December 1918. It was not the 'flu that usually killed its victims, but the pneumonia which resulted from it. Young and old were killed off, often in a matter of hours.

Whitby suffered only 11 deaths, with a population of about 3,000 and an additional 1,000 patients at the military hospital, had only three doctors, one of whom developed a case of the 'flu himself but would not admit it. These over-worked physicians spent days without sleep attempting to treat those who were ill.

Most of the victims of the Spanish Influenza were young men in their 20s and 30s, married with families. On Oct. 11, 1918, the first cases of influenza were reported at the home of Joseph Giroux, a railway contractor who owned the first farm on Dundas Street east of the town limits at Anderson Street. The first victim to die of the epidemic was Arthur Wilkinson, a young married man who died on Oct. 15, leaving a wife and a little girl.

By this time, some of the stores in town had to close because all their staff were ill. On Oct. 12, the Board of Health closed the town's schools, churches and public library and suspended all public meetings in an attempt to stop the spread of disease. Movie theatres were also closed, as they were said to be the worst disseminators of the 'flu.

Whitby's second influenza victim was William Anderson, a 20-year-old shop clerk who died on Oct. 19. The sick list was growing larger every day, with two ministers from local churches and a number of teachers suffering from the 'flu. The third victim was James Forbes Fegan, a 56-year-old employee of the buckle factory, who died on Oct. 22. The next day, the first soldier's death at the military hospital was recorded. Harold G. Bates, 21, a resident of Toronto, died, followed on Oct. 29 by Private Robert Stuart. Bates was buried in Toronto, while Stuart's last resting place is Groveside Cemetery south of Brooklin.

The deaths were occurring more frequently now. William Westlake, a store clerk, died on Oct. 27 and the next day Leslie Moore, a livery stable operator died, leaving a wife and two children who were also ill with the 'flu. On Nov. 4, the Board of Health reopened the public library but the schools and churches remained closed.

These Red Cross nurses were on the streets of Whitby, raising funds to assist the victims of the Spanish Influenza epidemic of 1918, as well as families of soldiers serving overseas in the First World War. From left to right are: Kate Lavery, Wilma Johnson and Temple Proctor.

No public meetings were allowed. By Nov. 8, with no new cases reported, the schools, churches and movie theatres reopened, but the Board of Health had proved too hasty in its decision.

By Nov. 13, three teachers at the Collegiate Institute were ill and many children were coming down with the 'flu. Realizing the danger was not over, the Board of Health closed the schools again. They would not reopen until after the Christmas holidays.

The town's sixth victim was James Noble, a 20-year-old married man. Will Maynard of Brooklin died Dec. 6, and George Percy Head, 33, a resident of Port Whitby and a hospital attendant, died early in December.

The Ontario Ladies' College (now Trafalgar Castle School), with an enrolment of more than 100 students, imposed a strict quarantine, with no students allowed to leave the building and no visitor allowed to enter. These precautions saved the college from having any cases of the 'flu. One of the young students quarantined at the Ontario Ladies' College was Catherine Burwash (1902-1984) who for more than 30 years was a much loved teacher at Whitby's high school. She retired in 1964 at Henry Street High School.

By mid-December, 1918, the crisis had passed. No new cases of the 'flu were reported, and by January, it was back to normal for the Town of Whitby. Health officials stated the town was lucky in having escaped the worst of the epidemic.

Former Whitby residents succumbed to the 'flu in other parts of Canada. In Regina, Saskatchewan, T. Aird Murray, the engineer who designed Whitby's first sewer system four years previously, died on Nov. 5 at the age of 52. In Toronto, where it was estimated there were more than 900 deaths in three months, some victims did not even get a death notice in the newspapers. One was Barnabas Gibson (1830-1918), Whitby's pioneer railway builder who constructed the Whitby, Port Perry and Lindsay Railway in the 1870s. He died in Toronto on Oct. 31. The only record of his death is his tomb stone in Mount Pleasant Cemetery. Gibson's palatial mansion, *"Ringwood,"* located at Victoria and Hopkins Street, was built in 1876 and designated an historic building in the 1980s. Owned by Lake Ontario Steel since 1963, it was converted into a job training centre by Durham College in 1998.

A number of widows of the men who were killed by the 'flu, remarried. One was Mrs. Arthur Wilkinson, who married Leo Smith after her husband died, and lived until 1982 when she died at the age of 88.

The Ontario Ladies' College (now Trafalgar Castle) was spared the ravages of the 'flu because the building was strictly quarantined in the fall of 1918. One of the quarantined students was Miss Catherine Burwash, later a Whitby High School teacher.

Street Names Honour War Dead

On Oct. 24, 1988, the Whitby Town Council unanimously adopted a recommendation from Councillor Tom Edwards (Mayor of Whitby from 1991 to 1997) that some of the town's new streets be named after the young men of Whitby who were killed in the First and Second World Wars. Edwards was a war veteran himself, having served in Africa and Europe during the Second World War.

The names of those killed, 40 in the First World War and 31 in the Second World War, are inscribed on the Whitby Cenotaph at Dundas and Green Streets. Many citizens of this town have not likely stopped to read the names or know any of the details about these young men who made the supreme sacrifice so that we may live in freedom. The Cenotaph does not tell us very much. There are the names and the regiments to which they belonged, but there are other things the sharp eye will pick up. One will notice on looking carefully, that three boys by the name of Brownwell, three named Fulton and two named Vanstone were killed in the First World War. The names Fallon and Wigston appear in the casualty lists of both wars.

It is a common misconception that most, if not all, war casualties occurred in battle. This is not the case. Many young soldiers died of disease or accidents before ever reaching the front line. Fred Elvidge was a victim of the great Spanish Influenza epidemic of October 1918. He died of pneumonia after contracting influenza while travelling by ship to France. The only son of the principal of one of Whitby's schools, he was buried at sea. Flying accidents claimed the lives of a number of Whitby men during both wars. Cullen Perry (whose story is told in another Chronicle in this book) was killed in a training flight on Feb. 3, 1918 at Alexandria, Egypt. It was suspected that he fainted while in the air and crashed as a result. Eleven days after Perry's accident, Allister McGillivray, the 19-year-old son of Judge Theodore

Robert Jackson Correll (1891-1916)

Charles Henry Wigston (1897-1918)

McGillivray (1862-1925) was killed in a training flight at Salisbury Plain in England. On Oct. 18, 1939, little more than a month after the beginning of the Second World War, John Ross Anderson, son of Ontario County's Deputy Sheriff John A. Anderson (1880-1974) was killed in a training flight in England.

Perhaps the most tragic accident was the death of Yestyn L. Thomas, a flying instructor at Ste. Therese de Blainville, Quebec, in 1943. He was teaching a new pilot how to fly, with the novice at the controls, when the plane crashed. Thomas was killed but the trainee survived with only a broken leg. Thomas's mother Mildred (1894-1989) was Whitby's last surviving Silver Cross Mother. The Silver Cross Mothers were the mothers of men killed in war.

Other freak accidents claimed the lives of Whitby residents before they even left Canada. Edgar Murray Eldridge was killed in a motor accident at Debert, Nova Scotia in 1941 and George Frederick Carter of the Royal Canadian Navy was killed at Halifax when a sentry's rifle accidentally discharged.

One of the first battle casualties from Whitby in the First World War was 25-year-old Robert Jackson Correll who was wounded in the battle of the Somme and died at the First Southern General Hospital at Birmingham, England, on Sept. 23, 1916. The writer of this book has a post card sent by Correll to his mother after being admitted to hospital. In very shaky handwriting he indicates that he is wounded but doing well, by crossing out lines on the printed card. The card was dated six days before he died. The news of Private Correll's death was received with great shock by the people of Whitby. The flags at the town hall and the post office were flown at half-mast as a tribute to him. Bob Correll, as he was popularly known, was a member of one of the oldest established families of Port Whitby. A son of Mr. and Mrs. Robert Correll, he was born at Whitby in 1891 and attended

William Charles Wigston (1921-1942)

school here. After finishing school he started working at the Martin Manufacturing Company (the buckle factory), which was one of Whitby's three large industries. He enlisted in the fall of 1915 with the 59th Battalion and attained the rank of Corporal. Anxious to take part in the actual fighting instead of being stationed in England, he gave up his stripes and joined the 5th Canadian Mounted Rifles which were sent to France to take part in the Battle of the Somme, one of the most costly engagements of the war. There were more than a million casualties in that battle, one of whom was Private Robert Correll of Whitby.

Another Whitby First World War casualty was Robert John Gunn Dow, well over six feet tall and a member of another pioneer family. He was killed at the Battle of Passchendale in Belgium on Oct. 30, 1917 at the age of 34. Michael Fallon was killed in action in August 1918. It is recorded that only a few days after he left Canada for France, his wife suddenly took ill and died in a hospital at Barrie, Ont. It is not recorded whether he learned of her death before he was killed. Corporal Gordon Vanstone died of wounds in August 1917. The first member of All Saints' Anglican Church to be killed in action, he was given a memorial service at the church, attended by many residents of Whitby. Fenton E. Brownwell and Charles H. Brownwell, sons of Jacob Brownwell (1855-1947) were both killed at Vimy Ridge on April 9, 1917. A third son, Berton P. Brownwell, was killed in action on June 20 of the same year.

When another generation went to war from 1939 to 1945, again a member of one of Port Whitby's oldest families was a casualty. He was John A. Watson, son of Harry E. Watson (1885-1968), who lived on Brock Street South. Jack Watson, as he was popularly known, was born at Port Whitby on April 25, 1919. He attended the old Brock Street School and was an outstanding athlete and swimmer. One of the first Whitby men to enlist when

John Allingham Watson (1919-1944)

the war broke out, Private Jack Watson was with the Stormont, Dundas and Glengarry Highlanders, one of the first Canadian units to enter the battered city of Caen after the invasion of Normandy in June 1944. On July 25, 1944, while he was pro-ceeding through France with his unit, a German shell burst near Private Watson. The concussion killed him instantly. He was given a funeral will full military hon-ours and buried beside another soldier, a good friend of his, who was killed the same day. John A. Watson rests today in the Canadian Military Cemetery at Bretteville sur Laize, in France.

Privates Correll and Watson had more in common than their deaths in war. They were both members of St. John's Anglican Church, where their families erected memorials to their memory. To the right of the main entrance of St. John's Church is a beautiful stained glass window dedicated to the memory of Private Correll. The win-dow depicts Jesus standing with arms out-stretched to receive a soldier in Crusader's armour of the Middle Ages. At the base of the window is the inscription: *"Greater love hath no man than this, that a man lay down his life for his friends."* The window was dedicated in 1927.

The lamp for the pulpit in this same church is dedicated in memory of Private Watson. The organ was also dedicated to the men of the church who were killed in both world wars: Privates Correll and Watson, Private Leslie Perry and Flight Lieutenant Robert W. Rea.

It was reported in the Toronto Globe and Mail on Feb. 23, 1944 that Jack Coleman, son of Ontario County Judge Dilly Benjamin Coleman (1890-1950) was reported missing and officially presumed dead. He had set out in a flying boat on anti-submarine patrol eight months earlier and did not return. His body was never found.

The Wigston family was one that suf-fered losses in both wars. Charles Henry Wigston, who became ill on the way to France, died in March, 1918. At the time of his death no particulars were available on the cause or where he died. In August, 1942, his nephew, William Charles Wigston, a pilot officer, was reported miss-ing and believed killed in the Middle East. His body was eventually recovered and buried in the war cemetery at El Alamein. The sixth Whitby soldier to die in the Second World War, he was honoured with a memorial service in the Baptist Church, attended by the Mayor Fred Rowe (1873-1959) and the Town Council.

The streets bearing the names of Whitby's war dead in the new subdivisions of the town are marked with signs bearing their surnames and a poppy, the symbol of remembrance. Portraits of these young men are located in the Town of Whitby Archives.

Hamar Greenwood – Whitby's Most Famous Son

If you ask any Whitby resident today if he or she knows anything about Hamar Greenwood, the response would be: *"Who was he?"* But for the first 50 years of this century, he was the talk of the town. A legendary character in his own right, he was clearly recognized as Whitby's most famous son. Many tales were told of his exploits and he was treated like royalty whenever he made a return visit to his home town.

Hamar Greenwood was born on Feb. 7, 1870 in a frame house which still stands at 208-210 Henry Street. His father was John Hamer Greenwood, a prominent lawyer and politician in Whitby. John Hamer Greenwood was born at Llanbister, Radnorshire, Wales, on Jan. 20, 1829 and came to Whitby in 1850 at the age of 21 to join his uncle John Hamer (1787-1872) for whom Hamer's Corners (Dundas and Anderson Streets) was named. Greenwood took any job he could find, which included mixing mortar and carrying bricks during the construction of the Ontario County Court House (now the Whitby Centennial Building) in 1853. He taught school while studying law and set up a practice in Whitby. In politics, he was Mayor of Whitby from 1872 to 1875 and again in 1883. He was described in his obituary as *"a fine public speaker and could hold the attention of an audience about as well as any*

The birthplace of Hamar Greenwood, 208-210 Henry Street, in 1975.

man in these parts." He was also described as a speculator who had interests in a clock factory and sewing machine works, and spent his money freely.

"Like many another he was several times crushed beneath the wheel of fortune but always managed to come out again in a short time," said his obituary. *"He was noted as a financier who could always wiggle out of a hole, but his enterprising and speculative nature pulled him back into the hole as fast as he could struggle his way out."*

John Hamer Greenwood died on July 15, 1902 at the age of 73, leaving a family of seven surviving children, all of whom grew up to be very successful in life.

The most remarkable of these was the oldest son, Hamar Greenwood. Among the legends that have grown up around him is the story that when he was born, his father was in such poor financial straits that he could not pay the midwife. It is also said that young Greenwood *"stole"* his brother's name. He was christened *"Thomas Hubbard Greenwood"* in All Saints' Anglican Church, but as a young man, he took the name *"Thomas Hamar Greenwood"* from his younger brother, William Hamer (1872-1923). Tom adopted the name *"Hamer,"* changing the *"er"* at the end to *"ar"* because he liked it. In his school days he was known as *"Tom,"* but as an adult he was *"Hamar."*

Hamar Greenwood was a rising star at the Whitby Collegiate Institute in the 1880s. He was president of the Debating Society, in which he took an active part. He led his team to victory in a debate on the resolution that *"The pen is mightier than the sword,"* but lost the resolution that *"Intemperance, as regards the use of liquor, opium and tobacco, has caused more misery than war."*

On May 6, 1887, Greenwood was elected the *"Dux"* (leader) of the boys at the Collegiate Institute. As the Dux he was required to present awards to the students who deserved them and to plant a tree in the school yard. Being elected as Dux by the

Hamar Greenwood in 1913.

student body was the highest honour at the Collegiate Institute.

At the time of his graduation in 1887, Greenwood wanted to be a teacher, so he enrolled in courses at the Model School (now Florence M. Heard School) where

teachers were trained. It was not long before he learned that a vacancy was open for a teacher at the school at Manchester, north of Whitby. He had just begun his training as a teacher and had not received his certificate, but he was determined to get that position. Never shy about expressing his will, he went to his favourite teacher at the Collegiate Institute, Anson G. Henderson (1852-1928) and said: *"There is a vacancy for a teacher at the Manchester School and you are going to get it for me."* Henderson, although surprised by his young student's affrontery, got him the job.

Henderson also played a significant role in Greenwood's military career. While still in High School, Greenwood joined the 34th Battalion on Militia (now the Ontario Regiment), of which Henderson was one of the officers. He went off to a military training camp at Niagara-on-the-Lake during the summer without telling his father. When his father found out where he was, he rushed off to Niagara to bring young Tom back. Greenwood, however, had other ideas. He was on sentry duty the night his father arrived to take him home. When his father tried to remove him from the camp, Greenwood arrested him for trespassing and threw him in the brig. He let him go, only when the father promised to return home alone.

On another occasion, Henderson told Greenwood that his unit of militia was short about 20 men for an upcoming inspection. Greenwood promptly went to Toronto, hired a hall, signed up the 20 needed recruits and marched them down Yonge Street. On inspection day, Greenwood's company was the only one on parade with a full complement of men.

Young Greenwood was also involved in an amateur theatre company which toured Ontario, putting on shows at small towns. On one occasion, when he found himself out of money, Greenwood sent a telegram to his father asking for some cash to get home. His father sent back a wire stating: *"The weather is fine and the walking is good."* Perhaps he was getting back for being arrested by his son at the Niagara Camp.

Greenwood owned a top hat and a long Prince Albert coat which he often put to good use. While he was teaching school, he saw a funeral proceeding to a nearby cemetery. He could hear the mourners expressing concern that the clergyman had failed to show up to conduct the burial service, so he grabbed his top hat, Prince Albert Coat and a prayer book and conducted the service himself.

Greenwood continued his education at the University of Toronto where he studied political science, but soon got involved in other kinds of politics. In 1895 a dispute arose when the University administration would not allow a certain article to be published in the school magazine *"The Varsity."* Demanding the right of free speech, the students went on strike. The leaders of the strike were Hamar Greenwood and William Lyon Mackenzie King, a future Prime Minister of Canada. The dispute was referred to a Royal Commission which recommended several reforms at the University. Greenwood made a name for himself as an accomplished public speaker, and despite his leadership of the strike, he was granted a Bachelor of Arts degree in political science in 1895. Forty-three years later, he was given an Honorary Doctor of Laws degree by the

Hamar Greenwood and R.S. McLaughlin at Parkwood, Sept. 4, 1938.

University of Toronto, when he made a return visit to the University in 1938.

After his university education, young Greenwood worked for a short time for the Department of Agriculture at Queen's Park in Toronto, but soon found that Canada was not big enough to hold his ambition. He decided to seek his fortune in England. In the summer of 1895, he worked his way over to the Old Country on a cattle boat, and landed with five dollars in his pocket.

Greenwood had a struggle getting started in England. He found that he was recognized as a good public speaker and began to travel the country making temperance speeches for a local agency. It is said that he was a strong temperance man, because his father had been a heavy drinker. He wanted to get enough money to go through law school in England and set up a practice, but the going was slow. All this changed one day when, while riding a London bus, he was involved in an accident. The bus turned over then threw him to the ground. He lay unconscious in a London hospital for eight days, and nearly died. When he recovered, Greenwood sued the bus company for damages, and with the money he received, he was able to set up his law practice at Gray's Inn, the leading law establishment in London.

Politics also attracted young Greenwood.

He attended Liberal meetings throughout the country, and in 1900, he was asked to run for election in Grimsby. He declined, however, feeling that he did not have enough experience yet. In 1903, Greenwood was called to the City of York to speak on behalf of a local knight who was standing for the York seat in the next election. Greenwood made such an impression with his speech that the Liberal organizers asked him to run for the seat instead of the local knight. When the election was held in January 1906, the Liberals won and Greenwood took his seat in Parliament for the City of York.

He held this seat from 1906 to 1910. During that period he was Parliamentary Private Secretary to Winston Churchill when Churchill was Under Secretary of State for the Colonies and President of the Board of Trade. When he visited Whitby in September, 1906 he brought with him a letter from Churchill which was published in the Whitby Keystone. This was probably the first Churchill letter ever to be published in a small-town Canadian newspaper.

When Greenwood made his first visit back to his home town in 1906, he was given a royal reception at the town hall, hosted by Mayor Arthur T. Lawler (1866-1928). The streets were decorated with flags and bunting and his friends in Whitby

cheered him as he rode in a carriage from the Whitby Junction Station (now the Whitby Arts Station Gallery) to the town hall at the present site of the fire hall at Brock and Colborne Streets. He was also the honoured guest at a garden party hosted by Mrs. E. Edmund Starr (1862-1932) at her home at Dundas and Palace Streets. Greenwood made another visit to Whitby in 1911 when he was the guest of Frank Burr Mosure (1862-1931) at his palatial mansion, Burr Lodge, on Centre Street South.

On May 23, 1911, Greenwood married Margery Spencer of Herefordshire, at St. Margaret's Church, Westminster, the church of the Members of Parliament. This was the same church where Winston Churchill was married in 1908. Among the guests at the wedding were Herbert Asquith, the British Prime Minister and future Prime Minister David Lloyd George; Canadian Prime Minister Sir Wilfrid Laurier and Lord Strathcona, the man who drove the last spike for the Canadian Pacific Railway. Frank Burr Mosure represented Greenwood's home town of Whitby.

When the First World War broke out in August 1914, Greenwood volunteered to organize a battalion of soldiers from Wales because his ancestors were from that part of Britain. On Jan. 1, 1915, Hamar

Greenwood was named a Baronet in the King's list of honours. Greenwood again showed his brashness when it came to this honour. Before going to the front with his Welsh battalion, he visited his friend Lloyd George, who praised him for his recruiting efforts and asked him if there was anything he wanted.

"Nothing for myself," Greenwood replied, *"but I have a little son and I should be glad to hand on to him a Baronetcy if I don't come back."*

Lloyd George consulted with Premier Asquith and Greenwood got his Baronetcy.

When Lloyd George was Prime Minister, he appointed Greenwood as Under Secretary for Foreign Affairs and Parliamentary Secretary to the Board of Trade. But a higher honour was to come. In April 1920, he was appointed Chief Secretary for Ireland, with a seat in Lloyd George's Cabinet.

As Chief Secretary for Ireland, Greenwood faced his most difficult challenge. For years, Britain and Ireland had been fighting over *"Home Rule"* for the Irish people, but as it is today, there were deep divisions between the Catholics who wanted independence and the Protestants who wanted to remain part of Britain. It was said that Lloyd George give the position of Chief Secretary to Greenwood because he

was a Canadian and the Irish might deal better with a Canadian than an Englishman. Greenwood and Lloyd George believed that the only way to keep order in Ireland was by force; therefore Greenwood was not well liked by the Irish. He was one of those who signed the treaty of 1922 creating the Irish Free State, but his work for Ireland severely hampered his political career. He was the last Chief Secretary for Ireland, serving from 1920 to 1922.

Greenwood lost his seat in Parliament in 1922, as did Winston Churchill, and like Churchill, he changed parties, becoming a Conservative. He was re-elected to Parliament as a Conservative for east Walthamstow in 1924 and served till 1929. From 1933 to 1938, he was Treasurer of the Conservative Party.

Greenwood made another triumphant visit to Whitby in September 1924, where he was tendered a testimonial dinner by the Town Council at the Ontario Ladies' College (now Trafalgar Castle School). It was on this occasion that Lady Greenwood presented the town's loving cup to Teddy Rowe, *"The Empire's Bonniest Baby."*

In June 1929, Hamar Greenwood was named a Baron, with a seat in the House of Lords. He took the title *"Baron Greenwood of Llambister, in the County of Radnor,"* reflecting his Welsh ancestry. In February

1937, he was elevated to the title of Viscount, and afterwards was known as *"Viscount Greenwood."* In 1938, the women of Whitby formed a Chapter of the Imperial Order of the Daughters of the Empire, and received his permission to name it the *"Viscount Greenwood Chapter of the IODE."*

On September 4, 1938, Viscount Greenwood made his last official visit home to Whitby to dedicate a memorial window to his parents in All Saints' Anglican Church. During this visit he was the guest of General Motors Chairman R.S. McLaughlin (1871-1972) and stayed at McLaughlin's home, Parkwood, in Oshawa. On this occasion he paid a visit to his birthplace on Henry Street and met with many of his old friends in Whitby who went to school with him.

In his last years, Hamar Greenwood became involved in the business sector in Britain. In 1934, he became chairman of Dorman Long & Co., the largest steel industry in England, and was president of the British Iron and Steel Federation from 1938 to 1939. He was also President of the Pilgrims Society which fostered friendship and co-operation between Britain and the United States. One of his last acts before he died was to arrange for the erection of a statue of U.S. President Franklin D. Roosevelt in Grosvenor Square in London.

One of the tragedies of Greenwood's life was that all his personal papers were destroyed when his rooms at Gray's Inn were bombed during the Second World War.

Hamar Greenwood died at his home in London, England on Sept. 10, 1948 at the age of 78. A memorial service was held at St. Margaret's Church, Westminster on Sept. 21, 1948, and he was buried at Codicote, Herefordshore with his wife's family. His wife, Viscountess Greenwood, died in 1968. Greenwood always like to tell the story that he met his wife in Kingston, Jamaica, during an earthquake.

Hamar Greenwood never forgot his home town of Whitby. He kept up a correspondence with many of his old friends and visited Whitby whenever he could. In 1939, he arranged to send a stone from Whitby Abbey, Yorkshire, England, to be installed in the wall of All Saints' Anglican Church. In 1933, he presented a portrait of King George V to the Ontario Regiment, of which he was a member for eight years. In 1948, his surviving family members donated a plaque in his memory which was placed under the Greenwood window at All Saints' Church. In the 1950s, the town returned his many favours by naming Greenwood Crescent after Hamar Greenwood.

The official reception at the dedication of the Greenwood window at All Saints' Anglican Church, Sept. 4, 1938. Left to right: Rev. E. Ralph Adye, rector of All Saints'; Hamar Greenwood, Viscountess Greenwood, Rev. Derwyn T. Owen, Archbishop of Toronto. In the background are two of Greenwood's children, Eric and Deborah.

Always interested in promoting Canadian interests in Britain, Hamar Greenwood published in 1913 a book called *"Canada As An Imperial Factor,"* which introduced Canada to British readers. A copy of this rare book is in the Town of Whitby Archives, along with all his correspondence with Rev. E. Ralph Adye (1897-1982), rector of All Saints' Church, regarding the Whitby Abbey stone and the Greenwood memorial window.

Hamar Greenwood was not the only member of his family to achieve high prominence in Britain. His sister, Florence Greenwood (1879-1975) married Leopold Amery (1871-1955) who served as Secretary of State for Dominion Affairs in the 1920s and Secretary of State for India during the Second World War. Florence Amery, known as *"Birdie,"* and her husband visited Whitby in January 1928, on a tour of the British Dominions. They too, received a civic reception at the town hall, and were treated like visiting royalty. While in Whitby, Mrs. Amery visited her birthplace, and the Greenwood plot in Union Cemetery, where she deposited some flowers. The author of this book had the pleasure of carrying on an extended correspondence with Mrs. Amery when she was in her 90s, when he was researching the life of Hamar Greenwood. He also had the pleasure of meeting her

The Greenewood window in All Saints' Church

son, Julian Amery, who was a prominent member of the British Parliament in the 1970s and 1980s.

Another sister of Hamar Greenwood, Mary Harriet Greenwood (1866-1953) made a name for herself in England. She trained as a nurse in the United States and after going to England, was stricken by blindness. Using her affliction to the best advantage, she joined Sir Arthur Pearson in providing aid for soldiers blinded in the First World War. For 25 years she taught Braille to these men and inspired hope and self-confidence in the victims of war.

William Hamer Greenwood (1872-1923), the brother from whom Hamar took his name, was a prominent man in the newspaper business in Canada. He was city editor of the Toronto World in the early 1900s and represented that newspaper in the Parliamentary Press Gallery at Ottawa. He was later managing editor and during the First World War he was director of publicity for the Canada Food Board. He finished his career as a promoter of banking and mercantile interests in Newfoundland, but illness struck him down at the age of 51 and he died at Toronto on Oct. 19, 1923.

The youngest of Hamar Greenwood's sisters, Gladys Greenwood (1886-1966) married the Hon. Simon Rodney in England in 1922 and became a member of the English aristocracy.

The remarkable Greenwood family remains today as one of Whitby's most successful and interesting historic families, rising from poverty and lack of education to the heights of British politics.

The School That Conveniently Burned Down

It is said that every child's dream is to see the school house burn down. In the 1950s there was even a *"burning school house"* piece in the fireworks that were set off on Victoria Day. It is quite another thing when the School Board wants to see the school burn down.

About 9:30 a.m. on a Sunday morning, July 4, 1920, George A. Ross (1858-1936) looked out the window of his home at King and Dunlop Street, and saw the old Henry Street Public School was on fire. The school stood, facing Henry Street, on the site of the present R. A. Sennett Public School. Ross turned in the alarm and the volunteer fire department with its *"Merryweather"* steam fire engine was soon on the scene. By noon, the fire was extinguished, having destroyed a wooden enclosure at the back of the school and the second floor and roof of the 66-year-old building. The only items salvaged were a teacher's desk and a couple of movable blackboards.

The old Henry Street School had been a source of controversy for many years. As early as 1893, it was condemned as unsafe and demolition was recommended. However, there was never enough money available to build a new school. As years went by it deteriorated further. In 1915 when renovations were made to the High School on Colborne Street, there was talk of refurbishing the

Henry Street Public School in 1919, one year before it was destroyed by fire.

Henry Street School. But there was still no money. By 1920, there was a desperate need to do something about the outdated school. Plans were made to construct a new $51,000 public school on the site and excavations for the basement had begun by the end of June.

There was a lot of talk around town when the Henry Street School conveniently burned down, three days after school closed for the summer holidays. It was widely reported that members of the school board had expressed the wish that it would burn down, and it was even said that the Chairman of the Board of Education had set the fire. The fire started in a dry wooden addition on the east side of the school which contained staircases to the second floor. It was rumoured that the fire had been set by a tramp, but nothing was proven as to the cause. The $3,000 insurance collected by the Board of Education, helped to finance the new school.

The Henry Street Public School was not always the subject of such derision and controversy. When it opened in September 1854, at a cost of $5,000, it was the finest school in Whitby and one of the best in the province. It was built of brick, two stories high, with two rooms. About 250 pupils attended it. When the Henry Street School was built there were only two other public schools within the limits of the new Town of Whitby which came into being in January 1855. There was a school house on Anderson Street at Hamer's Corners near the site of the present Anderson Collegiate, and a brick school house on John Street (now Dufferin Street) in Port Whitby, built in 1851. In 1855, the population of Whitby was 2,700. Records indicate there were 508 children of school age (five to 16), but only 431 attended school. School trustees reported that 231 children attended the Henry Street School during some part of 1855. Of these, 13 attended for one month or less and 87 attended for the entire school year. There were no laws making it mandatory to attend school, and in the 1850s, parents had to pay a fee to the town to send their children to school.

About two-thirds of the cost of operating the Henry Street School was paid for by the Town Council and the other third by the parents, in a levy of one shilling and three pence per child per month of school attendance. English currency of pounds, shillings and pence was used in Canada until 1858 when the country changed to the decimal system. The pound at that time was worth $5.00. Some families did not send their children to school on a regular basis since they could not afford the fees in addition to their taxes.

In 1855, the school had two rooms and two teachers, John Dundas (?-1870) who was paid $650 a year, and William Milne who was paid $360. Subjects taught at the Henry Street School were: reading, arithmetic, grammar, geography, history, writing, bookkeeping and algebra. However, only 17 of the 231 students studied history, two studied bookkeeping and one studied algebra. In 1856, Henry Street School had 300 pupils, but only 56 attended more than 200 days that year.

Two of the earliest teachers at the Henry Street school went on to make considerable contributions to the Town of Whitby. George Y. Smith (1833-1920) was later Mayor and a Judge of the Surrogate Court. John E. Farewell (1840-1923) who was a supply teacher at the age of 16 in 1856, became Ontario County's Crown Attorney and historian. One of the noted pupils of the school was Hamar Greenwood (1870-1948) who was Chief Secretary for Ireland in the British Cabinet from 1920 to 1922.

From its earliest days, Henry Street School suffered from overcrowding. In 1858, it was reported the average daily attendance was 140 while there were seats for only 100 children. A major reorganization of the school occurred in 1864 when it was divided into four rooms, and the enclosed staircase was built at the back. The front door was moved from the north to the west side, a porch was added and the old sheds removed. The renovations cost $350.

Only one photograph of the old school, from the back, has survived to this day, and accompanies this Chronicle. When the old school burned down, and the new one was being built, classes were held in St. Andrew's Presbyterian Church at Byron and St. John Streets and at the Whitby Public Library at Dundas and Byron Streets, during 1920-21. The new school, called King Street Public School, was opened in September 1921, with Robert A. Sennett (1889-1981) as principal. On Sept. 29, 1979, it was renamed the R. A. Sennet Public School.

They Danced in the Streets When The Paving Was Done

The citizens of Whitby danced in the streets when the first pavement on Brock and Dundas Streets was officially opened on Sept. 29, 1921. They had good reason to be merry, for this event ended years of having to cope with dirt roads that were dusty in the summer and muddy in the spring and fall. In the winter, carriages and automobiles had to contend with deep frozen ruts in the road.

Brock and Dundas Streets have always been the main streets for the Town of Whitby. Dundas Street, also known as Kingston Road, was the first road built through Whitby Township, about 1800, to link the town of York (Toronto) with Kingston. Brock Street was opened from Whitby Harbour north into Reach Township in 1831, serving as a route for farmers to ship their produce to the harbour. At the junction of these two main roads, Peter Perry built a store in 1836, where the Bank of Commerce is located, establishing what is now known as downtown Whitby.

Wagons, carriages, and later automobiles, sank up to their axles in the spring mud, making travel almost impossible at certain times of the year. By the end of the First World War, travel was increasing on Brock and Dundas Streets through Whitby. The Ontario Government was beginning to pro-

Bicycles in the parade passing Brock and Dundas Streets over the new pavement.

mote a Good Roads policy, and had paved the main highway from Toronto to Hamilton in 1916. Oshawa had its main roads paved in 1911, and the Whitby Council began to look at the costs of paving. The Ontario Government in 1921, announced that it was going to assume the Kingston Road as a provincial highway to be known as Highway 2. This made it eligible for provincial money to pave portions of the road in urban communities.

The Whitby Town Council managed to get an agreement for paving Dundas Street and convinced the Government to include Brock Street as well. Brock Street became Provincial Highway number 12 in 1923. Although the paved portion of the road done in 1921 included only the downtown section business section, it was a cause for celebration. The town council declared a holiday and invited Ontario's Minister of Highways, the Hon. F.C. Biggs, to perform the opening ceremonies at the Four Corners.

As many as 10,000 people from Whitby, Oshawa, Pickering and surrounding country converged on Whitby for the opening day. The town was gaily decorated with banners of welcome and all food and drinks were free. The official program began at 2 p.m. and lasted till midnight, with a parade in the late afternoon and a street dance on the new pavement after dark. More than 100 guest were invited to a banquet in the town hall at Brock and Colborne Streets where the fire hall is now located. Before the dance, The Whitby Amateur Athletic Association Minstrels held a concert of community singing, accompanied by the 48th Highlanders Band of Toronto.

The athletic association was in charge of the parade, led by the Highlanders Band, which included representatives from all the town's organizations, riding in brightly coloured automobiles. Mayor Ernest Harper (1867-1944) presided over the official ceremonies which took place at the Four Corners in front of the post office (later the site of the Bank of Montreal). The mayor, in his opening remarks, welcomed the distinguished guests, including representatives of the Warren Paving Company, which had the contract for the project. Albert Jackson (1870-1939), the town clerk, reviewed the history of the paving project and thanked the Minister of Highways for the Ontario Government's contribution of $100,000.

Never missing a chance to be a politician, Jackson, who was a former mayor of Whitby, took the opportunity to suggest to the minister that paving was also required on the government's road to the Ontario Hospital (now Whitby Mental Health Centre).

Biggs officially declared the paved road in downtown Whitby open at 4 p.m. In his speech he pointed out that the Provincial Government was paying the majority of the cost of the road work and explained how the province's good roads policy had replaced muddy roads with solid pavement, much to the delight of farmers and merchants who used the main highways.

Whitby was the first town in Ontario to sign an agreement with the Provincial Government to co-operate in the linking up of Highway 2 as a good roads project, said Biggs, as he congratulated the town council for its foresight. William Smith, M.P. said he was in favour of the province's good roads legislation, but expressed reservation at the opening ceremony about how the debt from such projects could be retired.

"If any person can tell can how those billions are to be paid, I will give them my farm," he declared.

W.E.N. Sinclair, M.P.P. (1873-1947), a Whitby-born man who would later serve as Mayor of Oshawa and leader of the Ontario

Liberal Party, declared the pavement in Whitby was one of the biggest projects ever undertaken in the town, but he did not think the progress made on the highway between Toronto and Oshawa was all it should be. He stated, however, that the good roads program was of great benefit to rural municipalities by improving business and bringing the town and the country together.

During his speech at the banquet in the town hall, Biggs defended the good roads program against the critics who said it cost too much. He said he *"stood foresquare to every wind, and most of it was wind,"* and much of the criticism levelled against his department was found only to be politics. *"The sooner the people realize that money spent on good roads is not an expenditure, but an investment, the sooner we start to get some,"* he said.

Once the political speeches were over, the concert and street dance followed, ending after midnight with the singing of the National Anthem and Auld Lang Syne.

Whitby was to benefit considerably from the new pavement and the assumption of the two main streets as provincial highways. The town soon lost its reputation of having the worst roads and the most garages between Toronto and Oshawa, and because it was a day's drive from Toronto to Whitby by automobile in the 1920s, many tourist stops were established in Whitby. The Spruce Villa Hotel was opened in an old farm house at the west end of the town in the early 1920s by Mrs. R.H. Weddel. She advertised *"luncheon served any hour, evening supper and home cooking. Special attention to motor parties. Accommodation over night, week-ends or by the week."* The Subway trailer camp also opened in the early 1920s as a tourist stop with cabins for over-night stays. A few years later, the Algoma Tourist cabins (now Canadiana Motel) and Ross Hill Cabins (on site of Owasco Volkswagen) were opened.

Throughout the 1920s, additional portions of Highways 2 and 12 were paved. Baldwin Street in Brooklin was paved by 1926, but as late as 1955, many of Whitby's residential streets remained unpaved. Although street pavement was late in coming to Whitby, many cement sidewalks were made as early as 1900, replacing the old wooden walks which existed in the downtown as early as the 1860s.

George Whitelaw (1870-1964) told the author that there was experimental paving done on Mary Street in 1889, the exact nature of which is not known today. Whitelaw remembered this paving particularly because a horse broke free from its hitching post at the Royal Hotel and ran up

The Fire Department's "Ever Alert" entry in the parade, Sept. 29, 1921.

Mary Street, leaving the impressions of its hoofs in the pavement.

Downtown Whitby did not get electric street lights until 1889. They were installed by the Ball Electric Light Company which had an electric plant on the east side of Brock Street, south of John Street.

Previously the downtown was lighted by coal oil lamps on poles which were kept lit by a man named *"Fish"* Taylor. Electric street lights were installed on Dundas Street outside of the downtown, in 1923 when the street was taken over as a Provincial Highway.

Whitby's Cenotaph Honours Those Who Served In Three Wars

June 3, 1924 was declared a half-holiday for Whitby's children so they could witness Ontario's Lieutenant-Governor dedicate the Cenotaph at Dundas and Green Streets. This fine stone monument was paid for by the Great War Veterans' Club, a forerunner of Royal Canadian Legion Branch 112, on a site donated by Ontario County Judge Theodore McGillivray (1862-1925). A parade formed at what is now Centennial Park, and marched north on Brock Street to the Four Corners, where it turned east on Dundas Street to the Cenotaph.

Those represented in the parade were the Whitby Citizens' Band, Boy Scouts, Board of Trade, Board of Education, Fire Department, Town Council, representatives of the 116th and 182nd Ontario County Battalions of the First World War, the 34th Regiment, the Lieutenant Governor, Col. Henry Cockshutt, and the veterans of Whitby. A platform was erected at the monument with reserved seats for the relatives of Whitby's men killed in the First World War.

The ceremonies opened with the singing of patriotic songs by the town's children, followed by an address by Mayor Richard N. Bassett (1880-1940). The massed bands then played the hymn *"O God Our Help In Ages Past"*, followed by scripture reading and remarks by the town's clergymen. The Lieutenant-Governor was then called upon to

A view of the crowd at the unveiling of the Whitby Cenotaph, June 3, 1924.

unveil the memorial and spoke of his recent tour of the battlefields of Europe. At the close of his speech, Col. Cockshutt pulled a rope attached to a Union Jack and the flag fell, unfolding at the base of the monument.

William D. Dykes, the town clerk, sang the solo *"There Is No Death"*, and Rev. Capt. S.E. Lambert delivered the dedicational prayer. A firing party composed of soldiers of the Ontario Regiment's *"C"* Company from Whitby fired a salute and a bugler sounded the Last Post amidst silence and bowed heads.

The hymn *"Fight the Good Fight"* was sung as flower girls and cadets from the high school, bearing about 50 offerings, formed a line that led to the monument where they laid their tributes at the base of the structure. Four soldiers with heads bowed and rifles reversed stood guard at the four corners of

Mayor Richard N. Bassett and Lieutenant-Governor Henry Cockshutt (in top hats) marching past Brock and Dundas Streets on their way to the Cenotaph.

the memorial. The Whitby War Relief Society presented a banner containing the complete honour roll which was hung on the memorial. The pianist was Robin Nicholson (1890-1970), who by coincidence, had been born in a house which once stood on the memorial site.

Each of the features of the Whitby Cenotaph has a special meaning, as outlined in the local newspapers in 1924:

"The whole is made up of fine light granite, which is purity itself. The composition of the

memorial is in three, namely the base, die and crown. This is in keeping with the great Three In One, by whose aid we have been able to overcome our trials and sacrifices and come through with flags still flying and the sword of victory in our hands. The base has three steps, Country, King and God, the top step being draped with the laurels of victory representing God, the crown of all things. The die has on each side three steps in the shadow of the cross on the top step. Near the bottom of the die is the outstanding battlement of strength from the Romans, surmounted by a beautiful bronze tablet. On the tablet is the inscription and crest underneath which is the honour roll of those who paid the supreme sacrifice. Below the honour roll is the Latin word "Resurgent" (they shall live again) showing our faith in the new life and the Resurrection.

"Above the tablet are the leaves of the allies with the maple leaf in the foreground. Near the top of the die is a sword on each side symbolic of victory with an inverted wreath in the centre and below the wreath are the words: "Pro Honoris Causa, 1914-1918" (For an honourable cause), showing victory through sacrifice. Surmounting the whole composition is the crown in the form of a Roman star of sacrifice draped with festoons. This is to represent the altar of Canadian honour and high spirit which although we passed through deep valleys and sorrow and sacrifice, still remains burning as a symbol in the whole world of our undying faith and integrity.

"On either side of the memorial are bronze plaques bearing the crests of the 116th and 182nd Ontario County Overseas Battalions. One beautiful point in the memorial is that it is in memory not only of those who fell but of all those who served in any capacity in the struggle for our humanity and civilization, the mothers, fathers and all who have a part."

On the original plaque were the names of 40 Whitby men who were killed in the First World War. Prominent among them are those of three brothers, two of whom were killed on the same day in the Battle of Vimy Ridge – Berton, Charles and Fenton Brownwell, and another three brothers, Andrew, James and John Fulton.

On Nov. 11, 1948, the names of 31 men who were killed in the Second World War were added to the Cenotaph. The special ceremony honouring this event, was unfortunately marred by the sudden death of 86-year-old John W. Bateman (1862-1948), a former mayor of Whitby, who dropped dead during the parade. He had been warned not to march that day, but he insisted on being part of the parade of veterans.

On June 16, 1985, the dates of the Korean War, 1950-1953, were added to the Cenotaph in a special ceremony. Although no Whitby men were killed in this war at least three participated in it.

Planning and raising of funds for Whitby's war memorial began in 1921, and took three years to complete. In 1928, the Cenotaph was first floodlit at night. As traffic became more congested on Dundas Street, and had to be rerouted every Remembrance Day, it was proposed in the 1960s that the Cenotaph be moved to Centennial Park. When asked to investigate this possibility, Town Clerk John R. Frost (1901-1983) discovered that if the site at Dundas and Green Streets was ever used for anything other than a war memorial, it would revert back to the Theodore McGillivray estate. The resulting legal problems have ensured that Whitby's war memorial will remain where it is.

At the dedication ceremony in 1924, the members of the Whitby Town Council decided to rent top hats which they considered befitting the occasion. According to John Frost, the council never paid the bill for them.

The program for the dedication ceremony, a copy of which is in the Town of Whitby Archives, contains a list of the Whitby men killed in the First World War, the poem "In Flanders Fields," and a picture and description of the Cenotaph. No record remains of who designed it, or the contractor who erected it at the corner of Dundas and Green Streets.

Teddy Rowe

The Empire's Bonniest Baby

The Town of Whitby achieved international fame for the first time in the summer of 1924 when one of its youngest residents was named "*the bonniest baby in the British Empire.*" Little James Edward "*Teddy*" Rowe (1922-1930), the two-year-old son of garage owner Thomas L. Rowe, was named winner over 60,000 other babies in the category of nine months to two years in a contest sponsored by the British Empire Exhibition at Wembley in London, England. Teddy Rowe received a cash prize of 100 pounds ($500) for his education in the competition which included children from Britain, Canada, Australia, New Zealand, South Africa and other countries of the British Empire, now called the British Commonwealth of Nations.

In the spring of 1924, the Toronto Daily Star sponsored the Ontario segment of the Empire-wide baby contest. The rules required that a health report be prepared for each baby, certified by the family doctor, and photographs taken for submission to the judges. On the urging of Teddy's two grandmothers, Thomas and Janet Ella Rowe took their son to Campbell's Studio in Oshawa on April 5, 1924 to have the portraits taken, and a medical certificate was obtained from Dr. Ralph T. MacLaren (1876-1956) who had brought young Teddy into the world. On the back of one of the pictures they recorded that Teddy was 31-1/2 inches high, weighed 29 pounds and had 16 teeth. Teddy just made it into the nine-month to two-year category, for the photos were taken one day before his second birthday. He was born at the Victorian Order of Nurses' Home on Dundas Street West, Whitby, on April 6, 1922. Thomas L. Rowe (1882-1959), an architect and civil engineer, came to Whitby from Toronto in 1913 to take charge of the construction of the Ontario Hospital, later the Whitby Psychiatric Hospital. When the hospital was completed in 1918 and his services were no longer needed, he purchased a garage and Ford motor dealership at Dundas and Centre Streets where the Scott's Chicken

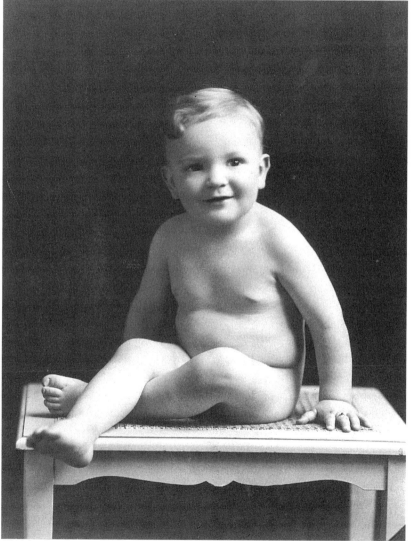

Teddy Rowe: *a portrait taken at Campbell's Studio, Oshawa, April 5, 1924. This is one of three pictures submitted to the British Empire Baby Contest.*

Villa is now. The Rowe family lived on the second floor of the garage and kept a summer cottage at Heydenshore Park.

The Toronto Star, which received 2,500 entries from across Ontario, placed Teddy Rowe second in his class, but he was elevated to first place by the judges in England. The Ontario judges included Fred Haynes, President of the Ontario Society of Artists, and Group of Seven artist Arthur Lismer, acting principal of the Ontario College of Art. Artist Sir William Orpen headed the English judges, who were selected by the National Baby Week Council of Great Britain. Patron of the Council was Queen Mary, wife of King George V.

On July 29, 1924, the banner headline on the front page of the Toronto Star read: *"Ontario Baby Heads Class in Empire Contest"*, accompanied by three photographs of Teddy Rowe. Representatives of The Star motored to Whitby to inform Thomas Rowe personally of his son's achievement. They found him at his garage and raced after him to Heydenshore Park to inform Mrs. Rowe and Teddy. Teddy took the news calmly, the paper reported, being more interested in throwing stones into Lake Ontario than his new-found fame. To his father, the news was "too good to be true". For several days The Star was filled with pictures and articles about Teddy Rowe's

Teddy Rowe and his mother in a decorated car, 1924.

accomplishment.

On Sept. 3, 1924, Teddy's parents took him to the Canadian National Exhibition in Toronto to receive his prize from the Honourable John S. Martin, Ontario's Minister of Agriculture. Also attending the presentation of the $500 was Whitby's mayor, Richard N. Bassett (1880-1940). Hundreds of women mobbed Teddy follow-

ing the ceremony, held at the Women's Building at the C.N.E. A few days later, Teddy was invited to open the Broadview Boys' Fair in Toronto by pressing a button to turn on the fair's electric lights.

On Sept. 12, it was Whitby's turn to honour two of its most famous sons, Hamar Greenwood and Teddy Rowe. Hamar Greenwood (1870-1948), a native of

Margaret Scott with loving cup given to her brother by the Whitby Town Council.

Whitby who had served as Chief Secretary for Ireland in the British Government, was in town for a visit to his old home on Henry Street. The Town Council presented him with a banquet at the Ontario Ladies' College (now Trafalgar Castle School), but it was Teddy Rowe who stole the show. Lady Greenwood (1886-1968) was called upon to present a silver loving cup from the Whitby Town Council to Teddy. On seeing the shining cup, Teddy cried: "*I want that*", much to the amusement of the distinguished guests.

In 1926, Thomas Rowe decided to give up the Whitby garage and return to Toronto. He was to have a long career in the city but young Teddy was not so fortunate. At the age of six, he contracted Scarlet Fever, his first serious illness, which weakened his heart. Two years later when he caught the 'flu, Teddy Rowe's heart gave out and he died on May 1, 1930 at the age of eight. The Whitby Town Council sent its condolences to the bereaved family. The Teddy Rowe story appeared to be over. But it was not.

In February, 1990, the writer of this book, in his capacity as Archivist of the Town of Whitby, wrote to The Toronto Star to find out if anyone knew anything about Teddy Rowe. All the information he had was the boy's name, the program from the dinner at the Ladies' College and a report of Teddy's untimely death. For years he had wanted to find out more about this little boy, but was unable to because the Whitby newspapers of the 1920s had been destroyed in a fire.

A few days after his letter appeared in The Star, he received a call from CBC Radio offering to do a phone interview about his search for Teddy Rowe. No sooner was the interview completed, than relatives of the long-lost baby began to call the archives with information. They told him that Teddy had a younger sister, Margaret Scott, who was vacationing in the Caribbean at the time of the interview. When she returned, they both did a live interview at the CBC studios in downtown Toronto. It turned out that Margaret Scott had the original photographs of Teddy Rowe taken by Campbell's Studio in 1924, a scrapbook of press clippings and the loving cup awarded by the Town of Whitby, bearing the names of the members of the Town Council.

Teddy Rowe was honoured again, 70 years after his winning of the Empire Baby Contest, on Sept. 10, 1994, when his story was the featured theme of Whitby's annual Heritage Day, sponsored by the Local Architectural Conservation Advisory Committee (LACAC). Margaret Scott and her family were special guests for the day. The Town of Whitby's loving cup and a silver bowl and spoon given to Teddy by a baby food company in 1924, were displayed at the Whitby Public Library.

Teddy Rowe had the distinction of bringing Whitby to world attention. Such an accomplishment has been recorded only twice since 1924: when the Whitby Dunlops won the World Hockey Championship in 1958 and Anne Ottenbrite won gold, silver and bronze medals at the 1984 Summer Olympics in Los Angeles.

Mother Nature's April Fools' Day Joke

Mother Nature played a cruel April Fools' Day joke on Whitby when she destroyed the beautiful steeples on St. Mark's United Church. The first week of April, 1929 was particularly disastrous for Southern Ontario, as high winds and severe flooding caused thousands of dollars of damage. A gale-force wind on April 1, which toppled the church steeples, was followed five days later by heavy rains which washed out roads and bridges from Pickering to Bowmanville, in the worst floods the district had seen since June 1890.

St. Mark's United Church, constructed as the Methodist Tabernacle, was one of the primary landmarks of Whitby. It was designed in 1875 by C.M. Mulligan of Hamilton. On the north-west tower was perched a steeple 165 feet high, 25 feet higher than the steeple of All Saints' Anglican Church. On the north-east tower stood a smaller steeple, 90 feet high. As the largest church steeple in Whitby, the spire on the north-west tower had been severely buffeted by winds for 54 years. Several years before it fell, it was reinforced from the inside with strong timbers after structural damage was discovered.

On the morning of April 1, 1929, a steady wind began to blow and by early afternoon it had reached gale force. A number of citizens had noticed the United Church steeple swaying back and forth in the wind. The danger of its falling was clearly evident.

Town Engineer Herbert Pringle (1885-1965) and Police Chief Herbert Gunson (1893-1948) arrived on the scene and set up rope barriers to keep back the crowd that had already gathered at the church. In mid-afternoon, the wind tore a large hole at the base of the steeple. At 5:45 p.m. the spire was seen to tilt to the south-east. For a brief second it hung in the balance, then crashed against the small steeple and toppled onto the lawn in front of the Church on Colborne Street.

The church was otherwise undamaged except for a few broken

Whitby Methodist Tabernacle with its steeples intact, C. 1895.

window panes. Great relief was expressed that the steeple did not fall through the roof. A number of church officials, including the minister, Rev. Archie L. Richards (?-1937) were at the scene to watch the steeple fall. As word passed around town that the steeple had fallen, an even larger crowd assembled. A few small boys ran forward to grab some shingles as souvenirs, but were warned away by Chief Gunson and the night watchman John Thomas (1885-1950) who had been called to assist the chief in crowd control.

It did not take the church officials long to act after the storm. On April 3, the small steeple on the north-east tower, was declared unsafe and torn down under the supervision of a local contractor, Russell J. Underwood (1883-1952). A stout rope and block and tackle were used to accomplish the job and the second steeple fell in almost exactly the same spot as the first.

It was estimated that it would cost $1,000 to replace the large steeple. This was far too much for a church to afford in 1929, so the board of Stewards decided to place brick battlements on the north-west tower and leave the north-east tower as it was because there was no damage to the brickwork. Russell J. Underwood was given the contract.

A newspaper reporter wryly commented at the time: *"Unlike steeples (the battlements) will not be visible for a distance, but on the other hand they more readily resist wind storms."*

The great wind storm of April 1, 1929, was followed by heavy rains on April 5 and 6, which washed out bridges in Pickering, Oshawa and Bowmanville. A steel and concrete trestle on the Canadian Pacific Railway at Lynde Creek was washed away, leaving only the railway tracks suspended in the air where the bridge used to be.

With the onset of the Great Depression six months after the steeples on St. Mark's Church were destroyed, there was no money to replace them. The only remaining record of these majestic spires is in photographs taken before 1929.

The small steeple being pulled down from its tower on the Whitby United Church, April 8, 1929

Brooklin's First Legion Branch Was Another Victim Of The Depression

Brooklin Branch No. 152 of the Royal Canadian Legion is a flourishing organization today, founded in 1966 by barber Fred Phillips. Few Brooklin residents realize that this is not the first Legion branch in Brooklin, or that when it was formed, it was given the same number, 152, as the original branch had in 1929.

On Oct. 3, 1929, the first organizational meeting of the Brooklin Legion was held, under the auspices of Oshawa Branch No. 43. A.J. Graves of Oshawa presided over the first election of officers and gave an address on the aims and objectives of the Legion at that first meeting.

The first officers for Branch 152 in 1929 were: President, Dr. James Moore (1872-1941); First Vice-President, William McCarthy; Second Vice-President, Arthur Boyes (1890-1971) and Secretary-Treasurer, Robert E. Wilson. The Executive Committee consisted of Messrs. Campbell, Shortridge, Ross, Harrison and Lockyer. Dr. James Moore, the first president, was a well-known figure in Brooklin. He and his brother, Dr. John Moore (1862-1937) were both doctors in the community, known as *"Dr. Jim"* and *"Dr. John"*. Professionally and personally they were great rivals, even though they were brothers. Bob Heron, who has served as president of the new Branch 152, was brought into the world by the first president Dr. Jim Moore.

Dr. Jim Moore was born in Reach Township and opened a medical practice in Brooklin in 1900. He was Medical Officer of Health for Whitby Township for many years. His extensive military background began before the First World War, when he was a company commander of a local battalion of the 34th Regiment, now the Ontario Regiment. In 1916 he went overseas as a medical officer for the 116th Ontario County Battalion, and was wounded at Hill 70 in France on Aug. 23, 1917. After being sent home to recover from his wounds, Dr. Moore entered politics, contesting the riding of South Ontario in the 1923 Provincial Election. He

Dr. Jim Moore, first President of the Brooklin Legion Branch No. 152, while on military service in England, 1916.

was narrowly defeated by William E.N. Sinclair (1873-1947) of Oshawa, who became leader of the Ontario Liberal Party.

Dr. Moore served as president of the South Ontario Conservative Association for many years and was a member of the Brooklin School Board. He was also District Deputy Grand Master for Ontario District of the Masonic Lodge. In 1931, he was appointed Registrar of Deeds for Ontario County, serving until his death on Dec. 17, 1941. Such a community leader with a distinguished military background was a natural choice to lead the new Brooklin Legion.

Nov. 4, 1929 was a gala night in Brooklin, as local residents, ex-servicemen and a large number of Oshawa veterans attended the charter night for the Brooklin Legion in the Whitby Township Hall (now Brooklin Community Centre). A.J. Graves, of the Oshawa Legion, presided over the meeting, while M. McIntyre Hood, a member of the Oshawa Legion and the provincial Legion executive, was the guest speaker who presented the charter. Hood delivered an impressive address on the aims and objectives of the Legion, stressing its creed of service to disabled men, widows and orphans.

In the 1920s, Canada's membership in the British Empire and the maintenance of a truly British spirit, figured prominently in

Legion logo.

Hood's address. In presenting the charter, he urged the members of the Brooklin Legion Branch 152 to note that the honour of the Canadian Legion (the word Royal was not added until 1965) was entrusted to their keeping. The charter was accepted by Dr. Moore, who gave a stirring speech.

Secretary Wilson outlined the new branch's program of activities for Armistice Day, as it was called then. They included a memorial service in Brooklin United Church on Nov. 10, 1929, conducted by Rev. Percy L. Jull (1880-1948).

The official ceremonies on charter night were followed with entertainment, which included vocal and piano solos by members of the community. The church parade the day before Armistice Day consisted of the Ontario Regiment band under the direction of A.J. Graves, Boy Scouts led by Scoutmaster William Agar (1885-1955) and members of Legion branches from Brooklin, Port Perry, Whitby and Oshawa, consisting of about 50 veterans. The Scouts formed a guard of honour as the veterans took their seats in the church, which was filled to capacity.

The Brooklin Branch of the Canadian Legion, which was formed with such enthusiasm in 1929 did not last long. There are no records in the surviving minute book of general meetings; only executive meetings. The last entry is dated Jan. 20, 1931 when it was agreed to give a ton of coal to a needy member. There is no official record of the disbanding of the first Brooklin Legion. It is likely that it could not be sustained during the Great Depression of the 1930s. Its members eventually drifted off to the Whitby or Port Perry branches.

For 35 years, Brooklin was without a branch of the Royal Canadian Legion until it was revived in 1966. Today its headquarters is in the Legion Hall at Baldwin and Campbell streets, a former hotel.

Whitby's First Yacht Club Was A Victim Of War And Water

For eight years during the Great Depression and the early part of the Second World War, Whitby had a flourishing yacht club at the harbour. Even though the Depression was at its worst and most Whitby residents could only dream of owning their own boats, a group of citizens met in October 1933 to establish a yacht club.

The officers for the club, elected at this inaugural meeting were: John Ham Perry (1892-1976), manager of the Dominion Bank, as president; G. Norman Irwin (1903-1983), owner of Red Wing Orchards, as vice-president; Dr. F. Stewart Mills, a dentist, as secretary and John R. Frost (1901-1983), Whitby's municipal clerk-treasurer, as treasurer of the club. Executive members include Donald A. Wilson (1891-1987), George Astley (1879-1938), Dr. Blake Beaton (1891-1982), Ernest M. Lomax (1886-1952), R. McArthur, R. Insole, Dr. George H. Stevenson (1893-1976), William F. Harden (1883-1949) and John Ferguson (1899-1983).

The new executive set fees for senior members, aged 21 and over, at six dollars, and junior members, under age 21, at three dollars a year. By November 1933, arrangements had been made for a lease of property on the east side of the harbour basin, south of the mouth of Pringle Creek. The follow-ing spring, construction began on a club house, a one-storey cottage style frame building set on piles driven into the marsh. It had an open verandah along the south front and a stone fireplace at the east end of the building. The clubhouse was a popular meeting place in the summer, with other organizations such as a duplicate bridge club using it for meetings. In the winter, members' boats were stored in the building.

At the inaugural meeting, held on Oct. 27, 1933, in All Saints' Parish Hall, Gordon D. Conant (1885-1953), Commodore of the Oshawa Yacht Club, offered all the help his club could provide, to get the new Whitby Club started, and said he would donate a cup for racing competition. Sailing instruction classes were offered in January, February and March of 1934, to prospective members. Plans were also made to purchase three boats as the nucleus of a fleet for the Whitby Yacht Club.

A year after the club house was constructed, Norman Irwin built a metal hanger behind the club house, where he stored his airplane, which, equipped with pontoons, could take off and land from the water at Whitby harbour.

In 1935, Mrs. Edward Bowman (1890-1973), wife of the Mayor of Whitby, christened *The Guardian,* a motor launch donated to the club by division Court Clerk Emily Macdonell (1864-1941). The Guardian was often used for cruises to Alcott, New York, directly across Lake Ontario from Whitby. The same year, Frederick H.M. Irwin (1890-1943) presented the club with a cup donated by his wife for the annual competition by dinghy skippers. The cup was known as the *"Inverlynn Cup,"* named after Irwin's residence, Inverlynn, at the corner of Raglan and Giffard Streets. The Moorelands Cup, named after the residence of William H. Moore, M.P. (1872-1960) at Frenchman's Bay, was donated by Moore for an annual race from Whitby Harbour to Moorelands.

Other trophies were the Emily Macdonell Cup, awarded to the top lady skipper; the Stonehaven Cup, donated by Norman Irwin for the winning skipper in the annual Whitby-to-Oshawa race, and the Gordon Conant Cup for competition between the Whitby and Oshawa Yacht Clubs.

The highlight of the year was the annual meeting, which featured a banquet at the end of October, when the cups were awarded and the officers for the new year elected. Commodore T.K. Wade, of the Royal Canadian Yacht Club, Toronto, was the guest speaker at the 1936 annual meeting. Winners of the cups that year were: William Ruddy, the Inverlynn Cup; Ward Irwin, the Stonehaven Cup and Regatta Cup; John

The Whitby Yacht Club's club house and Norman Irwin's airplane hanger, 1935.

Perry Jr., the Junior Cup and M. Carther, the ladies' cup. The Whitby Yacht Club was one of the first on the north shore of lake Ontario to have lady skippers.

At the 1937 annual meeting, it was announced that the Royal Canadian Yacht Club was going to follow Whitby's example and have lady skippers for the first time in the 1938 season.

In its heyday, the Whitby Yacht Club had about 100 members of all ages and all boats were owned by the club. The future seemed secure for the club until Sept. 3, 1939 when the Second World War began. In October, John H. Perry, who had served as the club commodore since its founding, joined the army and went overseas. Other members and officers soon followed. Norman Irwin left Whitby to command an air base at Aylmer, as part of the Commonwealth Air Training Plan. It was left to the older mem-

The club house, looking west toward the Ontario Hospital, 1935.

bers to take over command of the club as the younger ones went off to war. Frederick H.M. Irwin (no relation to Norman Irwin) took over as commodore in 1940 and Samuel Trees (1885-1957), owner of the blanket and buckle factories, was the last commodore in 1941. By the end of the year, the club ceased to operate. The clubhouse stood empty through the war and post-war years. High water levels in the late 1940s did much structural damage to the club house, as the water of lake Ontario rose over the floor. The building had settled badly when a reporter from The Times-Gazette, Whitby and Oshawa's local newspaper, inspected the site in July 1948. He found the *"Guardian"* considerably damaged by water, and the parts in the locked cupboard rusted beyond use. The

furniture was heavily water damaged and the whole place was described as *"a sorry mess."* In the spring the floor of the club house was under three feet of water. By April 1951, the stone chimney had collapsed, and in August, the building was demolished.

After more than a decade with no sign of the club being revived, the remaining members met in 1953 to decide what to do with the club's assets of $3,000. According to the charter, only paid-up members could serve on the executive, so a group of former members paid their dues and held one meeting to dispose of the assets. On a recommendation of John R. Frost, the $3,000 was given to the campaign to build a new community arena.

Three years later, when the Town of Whitby Purchased Samuel Trees' mansion at Dundas and King Streets for a town hall site (now the Whitby Public Library), five of the old yacht club's trophies were found in the house. Frost took them to the town hall before the Trees house was demolished in the summer of 1958. All have disappeared, except one, which is in a display case at the new Whitby Yacht Club. Some relics of the first yacht club are now in the Town of Whitby Archives, including the club's bank book for 1933 to 1937, a list of club rules dated 1938, and rules for the Inverlynn Cup, dated 1936. The pictures which accompany this chronicle were taken by Norman Irwin on what is likely the first 35-millimetre film ever used in Whitby.

An attempt was made to re-establish a yacht club in 1957, but it failed. In 1967, the year Whitby Harbour was designated as a recreational harbour by the federal government, the present Whitby Yacht Club was established on the west side of the harbour. For 32 years it has been an active and flourishing member of the community.

It Took Years To Get Rid Of These Derelict Ships

Nobody likes having someone else's garbage dumped in their back yard, especially when they don't know who was responsible for dumping it there. The Town of Whitby was placed in such a position in the 1930s when it wanted to have three derelict freighters removed from the harbour.

The boats were a wooden grain freighter, *"The City of Windsor,"* a schooner, the *"Island Queen"* and another unidentified boat. These three boats had been towed into Whitby Harbour in the early 1920s and left there, beached in the shallow water of the harbour basin.

About 1930 the Town Council and the Whitby Chamber of Commerce began negotiations with the federal government's Department of Public Works to have them removed. The town had tried to find out who owned the boats and who was responsible for leaving them in the harbour to rot, but got no results. Since the culprits could not be caught, the federal government had to be approached because it owned the harbour and was responsible for any improvements made there. However, since Canada was in the depths of the Great Depression, the government was reluctant to spend a lot of money on clearing old boats from an unused harbour.

Whitby Harbour had not seen any ship since 1929 because the water level had

Three men in a row boat passing the hull of "The City of Windsor" in the Whitby Harbour.

The Prince Edward Island ferry at Whitby Harbour in August, 1987.

dropped several feet and a sandbar blocked the entrance. The old hulks were considered another menace to navigation. *"The City of Windsor,"* 500 feet long, was not considered such a menace by the residents of Port Whitby and the unemployed of the town. It was a good source of firewood for the winter. In the summer of 1933, local residents rowed out to the big wooden freighter and stripped it of its superstructure. It was estimated that the wood from the old boat would heat Whitby homes for several winters.

The Town Council became alarmed,

because if too much wood was stripped from the boats, they could not be towed away. The back of *"The City of Windsor"* had already broken, leaving the stern submerged and the bow high out of the water. The *"Island Queen"* had been stripped to the water's edge. Even if the boats were burned to the water's edge, it would cost a considerable amount of money to dig out large sections of the hulls lying under the water.

In July 1933, the small unidentified boat was towed to Toronto by a salvage tug, but the others remained. The town council con-

tinued to petition the federal government to have them removed. Finally, in 1935, the government consented. *"The City of Windsor"* and the *"Island Queen"* were towed out into Lake Ontario and sunk, not far from Whitby harbour. It is likely that divers would still be able to find them in their watery grave.

Whitby experienced another derelict boat problem 50 years later, when a Prince Edward Island car ferry was tied up at the wharf for five years. The ferry was acquired by McNamara Marine in 1971 and converted to a floating electrical generating station. It was sold to a private owner who planned to take it to Haiti. A revolution toppled the Haitian government, terminating the agreement with the ferry's Whitby owner. From 1987 to 1992, it lay moored at the dock in Whitby Harbour. Concern was expressed about toxic PCBs on the boat, and in stormy weather the ferry caused damage when bumping up against the concrete wharf. Mayor Bob Attersley tried to have it removed, with no results. Some people jokingly referred to the ferry as *"Bob's Navy."* It was finally towed to Toronto on June 2, 1992.

Whitby Harbour is presently being transformed into a beautiful recreational facility for the town with money being provided by the Rotary, Kiwanis and Lions Clubs. Among the developments of the past 30 years are a public marina and a yacht club.

A Retired Minister Gave Whitby Its House Numbers

Whitby owes its system of house numbering to James Roy Van Wyck (1877-1941), a retired Presbyterian minister who provided this service to the town, free of charge, in the depths of the Great Depression. Many Whitby residents find it surprising that the town had no house numbering system until the summer of 1935. Oshawa houses had been numbered for years, and Whitby, with a population of about 4,000, had reached the point where such a system was needed. Until 1935, residences and businesses were listed in the telephone book by the street on which they were located. In Whitby, everyone knew everyone, so there was no need to number the houses. There was no mail delivery, so numbers were not needed by the post office. All mail was picked up by local residents at the post office at Brock and Dundas Streets. Although the town had reached the size where a numbering system would be an advantage, all that was needed was for someone to organize it. That person was Rev. Dr. James Roy Van Wyck.

Van Wyck came to Whitby in 1929 from Bay City, Michigan, on his retirement from the ministry, and lived at 205 Byron Street North. Early in 1935, he approached the Town Council and offered to set up a street numbering system at no cost to the taxpayers. Under Van Wyck's system, each block was numbered by a hundred. For instance, the first block south of Dundas on Brock Street was the 100 block; the second, the 200 block and so on. Buildings on the west side of the street had even numbers and the east side had odd numbers. On streets running east and west, the even numbers were on the north side and the odd numbers on the south. Van Wyck had to be careful to assign numbers for vacant lots between existing homes, so they could be used when new homes were built in these spaces.

The Whitby Gazette and Chronicle of June 20, 1935 reported that: *"House and business block numbering in Whitby is well under way, under the direction of Rev. Dr. Roy Van Wyck, whose plan was approved by the town council a few weeks ago. On houses and business places, listed below, numbers have already been established, and numbers are available at local hardware stores. Next week, a further list will be published and in the meantime, Dr. Van Wyck will be pleased to furnish any information required."* Below this notice were lists of the numbers for buildings on the north and south side of Dundas Street from Brock Street to the western limits of the town near Jeffrey Street, along with the owners' names.

During the summer of 1935, each Whitby residence was mailed a post card with the following message on it:

"Dear Friend:

"The Town of Whitby Council accepted my offer for free service in setting up a house numbering system in Whitby. You will find the number assigned to you on the address side of this Post Card. Please do your part. As soon as possible, place the assigned number at your front door. Thanking you for your co-operation in making this effort for a more efficiently organized town a success.

Sincerely yours,
J. Roy Van Wyck.
July 24, 1935."

The Town of Whitby Archives acquired one of these post cards at a stamp show in Toronto in January 1994. It is the only one known to have survived out of hundreds that were mailed to Whitby households and businesses. It is addressed to *"Mr. Kirk, 924 Brock St. S., Whitby."* He may have been J.C.M. Kirk, who gave a collection of First and Second World War badges to Branch 112, Royal Canadian Legion.

Van Wyck was an interesting personality who played an important part in Whitby's history for 12 years, as well as providing its house numbers. The son of a Presbyterian minister, Rev. James Van Wyck, he was born at Belleville in 1877. He graduated from Victoria College, University of Toronto, in 1902 as a silver medalist in philosophy.

After his graduation from Knox College, the Presbyterian ministerial school in Toronto, in 1906, he was a missionary in the Yukon before he went to Westminster Mission Church in Hamilton, followed by a pastorate in St. Andrew's Presbyterian Church at Chatham. In 1916 he accepted a call to the First Presbyterian Church in Bay City, Michigan, where he served for 13 years. In 1920, he was elected moderator of the Synod in Bay City.

When he retired to Whitby in 1929, Van Wyck had a library of 4,000 books in his house on Byron Street.

On May 30, 1933, Van Wyck was unanimously appointed an honourary member of the new Rotary Club of Whitby, because of his services to Rotary in Bay City. In his acceptance speech he urged a better understanding between Canada and the United States. This excerpt from that speech applies to today's society as much as it did in 1933.

"It is unfair to judge the people of the United States by the fact that their large cities have many criminals. There are criminals in Canada, but we would resent being judged by them."

He saw Canada serving as a link between Britain and the United States, which proved true especially during the Second World War.

Once a year, Van Wyck addressed the

House Numbering in Whitby

Dear Friend:—

The Town of Whitby Council accepted of my offer for free service in setting up a house numbering system for Whitby.

You will find the number assigned to you on the address side of this Post Card.

Please do your part. As soon as possible place the assigned number at your front door.

Thanking you for your co-operation in making this effort for a more efficiently organized town a success.

Sincerely yours,

J. Roy Van Wyck.

July 24, 1935.

The post card sent to Whitby residents by J. Roy Van Wyck in 1935, announcing his house numbering system.

Whitby Rotary Club, his speech in 1934 being on the economic system of Canada during the Depression. In 1935 he spoke on the life and works of Mark Twain.

Van Wyck died at his Whitby home at the age of 64, on March 3, 1941, and was buried in Hamilton. His wife, Edith, lived on in Whitby until her death on June 21, 1953. They had no family to carry on the work of this important contributor to Whitby's growth and development.

Norman MacCarl:
The First Shareholder of Maple Leaf Gardens

For more than 65 years, Toronto's Maple Leaf Gardens has been Canada's greatest hockey shrine. It was here that Foster Hewitt broadcast the Leafs' games every week with his famous call: "He shoots; He scores." It was here that the Whitby Dunlops first played the Russians on Nov. 22, 1957 before winning the World Hockey Championship four months later in Oslo, Norway.

But Whitby's connection with Maple Leaf Gardens goes back much further, indeed to the founding of the Gardens by Conn Smythe in 1931. Few of today's Whitby residents are aware that the first shareholder in Maple Leaf Gardens was a Whitby man, Norman R. MacCarl (1884-1939), an older brother of Walter F. MacCarl (1895-1984) who owned a hardware store on Brock Street South for many years.

When Norman MacCarl died in 1939 at the age of 54, Conn Smythe wrote a special tribute to him in the Gardens' magazine, "Maple Leaf Hockey News".

"In 1931, when we were trying to raise funds to build the new Gardens, we had an office on King Street," Smythe recalled. *"One morning, Mr. MacCarl, dressed in the ordinary clothes of a mechanic, stumped into my office on his crutch and said he would like to invest some money in the Gardens. I asked him how much and he said that he wouldn't say until he found out if he could buy the first*

Norman MacCarl in the Leafs' dressing room in the 1930s, standing behind "King" Clancy and "Busher" Jackson.

share issued by the Gardens. Getting in touch with Ed Bickle, who was the brains of the stock end of the business, we were informed that it would be quite easy to do this, and we passed this information back to MacCarl.

"He surprised me, and everybody in the office by laying down a thousand dollars and became Shareholder Number One, with a thousand dollars staked in what at that time was thought to be quite a venturesome investment —

Maple Leaf Gardens."

Smythe went on to recall that MacCarl became a devoted fan and supporter of the Toronto Maple Leafs.

"At the end of the night (of each game) whether we had won or lost, usually when we had lost, he used to stump into the dressing room and tell the boys that they were still a great team and he was proud of them. Then, at the Annual Meeting, he always made a hit with the directors by getting up and moving a vote of confidence in the directors and the management, saying how wonderful they were, and adding a tasty bit at the end as a comparison, how rotten the referees were in the National Hockey League."

Norman MacCarl was born on Oct. 26, 1884, the son of John MacCarl, Whitby's streets foreman for 27 years. He was one of a family of seven boys and two girls who grew up in a brick house at 215 Wellington Street. At the age of seven he lost one of his legs because of complications from an infected knee, and had to use an artificial leg for the rest of his life.

After attending public and high school in Whitby, he earned enough money through a newspaper route and working for local farmers, to put himself through Shaw's Business College. Moving to Toronto, he operated a pool room on Queen Street for a few years, before working for the Toronto Street

Railway Company which later became the Toronto Transit Commission. He spent 27 years with the TTC, as a dispatcher at the Coxwell Street terminal.

Although he could not take part in competitive sports because of his disability, he was a close follower of sports, especially hockey. He could swim, ride a bicycle, and skated on Whitby ponds using a skate and a spiked crutch. As Shareholder Number One of Maple Leaf Gardens, he frequently sent programs home to Whitby to his friends and brothers' children. He was considered an authority on the Maple Leafs in his home town.

Particularly fond of children, MacCarl organized and conducted picnics a couple of times a year for the motor-men's children of the TTC at his own expense.

Norman MacCarl's younger brother, Walter, entered the hardware business in 1911 in George M. Rice's store north of the Bank of Commerce on Brock Street. Except for service in the First World War, he operated a hardware business in Whitby until his retirement in 1967. Walter's son, Ralph MacCarl (1924-1996), a nephew of Norman, carried on the business until he retired in 1984. The MacCarl family's sporting interest was carried on by Ralph's brother Neil, a recently retired sports reporter for The Toronto Star.

The Toronto Maple Leafs played their last game in Maple Leaf Gardens on Feb. 13, 1999, and then moved to the Air Canada Centre adjacent to Union Station, ending a 68-year association with the hockey palace on Carleton Street.

Whitby Men Who Have Served In The National Hockey League

Ross Lowe
Boston Bruins, 1948-50
Montreal Canadiens, 1950-51

Peter Vipond
California Golden Seals, 1967-76

Dunc Wilson
Toronto Maple Leafs, 1973-78
Vancouver, 1970, 1972, 1979
New York Rangers, 1976-77
Pittsburg Penguins, 1979

Mike Keenan (Coach)
Philadelphia Flyers, 1984-87
Chicago Black Hawks, 1988-92
New York Rangers, 1993-94
St. Louis Blues, 1994-96
Vancouver Canucks, 1997-99

Gary Roberts
Calgary Flames, 1986-96
Carolina Hurricanes, 1997-

Joe Nieuwendyk
Calgary Flames, 1987-95
Dallas Stars, 1995-

Brad Balgarno
New York Islanders, 1987-88

Keith Primeau
Detroit Red Wings, 1990-96
Hartford Whalers, 1996-97
Carolina Hurricanes, 1997

Adam Foote
Quebec Nordiques, 1991-95
Colorado Avalanche, 1995-

Wayne Primeau
Buffalo Sabres, 1994-

Jamie Allison
Calgary Flames, 1994-99
Chicago Black Hawks, 1999-

John R. Frost Kept Whitby On The "Straight and Narrow"

No person in Whitby's recent history was probably better known than John R. Frost (1901-1983), Clerk-Treasurer and later Administrator of the town. In a career which spanned 47 years, he saved Whitby from bankruptcy during the Great Depression of the 1930s and guided it into the modern post-war era with its rapid residential development and industrial expansion. At Frost's retirement dinner in January 1971, former Mayor Harry W. Jermyn said: *"At the inaugural meeting of Council, the councillors would get up and say what they were going to do. After the meeting, Mr. Frost would tell them what they could do."*

"Frostie", as he was known to his friends in Whitby, was born at Castle Douglas, Scotland and got his financial training in the counting house of Lewis's Department Store in Liverpool, England. At the age of 22, in 1923, he decided to join his half-brother, William D. Dykes, a successful businessman in Whitby who was in charge of the Greater Canada Improvement and Land Company. Frost stepped off the train at the Whitby Junction Station (now Whitby Arts Station Gallery), with 25 dollars in his pocket on April 3, 1923. It was 3 a.m. and there was no one at the station to meet him. He checked his baggage and walked uptown to the Four Corners at Brock and Dundas Streets where he met

John R. Frost in 1929.

John Thomas (1885-1950), the night watchman.

"Pardon me," inquired Frost. *"Do you know where Mr. Dykes lives?" "Yes, I know,"* was the reply. *"Then, would you mind telling me where he lives,"* he asked. *"Three blocks east on the north side of the road." "I'm sorry,"* replied Frost, *"but I don't know east from west. Which way is east?"*

This was his introduction to Whitby.

John Frost's first job in Whitby was scrubbing the floor of the town armories (where the dental building is on Dundas Street beside the Cenotaph) for five dollars. He was later able to get a job tightening bolts on the rails of the Toronto and Eastern Railway which was being built through town on Mary Street. Within a few days, the railway went bankrupt and he lost his job.

Luck was soon to change for John R. Frost. Mayor Richard N. Bassett (1880-1940) quarreled with the Clerk-Treasurer, Albert W. Jackson (1870-1939) and Jackson resigned. William D. Dykes was appointed to the position and hired Frost as his assistant. His appointment was not popular at first for the townspeople said *"Albert Jackson did not need an assistant, so why should Mr. Dykes?"* Frost soon proved his worth by taking over the treasurer's job and balanced six tax rolls from previous years that the tax collector had failed to complete. He shared his office in the Town Hall at Brock and Colborne Streets with the Chief of Police, Charles F. McGrotty, night watchman John Thomas and a typist. At the back of the room was George W.P. Every (1880-1933), manager of the Public Utilities Commission and his secretary, Marcia Ross (1889-1979).

At the end of 1924, frost was paid fifteen dollars a week for his services. Two years later Dykes resigned as Clerk-Treasurer and Frost got the job, one he would hold for 40 years. His office was open from 10 a.m to 4 p.m. according to the town bylaws, but he often stayed till 5 p.m. to accommodate out-of-town visitors who had business with the corporation of the Town of Whitby.

As Clerk-Treasurer, Frost found his duties expanded considerably. At the end of each year he was required to present the town's financial statement to the ratepayers at a public meeting. After the financial statement was examined carefully, to see why Mr. Jones was paid 50 cents more than Mr. Smith, up to 500 people would cram into the town hall for nomination night. As Clerk-Treasurer, Frost presided over the nomination meetings for the municipal elections. These could be riotous affairs. At this first nomination meeting, Frost had two nominees swinging at each other over his head, while the crowd yelled: *"Go to it."* The speeches left nothing unsaid. One candidate for Mayor, in describing his opponent, cried: *"Who is he? What is he? I go to the Registry Office, I go to the Sheriff's office and all I can find are judgments against him."*

Following the nomination meeting, Frost acted as returning officer of the election, in charge of the town's five polling stations. As returning officer, he could not vote in a

municipal election, and did not cast a ballot until the 1969 election when William H. Wallace was returning officer. As clerk, he was allowed to break a tie in an election, a privilege he exercised only once. The tied vote was for low man on council and Frost chose the incumbent. *"It was the only municipal vote I cast in 45 years,"* he said, *"and everyone knew how I voted."*

During the 1927 election, one candidate who had been nominated and qualified, decided he did not want to run for office. When he approached Frost to have his name taken off the ballot, the clerk told him because he qualified, his name had to remain. On election day, the unwilling candidate stopped each person he met on the street, saying *"Please don't vote for me, sir."* He was not elected, much to his relief.

Another duty of the clerk was to issue marriage licences at five dollars each. On one occasion, a widow and a sailor came to Frost's office and asked for a licence. While he was writing the licence the widow asked Frost: *"Do you think I'm making a mistake?"* *"Frankly, I don't know,"* replied Frost. *"I'm not married."* The couple were duly united without further questions. Marriage licences issued through the clerk's office were valid for three months so that the marriage would be performed soon after the licence was issued. One day, Frost received a call from a

secretary at the Crown Attorney's office. She said her boss had married a couple three months previously, and they wanted to know if they had to renew the licence.

Frost had several other jobs to perform as well as Clerk-Treasurer. He was secretary for organizations like the Board of Health, Housing Commission and Police Court and was also treasurer for the Whitby Street Fair, a forerunner of the County Town Carnival. The first year of the Street Fair, 1926, he found himself deluged with $800 in change and had to devise a system to sort out the quarters, dimes and nickels that came into his office.

Frost's life was not all work, although the hours were long. He often acted as tenor soloist as minstrel shows presented in the old Town Hall by the Whitby Citizens' Band. In his first show in 1925 he sang a number called *"Linger Awhile."* As he finished the song, a member of the orchestra handed him a bouquet of leeks, onions and carrots. A note attached to the bouquet read: *"May the odor of these leeks and onions remain with you as long as the memory of your song remains in our hearts."* It was a present from one of the secretaries in the town office.

John Frost was appointed treasurer of the new Whitby Chamber of Commerce in 1928 and joined the Whitby Rotary Club

Whitby Municipal Office Staff, 1928. Left to right: John R. Frost, Clerk-Treasurer; Helena Richardson, Clerk's Secretary; Marcia Ross, Public Utilities Commission Bookkeeper; Herbert Gunson, Police Chief.

Rotary Club to buy the shares of the club and pay off the taxes. Thus, he managed to save what he called *"one of the finest bowling greens between Toronto and Montreal."* The lawn bowling green remains on the same site to this day beside the Seniors' Activity Centre. In 1973, the Rotary Club sold the land behind the bowling green to Central Mortgage and Housing for construction of a senior citizens' apartment building. The tennis courts became a parking lot and were relocated at Iroquois Park.

Whitby suffered financially during the Depression, but it could have been much worse without Frost's able management. He served for a few years as welfare officer, issuing food vouchers for use at local stores instead of money. Everyone on welfare was laid off relief on the first of May and told to get a job. They could re-apply in September when there were always fewer welfare cases. By the end of 1933, 70 families were on relief. Transients spent the night in the lock-up in the basement of the Town Hall. They slept on canvas cots provided by the Chamber of Commerce. The police department issued them meal tickets for which the town paid 25 cents each. Stone and wood piles were provided behind the town hall to give work to the unemployed. The wood had to be cut for fuel and the stone was broken for use on the roads. Starting in

when it was formed in 1933. As president of the Rotary Club in 1942-43, Frost saved the Whitby Lawn Bowling and Tennis Club from extinction. Founded in 1927, the club suffered badly during the Depression of the 1930s and by 1942 owed $1,200 in back taxes. The Council decided to sell the club's land for taxes, but Frost convinced the

Whitby Municipal Office Staff, 1955. Back Row: Verna Atkins, Robert Harding, Forbes McEwen. Front Row: Helena Richardson, John R. Frost, Verna Sandford.

saying this was the easy way out and would mean more financial trouble in the future. In an effort to collect outstanding taxes, Frost hired a man on commission to go door-to-door to collect the taxes. The tactic worked very well, for whenever the man was seen at a house, it was known that the occupants owed taxes. Not wanting their neighbours to find out, those who owed money quickly paid up. Frost described this process as a psychological thing. In one case, the town seized a businessman's store for back taxes and he had to purchase it back from the town in order to regain title to it. While other municipalities went bankrupt, Whitby remained solvent during the Depression, never stopping payment on its debentures. The reputation gained by the town at this time had a strong impact on its ability to sell debentures ever since. But in spite of his best efforts, Frost found that the Town Council had to cut his salary by $160 in 1933.

Due to Frost's efforts, Whitby gained another important facility in the 1950s. In the 1930s the town had a flourishing yacht club at the lake, but it disbanded when its executive and members went overseas to fight in the Second World War.

When the club did not re-form after the war and there was no likelihood that it would, Frost got approval to give its $3,000

1933, transients had to cut a certain amount of wood before being issued meal tickets. One transient, smoking on his canvas cot in the basement of the Town Hall in 1939, started a fire which almost burned the building down.

The greatest problem faced by Frost during the Depression was the collection of taxes. By 1934, the tax arrears amounted to nearly $72,000 and the banks wanted to call in the town loans. Frost appealed for help from the Ontario Railway and Municipal Board which suggested he issue debentures to cover the losses. Frost refused,

in assets to the fund to build a new community arena in 1953/54. As treasurer of the yacht club, Frost was in charge of this money.

Whitby obtained some of its industrial land at Lake Ontario through the efforts of John Frost. During the 1930s, the water level at the lake receded considerably, exposing large tracts of land at the harbour. Frost learned from the Registry Office that the original deeds of the property issued to John Scadding at the beginning of the 19th century stated that he owned land *"to the water's edge."* Frost got the town assessor to assess the land gained by the receding water to the Estate of John Scadding. If taxes were not paid on these lands for three years, the town could advertise the land for sale to the highest bidder. When the three years were up, Frost sold the land to the Town of Whitby, gaining at least 10 acres of prime industrial land for future development. Subsequently, in the 1950s, the Town of Whitby for one dollar traded some of this property for Federal Government land to enable Bathrust Containers to build a factory near the lake.

During the Second World War, the town formed an Air Raid Precaution Committee with Frost as secretary. Regular air raid drills were held under his supervision. Frost also served as chairman of the Whitby War Effort Committee's salvage committee. Long before the days of blue boxes and recycling, the people of Whitby willingly gave their newspaper, tin cans and scrap metal for the war effort. At the end of 1942, Frost reported 82 tons of salvage collected at a profit of about $600 which was spent on cigarettes and other comforts for the town's servicemen overseas.

A veteran of the First World War, Frost was called upon to drill would-be soldiers at the High School Grounds, because of his military training.

After the Second World War ended, Frost was Whitby's unofficial Industrial Commissioner, responsible for bringing industry from Toronto to the town. The big break came in 1947 when Dunlop Tire and Rubber Company announced it would move its factory to Whitby. Many years of negotiations on details followed, with Frost and Mayor Harry Jermyn taking a leading role. The negotiations were so delicate and secretive that meetings were held with Dunlop officials in cars on back roads instead of at the Town Hall. Finally, in 1954, construction of the Dunlop plant began, bringing 600 jobs to Whitby.

A member of Composite Masonic Lodge, Frost was the last person to receive a degree in the old Masonic Hall on Brock Street north and the first to receive a degree in the new hall next to the Bank of Commerce in 1926. He was in charge of the sale of the old lodge and the building of the new Masonic Temple on Cochrane Street in 1963/64, and arranged for some of the lodge property to be the site for the new St. Andrew's Presbyterian Church in 1967. On July 6, 1967, he and Mrs. Lloyd Campbell, daughter of former minister Rev. David Marshall (1890-1964) turned the sod for the new church.

In 1966, Frost was appointed Clerk-Administrator of the Town of Whitby, and when amalgamation of the Town and Township of Whitby occurred in 1968, he was named Administrator, in charge of all the municipal departments. In tribute to his services to Whitby, John Frost was awarded the Canada Centennial medal in 1967, and on his retirement in January 1971, he was the first individual to receive the Freedom of the Town of Whitby. Previously it had been granted to Ontario's Fire Fighters in 1939 when they held a convention in Whitby, and to the Ontario Regiment which celebrated its centennial in 1966. Frost Drive, in the Otter Creek subdivision, is another tribute to his memory.

On New Year's Day, 1936, John R. Frost married Marjorie Baker, a Whitby school teacher. She still lives in Whitby.

The Whit-Knit Club Was Active On The Home Front

Throughout the Second World War, a group of Whitby women provided a valuable service for the town's military personnel serving overseas. Known as the Whit-Knit Club, the girls knitted socks, provided candy and cigarettes, and raised money for a number of war charities.

The Whit-Knit Club, which stood for *"Whitby Knitters"*, was formed by 15 young women late in 1940. After doing work for a while for other organizations, they decided to form their own club, which was chartered under the War Charities Act, on June 25, 1941.

The Whit-Knit Club expanded its membership, elected an executive, framed its own rules and regulations, and began an ambitious program to aid the men who had gone off to war. Meeting once a week at the homes of various members, each woman paid a monthly membership fee of 50 cents so the club could purchase wool. The group's aim was to send a pair of knitted army socks to every Whitby man overseas. By September 1941, more than 100 pairs of socks were shipped to Whitby men and the club began work on a second shipment.

The second shipment, as well as socks, included a carton of cigarettes for each soldier, a large chocolate bar and a package of razor blades. To finance their expanded

Members of the Whit-Knit Club cut lawns to raise money to aid Whitby's servicemen. Left to right: Jean Heard, Grace Richardson, Mary Mathison, Verna Reid, Vera Richardson, Alice Threadgold, Betty Lawler, Ruth Ball, Madge Heard, Eileen McBride. This photograph was taken in Russell Hatch's yard at Byron and Dunlop Streets in the summer of 1943.

operations, the members of the Whit-Knit Club began doing odd jobs in their spare time, such as cutting lawns. It was hard work, as the women had to push old-fashioned hand-propelled mowers. Other sources of revenue included baby-sitting, waiting on tables and hosting dances.

An anniversary dance was held by the club at the Whitby High School on Colborne Street on Oct. 24, 1941. The members also acted as waitresses at a Rotary Club dinner at the Ontario Ladies' College (now Trafalgar Castle School).

They received much favourable publicity,

both from the Oshawa Times-Gazette and the Toronto media. In an article published in the Toronto Daily Star on Sept. 24, 1941, Mayor Fred Rowe said: *"These girls nearly all have regular jobs of their own during the day time, but they unselfishly give many of their leisure hours to help brighten the lives of our boys on overseas service. This club is certainly something Whitby can be proud of."*

In September, 1941, the club members were: President, Alice Threadgold; Secretary, Ella Muir; Treasurer, Betty Lawler; *"Babs"* Muir, Vera Richardson, Grace Richardson, Eileen McBride, Verna McNeill, Jean Sheppard, Mary Mathison, Jean Heard, Madge Heard, Mary Anderson, Ruth Ball and Elizabeth Correll.

Half the proceeds of one of the club's dances was given to aid British bomb victims, while money was also provided to the Whitby War Effort Committee and the Red Cross Society.

In October 1942, about 200 people, many from out of town, attended the Whit-Knit Club's second annual dance in the high school auditorium. Bridge and euchre tables were set up at the dance. A number of airmen from the flight training school at the Oshawa airport were introduced by Elizabeth Correll, who acted as hostess.

Patrons and patronesses for the event were Mr. and Mrs. Andrew Muir, Mrs. John H. Perry, Mrs. R.B. Insole and Miss Jean Heard, president of the club for that year.

By the end of 1943, the Whit-Knit Club has provided 321 soldiers, sailors and airmen with parcels at a cost of two dollars each. The average proceeds from each of the club's dances was $150. Among the organizations receiving money from the Whit-Knit Club were the Town of Whitby, Red Cross, Salvation Army, British War Victims' Fund, Whitby War Effort committee and Chinese and Greek War Relief.

The club kept a scrapbook of press clippings and letters from the Whitby boys thanking the members for their gifts. In a letter dated June 17, 1941, Bill Brown (1898-1973), serving with the Canadian Post Office overseas, said: *"The spirit of your club members is grand and I hope you girls will continue on in the same way, for you can hardly realize how much it means to hear from friends at home. I am certainly pleased to answer your friendly note and to say that the socks are such a good fit and that I also thought it a nice touch to finish them off with your club colours,"* (khaki and gold for enlisted men and black for officers). After the war, Bill Brown returned to Whitby where he served as postmaster from 1947 to 1963.

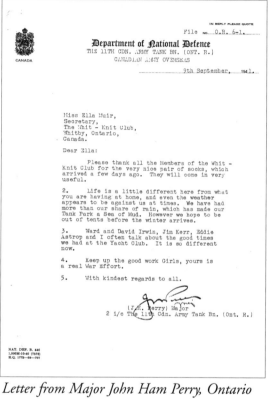

Letter from Major John Ham Perry, Ontario Regiment, to Ella Muir, Secretary of the Whit-Knit Club, Sept. 9, 1941. Major Perry (1892-1976), a grandson of Whitby's founder Peter Perry, is thanking Miss Muir for a pair of socks sent to him by the club, and gives some news of Whitby men from the old Yacht Club, of which he was Commodore before going overseas.

The Ship That Took Whitby's Name to War

During the dark days of the Second World War more than 100 ships named after Canadian towns and cities patrolled the North Atlantic, protecting our country from Nazi attacks. Among these ships was a Corvette named the H.M.C.S. Whitby, sponsored by the citizens of our town. For nine months it was part of the Royal Canadian Navy's fleet which helped win the war.

Early in 1943, the Whitby Town Council received a request from the Federal Government to assist in the outfitting of a ship that would bear its name. The Council turned the project over to the Whitby War Effort committee under the chairmanship Francis McIntyre (1891-1958), a local hardware dealer and former president of the Whitby Chamber of Commerce. A separate Corvette Committee was then formed under the chairmanship of James Bell.

The purpose of Canadian communities adopting war ships of the Royal Canadian Navy was to provide for the crews of these vessels the amenities that could not be provided by the government. The sponsorship gave sailors an identity with a certain place in Canada and a civic family to correspond with during their long days at sea.

On Sept.18, 1943, a delegation from the town of Whitby attended the launching of the H.M.C.S. Whitby at the government

Whitby Town representatives at the launching of the H.M.C.S Whitby at Midland, Ontario, September 18, 1943.

Back Row: Mayor Fred Rowe, Clerk-Treasure John R. Frost, War Effort Committee Chairman Francis McIntyre, Deputy Reeve James H. Ormiston, Rev. A.E. Ingram, Mrs. John S. Leitch, Reeve Robert M. Deverell, Councillor Robert McNee.

Front Row: Councilor Andrew Muir, Councillor Peter Draimin, Councillor Warren J. Mowat.

shipyards, at Midland, Ontario. The delegation consisted of Mayor Fred Rowe, Reeve Bob Deverell, Deputy Reeve James H. Ormiston, Councillors Robert McNee, Andrew Muir, Warren J. Mowat and Peter Draimin, Clerk-Treasurer John R. Frost and Francis McIntyre. The launch date was declared *"Ships for Victory Day"* by the Department of Munitions and Supply. The H.M.C.S. Whitby was one of the 12 ships launched that day. The launching was performed by Mrs. John S. Leitch, wife of a Midland shipping official, and the blessing was given by Rev. A.E.W. Ingram, rector of St. Mark's Anglican Church at Midland.

The H.M.C.S. Whitby, which cost $700,000, was designed to escort convoys, patrol the Canadian coast line and act as a defense against Nazi Submarines. Two hundred feet long and 33 feet wide, it carried four-inch machine guns and depth charges and was manned by a crew of 70. On April 13, 1944, Lieutenant R.K. Lester, skipper of the H.M.C.S. Whitby, was given a dinner at the Royal Hotel on Brock Street North by the Times-Gazette, the Oshawa-Whitby newspaper which was published three times a week, Tuesday, Thursday and Saturday. James H. *"Scotty"* Ormiston (1889-1957), its Whitby editor, presided as chairman.

Lieut. Lester was a veteran of naval warfare, being an anti-submarine control officer aboard the H.M.C.S. Wetaskiwin in 1942. He was mentioned in dispatches during the sinking of U-Boats that year. Before attending the dinner in his honour, Lieut. Lester and the crew of the H.M.C.S. Whitby visited William H. Moore, M.P. (1872-1960) at his home in Dunbarton. At the dinner, attended by the Town Council, Public Utilities Commission, Library Board, Ministerial Association and representatives of local industries, Lieut. Lester was presented with a set of brass match cases for his crew, manufactured by Whitby Malleable Iron and Brass Company, popularly known as the buckle factory.

A library of 100 books was also presented by the public library board, each book being inscribed by a Whitby citizen who donated it. This gift was augmented by 100 additional books given by the Viscount Greenwood Chapter of the Imperial Order of the Daughters of the Empire, which was founded in Whitby in 1938 and named after the town's most famous son, Hamar Viscount Greenwood (1870-1948).

By May 1944, the H.M.C.S Whitby was commissioned and due to leave Canada for active service in July. On June 20, 1944, a civic reception at the Town Hall was provided for 50 members of the crew of the ship, who arrived from Toronto by bus. Following a parade led by the band of the H.M.C.S. York and the Oshawa Sea Cadets, the crew was tendered a supper in the Council Chambers. Following speeches by Mayer Rowe, Francis McIntyre and J.H. Ormiston, Lieut. Lester introduced his officers and crew. Ormiston presented a photograph of the ship taken a few days before and spoke of the bronze plaque bearing the Whitby town crest given to the ship some months earlier by the town council. A number of Whitby organiza-tions announced at this reception the gifts they were providing to the H.M.C.S. Whitby. Branch 112 of the Canadian Legion presented a record player and records, while downtown merchants gave a sound system which was paid for by subscription from the business community. Other gifts included electrical appliances, musical instruments and a washing machine. In all, 15 cases of goods from the citizens of Whitby had been shipped to Midland during the ship's construction.

The supper, which was followed by a dance was provided by a committee of Mrs. Frank Wells, Mrs. Fred Marsh and William Harden (1883-1949), chief chef at the Ontario Hospital (now the Whitby Mental Health Centre). The dance committee consisted of Misses Alice Threadgold and Eleanor Correll. Robert Anderson, caretaker of the high school, was in charge of decorating the town hall with flags and coloured lights.

Ten days later, on June 30, 1944, the H.M.C.S Whitby paid a visit to its sponsoring town. It had been hoped that the ship would be able to tie up at the wharf at Port Whitby, but the water channel was not deep enough. Instead, the ship was anchored about a mile off the pier, and groups of Whitby citizens were taken by small boats to tour the town's adopted warship. Because of gasoline rationing, power launches were not

The Commissioning Crew of the H.M.C.S Whitby, June 6, 1944.

available to take citizens to and from the H.M.C.S Whitby. Therefore, they had to find their own transportation.

The H.M.C.S Whitby sailed for an unknown destination after its visit to Whitby and spent nearly a year on patrol in the North Atlantic. The sailors were well supplied with gifts of tobacco, letters and supplies by the citizens of Whitby for the duration of the war.

In July 1945, the H.M.C.S Whitby and 87 other Corvettes were decommissioned and turned over the War Assets Corporation for disposal. Most of the ships were dismantled at Sorel, Quebec, and soon became only a memory. Official records state that the H.M.C.S Whitby was commissioned at Midland on June 6, 1944, and arrived in Halifax on August 16, owing to repairs at Sherburne. Following

time at Bermuda in September, the ship arrived at St. John's Newfoundland on Sept. 30. On Oct 5, she sailed for Londonderry to join the group with which she served until June 1945 when she returned to Canada. The crew was paid off on July 16, and the ship placed in reserve in Sorel. The H.M.C.S Whitby was not broken up immediately like some of the other Corvettes, but was sold in 1946 for merchant service and reportedly named *"Bengo"*. Its final fate is not known. It is believed that 235 serviceman were members of the ships crew's at various times during the war.

One souvenir of the H.M.C.S Whitby was returned to the town for which it was named, after the war. On April 7, 1948, the ship's bell was presented to Mayor William Davidson (1889-1965) at a special ceremony in the Whitby Town Hall by Lieut. P.C. Benson of the Royal Canadian Navy. In 1959 the bell was presented to the Canadian Legion (now Royal Canadian Legion) by Mayor Harry Jermyn, who built

in into a speakers podium. Legion president Harry Inkpen was instrumental in acquiring the bell from the town hall and giving it a permanent home.

In January 1984, the Whitby Town Council granted $100 to place a plaque in the H.M.C.S Sackville, the last of the 100 Corvettes named after Canadian cities and towns 40 years previously. The Sackville is now a floating exhibit at the Maritime Museum in Halifax, Nova Scotia, where the H.M.C.S Whitby plaque is seen by thousands of visitors a year.

A book for the *Library of the*
CORVETTE "WHITBY"
from the personnel and friends
of the
Whitby Public Library
With the Compliments and Best Wishes of
Name *Rev. A. G. Channen.*
Address *Whitby.*

(Paste on inside front cover of book)

A book plate from a presentation copy of Mark Twain's "Huckleberry Finn", presented to the Corvette "Whitby" by Rev. A. G. Channen of All Saints's Anglican Church

Whitby "Took On A Mardi Gras Appearance" At The End Of The War

Like many other communities in Canada, Whitby celebrated the end of the Second World War with great rejoicing, prayers of thanksgiving and parades. Tuesday, May 8, 1945 was officially declared V.E. Day (for Victory in Europe) although some of the celebrations began on May 7, the day that Germany surrendered. Services were held in Whitby's churches that day, one of which was at the Baptist Church at Centre and Colborne Streets (demolished in 1977). One of the features of the service was *"Reading of the honour roll with a moment's silence after the name of each one who has paid the supreme sacrifice, followed by a prayer from the congregation for all who mourn and all who are left to face life handicapped because of the war."*

On May 8, one of the largest parades Whitby had seen in many years, marched from the Town Park (now Rotary Centennial Park) to a service at the Cenotaph at Dundas and Green Streets, and back to the park for a community service of thanksgiving. Practically every organization in the town was represented, including the town council, the Canadian Legion and its newly-formed ladies' auxiliary, children from all the schools, the fire department, Boy Scouts, Girl Guides, Cubs and Brownies and members of the Whitby Ministerial Association. The parade was led

Public school students bearing flags: Gerald Walsh, William Rowley, Bob Bradley, Ron Atkinson, John Greer, Carl Disney.

by the recently reorganized Whitby Citizens' Band.

At the Cenotaph, a wreath was laid by Mayor Robert Deverell (1885-1962) in recognition of the 31 Whitby men who had been killed in the Second World War and the 40 killed in the First World War. Rev. David Marshall (1890-1964) of St. Andrew's Presbyterian Church, conducted a

brief service that ended with the playing of the bugle by Jim Wilde (1899-1984) as the crowd stood bare-headed in respectful silence.

The parade then re-formed and, joined by the public and high school students, proceeded to the town park. At the park, Reeve Robert McNee (1890-1962), chairman of the V.E. Day committee, addressed the

High School Cadets lined up at the Cenotaph on V.E. Day, Des Denyer, Everett Fleming, John Archibald, Stuart Roblin, Wilmot Gates, George Rae.

Government, Dr. Donald R. Fletcher (1885-1956) addressed the crowd. He was followed by a Thanksgiving Prayer sung by the massed children's choir.

A hush fell upon the crowd as loud-speakers set up in the park brought the voice of King George VI in his address to the Empire, which was clearly heard throughout the park. Following the King's message, Rev. Clifford G. Park (1900-1993) of the Whitby United Church (now St. Mark's) offered a prayer of thanksgiving. Rev. Langford read an Intercessionary Prayer for the King, followed by the Prayer of Dedication, read by Rev. Hugh G. Crozier (1873-1965), a retired United Church minister. Rev. A. Gordon Channen (1906-1960) of All Saints' Anglican Church, pronounced the benediction. Following the service in the park, the parade re-formed and marched uptown where it dispersed.

In the evening, a Victory Dance was held in the town hall at Brock and Colborne Streets when the fire hall is now.

When the official word of Germany's surrender was heard over the radio at 9:30 a.m. on May 7, people rushed into the street waving Union Jack flags they had saved for weeks in anticipation of the event. The Times-Gazette, Whitby and Oshawa's newspaper, stated the downtown business section *"took on a Mardi Gras appearance,"* although

gathering, after which a prayer of invocation was read by Rev. F.T. Darnell of the Baptist Church. This was followed by a word of introduction by Rev. Douglas B. Langford (1876-1949) of St. John's Anglican Church. Mrs. Vernon Rowe (1903-1958), Whitby's school music teacher, for whom a public school was named in 1959, led a massed choir of children, singing *"O God Our Help in Ages Past,"* followed by a prayer for the dead by Rev. Marshall.

Mayor Deverell asked the townspeople to curb their celebrations with thoughts of those who had paid the supreme sacrifice, and to go forward with a grim determination to defeat the forces of Japan, which did not surrender until the end of August. As a representative of the Dominion

most industries continued to work up to 5 p.m. At 3 p.m. sharp, the siren behind the town hall sounded, making the news official. By 5 p.m. the taxis stopped running and most stores hung out signs stating they were closed until Wednesday, May 9. Hotel beverage rooms closed long before that hour and the brewers' warehouse also closed.

Although V.E. Day was a time for celebration for most Whitby residents, it was a time of stress and sadness for others. One girl attending the celebrations fainted during the service because her father had been killed during the war. Whitby's chief constable William J. Elliott (1885-1964) reported that everything was orderly and there was no trouble during Whitby's V.E. Day celebrations. The only incident worth reporting was a car stolen from a residence on the night of May 7.

The Times-Gazette of May 10, 1945 contained the following message from the celebrations committee: *"Thanks to the citizens of the Town of Whitby and particularly those who took an active part in the V.E. Day celebration for the splendid response and co-operation given, which made the proceeding commendable and successful. R. McNee, Chairman, Whitby Town Council, V.E. Day."*

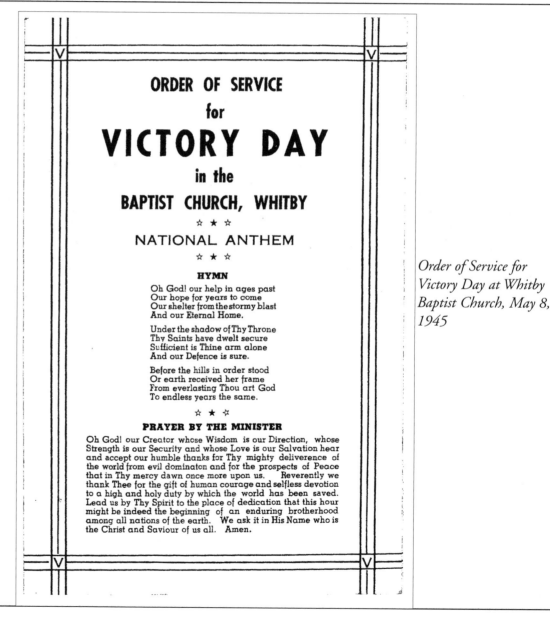

Order of Service for Victory Day at Whitby Baptist Church, May 8, 1945

Arthur Allin's Gift To Whitby

Most people when they make a will, give money to their relatives, but Arthur Allin (1869-1945) gave Whitby a new Town Hall. Allin, who died on March 11, 1945, was a wealthy bachelor who made his fortune by careful investment. He was a world traveller who had also accumulated a considerable collection of fine art during his travels.

Allin had a very specific idea in mind when he drew up his will on Dec. 20, 1944. After providing enough money for his two unmarried sisters, Marion and Lillian, and a number of organizations in Whitby, he directed that the residue of his estate be turned over to the town for the construction of a new town hall. Since 1912, Allin had lived in a large brick house at the corner of Green and Colborne Streets (now a restaurant), opposite the town hall which was located where the fire hall is now at Brock and Colborne Streets. Every day, Allin looked out his front window at the town works yard behind the municipal building. He was annoyed at the junk he saw piled in the works yard, and considered the town hall, built in 1877 to be a disgrace to the Town of Whitby. When he died, Allin left an estate of nearly $300,000. After sister Marion's death in 1949, the estate was settled, leaving $113,366 to the town. The town council invested the money and by the time a new town hall was built in 1959/60,

the fund had grown to $146,000.

It was ten years after Allin's death that the Town Council began to consider construction of a new municipal building. The biggest problem facing the council was where to build it. A proposal to construct the hall in Centennial Park, the site of the first town hall from 1857 to 1879, was defeated when ratepayers demanded that parkland be preserved. In 1958, the council purchased the Samuel Trees estate on the block bounded by Dundas, Henry, Colborne and King Streets. The council had the Trees house demolished and turned the sod for the new town hall on Sept. 22, 1959. The town hall, a one-storey concrete and stone building, was officially opened by the Hon. William K. Warrender, Ontario Minister of Municipal Affairs, on Nov. 4, 1960. A modern marvel for its day, the Whitby Municipal Building was featured on the cover of the Royal Architectural Institute of Canada Journal of August 1961.

With the rapid growth of Whitby in the 1960s and 1970s, Arthur Allin's town Hall soon became too small. A new municipal building on Rossland Road replaced it in 1977, and the old town hall became the home of the Whitby Public Library. A plaque on the wall at the front entrance dedicates the building to the memory of Arthur Allin.

Allin was an influential figure in Whitby's history for more than 50 years. The son of Lewis Allin a book and stationery dealer who had a store on Brock Street South, Allin, early in life, decided to become a druggist. After graduating from the Ontario College of Pharmacy, he worked as a clerk in Toronto for six years before purchasing the drug store at Brock and Dundas Streets (now Van Belle Flowers) from James McCullough in 1896. For 48 years, Allin operated his drug store, with the exception of three months in 1931 when he retired and sold the store. Retirement was not to his liking, so he bought back the store for considerably more than the selling price, and continued to operate it until ill health forced him to retire again in December of 1944.

On his final retirement, Allin gave the store to his two clerks, Frank Gray (1897-1976) and Norman Cormack (1906-1993) as a Christmas present. Both had served in Allin's store for more than 25 years. They carried on the Allin drug store until 1969 when Gray retired and Cormack went into partnership with Donald Courtice (1917-1996). Norman Cormack retired in 1987, after serving more than 60 years as a druggist.

A public-spirited man, Allin served on the Public Utilities Commission in Whitby

Arthur Allin standing in front of his store at Brock and Dundas Streets, 1904.

from 1915 until his death 30 years later. He was a charter member of the Whitby Rotary Club when it was formed in 1933, serving as the club's first treasurer.

Arthur Street was named after Arthur Allin, in 1955, in recognition of his contri-butions to the Town, and there is a plaque in his memory in the Whitby Royal Canadian Legion Hall.

Laying of the corner stone for Arthur Allin's Municipal building, July 19, 1960. Left to right: Police Chief George Rankine, Councillor Paul Coath, Councillor Joyce Burns, Rev. David Marchall, Councillor William Davidson, Tommy Thomas, M.P.P.; Dr. Matthew Dymond, M.P.P.; Mayor Stan Martin. In front at left, Architect C.F.T. Rounthwaite. (Photo by Bill Stannett)

Fred W. Browne Paid Whitby Back Many Times For A Family Mistake

On Nov. 21, 1947, a 77-year-old former student at the Whitby High School presented three prizes in his name to deserving students at the high school's Commencement exercises. The presenter of the award was Fred W. Browne (1870-1956), who in the 1940s and early 1950s gave away thousands of dollars to worthy causes in the Whitby-Brooklin-Columbus area. When he was attending the Whitby Collegiate Institute in 1887, Browne won the school prizes for art, penmanship and geometry. Sixty years later he decided to establish the Fred W. Browne Memorial Prizes in these same subjects, as a tribute to his old school.

Shortly before the 1947 Commencement exercises, Browne set up a trust fund of $1,000 to be administered by former Whitby Mayors Ed Bowman (1892-1969) and Fred Rowe (1873-1959). Prizes of $100 each were awarded in 1947 to Jean McMinn for Grade 9 art, Marjorie Harris for Grade 11 penmanship and Fred Kahn for Grade 12 Geometry. The prizes are still awarded today for Grade 11 Mathematics.

It is said that Fred Browne devoted the later part of his life to philanthropy to pay back the community for a loss his family had accidentally inflicted many years before. In 1922, Fred's brother George Browne (1883-1966) was caretaker of St. Paul's Anglican Church, on the Columbus Road, half-way between Brooklin and Columbus. One day, when he was burning leaves in the church yard, the fire got out of control and burned down the frame church. Although it was an accident, Fred always felt he had to make amends for this unfortunate occurrence.

The story of Fred W. Browne's life reads like the rags-to-riches tales in the Horatio Alger books – a boy of modest means achieves great wealth and success. Fred Browne, one of five sons of William H. Browne (1837-1894), an Irish pioneer whose father came to the Whitby area in 1836, was born in a log cabin near Columbus, on Oct. 12, 1870. The Browne farm, one mile north and one mile

Fred W. Browne, Whitby's philanthropist

west of Columbus, was later owned by the Howden family. John Dundas Howden (1841-1927), Whitby's postmaster for 39 years, was Fred's uncle.

Browne attended the Columbus Public School, long since gone, where he won first prize in proficiency. After graduating from the Whitby Collegiate Institute, he attended a military college connected with the Stanley Barracks on the Canadian National Exhibition Grounds in Toronto, reaching the rank of second lieutenant in three months. Brown started his successful business career as a grocery clerk in Lindsay, where he was placed in charge of the liquor department, earning five dollars a week. After four years in Lindsay, he spent two years as a clerk for Whitby grocer Thomas Lawler (1828-1895) who kept a store where the Golden Gate Restaurant's dining room is now.

Upon the death of his father, Browne managed the family farm for a few years, before selling it and moving to Toronto in 1894, where he joined the grocery department of the Robert Simpson Company at the corner of Queen and Yonge Streets. The Simpson store burned down a year later, but was rebuilt and Browne was promoted to assistant manager of the grocery department. On May 24, 1898 he was married to Annie McIntyre, a clerk at the Simpson

St. Paul's Anglican Church, the church accidentally burned down by Fred Browne's brother. St. Paul's Church was built about 1835 by Rev. John Pentland, about a mile West of Columbus. All that remains of the site today is a graveyard, the first Anglican cemetery established in Whitby Township, which is still used for burials. Fred Browne's parents and his brother George are buried in this cemetery. The photograph dates from Circa. 1907.

store. When Robert Simpson heard of Browne's marriage, he gave him a raise to nine dollars a week.

In 1905, after Robert Simpson's death, Browne set out on his own, opening a grocery store at the corner of Carlton and Ontario Streets in Toronto. When the property across the street was being developed,

he bought the stores and in three years his new businesses were completely paid for. After 31 years in the grocery business on his own in Toronto, Fred Browne retired in 1936, with a considerable fortune to his credit. He moved to Leaside and started giving money to many organizations in Toronto, Whitby and Oshawa. Although reluctant to talk about his donations, he admitted that by November 1947, he had given away approximately $15,000.

"I never regretted giving away a penny of it," he said, *"because I was always brought up with the thought in mind to always be of a charitable nature."*

In October 1946, Browne paid for the restoration of the Bible Christian Cemetery west of Columbus. The broken and neglected stones were gathered together and placed in a cairn as a memorial to the pioneers of the area where Browne was born and grew up. In 1950, he acquired a copy of the Tremaine map of Ontario County, printed in 1860, a rare relic, and presented it to the Ontario County Council. For years it hung in the old court house (now Whitby Centennial Building) and is now in the committee room behind the council chambers in the Durham Region headquarters.

In 1952, when Browne heard that the original address on parchment from the Mayor and Council of the Town of Whitby to the Prince of Wales on his Canadian tour in 1860, was for sale at an auction house in London, England, he purchased it and gave it to the town. This historic document is now on display at the Town of Whitby Archives, along with one of Browne's high school certificates for proficiency in art, dated June 1, 1887.

Browne always took an interest in St. Thomas' Anglican Church, which his family attended in Brooklin. On May 10, 1936, he participated in the unveiling of a plaque in the church, commemorating the 100th anniversary of the arrival of the Browne family in Canada. Anglican Archbishop Derwyn T. Owen dedicated the plaque and subsequently Browne also donated a Hammond electric organ to the church, followed by a set of chimes.

In 1892, Browne joined Mount Zion Masonic Lodge in Brooklin, of which his father had been Worshipful Master in 1882-83. On the occasion of the 50th anniversary of his joining the lodge, Browne and his two surviving brothers donated a pair of Union Jack flags. Ten years later, in 1952, when he received his 60-year jewel, he donated $1,000 to Mount Zion Lodge to help pay the cost of its new hall in Brooklin.

The Uxbridge Cottage Hospital, Whitby's Fairview Lodge and the Brooklin Spring Fair were all recipients of generous gifts from Fred W. Browne. It will probably never be known how much money he donated and all the organizations that received it. In Toronto, he was a member of St. Peter's Anglican Church, contributing a considerable sum to paying off its mortgage.

Fred Browne's wife Annie died at their home in Leaside on May 8, 1944. In 1953 he married Kathleen May Read (1896-1989), widow of James M. Read (1889-1947) who was superintendent of the Ontario County House of Refuge at Whitby for 13 years. On the death of her first husband, Mrs. Read was named superintendent, and became the first administrator of Fairview Lodge when it opened in December 1951. She retired in 1953, shortly before she married Fred Browne, and died on Dec. 20, 1989 at the age of 93.

Fred W. Browne died at his home in Willowdale on June 9, 1956 at the age of 85, and was buried beside his first wife in Forest Lawn Mausoleum, Toronto. Rev. Kenneth W. Scott, of the Browne's old church, St. Thomas' in Brooklin, took part in the funeral service. A man who gave much to his community, Fred W. Browne is still known today through the prizes handed out in his name at Henry Street High School.

Next to R.S. McLaughlin of Oshawa, who gave millions of dollars to his city for beneficial projects, Fred Browne is the Whitby-Oshawa area's second greatest philanthropist. Although many of his gifts have been recorded, it is likely that there are a number that received no publicity and are unknown today. He is someone who should be remembered by today's generation.

How Two Clerical Errors Gave Thickson's Point Its Name

A bureaucratic blunder, not once, but twice, changed forever the name of one of Whitby's most historic sites. And it all began with a bridge. Many Whitby residents are not aware that Thickson's Point, at the end of Thickson Road, and Thickson Road itself, have borne the name of Thickson for only 51 years. The original names were Corbett's Point and Corbett's sideroad.

The story of Thickson's/Corbett's Point began 170 years ago when lots 19 and 20 in the Broken Front Concession on the shore of Lake Ontario, were settled by John Corbett (1791-1853). Corbett purchased lot 19 in 1827 and lot 20 in 1833. The land was at the mouth of Corbett Creek, forming a small marsh and a strip of beach along the lake shore which was to be a popular picnic spot since earliest pioneer times. Today it is known as Thickson's woods, and is the site of a number of homes. John Corbett and his descendants let the residents use the point for picnics and summer camping. The earliest record of a picnic at Corbett's point is in the Whitby Chronicle of 1857, but use of the camp grounds goes back long before that time. Every summer, church, fraternal and business groups made use of Corbett's Point. The Ontario Ladies' College (now Trafalgar Castle School) held picnics there on the day of its May Court Festival, and delegates to the summer missionary conferences which

Delegates from Ontario Ladies' College missionary conference at Corbett's Point, July, 1913.

began at the school in 1906, travelled to the site on hay waggons.

On Jan. 30, 1919, Jane B. McIntosh, a descendant of the family of John Corbett's wife, sold 110 acres of lot 20, east of Corbett's sideroad to James Norman Thickson (1884-1967) for $1,000. Thickson proceeded to subdivide the property into cottage lots and sold them to clients over the next 30 years. A prominent citizen of Oshawa, Thickson was born on Jan. 5, 1884 at Bowmanville and moved to Oshawa in 1906, where he operated a garage until his retirement in 1947. During the Second

World War, he was administrator of the Oshawa office of the Wartime Prices and Trade Board. A Mason for more than 50 years, and an active member of Simcoe Street United Church, he died on Christmas Day, 1967, at the age of 83.

The strange saga of the change of Corbett's to Thickson's Point commenced in 1939, when construction of Highway 401, then known as Highway 2-A, began through Whitby and Oshawa. In 1941 bridges were built across the new highway at Brock and Henry Streets in Whitby, and several locations in Oshawa, but there was no bridge or cloverleaf planned for the Corbett side road, leading to Corbett's Point.

When he found out about this, Thickson approached the Department of Highways at Queen's Park to try to obtain a cloverleaf on the road to his cottage development. Eventually, permission was granted by the Ontario Government. In 1947, a bridge was built, and there was where the trouble began.

On all the bridges constructed on Highway 401 in 1947, the name of the street crossing the highway was chiselled onto each bridge. This had not been done on the 1941 bridges. To Thickson's surprise, the name "Thickson Road" was chiselled on the new bridge under the Province of Ontario's coat of arms. A few of his friends

kidded him about it, and secretly, he was rather pleased that his name had been placed on the bridge.

However, the name bothered some residents of the area who felt the Corbett name should be on the bridge. After all, it had been Corbett's side road as long as anyone could remember. The residents approached local MPP T. Kelso Creighton (1892-1973) of Oshawa, asking that the name be changed back to Corbett Road.

Early in 1948, Thickson was surprised when one of his friends came up to him and said: *"What crime did you commit? They're taking your name off the bridge."* Thickson went to have a look and found that his name had been removed from the bridge. Apparently, Creighton's comments to the Minister of Highways about the complaints he had received, produced this result.

Now, Thickson was angry. It was one thing to name a road after him without his permission. This he did not mind. But to remove his name from the road and bridge! That was too much. He determined that from then on, Corbett's Point would be known as Thickson's Point, and to make sure, he signed documents at the Land Registry Office to give that name to his property.

How Thickson's name got on the bridge in the first place is a bit of a mystery, but one

possible explanation was offered to him. A clerical error appears to have been the cause. When he approached the Provincial Government about establishing a cloverleaf, Thickson was given copies of blueprints for it, which bore the notation: *"Thickson's Road."* Although that was not the official name of the road, a clerk might have written the name on the road because Thickson had been lobbying for the bridge. When the bridge was built, the authorities, based on this blueprint, assumed that the proper name was *"Thickson's Road."*

"I'm gong to call my property Thickson's Point, since this stupid action has caused me so much embarrassment," Thickson told The Toronto Telegram in March, 1948, after his name was removed from the bridge. *"Since the area was never registered, it has been my responsibility throughout the years to maintain roads and conveniences, and it's therefore logical since I still own the greater part of the property, that I can call it what I choose."*

It was a case of two wrongs don't make a right, first the naming of Thickson Road on a map by a clerk, and the decision to remove the name once it had been placed on the bridge. Thus, 120 years of history were changed at the stroke of a pen and a chisel.

The Citizens of Brooklin Saved This Park for the Community

Located in the centre of the hamlet of Brooklin is a small triangular tract of land known as Grass Park. A popular picnic spot for nearly a century, it is named, not for the green grass that grows there, but for its long-time owner Charles J. Grass (1861-1941).

The story of Grass Park begins nearly 150 years ago, when the site was purchased in 1855 by Joseph Wilkinson, who built the Globe Hotel. A large frame building facing Baldwin Street, the Globe Hotel was the centre of social and political life in Brooklin, until it was destroyed by fire on Feb. 11, 1885. Four years after the fire, Charles Grass, a native of Columbus, built the large frame house south of the Globe Hotel site, where he lived for the remainder of his life. For many years he operated the Brooklin Flour Mill, further east on Cassels Road. Since his house overlooked the site of the old Globe Hotel, Grass took an interest in the property and purchased it on May 28, 1907 from the Thomas Chinn family, the last owners of the hotel.

For the next 34 years, Grass maintained the property as a park at his own expense. He planted trees and made arrangements with the Brooklin Horticultural Society and the Ontario Department of Highways to install picnic tables. In return, the Whitby Township Council placed a low assessment on the park so Grass would not have to pay

The Globe Hotel, on the site of Grass Park, as it appeared in 1860.

much money in taxes. Grass Park became a popular picnic spot starting in the 1920s when motorists driving north on Highway 12 would stop there for a rest and a meal. Grass maintained a water supply at the park from an old well originally used by the

Globe Hotel.

Before his death on Dec. 11, 1941, Charles Grass willed his park to the Township of Whitby, but the Township Council turned down the bequest. On the death of his wife Jennie in 1949, their

Grass Park looking west toward Baldwin Street, from a 1924 post card.

daughter, Harriet Fraser offered to sell the property for $1,600. It was agreed that the site because of its shape and size, was unsuitable for development, and most residents felt it should remain as a park, but the Township Council was unable to agree on a price.

In June of 1951, Mrs. Fraser again offered the park to the township, stating if the asking price of $1,600 was not paid within 10 days, she would sell the land for development. At a special meeting held in the Township Hall (now the Brooklin Community Centre), on June 8, 1951, anxious Brooklin residents who finally realized that they could soon lose their beautiful park, decided to form a committee to conduct a canvass of the village to raise the required money. Although the park had been considered unsuitable for development in 1949, Counsellor William Heron stated that as long as it was a registered lot, it could be used for building. Since taxes were always paid on the park, the township did not have the right to expropriate the land. Although it was located on a provincial highway, the park would not get any provincial grants to save it.

The committee formed at the public meeting to conduct the canvass consisted of Arthur J. Cook, chairman; Mrs. James White, secretary; and Morley Ross, Mrs. William A. Heron, Mrs. Mabel Richardson,

THE GLOBE HOTEL
BROOKLIN.
THOMAS CHINN, - - Proprietor.

Best Liquors and Cigars. A well supplied table. Airy bed-rooms. Confortable stabling and large yard room. Charges moderate.

Mr. Chinn is determined to spare no pains to make the Globe a comfortable and quiet resort for the travelling public.

This advertisement for the Globe Hotel, then owned by Thomas Chinn, appeared in The Brooklin Times, of June 13, 1882, three years before the building was destroyed by fire.

Miss Louella Mowbray, Mrs. Ernest H. Patterson, Mrs. Frank Ormiston, Ellis Pascoe and Mrs. Norman J. White, as collectors.

Brooklin was divided into districts, in which each of the collectors went door-to-door asking for contributions to save the park. People not at home at the time of the canvass were asked to leave their contributions at the Brooklin branch of the Bank of Commerce. Mrs. Fraser, who lived in Gravenhurst, gave the committee more than the 10 days she had allotted to raise the money, for it took until July 6, 1951 to

obtain the entire $1,600.

On July 13, 1951, the Daily Times-Gazette, Whitby and Oshawa's local newspaper, published the names of 162 persons who had contributed to the park fund, along with amounts collected. The largest donations were $200 from Gerald M. Brawley (for whom Brawley Road is named) and $125 from A.C. Ransom. The lowest contribution was 25 cents from an anonymous donor. A *"friend"* gave two dollars and another anonymous donor contributed 50 cents. All the rest of the contributors were named, each giving two, five or ten dollars.

The $1,600 was turned over to the Whitby Township Council to pay Mrs. Fraser, and the park was registered as public property on July 10, 1951. A provision was made that if Brooklin was ever incorporated as a village, the park would become the property of the village rather than the township. In 1968 when the Town and Township of Whitby amalgamated, Grass Park became the property of the new Town of Whitby.

In recent years, the park has been maintained by the Town of Whitby Parks and Recreation Department and the Brooklin Horticultural Society.

Thanks to the dedication and perseverance of Brooklin's citizens nearly 50 years ago, this fine community park was saved and maintained for future generations.

Dr. Horace Bascom, The Oldest Civil Servant In Ontario

When Dr. Horace F. Bascom (1863-1956) retired as Sheriff of Ontario County in 1955 at the age of 92, he was the oldest civil servant in Ontario. It was said that he remained in office so long because there were no pensions or retirement allowances for civil servants in 1955. The inspector of legal offices for Ontario had told him he could *"die with his boots on"* if he wanted to. When he finally did retire, after holding various court positions for 43 years, he was the oldest sheriff in the province.

Dr. Bascom really lived two lives – 24 years as a medical doctor in Uxbridge and 43 years as a county court official in Whitby. Born in Uxbridge on April 26, 1863, he was named after the noted American journalist Horace Greeley, who coined the phrase *"Go West Young Man"*. In the 1880s he was an athlete of considerable accomplishments who won the Ontario tennis doubles championship.

In 1884, Dr. Bascom graduated from the Toronto School of Medicine and for three years was a doctor in Cuba, Jamaica and England, where he was named a Fellow of the Royal College of Surgeons. After a year as an intern and house doctor at the Toronto General Hospital, he returned to Uxbridge in 1888 to be a country doctor. He often told the story of how he had to perform an appendectomy at night on a farmer's kitchen table, with the only light provided by the

Dr. Horace Bascom (left) being congratulated on his retirement by Oshawa Lawyer Thomas Kelso Creighton, April 27, 1955.

headlights of his car shining through the window.

Dr. Bascom played an important part in the only two murder cases in Ontario County which resulted in the execution of the accused. He served as the coroner for the inquest into the death of Mrs. Archie McLaughlin and her two children in

Uxbridge in 1909. It was believed that they were killed in a house fire, but an autopsy by Dr. Bascom revealed that they had been poisoned before the house burned. Mrs. McLaughlin's husband was charged with their murder, tried at the Court House in Whitby, and hanged at the County Jail in July, 1910. It was revealed at the trial that McLaughlin killed his wife and children and set fire to the house to cover up the crime so he could run off with another woman, Miss Alma Nix.

When he was sheriff in 1946, Dr. Bascom had to arrange for the hanging of George Bilton who had killed a woman and her daughter in the woods near Ajax, by bashing their heads with a rock. Bilton was hanged in the Whitby jail, the last person in Ontario County to receive such a sentence. He was buried in an unmarked grave in St. John's Anglican Cemetery with the rope still around his neck.

After a long and successful career as a doctor, Dr. Bascom came to Whitby to accept the positions of Registrar of the Supreme and Surrogate Courts and Clerk of the County Court in 1912. In 1935, he accepted the position of Sheriff of Ontario County, a position he held for 20 years. In 1913 he had a large American Colonial style house built at the corner of King and St. John Streets in Whitby, only a block from his office in the Court House.

During the First World War, Dr. Bascom was medical officer for the 34th Ontario Regiment, examining all recruits before they went overseas. From 1912 to 1948, he was a member of the Whitby Board of Education, serving as chairman for nine years. His recreation consisted of playing cards at the *"Millionaires' Club"* in a downtown Whitby store in the evening. He was also an accomplished golfer. He smoked big black cigars most of his life and still drove his car at the age of 90.

Dr. Bascom died at this King Street home on Nov. 4, 1956 at the age of 93, and was buried in his home town of Uxbridge, where his uncle had been the first mayor.

After the death of Dr. Bascom's wife in 1959, his home was sold to Duncan McIntyre (1903-1969), a former Reeve of Whitby and Warden of Ontario County. A lawyer, McIntyre was one of the founders of the Whitby Historical Society. He was born in the house diagonally across the road at the 320 St. John Street West. The Bascom house has been designated under the Ontario Heritage Act, being the only American Colonial style home of its kind in Whitby. It is now the home of Rick McDonnell, former chairman of the Local Architectural Conservation Advisory Committee (LACAC).

The longest-serving employees of Ontario County in 1955: Allan Lavis (22 years), Dr. Horace Bascom (43 years), Kay Barton (26 years), Isobel Davey (32 years). They are standing on the north steps at the County Court House (now the Centennial Building).

Whitby Showed The World How To Play Hockey

From 1955 to 1960, Whitby made hockey history with a team called the Whitby Dunlops. Never before had a team from a small Canadian town of 10,000 people made such an impact nationally and internationally. In their short career in Whitby, this team won one Provincial Senior *"B"* championship, two National Senior *"A"* championships, and the World Hockey Championship. For the first time, the name of Whitby, Ontario, became known all over the world.

The Whitby Dunlops actually began in Oshawa in 1952 when Wren Blair and sponsor *"Sam"* Smith of Smith Transport, formed a Senior *"B"* hockey team called the Oshawa Truckmen. Blair already had hockey experience, managing teams in Oshawa's Mercantile League. The nucleus of the *"Truckmen"* consisted of a number of former Oshawa Generals players who were then competing in the Toronto Mercantile League. Among those who later were Whitby Dunlops' hockey stars, were Doug Williams and George Samolenko. The Truckmen led the league in 1952-53, but were eliminated in the playoffs. Everything looked good for a successful season in 1953-54, when, six days before the opening game, on Sept. 15, 1953, the Oshawa Arena burned down. The Truckmen lost not only their home ice, but all their equip-

The Whitby Dunlops World Championship Hockey Team, April, 1958

Back Row: Jack Donlevy, George Samolenko, Alf Treen, "Bus" Gagnon, Don McBeth, George Gosselin, Connie Broden, Stan Waylett.

Middle Row: Fred Etcher, Roy Edwards, Gordie Myles, Frank Bonello, Harry Sinden, Sandy Air, John Henderson, Wally Brabin.

Front Row: Ted O'Connor, Eddie Redmond, Wren Blair, Sid Smith, Bill Hannah, Tom O'Connor, Bob Attersley.

Tom Puckrin and Charles Chaytor with the Whitby Dunlops "World Champions" sign, Brock Street South, March, 1958.

ment.

Always a decisive manager, Wren Blair had signed up the Bowmanville arena for his team, three hours after the fire. Joe Bolahood, of Oshawa Sportshaven provided new uniforms and equipment on extended credit. The team did not even miss their opening game. Having recovered from the disaster, the Truckmen defeated Kingston, Stouffville and Simcoe to win the Ontario Senior *"B"* Championship of 1954. They were the first team ever to win the championship without a home arena.

Realizing that the Truckmen needed a permanent home, Blair contacted Norman Irwin (1903-1983) and Donald Wilson (1891-1987) who were building a new community arena in Whitby. The crowds at Bowmanville had been disappointing and Smith Transport had withdrawn its sponsorship of the team. The Senior *"B"* team, however, struggled on, playing without pay and splitting any income from ticket sales. Whitby Mayor Harry Jermyn and Industrial Commissioner Charles Chaytor (1912-1977) expressed an interest in bringing Blair's team to Whitby and offered him all the help they could. The only provision was that it be now the Whitby, rather than Oshawa Senior *"B"* team. A secure future was at last attained when the town officials obtained sponsorship from the Dunlop Tire and Rubber Company, which was moving into its new Whitby factory in 1955. When the delicate negotiations hung in the balance, the Senior *"B"* team played the Kingston Goodyears at the new Whitby arena, with Dunlop officials in attendance. The rivalry of the two tire companies and an offer of $10 to each Whitby player who scored a goal, resulted in a 4-3 win for the Truckmen. The next day, they officially became the Whitby Dunlops, with the Dunlop Company as their sponsor. In the 1954-55 season they reached the playoffs, but were defeated by Kingston in the semifinals.

In 1955, Bob Attersley, a former Oshawa General, joined the team and became its highest scorer. *"Bus"* Gagnon, and another former General, Sandy Air, also joined, along with Eddie Redmond of Peterborough and goalie Jack Donlevy. During the summer of 1955, Blair managed to sell 24 memberships at $100 apiece to Whitby businessmen. Dunlop gave the team $2,500 for the advertising rights and enough programs were sold to raise the club's financial resources to $6,000. Ontario County Judge John A. Pritchard (1901-1961) was elected president and Norman Irwin vice-president.

In the 1955-56 season, the *"Dunnies"* as the team was affectionately called, lost only five of 48 games. They won the 1956 Ontario Senior *"B"* championship easily, but Wren Blair had bigger things in store for his team. He wanted to elevate the *"Dunnies"* to Senior *"A"* level, so they could play for the Canadian National Championship represented by the Allan Cup. The only Senior *"A"* league at that time was the western league, which refused to include the Dunlops. Blair succeeded, however in persuading the entire eastern league to rise to a Senior *"A"* level, and the Dunnies were ready to take on all comers. Sportscasters initially laughed at the Whitby Dunlops,

The Dunlops' World Championship victory parade on Highway 401 heading for Ajax, April 2, 1958.

calling them the *"Cinderella team"*, not expecting them to fare well in the Senior *"A"* ranks. Blair surprised everyone by winning the 1957 Allan Cup, with the Dunlops being the first team ever to do so in their first Senior *"A"* season. The Dunlops first eliminated the Kingston Frontenacs and Belleville McFarlands to win the Eastern

Ontario championship. They went on to defeat the Kitchener-Waterloo Dutchmen and then the North Bay Trappers. The North Bay series moved to Toronto's Maple Leaf Gardens, because the Whitby arena could only hold 2,000 people. The first two games in Toronto drew 12,000 fans. In game 7, before 15,000 fans, the *"Dunnies"* defeated North Bay and went on to the finals against the Spokane Flyers. The Whitby Dunlops defeated Spokane in four straight games, making hockey history.

But Wren Blair was not finished yet. Less than two weeks after the Allan Cup win, he travelled to Edmonton to the annual meeting of the Canadian Amateur Hockey Association. His mission was to persuade the CAHA to have the *"Dunnies"* represent Canada in the 1958 World Hockey Championships in Oslo, Norway. His proposal was accepted unanimously.

In the last months of 1957, and early months of 1958, hockey fever hit Whitby. A lot was riding on the world championship series. In 1956, the Kitchener-Waterloo Dutchmen had been defeated by the Russians, and the following year, Canada had not competed as a protest against the Russian invasion of Hungary. It was clearly a time for a Canadian win. Dunlop Rubber Company underwrote much of the expenses for the eight-week tournament, to the tune of $30,000, and agreed to reimburse the players for salaries they would have lost being away from work. The International Ice Hockey Association provided another $40,000 to cover expenses. More funding came from the Whitby Dunlops Booster Club, formed in 1957. Two of the club members, Donald Dulmage (1927-1966) and Stuart Roblin (1927-1998) had created the team's rallying cry *"Go Dunnies, Go"*, which fans shouted at every game.

On Nov. 22, 1957 at Maple Leaf Gardens, the *"Dunnies"* got a taste of what was to come, when they played the Moscow Selects. They proved their worth by defeating the Russians 7-2.

Early in 1958, a fund was set up to provide $5,000 to send four players who could not compete because of injuries, to the World Championships. After all they had done for the team, it would not be right for them to miss the series. On Jan. 29, 1958, 104 persons paid $10 a plate to attend a *"Bon Voyage"* dinner for the Dunlops at the Whitby Legion Hall. It was a great success, even though the person responsible for printing the program had put *"Oslo, Sweden"* instead of *"Oslo, Norway"*, on the cover.

The *"Dunnies"* played their last game before leaving Canada, shooting to a 2-2 tie with the Sudbury Wolves at the Whitby Arena, before 1,600 fans. They then travelled by bus to New York City, where they boarded the ocean liner *"Queen Elizabeth"* for the trip to Europe. Following a 14-game exhibition tour, they were to play in the World Championships from Feb. 28 to Mar. 9, in eight action-packed games. The teams they had to defeat were from East Germany, Poland, Norway, Finland, Sweden (defending champions), Czechoslovakia, the United States and Russia. The *"Dunnies"* easily defeated these teams, one by one, with scores of 14-1 against Poland, 12-0 against Norway, 24-0 against Finland, 10-2 against Sweden, 6-0 against Czechoslovakia and 12-1 against the United States.

Canada and Russia were both undefeated when they met for the final game on March 9, 1958. At that time, there was no television broadcast, so fans had to listen to the game on radio. The streets of Whitby were deserted, as the citizens of the town gathered in front of their radios at 1 p.m.. The Dunlops had received 10 bushel baskets of telegrams from Canadian hockey fans, the provincial premiers and the prime minister, all wishing them luck and expecting them to *"bring home the bacon"*.

Wren Blair and his team found the tension almost unbearable. Bob Attersley was Blair's star player, and he knew that *"in many ways, as Bobby goes, so goes the game"*.

Model of the World Hockey Championship cup at the Four Corners, March, 1958.

him. *I knew we had to get a goal."*

At this crucial moment, Blair remembered that Attersley was president of the Young Conservative Party, and Conservatives were the farthest thing away from a Communist.

"I stood and looked at him and said: 'The way you're playing, I'm beginning to doubt your political beliefs. Don't show me; show those Russians.' Three or four minutes later he scored a goal. He was angry. In the third period Connie Broden scored, but three minutes later the Russians scored. Three minutes from the end of the game, Alexandrov broke away on Roy Edwards, our goal tender. I couldn't watch the play. He hit the top crossbar. The Russians had been stopped. Bobby took the puck and scored the winning goal three minutes from the end. The score was 3-2."

When Attersley scored the winning goal, the commentator shouted *"Atta-boy Attersley. The Canadians have scored and it is 3-2. The goal was scored by Atta-boy Attersley".* The name stuck and whenever the game is remembered, old friends and hockey fans still call him *"Atta-boy Attersley".*

Shortly after the winning goal, Bus Gagnon scored the last of four goals for the *"Dunnies"*, making the final score 4-2 for Canada. Attersley set up Gagnon's goal for a total of two goals and one assist in that historic game.

As team captain Harry Sinden accepted

In a tribute to Attersley, on his retirement at Whitby's Mayor, in 1991, Blair recalled the scene in Oslo:

"Prior to the game I could almost feel the players were going to squeeze the sawdust out of their sticks, we were so uptight. Russia got the first goal. Bobby was not playing his usual game. His face was white, the intensity was so consuming. It was 1-0 at the end of the first period. Late in the second period, Bob came off the ice. I looked at him and he barely looked at me. I thought, 'What's the worst thing I could say to him to get him going?' He was normally not bothered by me pushing

the world championship cup, the crowd sang Canada's national anthem.

"As 'O Canada' was played at the end of the game, I could gradually hear voices", Wren Blair recalled. *"It was our entire team on the blue line singing. By the end they were booming it out like the Mormon Tabernacle Choir."*

Seconds after the game ended, Whitby's fire siren sounded, and people poured into the streets. Traffic was backed up for four miles on Highway 2 as revellers let off fire crackers, cheered and waved flags. One car was decorated with a sign reading *"We mopped the Ruskies; We Dunnies have gone"*. Works foreman John Rae (1905-1963) was ready for the win. He had painted signs reading: *"World Champions in Oslo, Norway, 1958"* before the game. Within minutes of the win by the Dunlops he unveiled these signs at the entrances to the town.

The Whitby Dunlops returned to a heros' welcome, and participated in a parade which travelled through Whitby, Oshawa and Ajax, on April 2, 1958. But the Whitby Dunlops were not finished yet. They went on to win the Allan Cup a second time in the 1958-59 season, the only team to do so immediately after winning a world championship. In 1960, the Whitby Dunlops disbanded and Wren Blair went on to a professional hockey career. They had won everything there was to win. There was no place else to go.

Over the years, the Whitby Dunlops team members have played important roles in hockey. Wren Blair in 1962, assisted in reactivating the Oshawa Generals, who were without a home since their arena burned nine years previously. He was responsible for signing 14-year-old Bobby Orr to the Generals, thus starting one of the legendary careers of hockey history. In 1966, Blair became coach and general manager of the Minnesota North Stars in the National Hockey league. He was a part owner of the Pittsburgh Penguins for two years and was later director of player personnel for the Los Angeles Kings. He is now a part owner with Bob Attersley, of the Kingston Frontenacs Major Junior *"A"* hockey team.

Blair, along with four former *"Dunnies"*, Bob Attersley, Harry Sinden, George Samolenko and Fred Etcher, joined the Kitchener-Waterloo Flying Dutchmen as Canada's hockey entry in the 1960 Winter Olympics in Squaw Valley, California. Although the Canadian team outshot the Americans 51-17, they lost the gold medal to the United States 2-1 in the final game. It was especially frustrating for Attersley, who hit the crossbar three times but could not get the puck in the net.

Bob Attersley decided to open a tire business in Whitby, rather than pursue a professional hockey career. He was elected to the Whitby Town Council in 1964 and was the town's longest-serving Mayor from 1980 to 1991. He made Whitby *"The Home of the Marigold"*, and successfully promoted Whitby through two recessions and the building boom of the mid-1980s.

Harry Sinden, the captain of the World Champion *"Dunnies"*, went on to be coach and general manager of the Boston Bruins, and was coach of the famous *"Team Canada"* that defeated Russia in the first Canada Cup series in 1972.

On Aug. 14, 1981, the Whitby Dunlops were inducted into the Hockey Hall of Fame in Toronto, with Attersley's and Sinden's sweaters being part of a permanent display. The *"Dunnies"* held a 25th anniversary reunion in 1983 and on May 2, 1998, they were the first inductees in Whitby's own Sports Hall of Fame at Iroquois Park, on the 40th anniversary of their World Championship win.

In all of Whitby's history, only three times did the town gain prominence at an international level — when the Whitby Dunlops won the World Hockey Championship in 1958 and when Anne Ottenbrite won gold, silver and bronze medals at the 1984 Summer Olympics. The third time was when Teddy Rowe was chosen as the British Empire's Bonniest Baby, in 1924.

The World Champion Whitby Dunlops Played Here

The Whitby Community Arena where the world champion hockey team the Whitby Dunlops once played, is just a memory now, but 40 years ago it was the town's leading sports and community centre. Located on the west side of Green Street between Gilbert and Ontario Streets, it was a large cement block building. The liquor store and an office building stand on site today.

The Whitby Community Arena was not the first to stand on this site. A frame arena for skating and curling was built in 1889 by William Barnes (1820-1892) and George Cormack (1830-1894), following a fire which destroyed Whitby's curling arena at Brock and Mary Streets (now the site of Pearson Lanes) in 1888. In 1913 Fred Burns (1872-1932) purchased the old arena and enlarged it. Whitby by this time had became a prominent hockey town, but its greatest days had not yet been achieved. In 1936, the arena was purchased by Norman H. Taylor of Bowmanville, who operated it until 1949.

By that time the old arena was in very poor condition and its future was uncertain. The Kinsmen Club of Whitby came to the rescue, offering to take over the management of the arena and make necessary repairs, but the project proved too much for the club's finances. The arena, built like a barn, was so cold that patrons of the hockey

The Whitby Community Arena under construction in the fall of 1953.

games used to take flasks of whiskey with them to keep warm. The ice was not artificial, but natural, depending on the weather for its texture. In spite of the primitive conditions, Whitby was able to produce an Ontario Juvenile Champion hockey team in 1944 and a provincial champion Junior "C" team in 1946.

By the summer of 1953 it was realized that the old Taylor Arena was beyond repair and would have to be demolished. Plans were formulated to build a new arena on

The completed arena in 1955, before an addition was put on the front the following year.

the same site, and an arena board was formed to oversee its management. Donald A. Wilson (1891-1987) was secretary for the board. His work for the arena was recognized when he received the Peter Perry Award as Whitby's first outstanding citizen in 1955.

In August, 1953, T.L.Wilson of Cannington, was awarded the contract to demolish the old arena. The ancient structure was taken down, piece by piece, and reerected at Chatsworth, a community near Owen Sound. The Chatsworth Community Centre Committee purchased all the lumber and sent men to Whitby to assist in its removal.

By the early part of September, the old arena was gone and construction began on the new one under the supervision of the T. L. Wilson Lumber Company. The new arena was 248 feet long and 96 feet wide, with the front facing Ontario Street. Included in the structure were four dressing rooms and a hall, where meetings could be held. This hall was the home of the Whitby Rotary Club for many years, and it was there that Judge John E. Pritchard (1901-1961) delivered of his speech at Whitby's Centennial in 1955 that led to the creation the of Peter Perry Award.

Under the chairmanship of Francis McIntyre (1891-1958) the Community Arena Board conducted the subscription drive which raised $60,000 of the estimated $97,000 needed to build the arena. Service clubs assisted in the project, the Rotary Club paying for the arena's cement floor.

In September 1953, the Oshawa Arena was destroyed by fire. McIntyre offered the use of the Whitby arena to Oshawa immediately, even though the foundations had barely begun. The new Whitby arena became the home of the Oshawa Truckmen, an exceptionally fine hockey team, which under its new sponsor, Dunlop Tire, became the Whitby Dunlops.

The construction of the framework of the new arena began at the end of October, 1953, with hopes that it would be completed by mid-December. The arena went into operation early in 1954, but it was not until Sept. 29 of that year that the official opening was marked with a game between the Toronto Maple Leafs and the Pittsburgh Hornets. This exhibition game was arranged through the efforts of the Town of Whitby and Conn Smythe, owner of Maple Leaf Gardens. A copy of the official program is in the Town of Whitby Archives. Hockey legends *"King"* Clancy and Howie Meeker were coaches for the Maple Leafs and the Hornets, respectively, during this game.

The Ontario Government assisted in the construction of the community arena by providing a grant of $10,000 under the Community Centres Act.

The arena's glory days lasted from 1954 till 1959 when the Whitby Dunlops won two Allan Cups and a world championship for the town. The arena was the site also of trade fairs by the Chamber of Commerce in 1961 and 1962, displays by the Boy Scouts, and even dog shows. Its days of use came to an end in July 1972 when new Provincial Standards for arenas were passed by the Ontario Government. Both the Whitby and Brooklin Arenas could not meet these standards, and had to be demolished. A new arena was built at Brooklin, and the first ice pad at Iroquois Park replaced the old Whitby Arena in 1974.

The writer of this book had a strange experience during the demolition of the old arena in the summer of 1972. In the darkened building as the workers proceeded with demolition, he could hear the Canada-Russia hockey series of 1972, on a worker's radio, echoing through the arena as Paul Henderson scored his famous game-winning goal for the first Canada Cup. It was as if the ghosts of the Whitby Dunlops were playing again as their old home came down.

30 Years Of Promoting Canadian Unity

Whitby's exchange visits with the City of Longueuil, Quebec, which have been maintained for 30 years, are recognized as the longest and most successful *"Twinning"* program in Canada. Through the F.L.Q. crisis of 1970 and the Separatist referendums of 1980 and 1995, the relationship between Whitby and Longueuil has remained strong and steady. Citizens of both communities have experienced life in their twin town and Canadian unity has been strengthened through the efforts of Whitby and Longueuil.

The twinning of Whitby and Longueuil began with a 1967 Centennial project by the Fifth Whitby Venturers, under the leadership of Benny LaHaye of Whitby. The Venturers took a canoe trip from Whitby to Expo '67 at Montreal, and on this trip met a citizen of Longueuil who introduced them to Longueuil's Mayor Marcel Robidas. Robidas, who had already set up a twinning program with a French-speaking community in Louisiana, U.S.A. suggested that a *"Twinning"* or *"Jumelage"* as it is called in French, could be arranged between Longueuil and Whitby. As a Centennial project, twinning of French and English-speaking communities in Canada was being promoted by the Quebec Federation of Mayors and Reeves, of which Robidas was a member.

Members of Whitby Venturers' Expo '67 Canoe Trip in Centennial Parade, Aug. 5, 1967. (Photo by Bill Stannett)

Longueuil, the fourth largest city in Quebec at the time, is located on the south shore of the St. Lawrence River, near Montreal. The community was founded in 1657, when King Louis XIV of France granted the Seigneury of Longueuil to Sieur Charles LeMoyne, the equivalent of Whitby's Peter Perry. Like Whitby, Longueuil was named a County town in 1791 and became the site of a Land

Mayors Marcel Robidas and Desmond Newman signing the Twinning Protocol, June, 1969, pictured on cover of Longueuil Municipal Bulletin.

Registry Office in 1857. In 1870 it was officially named as a municipality. The old section of Longueuil has centuries-old French homes and a fort. It became a tourist centre at the time of Expo '67, linked to Montreal by the Metro (subway) system, as Whitby is linked to Toronto by the GO-train. As Whitby is the home to many people who work in Toronto, Longueuil is home to commuters working in Montreal.

Preliminary meetings to arrange the twinning of Whitby and Longueuil took place between officials of both municipalities in 1968, and the first exchange visits were held in 1969. Mayor Desmond G. Newman appointed Councillor Tom Edwards to be Whitby's twinning chairman, and he held that position nearly every year until he became Mayor at the end of 1991. In June 1969, 75 Whitby residents travelled to Longueuil on the first twinning visit, and 71 Longueuil citizens came to Whitby in August. The official twinning protocol was signed by Whitby and Longueuil during these visits. Mayor Newman presented Mayor Robidas with the Whitby Mayor's Medal, and in 1972, Mayor Robidas presented Mayor Newman with the Order of Merit of Longueuil, the first time it was presented to a person who was not a citizen of the French-speaking community. Whitby also benefitted by adopting Longueuil's program of issuing a municipal bulletin to the ratepayers. Whitby's municipal bulletins were published for nearly 20 years. Many personal friendships developed between Whitby and Longueuil citizens which have lasted for years.

Whitby and Longueuil's twinning was officially recognized in 1979 by Ontario's Lieutenant-Governor Pauline McGibbon when she took part in the exchange visit at the Whitby Municipal Building. In 1991, 150 people, the largest number ever, took part in the twinning exchanges, despite the failure of the Meech Lake Accord to bring Quebec into Canada's Constitution. Tom Edwards stressed that the real meaning of twinning was non-political and it was designed to bring people together to learn about each other. The true spirit of twinning was demonstrated during the great ice storm of January 1998, when Whitby sent a number of employees from its Works Department and Whitby Hydro to Longueuil to assist in restoring power to the ravaged community.

Modern Whitby Began With 1968 Amalgamation

The modern age for the Town of Whitby began with the amalgamation of Whitby Town and Township on January 1, 1968. Six years before the Region of Durham was created and changed the boundaries of its member municipalities, Whitby led the way in creating the first viable unit of the Regional Government. No political event in the history of this community was more hotly debated at the time, since the choosing of Whitby as the County Town of Ontario County in 1852. And no other event was to have such a large impact on the town's future.

From 1855 to 1967, the Town of Whitby was a small urban community surrounded by a rural township. Whitby's boundaries stretched from Lake Ontario to Rossland Road and from a point east of Anderson Street to a point west of Jeffrey Street. In 1967, the town's population was 15,000. Whitby Township, with a population of 8,000 was a farming community containing the hamlets of Ashburn, Brooklin, Myrtle and Myrtle Station. Whitby Township's political headquarters was centred in Brooklin. When amalgamation came into effect, Whitby became a mixed urban and rural municipality of 56 square miles, stretching from a point east of Garrard Road to Lakeridge Road and from Lake Ontario to the Scugog

The First Council of the New Town of Whitby, 1968-69. Back Row: Dr. Kenneth Hobbs, Sam Hollingsworth, John Goodwin, Vernon MacCarl, Robert White, Tom Edwards. Front Row: Hugh O'Connell, Reeve Gordon Hanna, Mayor Desmond Newman, Deputy Reeve Bob Attersley, Heber Down. (Photo by Bill Stannett)

Township boundary, with a population of 23,000.

As early as 1962, discussions began between the councils of the Town and

Township of Whitby on some form of annexation so the town could obtain some of the township's prime industrial land. Almost all the town's industrial land was

Durham District Board of Education Headquarters.

than a partial annexation. Leading the Township forces were Reeves Heber Down, John Goodwin and John Dryden. Leading the Whitby Town Council was Mayor Desmond G. Newman, the youngest mayor in the municipality's history, being elected in 1966 at the age of 34. Mayor Newman proved to be a far-sighted individual who foresaw regional government before it was even clearly defined by the Provincial Government. Under his leadership, Whitby was prepared for this eventuality before any other municipality in the future Regional Municipality of Durham. The proposed *"marriage"* of Whitby Town and Township was carefully scrutinized by the Ontario Municipal Board, which approved the proposal in July 1967, to take effect on January 1, 1968.

The birth of the new Town of Whitby was heralded with a 100-gun salute in front of the fire hall at midnight on New Year's Eve, at which Mayor Newman, Councillor Vernon MacCarl, Fire Chief Warren Mowat and fire fighters Jim Corner and John Heard (1912-1981) officiated. On Jan. 1, 1968, new signs reading *"Town of Whitby"* were erected at the entrances to the expanded town, but some were promptly torn down by residents of the former township who did not favour amalgamation.

already taken or built upon. The catalyst came in 1963 when Lake Ontario Steel and Sklar Furniture began construction of factories on township land east of the town boundary and south of Highway 401. Whitby Town proposed that these lands be annexed from the township.

For the councillors of Whitby Township this was not a good idea. They wanted the town to take all or nothing. Having seen Oshawa annex parts of East Whitby Township over a period of years, the Township Council wanted a total amalgamation of the two municipalities rather

The inaugural meeting of the first council of the new Town of Whitby was held in the municipal building which is now the Whitby Public Library on Dundas Street West, on January 6, 1968. The council consisted of Mayor Desmond Newman, Reeve Gordon Hanna, Deputy Reeve Bob Attersley and Councillors Heber Down and Sam Hollingsworth of the North Ward, John Goodwin and Bob White of the East Ward, Vernon MacCarl and Tom Edwards of the Centre Ward and Hugh O'Connell and Dr. Ken Hobbs of the West Ward. The town was divided into a ward system to provide the best representation for its various inhabitants. The original old town of Whitby was the Centre Ward, the East Ward extended from Garden Street to the Oshawa border, the West Ward from Henry Street to Almonds and the North Ward from Taunton Road to Scugog. These boundaries were amended for the 1997 election.

Thirty-seven special guests from the Provincial Government, former Town and Township Councils and neighbouring municipalities attended the inaugural meeting.

Judge Alex C. Hall (1904-1971) of Ontario County, administered the oath of office to the councillors and staff. The municipal staff were: John R. Frost,

This sign welcomes you to Whitby, Durham's Business Centre.

administrator; William H. Wallace, clerk; Forbes N. McEwen, treasurer; Walter Evans, engineer; George Thwaites, director of social services and Alex Craigie tax collector and deputy treasurer. Rev. Father Leo J. Austin (1916-1984) of St. John the Evangelist Church, gave the invocation and Rev. John McLeod of the Whitby

Baptist Church pronounced the benediction. One of the first acts of the council was to adopt a new corporate seal.

In his inaugural address, Mayor Newman stressed industrial development and proposed construction of a heliport and sports stadium. Following the inaugural meeting a reception was held for the council by the Whitby Historical Society in the Centennial Building, with a symbolic cake being cut by municipal officials. Behind all the fanfare, there were the ratepayers, watching amalgamation with great interest.

Mayor Newman wanted to create a new identity for Whitby in a future regional government, but he neglected to realize the strong sense of identity felt by the residents of Brooklin and the other hamlets. When they found out their post offices would no longer be listed in directories and "*Brooklin*" signs would disappear from the highways, a mass protest meeting was staged at the town hall. At that memorable meeting, Brooklin's *"grand old man"* Heber Down (1889-1972) spoke on behalf of his community on the right to retain the names of Ashburn, Brooklin, Myrtle and Myrtle Station.

"I am not going to get into any argument with the mayor because he went to college and I only went to public school," he declared as the meeting broke into laugh-

Cullen Gardens and Miniature Village.

ter. Down's eloquence persuaded the mayor and council to retain Brooklin and the other hamlets' names. Brooklin today has its own Royal Canadian Legion branch, Kinsmen, Lions and Optimist Clubs, Oddfellows and Masonic Lodges, Brooklin Spring Fair and the Brooklin Redmen, six-time winners of the Mann Cup as Canada's national senior lacrosse champions.

Another area of discontent was the *"Corridor"* between Thickson Road and Oshawa. This part of Whitby had no sewers or water and the new town was heavily strained to finance these much needed ser-vices in a community that had been basically farm land a few years before. Not long after amalgamation, a ratepayers' association was formed in the Corridor area to negotiate with the town over sewers and water and with developers who soon started to build homes in the new town's east end. One local group was formed, calling itself CRAP (Concerned Ratepayers Against Pollution) to lobby for the sewers. Whitby's largest shopping centre, The Whitby Mall, was built at the corner of Dundas and Thickson Roads in 1968/69, and throughout the 1970s developments such as Whitby Town Estates and Blue Grass Meadows were built in the Corridor area. At the same time, the West Lynde subdivision was built between Annes Street and Lynde Creek in the West Ward.

After amalgamation, Whitby became a significant player with larger municipalities between Toronto and Oshawa. The town gained national recognition in July, 1971 when a proposal was unveiled to construct a massive sports facility called Iroquois Park. A committee of Whitby citizens came up with a plan to hold a nation-wide lottery based on similar lotteries in Europe to raise the funds to build a facility which would resemble a combination of the Skydome and Canada's Wonderland. Mayor Newman acted as spokesman at a gala press conference at the Royal York Hotel in Toronto, attended by the big-city media. Part of the Iroquois Park proposal was a Disneyland style theme park. The press caught hold of this concept and promptly called it *"Desneyland"* after Mayor Des Newman.

Only one factor stood in the way of the original Iroquois Park proposal. The lottery had to be approved by the Provincial Government. After a long delay, the Province decided not to approve the nation-wide lottery, but ended up using the concept proposed by Whitby as a basis for the future Wintario lottery. Iroquois Park as originally proposed, was never built, but after both Whitby's arenas were condemned as unsafe under new provincial guidelines in 1972, plans were made to build a new arena on the Iroquois Park site. The arena was opened in 1974, followed by an indoor swimming pool in 1975. Another arena was built in 1987, and with the help of private funding, another four ice pads were opened in 1997, along with a restaurant and several baseball diamonds. Iroquois Park Sports Centre is now billed at Canada's largest municipal sports centre.

In 1998 a Sports Hall of Fame opened in Iroquois Park with the Whitby Dunlops being inducted on the 40th anniversary of

Downtown Whitby, Dundas Street looking east from Brock Street.

winning the World Hockey Championship.

Another significant result of amalgamation was the moving of the municipal centre of the town to Rossland Road. Mayor Newman envisioned a new town centre in 1972 when there was yet no development

north of Rossland Road. There was much controversy about the new location for the municipal building, but it was opened in January 1977, designed by noted Canadian architect Raymond Moriyama. In the intervening years, a civic recreation complex was opened in 1991 beside the municipal building and a new land registry office was opened across the road the same year. North of the Court House at Rossland and Garden Streets is a large shopping plaza and office complex. Further development space is available north of Rossland Road between Brock and Garden Streets.

On October 1, 1973, elections were held for the Council of the new Regional Municipality of Durham, which came into effect on January 1, 1974. Under Regional Government, Whitby's Town Council was reduced from 11 members to 7. Desmond G. Newman was Mayor and Regional Councillor, Gerry Emm and John Goodwin were Regional Councillors and the local councillors were Don Lovelock for the North Ward, Tom Edwards for the Centre Ward, Joy Thompson for the East Ward and Jim Gartshore for the West Ward. Whitby, which had been the County Town of Ontario County for 121 years, became the seat of the Regional Headquarters. After a long debate, Oshawa Regional Councillor Mike Breaugh was quoted in a local newspaper as stating that the regional headquarters were *"in a corn field"*. In 1999, that corn field is the active commercial and administrative centre of the region at Rossland Road and Garden Street.

New housing development at Brooklin.

Whitby became a tourist centre in 1980, when Len Cullen opened Cullen Gardens and Miniature Village in a creek valley off Taunton Road. Cullen had owned adjacent land since 1955 where he grew plants and trees for his Weall and Cullen Nurseries. Cullen Gardens is now an internationally-known tourist attraction visited by more than half a million people a year. The establishment of Cullen Gardens opened Whitby's eyes to the possibilities of tourism and resulted in the town building a tourist information centre in Rotary Centennial Park in 1982. This centre is now operated by the Whitby Public Library.

Len Cullen saved Whitby's oldest building, the Jabez Lynde house, a relic of the war of 1812. He moved it from a site proposed for development, to Cullen Gardens

Fred Martin, Whitby's Town Crier, at Cullen Gardens.

and opened it as a living museum in 1988. Here, visitors can see members of the Lynde family going about their daily life as it was in the 1850s. Cullen has also rescued a number of other old homes from the Whitby area and plans to incorporate them in a centre of boutiques called *"The Prettiest Street in Ontario."*

Whitby's designation as a recreational harbour in 1967 has transformed the waterfront from a dormant neglected part of town to a thriving play area. A new Whitby Yacht Club began in 1967 and for a time was the fastest growing yacht club on Lake Ontario. A modern clubhouse in 1973/74 replaced the original clubhouse, a building from the old buckle factory. While the club house was being built, Whitby Yacht Club hosted the Thunderbird Worlds Sailing Championship Race in 1973. In 1979, the Port Whitby Marina was established by the Town in the harbour basin. Whitby Harbour was linked with other waterfront communities from Hamilton to Trenton by a Waterfront Trail in 1995. Board walks have been built along the lakeshore and the Rotary and Lions Clubs have developed parkland, walkways and a gazebo at the harbour. The Kiwanis Club has developed playgrounds and other facilities at Heydenshore Park. The Sailwinds condo-

minium is the first of a number of select housing developments planned for the harbour area, depending on the strength of of the economy and the housing market.

To the west of Whitby Harbour is the Lynde Marsh, one of the finest wetland areas left on the north shore of Lake Ontario. Housing developments under construction near the marsh have caused much concern about the protection of this natural area. In 1974 the west half of the Lynde Marsh and the Cranberry Marsh were purchased by the Central Lake Ontario Conservation Authority as a conservation area. An additional $4.5 million has been pledged by the Provincial Government to acquire the eastern portion of the marsh for public use.

Also, along the lakeshore, the original Ontario Hospital built from 1913 to 1925, was replaced in the 1990s by a new single-building hospital. The hospital lands are now being developed for housing, which should provide for a population of 5,000 between the harbour and Lynde Marsh, south of Victoria Street.

Whitby, in 1999, with a population of about 80,000, is the fourth fastest growing municipality in the Greater Toronto Area, with an increase in population of 3.8 per cent between 1991 and 1996. The population of Brooklin is approximately 3,000

Iroquois Park Sports Centre.

per cent open space and hazard land. In 1998, the town issued more than 109 million dollars worth of building permits. Approximately 80 per cent of Whitby's residents live in single family homes. The economic boom of the 1980s saw the population of the town grow from 35,359 in 1980 to 59,152 in 1991. Many of these new residents are commuters who work in Toronto. The old historic homes of Whitby have attracted a number of new residents who have restored these buildings and had them designated under the Ontario Heritage Act. The Town of Whitby now has nearly 50 designated buildings.

Of Whitby's 287 industries in 1999, 274 are manufacturing companies. Thirty-nine per cent of these export their products, mostly to the United States, 36.6 per cent import their goods and 24.4 per cent both import and export. Thirty-six per cent of Whitby's industries are unionized.

Whitby's newest industrial site is 140 acres west of Iroquois Park on the north side of Victoria Street. The first tenant will be Ryder Grocery Services which is constructing a 437,275 square foot office and warehouse building which will be a distribution centre for Sobey Foods. South of Highway 401 and west of Thickson Road EAM-MOSCA Canada Ltd. is construct-

and is expected to increase to 10,000 by the year 2001. For years, Brooklin was not permitted to grow because it did not have municipal sewer and water services linked to Lake Ontario. These were provided in the early 1990s. The first major growth in Brooklin in the 20th century was from 1955 to 1959 when 600 homes were built in the Meadowcrest Subdivision. Water from wells and sanitary services from septic tanks sustained Brooklin at 1,800 people until the development of the 1990s. Projected population for the Town of Whitby in 2001 is 91,589. With an area of 56.87 square miles, Whitby is presently 25 per cent urban, 45 per cent rural and 30

ing a 37,000 square foot building for manufacturing small strapping machines. On Consumers Drive, north of Highway 401, AMC Theatres of Canada is constructing a 24-screen entertainment centre. Also under construction are a Chapters Book Store, fitness facility and restaurants. Northampton Inns are constructing a 90-room four-storey motel on Consumers Drive near the Brock Street-Highway 401 interchange. Opened in 1999, is a 79,000 square-foot Canadian Tire store on Consumers Drive, the third store this company has had in Whitby since 1960.

In 1999, Whitby has industries, manufacturing a great variety of products. Commercial and industrial development in 1998 exceeded 46 million dollars, representing an increase of 418 per cent over 1997. The town's largest industrial employers are Mackie Automotive and Co-Steel LASCO, with more than 640 employees each. In the public sector, the largest employers are the Durham District School Board with 1,500 employees and Whitby Mental Health Centre with 840.

Whitby's industrial development began after the Second World War, when William J. Anderson Company, Empire Pant and Boys' Wear, Canadian Silica and Natlie Knitting Mills moved from Toronto. All of these companies ar no longer in business.

Whitby's big break came when the Dunlop Tire and Rubber Company announced it was moving from Toronto to Whitby. The plant opened in 1955 with 600 employees, quickly followed by MacMillan Bathurst, Ralston Purina and Dupont. Of these, MacMillan Bathurst and DuPont are still active in Whitby. CoSteel LASCO was built in 1964, while Andrew Antenna and Croven Ltd. were opened in Beech Street in the 1950s. In the 1970s, industry began to move into the Hopkins Street Industrial Park, and in the 1980s into the Thickson Road Industrial Park. One of the major companies to locate in Whitby in the 1980s was McGraw-Hill Ryerson Ltd., a book publishing company which built near Lake Ontario. Among the industries in Whitby today are E.D.S. of Canada Ltd. (computer systems), Lear Corporation (motor vehicle seat systems), Novartis Pharmaceutical Canada, Liquor Control Board of Canada warehouse, Horn Plastics, Ball Packaging and Atlantic Packaging, Makita Canada Inc. (electric power tools) Woodbridge Foam (motor vehicle foam seats), Sony of Canada (electronic equipment) and WEGU Canada Incorporated (rubber products).

One company of interest is J.H. McNairn Ltd. which makes food wrap and wax paper. The company was founded in the 1890s in Toronto by James H. McNairn (1837-1927) who was station master at the Whitby Grand Trunk Railway station in the 1860s. The company, which moved to Whitby in the 1970s, may or may not have known that its founder once lived in Whitby.

Among the interesting attractions in Whitby is Hunter Farms at Brooklin, the largest Emu farm in Ontario. Guided tours are provided so people can see these exotic birds.

The Whitby Arts Station Gallery (the former Whitby Junction Railway Station) opened as an art gallery in September 1970. A refurbished 1929 London and Port Stanley Railway box car houses a professionally equipped print making studio used by students and artists. A number of exhibitions and art programs are carried on throughout the year. The Station Gallery building dates from 1903.

The Whitby Courthouse Theatre presents a number of plays each year in the Centennial building, utilizing the old Ontario County Court Room. There are plans to expand this theatre in the near future.

For many years, Whitby has been known for its County Town Carnival. The original carnival ran annually from 1966 to 1982, and was revived in 1995. The County

McGraw-Hill Ryerson Limited.

Town Singers have performed in Canada, the United States and Europe. In 1973 they helped establish an official twinning between Whitby and Feldkirch, Austria. A Feldkirch choir, the Liederhort Tosters, came to Whitby to perform and the County Town Singers performed in Feldkirch in the 1970s. The County Town Singers sang at an International Lions Club convention in the United States and at Expo '86 in Vancouver.

An attraction of ever increasing interest in Whitby is Camp X, an espionage training facility established on the shore of Lake Ontario between Whitby and Oshawa, by Sir William Stephenson, *"The Man Called Intrepid."* From 1941 to 1946 it was operated by British Security Co-ordination, to train agents who parachuted into Nazi occupied territory to lead resistance movements and provide valuable information to the invading allied armies. After the Second World War, from 1946 to 1969, Camp X was a Canadian Government communications centre. Ian Fleming, the author of the James Bond spy novels took his training at Camp X and applied it in his writing. When Igor Gouzenko, the Russian embassy clerk, defected in 1945 with secrets about his country's espionage in Canada and the United States, he was hidden at Camp X. Camp X was demol-

Town Carnival features activities by the various organizations of the town, centered around the Four Corners, during the last weekend in June. The original carnival was started by the Whitby Chamber of Commerce, under Jack Woodward, who headed the carnival committee for many years.

Whitby has gained international recognition through the County Town Singers, formed in 1967 as a Centennial project by Joe Wainwright (1920-1987). The County

ished in 1971 after it was sold to the Town of Whitby and City of Oshawa. Only one Camp X building exists today, a small frame structure which was moved to the Animal Shelter on Thickson Road, through the efforts of Muriel Sissions (1903-1992).

The publication of Sir William Stephenson's biography, *"A Man Called Intrepid"*, in 1976 awakened a new interest in Camp X. Whitby and Oshawa political figures proposed in 1978 the rebuilding of Camp X as a tourist attraction, but the plan did not develop. Although located in the town's industrial area, a portion of Camp X was dedicated as Intrepid Park by the Town of Whitby and a monument to the men and women of Camp X was unveiled by Ontario's Lieutenant-Governor John Black Aird, on August 9, 1984. A book on the history of Camp X by David Stafford, published in 1986, kept interest in Camp X alive, and many articles about its mysterious role in World War II have been published in local and Toronto newspapers. At least two television documentaries on Camp X are planned for 1999 or 2000. Intrepid Park, accessible by the Waterfront Trail, was the scene of a special Remembrance Day ceremony on Nov. 11, 1998, attended by some of the people who worked at Camp X.

Another Whitby attraction is the

Brooklin Spring Fair on the first weekend in June. Founded in 1913 (although some sources say 1911), it has grown from a small agricultural fair to a multi-faceted four-day event, which had its largest attendance in 1999.

The new Whitby Mental Health Centre, which opened on Sept. 15, 1996, with 325 beds and 840 employees, will soon be turned over to the private sector, after nearly 90 years as a Provincial Government facility.

Highway 401 was opened through Whitby to Oshawa in 1947, with interchanges at Brock Street and Thickson Road. The highway is being expanded east from Pickering and approval was received in 1999 for construction of an interchange at Lakeridge Road (the Whitby-Ajax town line). Construction of Highway 407 south of Brooklin is projected after the year 2000, as far as Highway 35 and 115 in Clarington. A proposed link from Highway 401 to Highway 407 in the far west end of Whitby near Lakeridge Road is among future development proposals.

Whitby Hydro, which was founded in 1903 as a public utility, will become a commercial business by November 2000, when competition will be introduced into the electric business as it has been in telephones.

In the 1990s a new complex of municipal services was built on Taunton Road, east of Highway 12. This includes a works centre, fire department headquarters and Whitby Hydro headquarters. To the east on Taunton Road is the new Durham District Board of Education administration building, and Sinclair Secondary School, opened in 1995. These buildings were constructed on the site of the old Sinclair Public School, built in 1874.

Whitby's first senior citizens' housing, a 16-unit building across from the Centennial Building on Centre Street South, was opened in 1969, followed in 1974 by the Bowling Green Towers developed by the Whitby Rotary Club on Green Street. The Windsor Place seniors' apartments were opened in 1978 on Colborne Street, on the site of the old high school. The latest seniors' apartment development is expected to begin in 1999 at the corner of John and Ash Streets. A Seniors Activity Centre was opened beside the lawn bowling green in 1976, and expanded in 1995/96. The members of the centre raised $450,000, about 25 per cent of the total cost of the expansion.

In 1993 Durham College opened a Skills Training Centre in the former Cadbury plant and in 1998 the Durham Business Centre opened in the old Ringwood house

Atlantic Packaging.

mer of 1998, 12 episodes of the Walt Disney series *"The Famous Jett Jackson"* were filmed in Brooklin. Trafalgar Castle School was the location for the movie *"Strike"* about a girls' school, and several other films have been made in Whitby. In 1971, Inverlynn, the large estate at Raglan and Giffard Streets which has been owned by the McGillivray family and its descendants since 1870, was the site for the filming of the noted television series *"The Whiteoaks of Jalna".* Mazo de la Roche, the author of the Jalna books in the 1920s, was related to the Roche and Bryan families of Whitby.

Early in 1999, Mayor Marcel Brunelle set up a Millennium Committee called Whitby 2000 to plan celebrations of the end of the century and end of the millennium. A special celebration is planned at Iroquois Park at the stroke of midnight Dec. 31, 1999. In 1955, Whitby celebrated its centennial of incorporation as a town. In 2005, it will celebrate its 150th anniversary. As a new century and millennium begin, Whitby looks forward to the future with hope and enthusiasm.

(Photographs for this chapter are courtesy of the Town of Whitby Marketing and Economic Development Department).

at Hopkins and Victoria Streets. Durham College President Gary Polonsky announced in June, 1999, an expansion of the Skills Training Centre, including six class rooms, meeting rooms and a learning centre with 50 computer stations.

Since 1997, Whitby has had a web site on the Internet, which had received more than 640,000 hits by early in 1999. The average number of hits per day is 1,336.

Whitby has benefitted from the movie-making industry in Canada. In the sum-